# Policing Empires

"This original and fascinating history of colonial policing, is a must-read for anyone concerned by racist state violence. *Policing Empires* combines detailed research with a compelling and urgent argument challenging militarised policing across the Anglophone world in the 21st century"

**Adam Elliott-Cooper**, author of *Black Resistance to British Policing*

"Turning his keen and critical eye toward police militarization, Julian Go reveals how the modes, means, and technologies of the police were forged in empire's cauldron. This brave and provocative genealogy shows how the disdain of a racialized other and the fear of their revolt brought the tactics of imperial conquest home. Ambitious in scope yet effortlessly readable, *Policing Empires* takes us from the advent of the civil police in London, where the threat of Irish rebellion and the revolt of black Caribbean slaves shaped the formation of the modern police force, to the counterinsurgent practices developed and honed in the Philippines and in Vietnam which would be deployed in Harlem and Watts, but also in Chicago, Detroit, Oakland, Ferguson and Minneapolis. This book should be read by anyone invested in understanding the world in which we live, and certainly by those who hope to change it."

**Reuben Jonathan Miller**, author of *Halfway Home: Race, Punishment and the Afterlife of Mass Incarceration*

"*Policing Empires* painstakingly reveals the colonial roots of modern policing across the globe. Dismissing simple narratives of police militarization or individualized racism, Go shows how racialized fear of crime and the mobilization of counterinsurgency practices have been the organizing logics of the institution of policing."

**Alex S. Vitale**, author of *The End of Policing*

# Policing Empires

*Militarization, Race, and the Imperial Boomerang in Britain and the US*

JULIAN GO

OXFORD
UNIVERSITY PRESS

# OXFORD
UNIVERSITY PRESS

Oxford University Press is a department of the University of Oxford. It furthers the University's objective of excellence in research, scholarship, and education by publishing worldwide. Oxford is a registered trade mark of Oxford University Press in the UK and certain other countries.

Published in the United States of America by Oxford University Press
198 Madison Avenue, New York, NY 10016, United States of America.

Library of Congress Cataloging-in-Publication Data
Names: Go, Julian, 1970– author.
Title: Policing empires : militarization, race, and the imperial boomerang
in Britain and the US / Julian Go.
Description: New York, NY : Oxford University Press, [2024] |
Includes bibliographical references and index.
Identifiers: LCCN 2023013837 (print) | LCCN 2023013838 (ebook) |
ISBN 9780197621660 (paperback) | ISBN 9780197621653 (hardback) |
ISBN 9780197621684 (epub)
Subjects: LCSH: Militarization of police—United States. |
Militarization of police—Great Britain. | Police—United States—History. |
Police—Great Britain—History.
Classification: LCC HV7909 .G65 2024 (print) | LCC HV7909 (ebook) |
DDC 363.2—dc23/eng/20230512
LC record available at https://lccn.loc.gov/2023013837
LC ebook record available at https://lccn.loc.gov/2023013838

DOI: 10.1093/oso/9780197621653.001.0001

Paperback printed by Marquis Book Printing, Canada
Hardback printed by Bridgeport National Bindery, Inc., United States of America

*For Emily and Oliver*

# Contents

# Tables

# Figures

# Preface

In my more pretentious moments, I think of this book as the third installment of a trilogy of historical sociologies of the American empire. The first volume is my book *American Empire and the Politics of Meaning: Elite Political Cultures in the Philippines and Puerto Rico* (2008). That work explored the political dynamics of meaning-making during the American occupation of the Philippines and Puerto Rico during the first decades of the twentieth century. Among other things, it contended that America's colonial empire was founded upon signifying practices as they unfolded in contexts of unequal political power. Beyond the specific arguments of that book, *American Empire and the Politics of Meaning* was also an invitation for other scholars to join me in overthrowing the chains of American exceptionalist thought and begin studying US colonialism properly, without restraint.

The second volume is *Patterns of Empire: The British and American Empires, 1688–Present* (2011). That book examined the macrohistorical dynamics of the British and American empires over the past three centuries. It was a direct assault on exceptionalist themes. It sought to unmask the myriad of ways in which the United States is and has been an empire; to reveal how the historical dynamics and forms of American empire recapitulate those of its imperial partner and historical predecessor, the British Empire; and to show how those things about the American empire that are taken to reflect America's special character and values are actually responses to the agency of people in the colonial and ex-colonial world. Exceptionalism begone.

Despite the differences between these two early works, both books tried to better understand the American empire at a time (in the early 2000s) when many skeptical scholars could not accept the idea that the United States was ever an empire. Some of those skeptical scholars were located in the discipline of international relations and had pretensions to occupy positions of power in the American state. They therefore could not admit empire. Others included US historians whose refusal to admit of empire was rooted in their personal politics or disciplinary blinders. Those blinders did not permit them to look beyond the traditional borders of the United States, and they worked within academic incentive structures that compelled them to hold steadfast to American exceptionalism. (After all, if the United States is *not* exceptional, what use is the specialized knowledge that historians of the United States purportedly monopolize?)

By now, things have greatly changed. A younger generation of scholars, including historians, have produced new works on the US empire and its various components. Even if they still have not taken up the call to conduct more comparisons, there is less hesitancy to think of the United States as an empire and to take it as an object of serious study. This is good.

Both of my two earlier books on the US empire also shared something else: they explored the more global or peripheral dynamics of empire. They are about what happened "outside" the United States and Britain. They are about patterns and processes "over there" in the colonies and peripheries of imperial power. Even *Patterns of Empire*, despite its macro-scale focus on global dynamics, was about the peripheries of imperial power. One of its arguments is that what empires do and how they act, the forms they take and the strategies they deploy, and ultimately how they fare depend upon what happens in the peripheries rather than the metropole. Empires are made on the ground.

The present work is significantly different on this score. Rather than examining the dynamics of colonial rule on the ground or the historical forms and global dynamics of empire, *Policing Empires* is about how these things matter for the policing of marginalized populations within Britain and the United States. It examines how imperial interventions abroad have shaped police militarization in the United States and Britain from the very birth of modern policing. This book, therefore, is about how the margins constitute the center, how imperial experiences have not been appurtenant to operations of state power in the cities and heartlands of Britain and the United States but central to them. It is about how police on the streets of Chicago, Los Angeles, London, and Manchester (among many other sites) act like occupying armies abroad because, in a sense, they *are* occupying armies, not just learning from colonial and imperial experiences but also serving as extensions of them. The police that I see outside my window in South Chicago or patrolling the streets of Brixton in London are material traces of occult histories encompassing brutal imperial power in the colonial and ex-colonial world—histories connecting imperial intervention into lands deemed foreign and far away with the beat officers, stops and searches, crime maps, surveillance cameras, police raids, detective bureaus, rubber bullets, and riot shields in major cities and towns spanning Britain and the United States. This is a book about empire. But it is more precisely about empire's effects upon institutions of violence "at home."

By exploring the returns of empire upon policing, the present book's theoretical and methodological inclinations summon a different book of mine, *Postcolonial Thought and Social Theory*. One of the many insights of postcolonial thought is that our present modernity has been fundamentally shaped by histories of empire and its correlates of racialized power, colonial domination, and global capitalism. More crucially, and by the same token, the insight is that metropole and colony, center and periphery, or the "domestic" and "foreign" do not constitute separate, distinct spaces and histories untouched by each other but are mutually constituted. If conventional social scientific thought operates by an "analytic bifurcation" (as I call it in *Postcolonial Thought and Social Theory*) that would have us separate what happens in the United States or Britain from what happens in the imperial hinterland, postcolonial thought urges us to reconnect them and recognize their mutual constitution.

Unfortunately, the lessons of postcolonial thought have yet to be absorbed by the new scholarship on US empire. This scholarship does well to bring American empire into the analytic spotlight but, exceptions aside, much of the work reinscribes an exceptionalism of a different sort, continuing to analytically bifurcate what happens within America's traditional borders from what America does outside those borders. If it is now more acceptable in academic institutions to move from the study of America to the study of its colonies, it is less common to study the mutually constitutive relations between or across metropole and colony.

One hope of this book is to overcome this form of exceptionalism too. The book shows some of the many ways in which the histories of policing in both Britain and the United States are entwined not only with each other but also with the two empires' overseas excursions—how colonialism and imperialism "over there" have shaped policing "at home." In so doing, this book hopes to show that the insights of postcolonial thought and their invitation to overcome analytic bifurcation can also apply to the study of policing, and that policing in Britain and the United States is an effect an empire. This book, therefore, is not *just* about empire. It is about empire's returns. It is about policing in Britain and the United States as effects of the imperial boomerang.

As will be seen, one part of the story about policing and the imperial boomerang is the police deployment on America's and Britain's streets of coercive tactics, techniques, and technologies developed and perfected in the peripheral zones of empire. Many of the methods and modalities of power used by the police came to the United States from imperial zones like the Philippines and Vietnam. "Internal colonialism" is thus not a metaphor but a sociohistorical reality.

My own biography is not far from those same sorts of flows. My parents were born in the Philippines (in Iloilo, to be precise) and migrated to Detroit in the late 1960s for my father's medical residency. They can still remember the so-called riots on the streets of Detroit in 1967. Newly arrived wide-eyed immigrants from America's largest former colony, they watched from their small apartment window with fright and fascination as Black residents rose against police brutality. This was a brutality that, as we will see in Chapter 3, was not disconnected from the violence meted out by the US Army in the Philippines earlier in the century. One of Detroit's police units whose brutality invited the riots was the Detroit Tactical Mobile Unit, a descendant of the policing forms envisioned decades earlier by August Vollmer, a police innovator who had served as a soldier in the US Army during the Philippine-American War.

Originally, my parents planned to return to the Philippines after my father finished his medical residency. But the rise of Ferdinand Marcos to power in the Philippines, with the full support of the US government, thwarted the plan. The Marcos regime did not take kindly to my father's family in Iloilo. The fear of persecution pervaded the lives of my family in the Philippines.

Their fear was well founded. Marcos' henchmen, aka the Philippine Integrated National Police, soon became notorious for their violence and brutality against citizens. This Philippine police was indirectly if not directly funded by the US empire, and it was a legacy of America's earlier colonial intervention, when the US colonial state created the counterinsurgency force known as the Philippine Constabulary (which later became the Philippine National Police). Given this American-created and -funded police state, coupled with the threat of persecution, my father decided to stay in America. Like modern policing, my parents' very lives in America can be said to be an effect of empire.

So could mine. I was born in Detroit.

# Acknowledgments

It pleases me that I have more supporters to thank than enemies to spite. The following forums provided helpful spaces for developing some of the ideas in this book: the British Sociological Association lecture series "Post/Decolonial Transformations" (with Meghan Tinsley and Adam Elliott-Cooper), the Cambridge IR and History Working Group's workshop at Cambridge University (with special thanks to Ayse Zarakol, Jaakko Heiskanen, Duncan Bell, and Jason Sharman), the Criminology Seminar Series at Birkbeck College University of London (especially Sappho Xenaskis), the "Presence of the Past" workshop held in Schliersee, Germany (organized by Stephan Stetter and Klaus Schlichte), the Visiting Scholars Program of the Havens Wright Center for Social Justice at the University of Wisconsin (with special thanks to Mustafa Emirbayer), the John Jay College of Criminal Justice (Musabika Nabiha), the University of Montreal (Fréderic Mérand), Harvard University's History, Culture and Society Workshop (Ya-Wen Lei and Orlando Patterson), the MIT Economic Sociology Seminar (Nathan Eric Wilmers), the University of Florida's Political Science Department (Ben Smith), and the University of Florida's English Department (Malini Johar Schueller). Input from the sociology departments at the following institutions has been both invaluable and energizing: Princeton University (including Viviana Zelizer, Paul Starr, and Kim Lane Scheppele), the University of California, San Diego (Abigail Andrews), the University of California, Berkeley (Chris Muller), the University of Arizona (Daniel Menchik), the University of Georgia (Diana Graizbord), Stony Brook University (especially Nicholas Hoover Wilson, Crystal Fleming, and Kristin Shorette), McGill University (Poulami Roychowdhury), Colby College (Neil Gross and Damon Maryl), the University of Michigan (Müge Göçek), the University of Nevada, Las Vegas (Barbara Brents), the University of Texas at Austin (especially Harel Shapira), the University of North Carolina at Chapel Hill (with special thanks to Taylor Hargrove and Neal Caren), and the CUNY Graduate Center (Lynn Chancer, Thomas DeGloma).

At the University of Chicago, I have benefitted from critical comments and conversations at the following forums: the Department of Sociology's Colloquia Series (especially Forrest Stuart, Andreas Gleaser, Dingxin Zhao, and Linda Waite), the History and Social Sciences Workshop (including Steve Pincus, Andrew Abbott, Terry Clark, and Bill Sewell), the Politics, History, and Society Workshop (Marco Garrido, Lis Clemens, and Chris Williams), the Reproductions of Race and Racial Ideologies Workshop (especially Adom Getachew and Kevin

Irazoke), the American Politics Workshop (especially Sonja Castaneda and Maya Van Nuys), and the Chicago Center for Contemporary Theory (especially Lisa Wedeen, Kaushik Sunder Rajan, and Daragh Grant). I have been emboldened to complete this book by my colleagues in the Sociology Department at the University of Chicago, where I wrote much of this work (and specifically in my office, 319 SSRB, across the hall from the former office of August Vollmer, the "father of modern policing" and onetime professor at Chicago). Thanks to all of them for providing a collegial and stimulating environment, especially but not restricted to, besides colleagues mentioned above, Neil Brenner, Kimberly Kay Hoang, John Levi Martin, Kristen Schilt, and Robert Vargas.

This is a work of historical sociology, which means that, by its nature, hard-nosed territorial historians will balk at it. But I have been honored by the encouragement, aid, and/or critical feedback from wonderfully astute and collegial historians, including but not restricted to Simon Balto, Jonathan Booth, Adam Crymble, Simon Devereaux, Matthew Guariglia, Max Felker-Kantor, Wilbur Miller, Steve Pincus, and Ben Taylor. Thanks also to the following colleagues, friends, and interlocutors who offered criticism, commentary, or indispensable encouragement at various stages of this project, besides those mentioned already: Tarak Barkawi, Brenden Beck, Bart Bonikowski, Sarah Brayne, Sean Case, Neil Gross, Charlie Kurzman, Chris Muller, Lou Pingeot, Stuart Schrader, Alex Vitale, and Loïc Wacquant. Thanks also to Zophia Edwards, Ricci Hammer, Meghan Tinsley, Trish Ward, Jake Watson, and Sasha White, former PhD students who have since become invaluable colleagues, allies, interlocutors, and sources of inspiration.

The archivists at the following libraries have been especially helpful: the Hargrett Library at the University of Georgia (Mazie Bowen), the Manchester Central Library, United Kingdom (Sarah Hobbs), the Bancroft Library at the University of California, Berkeley, the Bristol Archives, United Kingdom (Sarah Taylor), and the National Archives at Kew, United Kingdom. Jessica Stinson, Berenice Martinez, Elizabeth Jones, and Fernanda Gutierrez Mello Vianna provided research assistance at different stages of this project. Research funds have been provided by the Boston University College of Arts and Sciences and the University of Chicago Division of the Social Sciences. Anonymous readers for Oxford University Press provided constructive comments, for which I am forever grateful. I am also grateful to James Cook for his steady support, acumen, and efficiency. He has been an ideal editor.

Finally, I want to thank my family. My wife, Emily, has been an unceasing supporter of all my ideas, good or bad, and has also never failed to tell me when they're bad. I don't know how I could do my work without her support and insight. My teenage son, Oliver, has also been helpful, in his own peculiar way. When Oliver was twelve and I was beginning this book, I asked him what he wanted to be when he grows up. He replied with a smirk: "I want to write boring books that no one reads, just like you, Dad." I appreciate his subtle and not-so-subtle digs. They keep me grounded, which is important for writing boring books that no one will read.

I dedicate this book, boring or not, to Emily and Oliver.

# Permissions Notes

1.

*Image:* Figure 1.1. "Percentage of Arrests"
*Source:* Made by author

2.

*Image:* Figure 3.1 "August Vollmer"
*Source:* "August Vollmer Portrait Collection" held by the Bancroft Library at the University of California at Berkeley (duplicated by the photoduplication services at the Bancroft Library).

3.

*Image:* Figure 4.1 "Fenian Guy Fawkes"
*Source:* Hathi Trust Digital Library and the University of California via https://victorianweb.org/art/illustration/tenniel/punch/14.html

4.

*Image:* Figure 5.1 "Hand to Hand Combat Training, Honolulu Police, ca. 1939"
*Source:* "August Vollmer Portrait Collection" held by the Bancroft Library at the University of California at Berkeley (duplicated by the photoduplication services at the Bancroft Library).

# Introduction

## A Civil Police?

It is not because the Indo-Chinese has discovered a culture of his
own that he is in revolt. It is because "quite simply" it was, in more
than one way, becoming impossible for him to breathe.
> —Frantz Fanon, *Black Skin, White Masks* (1952)

I can't breathe.
> —George Floyd (2020)

The militarization of policing is by now complete. Witness the weaponry, armor,
and vehicles used by police forces in response to Black Lives Matter (BLM)
protests. Whether in Ferguson in 2016 or Minneapolis in 2020, police have
greeted BLM and its supporters with flash grenades, riot gear, chemical irritants,
short-barreled 5.56 mm rifles based on the military M4 carbine, armored vehicles
with .35-caliber ammunition, and even Air Force drones. About the Ferguson
protests in 2016, observers were unequivocal: it was "a war zone."[1] Witness, too,
how police responded to Native American activists and their allies at Standing
Rock in 2016 and 2017. An array of different police agencies routed them with
rubber bullets, tear gas canisters shot from grenade launchers, and vehicles initially made for the military, like Bearcats, Humvees, and mine-resistant ambush-
protected vehicles (MRAPs). The clashes resulted in hundreds of injuries and at
least twenty-six hospitalizations.[2]

The irony must be noted: here are local police forces deploying military-
grade weaponry on citizens whose tax dollars have paid for that very same
weaponry. But police militarization involves more than just the use of military-
grade weapons and tanks. Sociologists Peter Kraska and Victor Kappeler define
militarization as the process by which the police adopt not only the material
components of the military but also "the cultural, ideological and organizational" components.[3] Militarization includes the police adoption of military tactics, technologies, templates, and training, not just military weaponry. Special
Weapons and Tactics (SWAT) units are a good example. These use military-style
training, clothing, tactics, and command structures along with military-grade

*Policing Empires*. Julian Go, Oxford University Press. © Oxford University Press 2024.
DOI: 10.1093/oso/9780197621653.003.0001

weapons—an entire military culture, emulating and deploying military mindsets and mentalities alongside MRAPs. Militarization also refers to personnel. In fact, military veterans are disproportionately represented in police departments. In 2017, about 19 percent of police officers were military veterans, while just 6 percent of the population at large were veterans.[4]

How did this happen? How have we come to a point where citizens of a presumably liberal democratic nation pay for police forces that look and act like an occupying army? By most accounts, it was not supposed to be this way. Policing in the United States is historically and self-consciously part of an Anglo-American tradition known as "civil policing." Born in Britain in the nineteenth century, this model of policing posits a firm distinction between police and military power. In 1829, Sir Robert Peel created England's first modern police force, the London Metropolitan Police, and he meant it to be a substitute for the deployment of military power on home soil—a "civil" police because it was supposed to be of, by, and *for* citizens. This is also the tradition of policing that the United States adopted in the nineteenth century when the first police departments were created, emulating the London model.[5] But police militarization violates the civil police ideal. This should make us wonder: how did we get here?

Police militarization is more than a quaint academic puzzle. It is also dangerous. One study finds that police officers who are military veterans are more likely to fire their weapons than those who have never served.[6] Even if police aren't war veterans, militarization can still shape their behavior. How can putting police officers in military garb, arming them with military-grade weaponry, and sending them off in MRAPs *not* impact officers' behavior? This is what the former police officer and now law professor Seth Stoughton calls "the warrior worldview." By this worldview, police officers "learn to treat every individual they interact with as an armed threat and every situation as a deadly force encounter in the making."[7] If all you have is a hammer, surely everything will look like a nail. And while the jury is still out, mounting evidence suggests that this point is not just theoretical. Studies reveal a significant causal connection between military hardware and violence: the more military equipment a police department has, the more violent the department is. Furthermore, having military equipment decreases the public's trust in the police, and it doesn't even reduce crime.[8] Perhaps all militarization does is transform social problems into military ones, forsaking imaginative possibilities toward change for quick, expensive, and lethal military solutions.

Militarization also has a racially *unequal* impact upon society. Let there be no doubt about it: police patrol, harass, and violently coerce racialized minorities at disproportionate rates. Research shows that SWAT units have descended upon the homes of Black residents with higher frequency than upon those of white residents, swarming citizens' homes as if they were attacking the compound of ISIS terrorists. In many cases, these residents did nothing illegal.[9] And police have typically patrolled Black communities like occupying armies. Patrisse Khan-Cullors, activist and founder of the Black Lives Matter hashtag, recalls growing up in a poor neighborhood outside Los Angeles where local police used "militarized responses and maneuvers" on an "almost daily basis."[10] Accordingly, she was "not shocked at the use of tear gas, assault weapons and tanks" at Ferguson in 2016.[11] If white Americans stood aghast at how police treated protestors, Khan-Cullors was hardly surprised.

There is thus a *racialized* pattern to militarization, a pattern whereby the militarization of American policing and racist suppression are tightly interwoven, braided together into a singular logic of coercion meted out to society's more underprivileged and marginalized members. It is as if militarized policing has been deployed primarily against nonwhite peoples to subdue them into submission, to forcibly discipline them into an overarching social order already fitted against them. At a town hall in Cincinnati on policing in 2020, one astute African American resident voiced the pattern simply: "To know as a taxpayer that [Cincinnati police] is receiving my hard-earned money to continue and consistently oppress my brothers and sisters is sickening. At this point we are paying slave masters with badges."

The puzzle of police militarization is thus bigger than just "How did we get here?" It is also this: why does militarized policing appear to be disproportionately directed at racialized minorities? Is it due to a few racist "bad apples" in our police departments who need anti-bias training? Or is something deeper at work?

"It has become rare in contemporary society," writes the sociologist Didier Fassin, "to interrupt the ceaseless flow of information presented as self-evident and take the time to reflect on why—or simply how—we have arrived at where we are."[12] This book aims to avoid this trap by uncovering the origins and development of racialized police militarization in the cradles of the so-called civil police: Britain and the United States. The book explores when, why, and how police militarization has occurred in Britain and the United States. It probes the origins of militarized police power from the beginning of modern policing and tracks it over time. It unearths the sometimes occult social logics that produce police militarization and the relations of power that give it substance and form. It charts and compares the mechanisms, modes, and modalities of police militarization in Britain and the United States and ponders the role that racialization plays in it all. It also shows some of militarization's many nefarious and often unintended effects. It offers "a history of the present," to borrow Foucault's phrase—or, more precisely, a *historical sociology of the present*. It uncovers the emergence, formation, and reproduction of militarized police power in Britain and the United States, thereby showing how the past shapes the present.[13]

While this book offers a history of the present, it also offers something bigger: a history of our *imperial* present. For as we will see in chapters to come, understanding police militarization in Britain and the United States requires us to cast our eyes beyond the traditional borders of both countries to consider global logics of empire—logics of imperial expansion, coercion, and racialized violence in the exploited peripheries of empire's metropolises. The history of these logics is not separate from the history of racialized militarized policing "at home." This book will show that empire is the fulcrum of modern militarized policing, if not of policing itself, and we cannot apprehend police and its militarization without grasping its coloniality—its *racialized imperiality*. This book, then, is not just a historical sociology of racialized and militarized policing in two nations. It is also about imperial assemblages of power, the effects of which have been felt at the peripheries of empire—from Madras and Ulster to Jamaica, Singapore, the Philippines, and Vietnam—as well as in the streets of London, Manchester, Savannah, New York, and Los Angeles, among many other places in between. This book is a *postcolonial* historical sociology of militarized police.[14]

But we are getting ahead of ourselves. Let us first unpack the idea of the "civil" police that militarization ostensibly transgresses.

## The Puzzle of Militarization

The model of the "civil police" was born with the London Metropolitan Police in 1829. This was a new thing. Prior to the London Met, neither England nor the United States had police departments as we know them today. Crime had been the purview of a hodgepodge of actors, ranging from private detectives to local constables and watchmen. And in the event of riots in the streets, mob violence, or unruly demonstrations and strikes, state officials had little alternative but to call in the army. The creation of the London Metropolitan Police changed all of that. It was the first full-time, professional, uniformed, and centralized department to manage crime and also handle disorder without relying upon the military. Sir Robert Peel, who helped create the new police, is said to have laid down the ideology with his principles of law enforcement, known today as "Peel's Principles." "The basic mission for which police exist," the first principle states, "is to prevent crime and disorder as an *alternative* to the repression of crime and disorder by military force."[15]

The London Metropolitan Police was also different from the type of police that had existed in Europe. At the time, many European countries had militarized police forces in the form of national gendarmeries, such as France's current Gendarmerie Nationale, the Prussian gendarmerie from the nineteenth century, or Italy's carabinieri. A legacy of Napoleon's conquest of Europe, these "state-military" police persist today. They are national in scope and are expressly militaristic in function, form, and content. Many are branches of the military, and they have been traditionally "armed and equipped like soldiers, stationed in barracks."[16] Part of state armies, they are *meant* to be militarized. With the London Metropolitan Police, Peel hoped to create an alternative to this state-military model: a civilian or "civil" police. A form of state power putatively most appropriate for democratic societies, a civil police force is separate from the military branch. It is staffed and run by civilians rather than soldiers. As the historian Charles Reith wrote in the 1950s, the basic idea of the new London Metropolitan Police was to create a police system "exercised indirectly by the people, from below, upwards," as opposed to the "despotic totalitarian police systems" represented by the French gendarmerie or the army, wherein authority came "from above, downwards."[17]

America's municipal, city, and county police forces today are of this sort exactly. They were explicitly modeled after the London Metropolitan Police. New York created the first London-style police in 1844. Most northern cities followed in subsequent decades. In the South, the earliest types of "police" were slave patrols and militias, but after the Civil War these were dismantled and replaced with modern police departments following the civil police model. They were all meant to be alternatives to a "tyrannical standing army," as the historian Wilbur Miller puts it.[18] Accordingly, like the London police but unlike European gendarmeries, they were put into the hands of civilian officials rather than the military. Adopting Peel's idea of civil policing, the early police officers in New York City were not even issued firearms, only truncheons like in London.[19]

Not only was this a new model of policing, it also introduced a comparably new distinction in the state's coercive powers that we take for granted today: a bifurcation between the "police" on the one hand and "the military" on the other. "An army," avers the historian C. A. Bayley, "uses force to defend a community from threats outside itself; a police force protects threats from within."[20] According to a US Congressional Research Service report, the civil police force embodies the "tradition" of "a distinct separation between military force and civil law enforcement."[21] The term "civil police" is thus fitting. The word *civil* invokes the idea of the "citizen"—as in a police force of, by, and for citizens—but it likewise summons the sense of "civility" and hence politeness and peace rather than brute force and violence. The "difference between the quasi-military and the civil policeman," declared former British police officer John Alderson, "is that the civil policeman should have no enemies. People may be criminals, they may be violent, but they are not enemies to be destroyed."[22]

This is why the militarization of policing is so puzzling. It transgresses the civil police ideal. As Melina Abdullah, the co-director of Black Lives Matter Grassroots, states in her response to police militarization in the United

States: "Our streets are not a war zone, and our people are not enemies of war."[23] But militarization does exactly that: it turns the streets into scenes of war. Police militarization blurs the lines between the army, state-military police, and civilian police while threatening to obliterate the distinction between citizen and foreign enemy. Militarization thus manifests what Nikhil Pal Singh calls an "ongoing slippage between policing and war that visibly characterizes the present."[24]

This slippage is seen even in the country where the civil police model was born: Britain. It is a common but mistaken assumption that the British police is America's peaceful, effective, non-militaristic counterpart—personified in the image of the friendly and peaceful "bobby on the street." In fact, in the United States, many of the first police departments did not routinely issue firearms to their officers, while some English police officers did have access to lethal weapons like cutlasses and even firearms. By now things have changed: US police are more armed than British police. But this difference is misleading. While only about 5 percent of officers in England are authorized to carry firearms, the majority of police departments in England nonetheless have armed response units (ARUs). Speeding to conflict sites in armed response vehicles (ARVs), which are like American SWAT vehicles, ARU members are clad in Kevlar body armor and carry "a cache of weapons including sniper rifles, automatic assault rifles, handguns, submachine guns and tasers."[25] Their raids have sometimes led to civilian fatalities.[26]

The late Stuart Hall, one of England's most renowned critical thinkers, alluded to this militarization in Britain as early as 1979. "It has become increasingly clear," he said in his Cobden Trust Human Rights Day Lecture,

> that the claim that the British police remains substantially an unarmed force, the only one in the world, is largely a semantic quibble. The fact that the accessibility to arms and similar equipment is still limited does not undermine the substantive fact that, for good or ill, in all those cases where it matters, the British police are now in effect an armed and fully equipped technical force.[27]

Hall might have also mentioned that even when British police are not carrying firearms, they nonetheless wield Mace, batons, and stun guns. In 2014 alone, the police in England and Wales used Tasers on citizens more than ten thousand times, down only a few hundred from the year before.[28] And since 1965, British police have been armed with tear gas. Furthermore, as we will see in later chapters, the British police have also adopted a military mentality and tactics that have contributed to heightened police brutality.

It is not just that the British police are militarized; it is also that it conducts racially disproportionate policing, just as in the United States. Britons coded as "Black" and "Asian" are subjected to stop-and-search and police uses of force at higher rates than those coded as "white." And while the actual numbers of police killings are small in Britain, Black Britons are more likely to die from policing shootings than whites, statistically speaking.[29] This is perhaps why so many racialized minorities in Britain joined the Black Lives Matter protests in the wake of the killing of George Floyd in 2020. The participants in the 160 protests across the country—including the fifteen thousand people marching in Manchester, the six thousand marchers in Cambridge, and the ten thousand in Bristol—were not only signaling solidarity with Black Americans. They were bearing witness to the racialized brutality of British policing on their own streets.[30]

The question again arises: how and why has this come to be?

## Making Sense of Militarization

To make sense of police militarization, some analytical tools would be helpful. But what tools? With what frames, concepts, or theoretical approaches are we to untangle the complexity that reveals itself to us as "police militarization"? Fortunately, in the wake of heightened attention to police violence in Britain and the United States, pundits, activists, and scholars have pondered and debated questions of policing and violence. This terrain of discourse is traversed by different modes of thought that might help us approach the problem of police militarization. Or they might not.

One dominant way of thinking about policing is *liberal reformism*. This is often represented in standard policing textbooks. It is also the near-official view of the state and the policing establishment. This mode of thought takes the model of the civil police and its associated "democratic policing ideal" seriously; hence it often quotes the founding principles of policing supposedly adumbrated by Sir Robert Peel. Policing, in this view, exists to protect the rights of citizens against criminals and disorderly disruptions to society. It is a necessary institution that can and should be deployed to protect us. As the scholar of English policing David Ascoli summarizes this mode of thought, the police "have been brought into existence to . . . protect the liberty of the subject against the license of the ill-disposed."[31] Or in the words of the United States Supreme Court in 1873, a police force is necessary for "the security of social order, the life and health of the citizen, the comfort of an existence in a thickly populated community, the enjoyment of private and social life, and the beneficial use of property."[32]

While this mode of thought has multiple implications for thinking about policing, it has specific implications for thinking about the militarization of policing. By this approach, militarization appears as a tragic aberration from policing's purpose. Not only does it violate Peel's stated principle regarding the separation of police from the military, it also violates the civil police's role in protecting rights.[33] Rather than protecting citizens' rights, police are more likely to violently violate them. The policy prescription follows. We must halt the flow of military materials to police agencies so police can return to their true mission and best realize the democratic policing ideal.

There are at least two limitations to this view. One is that it restricts the concept of militarization to the transfer of weapons only, overlooking that militaristic attitudes, ideologies, cultures, and tactics also pervade policing. A second limitation is more fundamental: liberal reformism mistakes seemingly noble ideals for historical reality. It takes as fact the rhetoric about the civil police that police departments themselves espouse. It assumes that the civil police's primary function is to protect the rights of citizens; it assumes that policing was at one point not militarized and only later became militarized. Policing used to serve its true purpose of serving the community and its citizens—or at least it was on the path toward fulfilling that goal—until militarization ruined it. Policing's past marks a prelapsarian state of innocence now corrupted by militarization.

This narrative is wrong. As we will come to see throughout this book, the so-called civil police has never been uncontaminated by militarism. Since its birth in Britain (and then later in the United States), the civil police model has been just that: a *model*—an ideal if not a myth. It is true that the birth of modern policing insinuated a bifurcation of state power between the police and the military, but this bifurcation was a theoretical one and was transgressed in practice from the outset. As we will see, police officials throughout modern policing's career have turned to military forces for templates, tools, and tactics; for ideas and ideologies; and for personnel and training programs. It would not be incorrect to say that, in some form or another, militarization has been a *constitutive* feature of policing. At most, as we will see in Chapter 1, police officials upheld the civil policing model as something to be *performed* in order to cover up the tracks of their militarizing moves. Given this reality, one might rightly claim that the attempt to demilitarize policing by proponents of liberal reformist thought is a fool's errand. Since the civil police has been militarized from the beginning, militarized mindsets and forms are baked into its character and operations, deeply ingrained in its very essence. Truly demilitarizing policing is impossible without abolishing the police entirely.

Such an argument about policing's deep-rooted militarization articulates with another way of thinking about the police in liberal democracies. We can call it *critical structuralism.* It can be rightly labeled "critical" because it contests the very premise of liberal reformism: that policing is meant to control crime, protect the rights of citizens, and thereby serve the community. According to critical structuralist thought, the liberal reformist premise is as unrealistic as it is naive; worse still, it dangerously reproduces the discourse of policing itself. The point of policing is not to attend to crime and disorder but rather to protect the property of the privileged and secure the conditions necessary for capital accumulation. The police indeed attend to crime, but repressing crime is just another way for the state to force the poor to live by wage labor rather than by theft. When not attending to crime, the so-called civil police is little else than a repressive state agency for disciplining workers into compliance. Marxist-inspired histories of American policing offer one version of this perspective. Policing "in its modern form," the historian Sidney Harring contends, "emerged from class struggle under industrial capitalism" as a means to repress the industrial working class while protecting the property of the upper class.[34] Some philosophers and sociologists similarly theorize "the police power"—which extends beyond the institution of police departments—as a matter of ensuring "security," where "security" is defined as the maintenance of capitalism.[35]

This mode of thought offers a different way of thinking about police militarization than liberal reformist thought. Foremost, it would not find militarization surprising. After all, by its nature, capital accumulation requires violence. Anything or anyone that stands in its way must be subdued, and militarized policing was born to fulfill the function. "The police power organizes and operates *as though* it is at war," announces Mark Neocleous, "precisely because *it is at war*"—a war against any impediments to capital accumulation. In this view, to even speak of "the militarization of policing" misses the picture. As "the police power *is always already at war*," it is also always already militarized. To even speak of something like "police militarization" or the "militarization of policing" is a dangerous misnomer that reifies distinctions between policing and the military.[36]

The critical structuralist mode of thought is powerful and important. It serves to demystify extant thinking about policing and militarization while upending liberal reformism's premise. But as a mode of historical investigation and social analysis, the critical structuralist approach raises as many questions as it ostensibly answers, offering some useful but ultimately restrictive analytic tools. For one thing, it does not offer the categories for apprehending the historical rhythms of police transformation and attendant accumulations of power over time. If, as critical structuralist thought has it, policing is always already militarized, then the history of police power emerges not as a history at all but rather as an infinite reiteration of the selfsame. Policing is and always has been exactly the same (militarized) and has always served the same singular function over time (capital accumulation).[37] We are left with a unidimensional and flat history, along with an incomplete understanding of complex formations of coercive power.

As we will see in forthcoming chapters, there *is* a history to the militarization of policing. This is a history replete with distinct temporal rhythms, discontinuities, and variations; a history of fits and starts, of particularities and distinctions, underlaid with certain logics and patterns. For example, as already noted earlier, from the very beginning the police in both the United States and Britain have been militarized. We will count the ways. But we will also see that the specific *timing*, *extent*, and *form* of militarization have varied. There have been *waves of militarization* over time: moments where police institutions adopt materials, methods, and mindsets from the military, punctuated by troughs of stabilization. At the birth of modern policing in London in 1829, some aspects of the states' war-making forms and practices were adopted, thereby initiating one such wave. The same is true for the United States in the 1840s through the 1860s. But these waves were followed by moments of relative calm—periods of time whereby the police did *not* militarize (as in not adding more militaristic elements to their repertoire)—only to give way to yet more waves or moments of militarization as police sought even more militarized tools, tactics, and technologies. Rather than a history in which policing is "always already" militarized, therefore, the history of policing is a *historical accumulation* of militarized means, methods, and modes by police, a history whereby police forces today have layers upon layers of militaristic components.

There are other variations besides these historical ones, both across Britain and the United States and across localities within them.[38] These will be explored in forthcoming chapters. The point here is this: if we were to stop at the notion counseled by critical structuralist thought that policing is "always already" militarized, we would overlook these dynamics and variations. Our analysis would flatten policing and war-making into one monstrous monolith whose parts are only understood in terms of their presumed singular function for capital accumulation. In the event, militarization would appear to be everywhere and therefore nowhere, and it becomes difficult to reach a critical understanding of the nuances, dynamics, and logics of power.

The gamble of this book is that we can do better by asking different questions. The question should not be "Is the police militarized?" Nor should it only be "What is the function of police?" It should rather be "When, where, how, and why have the police become militarized, and what are the possibly multiple logics governing it all?" Put differently, the analytic task of this book is to identify and explain waves of militarization, the moments of heightened borrowing from the military, and any other variations we might find. The gamble is that, by doing this, we will see new things.

One of those things has to do with *race*. Here is the other limitation of critical structuralist thought and liberal reformist thought alike: they offer us precious little by way of understanding *racialization* and militarization.[39] As noted earlier, there is something about militarized policing today that is deeply entwined with racialized social order. But liberal reformist thought reduces the issue of race to an aberration (a few "bad apples" or racist cops). Meanwhile, critical structuralism's emphasis on capital accumulation alone makes it hard to see race's possibly autonomous impact on policing or any deeper constitutive relations between police militarization and racial inequality. At most, critical structuralism would address race by reducing it to socioeconomic class. Yet, as we will see throughout the chapters to come, the logics of racialization connected to policing and militarization are not always reducible as such. While the role of policing in maintaining relations of class cannot be easily dismissed, and while race and class obviously intersect, racial ordering often plays a more subtly autonomous role in policing than either Marxist-informed critical structuralism or liberal reformist thinking would permit.

We hereby arrive at another mode of thought about policing. This is the mode of thought that sees policing as inextricably racialized. Refusing to reduce race to class and recognizing that the primary targets of policing have always been not just workers but more precisely nonwhite workers, this way of thinking about policing would locate the origins of modern policing not in London or New York but in the eighteenth- and nineteenth-century plantations of South Carolina. "The slave patrol was the first distinctly American police system," argues the historian W. Marvin Dulaney, "and it set the pattern of policing that Americans of African descent would experience throughout their history in America."[40] In his classic work on Reconstruction in the aftermath of the Civil War, W. E. B. Dubois revealed how slave patrols, manned by poor whites, served as the crucial mode of policing during slavery and then transmuted into postbellum forms of policing that continued to prop up Southern white supremacy.[41] Policing is a "war on black people," and its militarized forms follow directly from its function.[42] Other thinkers working in this tradition underscore the long history of militarized policing not only against African Americans but also against other peoples. They point to organizations like the Texas Rangers as early forms of policing that meted out violence against Indigenous peoples and immigrants.[43] The lawyer and activist Derecka Purnell summarizes: "Policing has always been used to control Black, Indigenous and immigrant labor."[44] To Robin D. G. Kelley, policing has long been a "cordon" to protect white supremacy, serving the interests not just of capitalism but of *racial* capitalism specifically.[45]

Throughout this book, we will see that the relationship between militarized policing and racial oppression is indeed long-standing and deep. But forthcoming chapters will also extend and sharpen the analytic lens offered by this approach. First, we need to avoid false continuities and more clearly trace the connections between prior state organizations of racialized coercion on the one hand and the civil police on the other. Historically, slave patrols and the Texas Rangers were among the first organizations in the United States to fulfill some of the state's policing powers, and indeed they were apparatuses of racialized violence. But they were *not* modern civil police departments. And slave patrols did not exist in London, Manchester, or Liverpool, yet the modern civil police was born in Britain and British policing has been racially disproportionate, as it is in the United States. If the roots of policing lie in slave patrols but Britain did not have slave patrols, why did Britain invent the civil police model and why is British policing racialized? Clearer genealogies of the entangled history of racialization and the civil police are needed.

Second, we need to expand the analytic capacities of this approach by exploring the potentially multiple and perverse ways in which racialization matters for policing. Most of the thinking on racism and policing examines the *effects* or *functions* of policing: how it disproportionately impacts racial minorities. But as we will see in the chapters to come, it is not just that militarized policing negatively impacts racialized minorities. It is also that racialized imaginaries generated militarized policing in the first place.[46]

Finally, we need to expand the lens of this view of policing to consider the broader international context of militarized policing; the transnational and even global scales at which racialized and militarized policing has operated (and continues to operate). As this book will show, to understand militarized policing in the United States and its historical dynamics, we need to look beyond policing within the traditional boundaries of the United States itself, and beyond the impact of militarized policing upon Black, Brown, and Indigenous peoples within the traditional borders of nation-states. We also need to look at more than the history of policing in Britain. We need to look at broader global relations of *empire*. To this issue we can now turn.

## Seeing Empire

Conventional critiques and modes of thinking about policing, from liberal reformism to critical structuralism, are often blinded by methodological nationalism. As we think about the militarization of policing in the United States, we assume that there is something called the "military," aimed at "foreign enemies" operating outside the boundaries of the nation-state. Then there is something called "policing," aimed at "citizens" operating inside the nation-state. Militarization is conceived as a process whereby modes of violence meant for foreigners outside are brought "inside": the foreign is imported into the domestic. Militarization means the domestication of foreign methods and means.

There is something to this way of thinking. Much of the world today is indeed organized into nation-states, whereby a simple division between the "domestic" and the "foreign" pertains. The danger is when methodological nationalism blinds us to another category of state-making, war-making, and subjecthood: empire. I use this term precisely, not metaphorically. Empire is a transnational formation of political domination, a formation of power whereby a center or metropole exerts control over other societies. Formal empire, or colonialism, has been the most typical form of empire, but informal empire is also common. While the former operates by the direct and juridical assertion of sovereignty over previously foreign territories and peoples, the latter operates through a panoply of assertions of power, including temporary occupation, threats of force, or politico-economic manipulation. It is typically exerted over ex-colonial territories. It is a kind of neocolonialism.

In both its formal and informal modalities, empire has been a dominant sociopolitical formation for centuries. It persists today. While most of the former formal colonies have gained independence—first in the nineteenth century with the decolonization of Latin America, and then later with the decolonization of many countries in the rest of the globe after the Second World War—some colonies persist. The United States continues to exert direct control over territories such as Puerto Rico, Guam, and the Virgin Islands. Furthermore, informal empire continues unabated. Postcolonial societies, enjoying nominal independence, are still subjected to various subtle and less subtle imperial interventions, forced into wider networks of continued control extending from Afghanistan to Central America. Empire remains.[47]

What does this have to do with methodological nationalism and the militarization of police? Consider the writings of the 1950s anticolonial activist and thinker Frantz Fanon. In his book *The Wretched of the Earth*, Fanon offers a scathing critique of French settler colonialism in Algeria:

> The colonial world is a world cut in two. The dividing line, the frontiers are shown by barracks and police stations. In the colonies it is the policeman and the soldier who are the official, instituted go-betweens, the spokesmen of the settler and his rule of oppression. . . . [T]he policeman and the soldier, by their immediate presence and their frequent and direct action maintain contact with the native and advise him by means of rifle butts and napalm not to budge. It is obvious here that the agents of government speak the language of pure force. The intermediary does not lighten the oppression, nor seek to hide the domination; he shows them up and puts them into practice with the clear conscience of an upholder of the peace; yet he is the bringer of violence into the home and into the mind of the native.

Fanon's observations here underscore the limits of methodological nationalism for thinking about police militarization. Fanon's world was a world of empires in which France was not a self-contained nation-state with "domestic" boundaries, where police operated, marking a difference from the "foreign," where the military operated. The French state was an *imperial* state, and in Algeria it had developed and deployed a system of violence to maintain its rule. This was a colonial modality of power where the "police" and the "military" operated together: a singular police-army force or colonial-military power operating according to the same principle of violence. In Fanon's world, the soldier and the policeman are both "agents of the government" speaking "the language of pure force," deploying the same brutal means and methods of coercion. And both do so for a singular purpose: to maintain the racialized order of colonialism, a world "cut in two." "The colonial world is a Manichean world," Fanon declares elsewhere in the text, and it is held intact by colonial-military power.[48]

Fanon helps us see that colonialism does not operate according to binary distinctions between "citizen" and "foreigner," or "domestic" and "foreign." Colonized peoples were never citizens enjoying full rights nor only foreigners to be ignored (or otherwise aggressed). They were putatively inferior and racialized *subjects* to be ruled, managed, and coerced. Similarly, colonial spaces were not "domestic" or "foreign" but somehow in-between and neither at once; they were novel spaces requiring new forms of statecraft and intervention, new practical grammars of coercion and violence. Empire entailed new technologies of rule and governmentalities fitted for the peculiar status of subjected peoples and territories. Tools and techniques—from coercive to legal to governmental—were devised to manage, control, or otherwise exploit subject peoples. Imperial peripheries and colonial societies, as the political scientist Alex Barder summarizes, were often laboratories of modernity, generating "new forms of violence, social control and, more generally, *disciplinary* practices."[49] And as Fanon highlights, those forms of violence involved unique configurations of militarized police and policing militaries that disrupt any fundamental bifurcation between them. "Trying to distinguish between the 'civilian' and the 'military' [modes of coercion] makes little sense" in colonial settings, writes the historian Emmanuel Blanchard.[50]

What Fanon finds in the French empire also applies to the US and British empires. During formal colonialism, both empires developed colonial policing systems to create, perpetuate, and defend racialized rule, thereby merging military forms and functions with the duties we associate with "policing" in metropolitan sites (such as crime control and maintaining social order). In the US empire, these systems included everything from militias in frontier territories to the Philippine Constabulary, the Puerto Rican Insular Police, and the American-run Gendarmerie of Haiti in the early twentieth century. The British Empire included coercive formations such as Caribbean slave patrols of the eighteenth century, the Royal Irish Constabulary and the Dublin Police of the nineteenth century, and the Malabar Special Police, the Uganda Police Service, and the Royal Hong Kong Police of the twentieth century.

The military stood by these forces, particularly for the purposes of quelling insurgencies in moments of "emergency" (such as the "Kenyan emergency" or the "Aden emergency" of the mid-twentieth-century British Empire). Militaries and colonial police were typically interchangeable in training, personnel, form, tactics, and weaponry. In addition, in both the US and British colonial empires, the military was often the de facto ruler of far-off lands, serving as the actual government of colonial societies until civilian government was created. In informal empire, the military takes on a primary role too. Armies invade, occupy, sometimes govern, cajole, or threaten weaker societies in the interests of the imperial center through efforts like America's "gunboat diplomacy" or Britain's "Opium Wars." Even in the period when formal empire was dying, between 1945 and 1971, "the British Army was involved in at least thirty-seven conflicts across a rapidly decolonizing world," notes the sociologist and activist Adam Elliott-Cooper.[51] Furthermore, military personnel often advised and armed local police forces, counterinsurgency units, and the armies of nominally independent postcolonial societies—all in the name of "nation-building" or "modernization."[52]

In both the US and British empires, therefore, rather than only aiming at "foreigners" as distinct from "citizens," the military has directed its power at colonial or neoimperial subjects through a variety of practices and modalities of intervention, ultimately helping to repress and suppress peripheralized peoples at the margins of imperial formations. To be clear, this has not been an unusual function for the military. In a certain sense, imperialism has been the raison d'être of militaries just as empires have been dependent upon militaries. The British colonial empire in the eighteenth and nineteenth centuries would not have been possible without the Royal Navy or the British Army. The reverse is also true: colonies supplied the majority of soldiers and raw materials for Britain's armed forces.[53] America's colonial expansion westward was not only eased by the US Army but occurred by the US Army's hand. In turn, the US Army owes much of its existence and development to westward expansion. Its primary function in the nineteenth century was to fight the so-called Indian Wars and suppress Indigenous resistance. Through the 1870s and 1880s, the US Army engaged in more than a thousand combat actions, killing at least six thousand Indigenous people. Two-thirds of all soldiers in the US Army were stationed in the western frontier.[54] By the turn of the twentieth century, the US military also played an important role in securing America's overseas colonial empire, extending from Puerto Rico to Samoa and the Philippines. This colonial experience in turn transformed the US military (as we will see in Chapter 3).

Put differently, what we typically refer to as "the military" must be seen for its role in what I will refer to as *imperial-military* regimes (or *colonial-military* regimes). These are loosely organized assemblages of coercion and control for creating and sustaining empires. They are agents of imperial and colonial power that claim a monopoly over the legitimate use of violence. If, as noted, "empire" is a transnational formation by which political power is unequally exercised over weaker populations and subjects deemed inferior, imperial-military regimes are the coercive components of those formations. They entail operations and practices of violence conducted by the imperial state and its agents on the ground. They include both the "military" and the colonial "police," along with other state organizations of power that go under different names but nonetheless use violence and its threat. These regimes are essential for imperial states to conquer new territory and peoples, rule them, and repress resistance. They also aid in empire's other tasks, such as dispossessing local populations, extracting raw materials, or deploying local labor in the interests of metropolitan capitalists and settlers. Imperial-military regimes are not only vital for sustaining imperial rule; by the very same token, they are vital for colonial and imperial capitalism.

To meet the imperatives of empire, these colonial and imperial-military regimes typically invent, deploy, and perfect a wide repertoire of tools and techniques. They use material *tools and technologies of coercion*, from swords and cutlasses to advanced firearms and weaponry of all kinds, along with accessories of war like tanks, helmets, and shields. Beyond these, imperial-military regimes also develop multiple organizational *forms, operations, templates, and tactics* for violence: modalities of distributing, deploying, arranging, and asserting bodies, materials, and forces to maximize capacities and meet strategic goals. These help regimes best use the tools and technologies at their disposal. They include military mindsets and cultures of power: ingrained modes of thought and behavior that maximize the power of bodies for coercion and its threat. Finally, colonial and imperial-military regimes develop *assemblages of knowledges*, schemas and entire epistemes about colonized terrains and peoples that serve as templates for understanding subject populations in the hopes of ruling them. These assemblages include seemingly benign systems for collecting information and various technologies of surveillance.

There is a history to these colonial and imperial-military regimes. They are complex assemblages of power with multiple forms and features. They develop and transmute over time. They are subjected to different forces and in turn unleash new forces. They expand, contract, rearrange, and transform. They mark out a history of empire and its coercive formations.

This history of imperial and colonial military regimes has unfolded alongside the history of policing in the United States and Britain. As the "civil police" was being founded in London in 1829, Britain was ruling territories across the Caribbean, expanding into India, and consolidating new forms of colonial rule in Ireland (among other places). When the first London-type police forces were formed in the United States in the 1840s and 1850s, America's military-imperial regime was conquering Mexican territories and creating present-day Texas, while slave patrols maintained white settler rule in the South. In the early twentieth century, as the "professionalization" and "reform" movement in urban policing was unfolding, the American state was conquering the Philippines, Puerto Rico, and Cuba. In the 1950s, when police departments in the United States were using new technologies to patrol increasingly nonwhite neighborhoods, the American state was funding, training, and running counterinsurgency units overseas and creating client regimes to shore up its global network of power as a bulwark against communism.

Despite all of this, most popular and scholarly discussions of police militarization overlook empire and the history of imperial-military formations. While extant analyses highlight that the police appropriate, emulate, or model various things from the military, they tend to portray the military as a homogenous, flat, and transhistorical regime of power. They overlook that military formations of modern states exercise a variety of functions entailing a diverse array of tactics and operations; they elide the fact that militaries are tethered to empire, the key player in colonial and imperial-military regimes. But once we recognize this, we can more clearly sketch the myriad ways in which the history of police militarization is not only synchronized with but also *shaped by* the dynamics and operations of empire. We can better see how the history of policing is entangled with imperialism and recognize that what is typically called "the militarization of policing" is in an effect of the *imperial boomerang*—a result of *imperial-military feedback*. This is one of the main claims of this book.

## Domesticating Empire, or the Boomerang Effect

The term "boomerang effect" (which we will use interchangeably with "imperial feedback") originates in critiques of European imperialism leveled by anticolonial thinkers such as Aimé Césaire, the Martinican politician, poet, and theorist. Césaire used the term to characterize Hitler's violent invasion and rule of neighboring European countries.[55] In Césaire's rendering, Hitler manifested in Europe what Europeans had always done to colonized peoples in the Caribbean, Africa, and Asia. Hannah Arendt too was alive to the notion of the "boomerang effect," enlisting it to refer to how "rule by violence in faraway lands" by the British "would end by affecting the government of England," such that "the last 'subject race' would be the English themselves."[56] Later, in the 1970s, the French philosopher Michel Foucault caught on. In his lectures at the Collège de France, published under the title *Society Must Be Defended*, Foucault, in one of those rare moments when he actually refers to colonialism, voices Césaire's insight:

> It should never be forgotten that while colonization, with its techniques and its political and juridical weapons, obviously transported European models to other continents, it also had a considerable boomerang effect on the

mechanisms of power in the West, and on the apparatuses, institutions, and techniques of power. A whole series of colonial models was brought back to the West, and the result was that the West could practice something resembling colonization, or an internal colonialism, on itself.[57]

In subsequent chapters, we will see that the waves of militarization in Britain and the United States are the products of colonial boomerangs. The militaristic means and methods that police have imported for home use originate in the frontiers and peripheralized spaces of empire, in effect transforming the "civil" police into not just a militaristic force but a *colonial* force on home terrain. This militarization-as-boomerang has occurred since the very beginning of the so-called civil police in London. It continued as the civil police popped up in other cities in England and also later in the United States. It has continued thereafter, all the way to the present.

Forthcoming chapters will track these flows, chart their forms and functions, and disclose their mechanisms and modalities. But what is at stake in this? Why shift the conceptual terrain from militarization to the boomerang effect? Part of the issue is historical truth. To say that police militarization is an effect of the colonial boomerang is more historically accurate. It gets at what really happened (and what is really happening today, as will be seen). Just as importantly, it offers much-needed analytic precision and explanatory weight. Empire has its own histories, its own rhythms and waves. Reckoning militarization-as-boomerang helps us see that waves of police militarization are partly structured by these historical dynamics of empire. Indeed, as will be seen in subsequent chapters, police militarization has occurred in the aftermath or during periods of redoubtable imperial expansion and reconfigurations of the imperial-military regime.[58] If we want to understand the historical waves of police militarization, we will do well to consider the dynamics of empire.

But recognizing militarization as an effect of imperialism is also important because it highlights the *raciality* of power. The boomerang effect means that police departments appropriate and deploy not just any materials, means, and mentalities of coercion; it means that they appropriate and deploy *imperial* or *colonial* materials, means, and mentalities devised to repress and rule imperial subjects deemed lesser and inferior. These tools and tactics are not the same as those used for trench warfare in Europe during the First World War, for instance. Rather, they were developed initially in the colonial context for *racialized* populations and hence for the purposes of maintaining a racialized social order. As we will see, these include everything from fingerprinting (which was originally created in British India in order to identify ostensibly unidentifiable Brown and Black populations) to pin mapping (initially created for colonial counterinsurgency campaigns) and beat patrols (which originated in plantation colonies). Understanding police militarization as a colonial boomerang effect therefore calls attention to the racialized character of the otherwise seemingly neutral process of so-called militarization.[59] It invites us to acknowledge the racialized "coloniality" or *racialized imperiality* of civil policing, alerting us to policing's origins in empire and its colonial character.[60]

In exposing the operations, modalities, and logics of policing's racialized imperiality, this book aligns with scholarship on policing that takes empire seriously. Historians Georgina Sinclair and Chris Williams have highlighted the "cross-fertilisation" of British policing at home and colonial policing abroad, unraveling how the latter influences the former and vice versa.[61] Scholars of policing in the American context such as Elizabeth Hinton, Jeremy Kuzmarov, Micol Siegel, Alfred McCoy, and Stuart Schrader have likewise explored some of the ways in which imperial coercion abroad has influenced policing within America's traditional domestic borders.[62] These works offer a promising aperture for apprehending the dynamics and logics of police militarization. This book draws upon them. But more investigation is required. Foremost, the larger patterns and logics of the boomerang effect need to be detected. Existing scholarship focuses on particular individuals or historical eras, thereby rendering it more difficult to detect and explain larger patterns and logics. Most of the emerging historiography on policing in the United States, for example, focuses on individual police officers who act as what I call *imperial importers*: energetic and enterprising individuals who serve in the military or colonies overseas, return home to take up important positions in police agencies, and then import the militaristic methods they have learned. This, as we will see, has been a key circuit of imperial influence upon domestic policing in both England and the United States. But it leaves open the questions of whether imperial feedback *only* happens through veterans, and whether those veterans always bring the boomerang home. In fact, we will see that there are veterans who become police officers but do not import military methods for policing. And there are imperial importers who do not have military experience.[63] Sometimes the boomerang returns, sometimes it does not, and we have not yet cottoned to why. Nor have we mapped the different routes by which it might return.[64]

Questions thus remain as to the conditions, causes, and paths of the boomerang.[65] When and why does the boomerang return? And through what means? This is a crucial question. By answering it, we also address the puzzle of militarization. Militarization is an effect of the boomerang; to explain the return of the boomerang is also to explain militarization. Accordingly, *explaining* rather than only tracing the boomerang effect is one of the main challenges that this book confronts.

## Logics of Racialization: From Citizen to Subject

To better understand the boomerang effect and police militarization, we might first listen closely to their victims, such as the founders of the Black Panther Party for Self-Defense in the United States in the 1960s. In 1967, Bobby Seale, a leading figure of the Black Panther Party, wrote: "The racist military police force occupies our community just like the foreign American troops in Vietnam." The organ of the party, *The Black Panther*, similarly announced: "The police action in Vietnam is no different from the police action in the Black Ghettos of America. The police occupy our black communities like a foreign troop occupies territory."[66] These statements register telling analogies between the policing of African American communities in the United States and imperial aggression abroad. But they also speak to actual connections rather than just analogies. In fact, as we will see in Chapter 5, the local police to whom Seale and Newton refer had been deploying some of the same military tools and tactics that were being used in Vietnam and elsewhere in the imperial world.

The Black Panthers thus put their finger on the boomerang effect precisely. But their critiques also help us dissolve the puzzle of militarization raised earlier in this Introduction. The puzzle is as follows. The civil police, theoretically, is for protecting citizens. Therefore, policing should be peaceful—indeed, "civil." The military-colonial police, meanwhile, are aimed at repressing ostensibly inferior subjects, and thereby employ "uncivil" tools—namely, violent militaristic methods. The militarization of policing through the boomerang effect means that these boundaries are transgressed. Citizens are treated like colonial subjects. But why? Why have police imported colonial methods used abroad for use on citizens? How is it that the so-called civil police have come to treat citizens as if they are enemies and colonial subjects, using the same means and methods that they use on the latter? Armed with the Black Panthers' insights, the answer is plain: the civil police use colonial modes of coercion on citizens and treat those citizens like colonial subjects because police see citizens *as* colonial subjects. And the primary modality for this categorical transformation—the key social code by which this miraculous transubstantiation of citizens into subjects occurs—is *racialization*. By racialization, citizens are constructed to be inferior, dangerous, and violent just like colonized peoples. Racialization thereby warrants, if not demands, the importation of militarized tools, tactics, and technologies.

As we will see in this book, this logic of racialization has been a primary driver of police militarization and its waves. Besides empire, it is the other part of the story for apprehending waves of militarization. For as we will see, while imperial-military formations make new tools, tactics, and technologies available to police, police have been more likely to draw upon and import those tools, tactics, and technologies as they face a perceived racialized threat.

To fully understand this, we must unravel two interrelated but analytically distinct processes: the *racialization of people* and the *racialization of crime and disorder*. First, the racialization of people: I draw this concept from the classic work by Michael Omi and Howard Winant. By their seminal definition, "racialization" means that a group of humans is turned into a group that is seen as biologically distinct. It refers to a process of " 'othering' social groups by means of the invocation of physical distinctions." Racialization is a way of turning society's members into a presumably inferior "race" and hence into society's alters. And while it is a mode of othering rooted in perceived biological differences, its power derives from the fact that it does not stop with biology. Phenotypical differences are presumed to index deeper differences in culture, character, and hence behavior.[67]

The racialization of people does not always generate singular derisive images. There have always been wide variations in racial classifications. A part of racism's power is that racism preys upon ambiguities to generate multivalent and polysemic discourses; it often works through and not in spite of fine-grained differentiations and deceitfully nuanced observations. In the early twentieth century, US colonial officials and settlers debated whether the "Tagalog race" was the same as the Comanche, while contrasting both with the Chamorros, whom they saw as peaceful "noble savages."[68] In the mid-twentieth century, British police drew lines among the newly arrived immigrants from the colonies, with one official claiming that Jamaicans "give practically no trouble," but the "same cannot be said" of the West Africans, whose "ethical conduct is deplorably low."[69] Racialization can also generate contradictory and ambivalent stereotypes of any single racialized group, invoking both desire and derision alternatively or simultaneously.[70] To wit: "They are racially inferior, but I like the way they dance."

Amid these complexities, one specific form of racialization is particularly potent for triggering police militarization. This form of racialization constructs racialized others as deviant, lawless, criminal, and menacing, collecting under signifiers of phenotypical or physical differences all the feverish fantasies of fear and horror. To draw from Achille Mbembe writing in a somewhat different context, this form of racialization invokes "a perverse complex, a generator of fears and torments, of disturbed thoughts and terror." It thus transforms would-be citizens into inferior groups to be contained, managed, kept apart and below, and eventually locked up—if not exterminated. The other, to again invoke Mbembe, becomes "a menacing object from which one must be protected or escape, or which must simply be destroyed if it cannot be subdued."[71]

Historically, militaristic policing in the colonies and imperial peripheries has been spirited by this type of racialization. Colonial discourse constructed colonized peoples not only as inferior to the colonizing community of citizens but also as irrational, violent, lawless, and hence prone to crime. The British colonial state classified entire communities and "tribes" in Kenya or India as inherently criminal.[72] Plantation owners, military officials, and state authorities typically theorized slaves in the American South, rebellious Moros in the Philippines, and rural Puerto Ricans as too ignorant to comprehend the law. All these constructions thereby justified unequal treatment. If the colonized are un-civilized, they must be treated with uncivilized methods. In fact, one common racialized assumption among colonial officials and settlers around the imperial world was that colonized people, as criminal brutes and savages, could *only* un-derstand violence. The related assumption was that colonized people, as fun-damentally foreign to the community of citizens, were essentially evil. To again invoke Fanon: "The settler paints the native as a sort of quintessence of evil." Thus warranted by this racialization, colonial regimes readily and often spoke "the language of pure force," in Fanon's words.[73] Indeed, racialization is why brutal colonial-military regimes of policing and counterinsurgency were formed in the first place.

What about racialization in the imperial metropole? There is a long-standing literature in social science highlighting that people who act against society's norms (i.e., those who deviate from social rules) are seen as deviant; when those rules have been codified as law, rule breakers become "criminal."[74] Race has been one of the dominant categories for this construction of deviance and criminality in metropolitan societies. To refer to just one example among many: in the United States in the early twentieth century, biological explanations of urban criminal behavior proliferated, constructing African Americans as inherently criminal even if they did not actually commit crimes. This was a pseudo-scientization of preexisting folk assumptions about the inherent tendencies of Black slaves (who were presumably kept in check only by the whip of their white masters). But the perverse logic was the same: criminals are not racialized, but racialized groups are seen as always-already criminals.[75]

Racialization in the colonies cannot be analytically separated from racialization in the imperial metropole. They have been reciprocal and mutu-ally supporting.[76] Colonial migration has often enabled this mutual relationship, as colonized peoples were often brought to the metropole to fulfill metropol-itan needs. In the event, metropolitan minorities and colonized peoples were literally one and the same, and it followed that the racialized discourse about them was the same too. In 1950s Britain, as more and more Black Caribbeans and Black Africans migrated to London, police referred to the neighborhoods in which they settled as "the colonies of London."[77] But the overlapping and mu-tual entanglements of metropolitan and colonial discourses of race also happen because of homologization, rooted in the pernicious structure of racial thought itself. The expansive classificatory grid of racist thought makes it possible to see ostensibly essential similarities between colonized peoples abroad and criminals at home who happen to look like them. Perceived phenotypical similarities facilitate shared classification. Homologies are created. Analogies are made. Equations are implied. To wit: Chinese migrants in California in the early 1900s were not exactly the Filipinos whom the American colonial state ruled overseas, but they were sometimes perceived to be *like* them.

Here lies the key to understanding the connection between metropolitan racialization and police militarization as boomerang effect. By racialization, metropolitan authorities and their allies make equations between the colonial alter and the criminal metropolitan subject. Through analogy or homology, metropolitan officials or the white upper classes construct equivalences between colonial and domestic populations, and this makes the application of colonial means and methods of coercion possible and justified. Because the brutes on the streets of the metropole are criminal and evil just like the savages in the colonies, both require the same treatment. Both are unworthy of citizenship and likewise unworthy of "civil" treatment. Without the use of weapons and tanks brought over from the Middle East campaigns, won't Black Lives Matter protesters loot and exact bloody revenge upon their white masters, just as Nat Turner did in 1831 and the Kikuyu did during the Mau Mau uprisings of the 1950s? The boomerang is thus summoned: warranted by racialization, militarized policing and the tools of colonial coercion are brought home to be put to use in order to maintain the racialized order. What we call "police militarization" is the result.

Still, if this is true, both the United States and Britain would have seen ceaseless and persistent militarization. Both countries have long had racialized minority populations in their midst, just as they have long had empires. Theoretically, therefore, racialization, analogization, and hence police militarization would be continual. But this is not exactly the case. As subsequent chapters will show, imperial feedback and hence militarization have tended to occur haphazardly, at particular moments and initially in specific places. Why?

The secret here is not just the racialization of peoples but the related *racialization of crime and disorder*. This refers to the attribution of seemingly criminal acts to racialized groups, typically sparked by threatening, unexpected, or ugly events and happenings.[78] In the face of frightful things, government officials and dominant groups blame racialized minorities. When an especially heinous crime occurs, authorities suspect that it was due to immigrants living in the obscene parts of town. To make sense of an outbreak of home break-ins, white families blame Black youths from the city. Faced with a seemingly sudden influx of migrant laborers, white residents stoke fears that the migrants will assault white girls or rob shops. After hearing about a bloody uprising in a colony in Asia, officials in Manchester or Los Angeles fear revolt among the city's racialized minorities. And so on.

In such cases, racialization acquires an added and particularly pernicious valence. It builds upon existing racist images, feeds upon itself, and sets off the racialization of crime and disorder to match the racialization of peoples. Racialized analogies between colonized and metropolitan populations that may have been latent become manifest, bursting to the surface to foment a sense of renewed racialized menace to order. Frightened white citizens, already stirred by preexisting images of racialized minorities—which empire, colonialism, and slavery made widely available—connect crime and disorder with minorities. They perceive an uncontrolled spread of lawless violence, murmuring silently or proclaiming loudly, "It is 'them.'" They begin to perceive a "crime wave" that threatens life, limb, and property, and they blame "them." Worse still, they worry that the once seemingly submissive minorities are finally planning revolt. They fret that the racialized groups' protests and demonstrations will spread like wildfire. In their racialized imaginaries, smashed windows from the night's protests are not just smashed windows. They are portents of violent insurrection, and the white community fears that it is the target. In brief, through a process Stuart Hall and coauthors call the "signifying spiral," a wider racial threat that portends violence and social breakdown is perceived, and analogization unfolds: the otherwise peaceful town or civilized city looks more like the wild frontier in the colonies, where white settlers, planters, and officials are outnumbered. White residents are disturbed and then triggered. They think of themselves as besieged settlers in a tumultuous dark colony.[79]

These are the scenarios that are most likely to summon the boomerang home. In face of perceived racialized threats from subjects in the metropole who are equated with colonial subjects overseas, state authorities look for tools and tactics to keep the barbarians at bay, to contain and suppress them. And they seek out those tools and tactics in the places that seem most appropriate: the frontiers and colonies of empire.

But who does the work? Veterans from the frontiers serving as police officials are the most likely to serve as imperial importers. But even if police officials are not themselves veterans, they can consult them, learn from them, and adopt their lessons. They can turn to veterans of the Philippine-American War, British campaigns in Northern Ireland, or the Vietnam theater. They consult counterinsurgency "experts" from the Mau Mau campaign, the Malayan emergency, or Afghanistan and Iraq. Either way, they bring the boomerang back, helping to equip the police with the tools, tactics, and technologies of imperial-military regimes. The process appears to us as "police militarization." But it is in actuality an effect of the colonial boomerang triggered by the racialization of crime and disorder.

## Questions of Theory and Method

The story sketched above identifies two sets of logics crucial for explaining the imperial boomerang effect and its manifestation as police militarization: empire and racialization. Waves of police militarization are the product of a historical conjuncture between the logics of imperialism on the one hand and logics of racialization on the other. The coércive formations of empire make novel militaristic means and methods of violent control available to police departments, but whether police avail themselves of those means and methods depends upon the racialization of crime and disorder and the perceived threats to order summoned thereby.

The converse is also true, as we will see in forthcoming chapters. Absent a racialized threat, the imperial militarization of policing is less likely to occur. Or if it happens at all, it is muted, with seemingly more benign and less violent tools adopted. Militarization might even be actively resisted or stopped short by knowing and indignant citizens. In such instances, the wave of militarization subsides, even if the tools and tactics remain. We will see, for instance, when white workers or elites fear that the police will use militarized police powers on them, they fight against militarization. When the imperial-military boomerang appears to be coming for *them*, police militarization faces barriers. It is only when there is a racialized threat to crime and disorder that imperial feedback and hence police militarization is likely. In the event, white authorities and citizens can be rest assured that if the "civil" police model is transgressed, it does not matter for them. Police militarization is meant for someone else.

It follows that race is not merely an effect of militarized policing but a cause. Rather than a sideshow to the presumably deeper structuring principles of capital accumulation and the need for class control, the code of race is fundamental, and doubly so. Racialization in the peripheries of empire feeds and justify new formations of violence; it generates militaristic forms of policing and control often requiring new tools, tactics, templates, and technologies. Racialization in the metropole, meanwhile, compels police officials to seek out novel tools, tactics, templates, and technologies and deploy them for use at home. As a social process occurring through but also behind the backs of individual racist police officers, racialization is thereby *constitutive* of police militarization, summoning the imperial boomerang that makes militarization possible.

This is only a broad sketch of the story told in chapters to come. There are variations across time and space to explore. Routes of importation, the particular actors involved, the groups that are racialized, the specific tactics or tools that are imported, the depths of militarization, resistance to militarization—all of these are variable. So too are the correlates and consequences of militarization as boomerang effect. We will explore these in the rest of the book. But we will likewise see that they are all variations on the same theme. The goal of this book is to capture the variations as well as the theme, to cast light on specific historical cases and moments but never lose sight of the subterranean logics of empire and racialization that undergird them. To cut through the messiness of overwhelming empirics and isolate dominant logics, necessarily bracketing other possible causal processes, people, and events—this is the goal. If the goal offends historiographical sensibilities that seek infinite complexity and radical contingency, so be it. The challenge is set: to excavate and expose logics that have been ignored or underexplored in our extant accounts of the supposedly "civil" police in the United States and Britain, thereby locating the *patterns* in the seeming madness of police militarization across time and space—from London to Los Angeles and Berkeley, from Savannah to New York and Manchester.

But how have these patterns been discovered? The theory of the boomerang effect and police militarization unfolded in this book has not fallen from the sky. Nor has it emerged from the presumably brilliant mind of a self-fashioned culture critic reading headlines and tweets in order to proffer profound theoretical insights. The patterns to police militarization explored in this book have been divined only through careful research guided by the methodological principles of comparative-historical social science and the philosophy of social science sometimes called "critical realism."[80] By these principles, we can identify social regularities, causal conditions, and occult causal mechanisms. There is no space to cover these principles in great detail. Here, though, are some general guidelines that constitute the comparative and historical methodology of this book. How can a historical sociology of police militarization be conducted?

First and foremost: identify the *sites of importation and hence militarization*, the spaces or localities of innovation. Where and when did the civil police turn to the military for organizational templates, tactics, and tools? In other words, which law enforcement agencies first adopted new military weapons or forms, thereby setting the standard for other law enforcement agencies to follow? Many of these agencies will likely be local police departments—city, county, or state law enforcement agencies—so look there. The federal government in the United States, or the national government in Britain, might have sometimes had a hand in encouraging militarization, so paying heed to national policies and programs will be important. But much of the story will probably be about local-level police, from London to New York and other cities. These are where the civil police model was born and where many of the waves of militarization began.

Second, examine the *importers*, the enterprising actors or *entrepreneurs* of violence work who aim to strengthen their departments, reform their ways, and transform policing by appropriating new coercive tools or organizational templates. Who were the officials, politicians, or police reformers that led the way in militarization? What is their background, their habitus, their identity, and their interest? Try to understand their understandings so that we can ascertain their goals. Even if full understanding is impossible, mobilize all evidence to recreate their contexts of meaning and motivation. Map the relations that shaped their actions and informed their importation. At the same time, take the broader context of the sites of importation into account. What was going on in London, Manchester, or Savannah at the time? To what were these innovative importers responding, exactly? Was it simply a rise in crime and disorderly events? What was the meaning of those events to the relevant actors?

Third: *compare across time and space* to ascertain patterns as well as the conditions and causes of police militarization. After locating the main sites of importation, see what the different sites shared and what they did not. Were the importers veterans? Were crime rates rising in all of them? Did certain events, like violent protests or grisly murders, precipitate militarization? Look for similarities, but also consider the possibility that there may have been different routes to militarization. Crucial for this comparative method is not just the logic of similarity but also the logic of difference. Locate other sites that are comparable to the sites of militarization but which did *not* militarize.[81] And compare across time. Investigate the historical period *before* the moment of militarization. What was different? And what was the turning point or series of events that ushered in the search for new tactics, tools, templates, and technologies? Explore the social conditions under which police militarization occurs.

Fourth: consider the *specific type of military methods and materials* that are domesticated, and their *origins*. What exactly did police appropriate and deploy to transform and hence militarize their departments? What did they choose to leave behind? What are the means and materials going into materialization? Firearms? Organizational templates? Tactics of force? And so on. Where did they come from? Can we discover their provenance, original functions, and form? Even if we cannot locate their precise historical origins, at least consider who was using them before the police appropriated them, where they were using them, and why. Conventional studies of police innovations in the United States or Britain tend to examine how police draw from each other, but we should also consider the ideological, material, cultural, and operational components of military-imperial regimes as possible sites of origination. Pay serious attention, therefore, to imperialism, its varieties of control and violence, and its tools of coercion. In short, put the forms of policing and the modalities of imperial violence into the same analytic field.

This means that one must *follow the relations*. Once key tools, technologies, templates, sites, actors, importers, and discourses are located across time and space, trace out the networks of relations that birthed or shaped those things, but do not stop at national borders. Recognize that policing has occurred in wider transnational, imperial, interimperial, and even global fields. If the analysis takes us all the way to far-off colonies and frontiers of empire, see what happens when you go there. And remember that this analysis, though a tool of transnational and global analysis, is not antithetical to comparison. Once different sites, events, and processes are compared, and once the relations are followed, transnational forms, flows, processes, and patterns can also be compared. Comparative analysis and transnational analysis are not intrinsically opposed methodologies.[82]

These are some of the principles that have guided the empirical investigation in the chapters to come. They have helped to reveal the patterns discussed in this book. They have served to identify the logics of empire and racialization at work in the making of militarization. They have thus led us to one of this book's conclusions: that police militarization is an effect of the colonial boomerang, brought home in the face of racialized threats. Put differently, police militarization is the long-standing practice of the imperial state domesticating the methods and tools of its armies abroad to herd, contain, and thrash imagined barbarians who have dared flood through the gates of its ostensible civilization.

## Looking Ahead

The chapters unfold in loosely chronological order, with each chapter covering distinct time periods, each marking the main waves of militarization. Chapter 1 explores the emergence of the idealized image of the civil police and its first institutional manifestation in the London Metropolitan Police created in 1829. The chapter illuminates how the racialization of crime and disorder, precipitated by the arrival of new Irish migrants to England's shores, triggered the formation of this novel form. The chapter also shows how the inventors of the civil police acted as imperial importers, drawing upon colonial forms and operations as they breathed life into the new police. Ireland will play a dominant role in the story, but Britain's Caribbean colonies will appear as well. The chapter also discloses the logic of performativity that the creation of the civil police engendered. The so-called civil police was born as an imperial-military form, but its founders tried to hide its militarism and replace it with performances of civility.

Chapter 2 examines the spread of the civil police model. After the London Metropolitan Police was created in 1829, other local governments in Britain copied it. The civil police then spread across the Atlantic, influencing the formation of the New York City Metropolitan Police in the 1840s and the Savannah police in the 1850s, among police forces in many other cities. The chapter shows how the racialization of crime and disorder triggered the birth of the new police in these cities and how the larger transatlantic interimperial network of cotton production and trade gifted their form, function, and targets. As the chapter shows, the new civil police in the transatlantic sphere was a response to the racialized subproletariat of cotton colonialism. The chapter further shows how these new police forces were modeled after the London Metropolitan Police but also had various colonial and imperial influences, including slave patrols. In addition,

Chapter 2 explores differences between the emergent policing formations in the different locations, including differences in armaments.

Chapters 3 and 4 explore the next wave of militarization in the two imperial metropoles. Chapter 3 looks at the police in the United States in the late nineteenth and early twentieth centuries. Historians refer to this period as the "professionalization" of policing, or the "reform era." This chapter unmasks these changes as effects of the colonial boomerang, made possible by America's new overseas expansion into colonies such as the Philippines. Again, the trigger for bringing the boomerang home was the racialization of crime and disorder, with a range of racialized populations serving as a repository for white residents' anxieties about urban development and industrial capitalism. These populations included European immigrants in the Northeast, Black urban migrants in the South, and the putatively criminal Chinese in the West.

Chapter 4 looks at Britain in the late nineteenth and early twentieth centuries. It will complicate the otherwise straightforward narrative of imperialism, racialized triggers, and imperial feedback told in previous chapters. For while the British Empire expanded significantly in this period, and while many veterans of empire took up policing positions, police militarization through the boomerang effect was limited. There was some development regarding firearms usage, crowd control, and surveillance, but these changes did not match the militarization of the American police around the same time. For instance, the efforts of London Metropolitan Police commissioner Charles Warren to militarize the force were halted. The chapter shows that racialization helps us understand this. Muted militarization in this period was due to a comparably limited racialized threat in the mid-nineteenth century. By the early twentieth century, the police did adopt colonial forms, such as fingerprinting, but this was due to the particular character of the perceived racialized threat rooted in new images of the criminal. And when some officials later tried to militarize the London Metropolitan Police further, those efforts too were halted.

Chapter 5 examines developments in American policing as the US empire transmuted from the strategy of colonial control overseas to the more informal modality of "tactical" imperialism. The chapter shows how the migration of racialized minorities to cities in the late 1950s generated a new series of racialized panics about urban crime and violence. If "white flight" to the suburbs was one product of those panics, another was police militarization, resulting in new policing units like New York's Tactical Police Force, whose bellicosity in turn had lasting effects. One effect was to trigger urban revolts that summoned the imperial boomerang yet again, with new tactics and tools from Vietnam and the British Empire domesticated for use on America's streets.

Chapter 6 finds a similar story unfolding in Britain beginning in the early 1970s. In Britain, a new round of militarization debuted in London, when the

London Special Patrol Group was repurposed from a seemingly benign crime-fighting unit into a heavily militarized force devoted to counter subversion and insurgency. The transformation, which can be named *counterinsurgenization*, occurred through the importation of recent counterinsurgency theories, tools, and techniques that had been developing in Britain's imperial peripheries, from Malaya and Kenya to Hong Kong and Northern Ireland. The original impetus was racialized threat, and in the 1980s the subsequent counterinsurgenization of British policing did not stop insurgency but provoked it. This perpetuated a larger cycle of militarized policing, insurgency, and militarization that continued into the early 2000s.

The Conclusion reviews, clarifies, and extends the analysis. It also surveys the landscape of militarization as boomerang effect in Britain and the United States in the first decades of the 2000s, revealing that the past indeed stages the present. The chapter ends on a note of hope. But the hope is not naive. It is informed by the lessons learned in the preceding chapters.

# PART I
# THE COLONIALITY OF POLICING

# 1

# The Birth of the Civil Police
# in London, 1829

Sir Robert Peel was likely not amused by some of the things that the London Metropolitan Police encountered in 1830. Previously, as home secretary of Britain, he had helped devise and implement the new police to replace the previous system of constables and watchmen. In 1829, his new force, sometimes called the "Peelers," finally hit the streets of London. Peel had meant the new police to be a "civil" force, a nonmilitary organization under civilian command, different from the British Army and from Continental police forces like France's gendarmerie—the heavily militarized force that, to the English mind, represented French tyranny. But in 1830, an anonymous poem circulated throughout London that challenged Peel's pretensions. Titled "The Blue Devils, or New Police," it staged a fictional address made by Peel to his new police, portraying Peel as leading an army heading into battle. It concluded as follows:

> By your rise and Charleys' fall,
> By our constitutional
> Regard for king and country all,
> Ye shall, ye shall be free!
> Lay the Hunts and Cobbetts low,
> Tyrants them in every row;
> At Spa Fields, or at Peterloo,
> Let us do, or die.[1]

The poem undermined Peel's pretensions regarding the new civil police. It portrayed the London Metropolitan Police as another army in disguise, equating its activities with the British Army's violent suppression of mass gatherings at Spa Fields in 1816 and Peterloo in 1819. In other passages, the poem referred to the new police as "Jenny Darbies."[2] This was the English way of pronouncing *gens d'armes*, or the gendarmerie, and the epithet painted the London Metropolitan Police as another despotic force and militaristic power—an odious incarnation of Napoleonic tyranny. Peel had attempted to present the new police as a non-military civil force, but the poem taunted the new police for being anything but.[3]

*Policing Empires*. Julian Go, Oxford University Press. © Oxford University Press 2024.
DOI: 10.1093/oso/9780197621653.003.0002

There was another event that must have disquieted Peel. On their new beats throughout the late Georgian metropolis, patrolmen of the London police often found themselves caught in scuffles with the public that devolved into violence. In one such incident in 1831, a year after the poem about the "Jenny Darbies" had circulated, a group of Irishmen launched "a serious riot and attack on several officers of the police." The police had been summoned to quell a "disturbance" in Ratcliff Highway in East London, a largely poor and working-class district where Irish immigrants settled. When the police arrived, a melee ensued, and "a desperate attack was then made by the Irish on the policemen." The serjeant on the spot, C.W. Wheeler, "was brutally kicked and trampled upon." Meanwhile, the other Irishmen called out, "Murder the police! Down with the Peelers!" and tried to chase them away.[4]

Why was such scorn heaped upon the London Metropolitan Police, despite Peel's efforts to make the new police palatable to the public? Why was the new police accused of being a military force when Peel and the other proponents of the new police meant it to be something different from a military force? We are invited to consider that the criticisms were not unfounded. Perhaps the new "civil" police, even though intended to be a nonmilitaristic alternative to the army, was actually just a different kind of army—an army in society masquerading as a civil power. Perhaps the police's performances of benign civil power masked a deep militarism that astute observers, like the Irish of the East End, were right to expose.

Perhaps, too, something else was going on. In his instructions to the new police force in 1829, Peel had told the officers that "the police seek and preserve *public* favor . . . by demonstrating absolutely impartial service to the law." But the fact that the Irish of the East End were so stridently and even violently opposed to the police suggests that maybe the police was not in fact acting impartially; that, although the police was dressed up to serve the "public" broadly, Peel's new police was concentrating its power upon certain classes (in this case, the Irish). Perhaps the London Metropolitan Police was not only a militarized force but also a *colonial* force of sorts. Perhaps too the militarization of the police and its colonial functionality were not incidental to each other but deeply intertwined, braided together into a pattern whose contours merit scrutiny.

This chapter examines the birth and operation of Peel's police in London in the 1820s and 1830s. It will consider the actual form and operations of the "Peelies," as the new policemen were sometimes called when they weren't charged with being "Jenny Darbies." It will also excavate the London police's militaristic structure and practices. But to fully apprehend the criticisms that the London Metropolitan Police encountered, the chapter will also bring us farther afield, far beyond London, to Ireland, the British Caribbean, and North America. This will unlock the secret of Peel's civil police and dissolve the mystery of the charges leveled against it.

## The "New" Police

It helps to begin by clarifying the novelty of the new police in London. As noted in the Introduction, "police departments" as we know them today did not exist prior to 1829. The word "policing" referred to a wide array of regulatory activities and governance rather than crime-controlling activities by an organized and centralized body of constables (i.e., state-appointed officers). The word "police" was most typically used as a verb: "*to* police" as opposed to "*the* police." It was only in the late 1700s and early 1800s that the word "police" began to acquire its more modern connotations, becoming increasingly associated with the repression of crime and the maintenance of order.[5] Even then, there was no singular institution in England tasked with meeting these imperatives. Instead, there had been a variety of different organizations dealing with a myriad of issues that would later come under the purview of the new police.

Consider first the issue of crime. Before the new police, London lacked a single professionalized organization charged with deterring, detecting, and detaining criminals. Constables were charged with bringing accused criminals before a justice of the peace, but they were not salaried professionals. They were paid fees according to the number of suspects they apprehended. Nor did they investigate crimes, do anything to prevent crime, or pursue the accused. If a thief robbed a victim, the *victim* was expected to pursue and detain. In theory, watchmen were supposed to help. These were groups of citizens, typically volunteers, who walked the streets at night. But the watchmen were unreliable. They were liable to drink or to sleep in the watch-houses rather than tend to their duties. Their prescribed duties were minimal. They mostly chased away vagrants, checked locks on gates, or ensured that the gas lamps operated properly. Their "patrols" were limited too. As late as the 1810s, watchmen in London were found to cover areas of little more than a single lane or courtyard. It all amounted to a "medley of local parish officers and watchmen" lacking central direction or command.[6]

The only other major organizations for managing crime included the Bow Street Runners, originally founded in 1749 (and consolidated properly as the Bow Street Runners only in 1785).[7] Operating at the behest of the chief magistrate of Bow Street and invented by two of those chief magistrates, John and Henry Fielding, the Bow Street Runners were essentially salaried constables who pursued thieves and other criminals. By the early 1800s, they had expanded their activity to also track and arrest conspirators, such as the Cato Street Conspirators in 1820. Another organization was the Thames River

Police. This had been initially created in 1798 as a private police for the West India Committee. It chased thieves robbing warehouses and pirates looting ships from the Caribbean. The prominent police theorist Patrick Colquhoun was one of the founders of the river police and helped pressure Parliament to put it under governmental control in 1800. But neither the Thames River Police nor the Bow Street Runners covered large swaths of territory. Nor did they cover all forms of crime.

The other issue was social disorder. None of the existing organizations handling crime were meant to manage large-scale disruptions. In the event of riots, strikes, or uproarious crowds, civil authorities in London and other cities or towns in England had little choice but to summon the military. This they had done repeatedly, calling upon thousands upon thousands of soldiers to control unruly demonstrators or crowds. To subdue the Gordon Riots in London in 1780, authorities ended up summoning almost twelve thousand soldiers. In 1815, authorities even called in heavy artillery to subdue the Corn Bill Riots. In 1819, the cavalry descended upon protestors at Peterloo near Manchester, injuring six hundred and killing eighteen. In anticipation of protests during Queen Caroline's funeral in 1821, the government called in eleven thousand soldiers (half of Britain's soldiers at the time).[8]

The London Metropolitan Police changed things. First, the Met expanded and *professionalized* policing as never before. In 1800, there had been about one thousand constables and fewer than seventy members of the watch—all operating under different local trusts in the metropolis. But with the new police, in 1830, there were 3,314 officers under central command.[9] No longer volunteers or low-paid locals who were prone to shirk their duties, the new constables were full-time salaried subordinates. They were expressly forbidden from engaging in any other business. They were uniformed, trained, and disciplined. They were taught a professional ethos.[10]

Second, the new police became the sole agent of crime control and institutionalized a new discourse of *crime prevention*. The London Met also replaced the constable and watchmen system and later absorbed the Bow Street Runners and Thames River Police.[11] The new police was thus a full-time watch, with large numbers of officers surveying their respective beats and providing a persistent presence. As the *Times* correctly observed, while the older system was mainly about apprehending criminals, Peel's new force adopted an entirely new theory: the main object of the new police was "*the prevention of crime*—not the execution of the criminal."[12]

The London Met also became the first responder to crises of public order. The military was no longer meant to deal with public order and maintain security in London (or in other cities, as the London police came to be emulated throughout England). That was now the role of the police. Peel explained in the

House of Commons discussion of his Metropolitan Police bill that "with a police established upon such a system . . . [we] would be able to dispense with the necessity of a military force in London, for the preservation of the tranquility of the metropolis."[13] The London Met thereby *conjoined two previously distinct objects of intervention:* criminality and social disorder. "Police duty," wrote former commissioner of the London police Sir Robert Anderson in 1902, "may be roughly divided into the two spheres of public order and crime."[14] Now a single centralized, hierarchical, and bureaucratic force, run at the top by police commissioners appointed by the Crown, which exerted indirect control through the Home Office and Parliament, was in charge of both order maintenance and crime control.

Finally, the new police inaugurated a new *bifurcated regime of power.* The police monopolized the means of coercion for dealing with "citizens" and subjects in the domestic territory, while the military was for foreigners or imperial subjects abroad. The police became the "organization authorized by a collectivity to regulate social relations *within itself* by utilizing, if need be, physical force," while the army was to operate "outside."[15] It is for this reason that the Metropolitan Police has been seen by scholars as a new type of organization and, most importantly, a "civil police." Besides its centralized and bureaucratic form and its dual function of preventing crime and managing disorder, it was to be a nonmilitary and hence civilian force. It was to be an organ of the government that looked after internal rather than external security, commanded by civilian officials rather than generals. Soldiers were not to be deployed against citizens; the police were. Military generals were not to control the domestic coercive apparatus; civilian officials appointed by the Crown were. Accordingly, Peel and the first commissioners he assigned to lead the force, Richard Mayne and Charles Rowan, limited the policeman's weaponry, allowing only a truncheon that was to be concealed from public view and used only as a last resort.[16] Further, they made uniforms mandatory for the new constables, but they chose blue uniforms, avoiding the traditional military red. This was to avoid the perception that the new police were the army.[17] "By contrast with the centralized paramilitary police used by Continental regimes to subdue and repress a hostile and non-complaint population," P. A. J. Waddington explains, "the British police were to be seen as a distinctly civil force which would support, not undermine, the traditional liberties of the British people."[18] This was at the heart of the idea and novelty of the new civil police.

But here arises the conundrum: while a key innovation of the London police was its "civil" character, meant as an alternative to the naked power and ostensible brutal violence of armies or militarized forces like the French gendarmerie, it was accused of being an army anyway, the "Jenny Darbies" worthy of contempt. Why?

## Constructing Crime and Disorder

To answer, we must first see why the new police was born in the first place. The London Metropolitan Police marked a significant change in forms of domestic power, but what led to its formation? This is partly a question about timing. Why did officials like Robert Peel start pondering, debating, and advocating for a new civil police system in the first decades of the nineteenth century and not later or before? A common explanation in existing historiography is that the new police was formed in response to new problems of crime and disorder. This explanation has much to commend it. It is true that crime and disorder had become significant problems in London by the 1820s. The very idea of "crime" as a phenomenon external to the normal operations of society was a relatively recent one, emerging among some writers in the late eighteenth century.[19] And in the early 1800s, this phenomenon of "crime" appeared to be on the rise.[20] Officials and the public began pointing to statistics suggesting that crime in the metropolis was increasing at horrifying rates. The press exacerbated such concerns, printing stories of thefts, robberies, and more gruesome crimes. In 1811 the brutal murders of two families in their homes near Ratcliff Highway prompted Parliament to appoint a committee to investigate ways of reforming policing in the city. By the 1820s, outlets such as the *Times* were printing daily reports of violence.[21] An 1828 parliamentary committee displayed statistics meant to show that crime had grown in London in disproportion to population growth, thereby revealing a frightening rise in "the immorality of conduct" in London.[22]

Whether or not crime was actually on the rise is immaterial; what matters is that there was a *perception* of rising crime.[23] Importantly, Sir Robert Peel was one of the officials who perceived a rise in crime. When he first brought his proposal for a new police to Parliament in April 1829, he offered statistics suggesting that crime had risen by 26 percent from 1821 to 1828, while the population had risen only 11 percent. Peel concluded that crime in England was worse than in Europe: a "comparison . . . not . . . very favourable either to the morality of the people, or to the security which the laws afford to property in this great metropolis."[24] Later, in 1826, Peel wrote that "the continued increase of crime in London and its neighborhood" was what compelled him to formulate a new policing bill. "I have given notice for an inquiry into the state of the Police in the district that surrounds the Metropolis," he wrote to a friend in Parliament, Sir John Hobhouse. "The continued increase of crime in London and its neighbourhood appears to me to call for some decisive measure."[25]

Besides the perception of increased crime was the fear of rising social disorder. While riots, disruptions to order, and even periodic threats of rebellion had been ongoing for decades, the early 1800s witnessed an escalation and culmination of sorts, animated by the political openings and economic insecurity left behind by the end of the Napoleonic Wars and the growing appeal of Radicalism among the discontented and displaced. The Luddite uprisings of 1811–1813, Spa Fields in 1816, Peterloo in 1819, the Queen Caroline Riots of 1821, the wage disputes and strikes in Monmouthshire and Staffordshire in 1822—these and many more public disturbances unsettled the establishment, evoking the image of riotous mobs running wild in the streets and even outright revolt. It did not help that the "mobs" (that is, workers) infused their recalcitrance with Radical and Jacobin ideologies. The French Revolution was never far from the minds of the English elite.

Surveying the empire from his post as home secretary (1822–1827), Peel was well aware of the threats; looking after them was part of his job. In just his first year as home secretary, and eight years before his Metropolitan Police Act, a series of strikes and riots erupted across the country from Staffordshire to Newcastle-on-Tyne, with more occurring elsewhere in subsequent years. The cotton industry was almost brought to its knees by strikes in Scotland, Lancashire, and the Midlands. In London too there had been rising trouble. According to one estimate, London was the site of riots or some form of major social disturbance every year from 1816 until 1829.[26]

In light of this, it makes sense that existing histories claim that the new police was created in response to a wave of crime and disorder. But these traditional explanations occlude something important: *who* exactly were these "criminals" and agitated workers that the new police was meant to control? In fact, the press, the public, and officials did not see crime and disorder as stemming from just anyone. Parliamentary committees investigating policing issues, along with other officials and the press, specifically blamed two groups: the migratory unemployed "vagrants" of cities, and the Irish pushed out by the colony's transition to export-oriented agriculture and drawn to the industrial cotton economy in England. As we will now see, these two groups were not distinct but often overlapped. Together they constituted the displaced, abject racialized subproletariat to whom the creation of the new police was a response. This is exactly what the existing historiography on the emergence of the new police overlooks.

## The Irish "Problem"

The ranks of unemployed and temporary laborers migrating throughout the kingdom had grown in the first decades of the nineteenth century, putting immense pressure upon the existing relief system, known as the Poor Laws. Writers and officials supporting police reform typically blamed these laborers for rising crime rates. In his writings, Patrick Colquhoun, who was highly influential upon officials working on policing issues, made repeated references to the "labouring people, who come to seek employment in the Metropolis" and end up "indigent." These people, he said, were "a principal cause of the increase of Crimes."[27] Colquhoun contended this was a "gangrene" that could not be removed by charity. A proper police was needed. "It is not pecuniary aid that will heal this *gangrene: this Corruption of Morals*," he announced. "There must be the application of a correct System of Police."[28] George Mainwaring's *Observations on the Present State of the Police of the Metropolis* (1821) reiterated the charge, blaming the "unproductive population . . . differing little from the barbarous hordes which traverse an uncivilized land" for crime. Mainwaring thus demanded "a change in our policing system."[29] Similarly, parliamentary select committees in 1818 and 1828 referred to the "poor and indigent" as "that class of persons who ordinarily commit crime."[30]

Yet the downtrodden and dispossessed to whom police reformers referred were not always English. Most were Irish migrants. It would not be unfair to say that in the eyes of most English, the "Irish" and underemployed or vagrant populations were one and the same. Of course, the Irish had long been coming to England's shores. But their numbers had increased by leaps and bounds in the early decades of the nineteenth century. Their increasing presence was concomitant with the menacing rise of the dispossessed and unemployed in England about which so many fretted. It was also concomitant with the appearance of rising criminality and disorder.

There is a background to this. The Union of 1801 between Ireland and the United Kingdom of Great Britain had served to further consolidate the power of the English landowning aristocracy in Ireland. This, along with England's increasing reliance upon Irish foodstuffs, spelled the collapse of Irish domestic industry. Land concentration followed, as did heightened agricultural production through intensified exploitation of tenants and cottiers.[31] Ireland was slowly transformed into an agricultural outpost of the empire, dramatically increasing its exports of grain to England after 1815 (given the Corn Laws) while expelling thousands upon thousands of Irish peasants from the land. Many of the dejected and dispossessed Irish looked to England. The development of steam packets between Ireland and other British ports facilitated the outward flow. The demobilization of Wellington's army in 1815, in which many Irishmen had served, also contributed to migration.

The cities that attracted the greatest share of England's Irish immigrants were Liverpool, London, and Manchester. Early on, London was a particularly attractive destination for the expelled, and even when Irish first came to Liverpool or Manchester, many eventually migrated toward London, landing in neighborhoods like the St. Giles Rookery. This was a tiny quarter that in 1816 had an Irish population of about six thousand adults and almost four thousand children. Though Irish migrants did not make up an especially large proportion of London's population, the sheer numbers are remarkable. In 1814, estimates of Irish-born poor in London reached fourteen thousand out of more than one million total London residents. This is an underestimate, because it refers to only the very poorest Irish in need of charity. Real numbers must have been higher. Also remarkable is the relative growth. The number of Irish in England rose from 40,000 in the 1780s to 590,000 by 1831 and 727,000 by 1852, marking a movement "perhaps nearly unparalleled in the history of the world," according to contemporaries.[32] We can assume London saw a similar increase. By 1841, when the first census that included data on birth location was taken, the number of London's Irish-born residents had reached seventy-five thousand.[33] And even though the Irish made up a small proportion of London's inhabitants, they remained the largest immigrant group in the city.[34]

The dispossessed Irish had come to England in search of work, but they were forced into the bottom sectors of society. Those who found work ended up laboring in the lowest-paying jobs, many of which were seasonal and hence temporary. Quite a number could not find work at all. Historians by now know the story: the Irish ended up serving as England's unemployed reserve army and its subproletariat—that is, the lowest-paid workers at the bottom of the country's socioeconomic hierarchy.[35] In London, the Irish served as the city's main unskilled laborers and seasonal laborers, collecting hay or performing other rural jobs in the environs of the metropolis. During harvest season, the hay laborers would come from Ireland in numbers of five thousand or more.[36] In the off-season, these casual workers were thrust into poverty, and it became commonly known that in the early nineteenth century "many of the most wretched of the London poor were Irish." Reports from the 1790s suggested that there were more than five thousand beggars in London and the majority were Irish.[37] Later, in 1827, the Trades Free Press noted that Ireland "inundates us with her miserable poor to gradually push tens of thousands 'from their stools,'" adding that "multitudes are daily poured upon our shores ready to invade the work of very labourer and operative."[38] The next year, a writer in the London Quarterly Review complained about the incoming Irish hordes "flocking to England in search of employment . . . the great body of which is in extreme misery."[39]

The presence of increasing throngs of the Irish subproletariat in metropolitan centers generated a backlash. Both needing and yet deriding them, the English constructed the Irish as fundamentally foreign, unalterably alien, and incorrigibly inferior. While disparaging views of the Irish had long circulated in England, the new immigration deepened and solidified extant conceptions of "the Celts" as "ignorant, uncivilized and violent" with "rude and barbarous customs."[40] In his 1804 book on the Irish peasantry, Robert Bell wrote despairingly of the "turbulent and barbarous habits of the lower orders of the people of Ireland."[41] A parliamentary report in 1836 claimed that Irish immigration was a prime example "of a less civilized population spreading themselves as a kind of substratum, beneath a more civilized community," and implied that the Irish were England's slaves: the influx of Irish hordes, the report asserted, was only possible because importing slaves was *im*possible.[42]

The fact that so many of the incoming Irish were Catholic further fed these fictions, and religious difference blended easily with cultural, civilizational, and ethnic difference. Biological difference was also noted. While scientific racism was not complete, references to Irish biology, blood, and stock increased in the first half of the nineteenth century, mingling with cultural explanations of Irish inferiority. English observers thus *racialized* the Irish migrants. They attributed high rates of typhus among London's Irish community to their biological inferiority.[43] Members of Parliament thought of the Irish as "aliens," not just "in language and in religion" but also "in blood."[44] Employers opined that the physiological character of the Irish made them more suitable than the English for manual labor. Later, English racialists would contend that Celts had more melanin in their skin than descendants of Saxons or Scandinavians.[45] But even before then, as one historian puts it, "similar skin colour did not prevent the racialization of the Irish."[46]

By this racializing discourse, stark differentiations between Irish and English also proliferated, prefiguring later claims that the Irish were the missing evolutionary link between Black slaves and English workers.[47] The physician James Kay's influential reports on the Irish in Manchester maintained that while English workers were typically "peaceful," the Irish were no different from "the savage." Worse still, according to Kay, the Irish threatened to culturally and morally infect the English population, teaching the latter their "barbarous habits."[48] The press picked up this racial theme of contamination and fretted about the disruptive presence of the Irish. This "immigration of Irish outcasts," said an editorial in the *London Quarterly Review*, would ultimately serve to reduce "the English labourer to the wretched condition of the Irish, that is, to the very lowest condition in which human beings have ever existed in any country calling itself civilised and Christian. These causes alone might but too well justify a fear that the foundations of society will give way, and the whole fabric be brought down."[49] State authorities formed investigative committees and held hearings about what might be done about Irish immigration and Irish poverty, at once building upon and perpetuating the construction of the Irish as a peculiar group with distinct racial and cultural characteristics. All of it fed rising upper-class anxieties about the putatively teeming hordes of Irish immigrants.[50]

## Racializing Crime and Disorder

As Irish migrants became England's racialized subproletariat, they figured into the English imagination as the "unproductive" and "vagrant" group that officials, the public, and the press blamed for crime.[51] A nascent criminology surfaced in proportion to the menacing ingress of Irish migrants. The main claim was this: by virtue of their race, culture, religion, and class, the Irish were predisposed to lawlessness.

The theory was not entirely new. In the mid-1700s, the small number of Irish then residing in London had acquired a reputation for being either "good servants" or desperate criminals. But the seemingly unstoppable inundation by Irish incomers in the early 1800s solidified the equation between them and criminality. "We hardly ever hear of a riot or a murder or a burglary," declared one witness at a hearing on mendicity in 1815, "in which some of these poor creatures [i.e., Irish] are not implicated."[52] In the 1820s, the *London Quarterly Review* decried not only that the influx of Irish immigrants increased crime but also that it likewise threatened public morality. The Irish immigrants brought with them "the tendency . . . to worsen the moral habits of our own people" and injure "the public peace."[53] *The Scotsman* opined in 1828 that economic stress in Ireland exacerbated the problem: "As there is more ignorance, degradation and misery in Ireland than in Scotland, the Irish are more likely to fall more easily into the habit of committing crime."[54] Other commentators remarked on the additionally deleterious impact of liquor as it merged with the Celts' presumed predilection for violent crime. The 1816 Select Committee on the Police of Metropolis declared: "The effects of liquor upon the Irish in every scene of depredation and murder, needs to only to be adverted to; it is certain that the abuse of this destructive stimulus foments and keeps alive the most atrocious and appalling crimes."[55] Sir John Fielding of the Bow Street Runners found Irishness and criminality to be so interlocked that, in his mind, one way to reduce crime in London was to prevent Irish immigrants from coming to England in the first place.[56]

Colquhoun had set the stage for this "Irishization" of crime. In his *Treatise on the Police of the Metropolis* (1806), Colquhoun explained that crime was due to the "enlarged State of Society . . . joined to the depraved habits and loose conduct of a great proportion of the lower classes of the people," and then pointed to immigrants in particular: "Let it be remembered also that this Metropolis is . . . the general receptacle for the idle and depraved of almost every country, particularly from every quarter of the dominions of the Crown." These "labouring people, who come to seek employment in the Metropolis," came from "the most remote quarters of Great Britain and Ireland" and ended up having to "live by petty or more atrocious offences."[57] Colquhoun thus declared "indigence" to be a "princip[al] cause of the increase in crimes" while believing that Irish migrants were disproportionately indigent.[58] Colquhoun further suggested that criminality was a Jewish trait as well as an Irish one, but his main concern was with the Irish migrants roaming the streets.[59]

A visit to England's courts would have confirmed Colquhoun's impressions. The best available data suggests that in the early nineteenth century, the Irish in London were "massively overrepresented among Old Bailey indictments for violent crimes."[60] This did not mean that the Irish were inherently more criminal. It likely reflected inequalities in sentencing due to racialized bias. To be sure, the Irish were *accused* of crimes at disproportionate rates. While Irish-born inhabitants constituted between 2 and 3 percent of London's population in the first years of the 1800s, more than 10 percent of those accused of crimes were Irish-born. Furthermore, the Irish faced more severe punishment than other groups. From 1790 to 1805, two-thirds of Irish murder convicts in London were hanged, while only one-third of non-Irish were sentenced to death for similar charges.[61] All of this both reflected and likely perpetuated the perception that the Irish tended toward violence and were resistant to law. When sixteen horrific and bloody murders in Scotland in 1828 were discovered to be the work of two Irishmen, William Burke and William Hare, no one in England appeared surprised.[62] "The Irish in London," wrote the historian Mary Dorothy George in her classic work, "were a police problem" as much as "a sanitary problem, a poor-law problem, and an industrial problem."[63]

This racialization of crime was partnered by the "Irishization" of social disorder. When state authorities, London's upper classes, and the press fretted over mass outbreaks of disorder, the Irish were on their minds. During the 1790s through the first decades of the subsequent century, agrarian protest, revolutionaries, and so-called bandits in the Irish countryside shook the English colonial state. London received near-mythic tales of horrific acts of violence by Irish rebels. In 1829, the same year that Peel's Metropolitan Police Act passed, Peel decried the "melancholy fact" that "for scarcely one year, during the period that has elapsed since the Union, has Ireland been governed by the ordinary course of the law."[64] He repeatedly fretted about Irish revolt.[65] The Irish challenges to English authority reinforced English stereotypes that the Irish were prone to violence. As secretary in Ireland, Peel held that the Irish were "very little advanced from barbarism," as he put it in 1816 in a letter to a friend, stressing the "murders and burnings and other atrocities" they ostensibly committed."[66] He referred often to the "Irishman's natural predilection for outrage and a lawless life."[67] Others agreed. "The very name [of Ireland] forces to our recollection images of shillelaghs, and broken heads, and turbulence of every kind," said an observer in 1834.[68] Police reformers like Colquhoun seemed to believe that violence was a distinctly Irish trait.[69] Richard Brooke's *Gazetteer* described the Irish in 1812 as "ignorant, uncivilized, and blundering . . . implacable and violent in all their affections" (though adding that they could also be "courteous to strangers").[70]

Violent rebellion in Ireland, twinned with the influx of Irish "hordes" to England, fostered fear among English authorities that Irish violence was coming to England's shores. Reports of violence among the Irish in London and other cities lent proof. Londoners were aghast at news of "pitched battles, every Saturday night" among the Irish in the area known as Calmel Buildings and drunken brawls on Sunday mornings in St. Giles, with "three or four hundred" Irishmen engaged.[71] In the earlier Gordon Riots (1780), the Irish had not been involved, but writers suggested that it was a blessing that they were not. Had they been, the riots could have been much worse.[72] The fear by the 1820s was that, in fact, the Irish *were* involved.

The related fear was all the more horrific to English authorities: not only were the lawless Irish arriving in droves, they were poised to bring English workers over to the barbaric side. The racializing discourse of Irish migrants as infecting English society and corrupting the otherwise pristine English worker thus acquired profound political resonance: the fear was that the Irish masses were bringing their insurrectionary tendencies to the metropole, allying with English workers to undermine imperial authority from within. After the 1798 rebellion, officials like the viceroy Lord Cornwallis feared that the main cause was not only Irish character and Catholicism but also Jacobinism. This intimated that violent colonial rebels and striking English workers were cut from the same ideological cloth.[73] Other authorities seamlessly connected Irish nationalism and English Radicalism. In 1828, the *London Quarterly Review* carried an article advocating strongly for police reform in London, but it also ran an article insisting that there were direct links between anticolonialists and English workers. After discussing how Irish migration generated more crime in London, it dramatically sketched a presumed plot by the "Irish conspirators" of 1798 to "send over as great a number of United Irishmen into this country as could be done without exciting suspicion" to "co-operate" with "their English associates" and incite revolutionary acts. It accused these "trouble-makers in Ireland" of creating an entire network of rebels and English allies. "The Guy Fauxites in that country . . . have boasted of the number of their countrymen in England, and reminded us that they are able, upon occasion, to make a glorious bonfire of London!"[74]

Those who concocted such theories can be forgiven. London, Manchester, Dublin, Monmouthshire, Cork, and Kerry: these and other spaces were all part of the same imperial field. And worker mobilization traversed it. In the early 1820s, some London Irish organizations like the Association for Civil and Political Liberty reached out to English Radicals for support.[75] Their efforts were reciprocated. The English Radical Henry Hunt allied with Irish leaders like Feargus O'Connor and together mobilized Irish migrants, supporting Irish causes like Catholic Emancipation. Hunt even advocated "Political Union in the cause of Universal Civil and Religious Liberty," hoping to attract twenty to thirty thousand Irish immigrant workers to London for a massive demonstration. The National Union of the Working Classes (NUWC), formed in 1830, likewise adopted Irish issues as their own and advocated Irish home rule.[76]

These connections reveal a "clear consecutive alliance between Irish Nationalism and English Radicalism between 1790 and 1850" that likely made it difficult for English elites to separate the two.[77] Some observers even claimed that the Irish were "more prone to take part in trades unions, combinations and secret societies than the English" and that the Irish were typically the "ringleaders" of those movements.[78] By the late 1830s, Black workers were added to this perceived threat to order from Irish Radicals. The press seized upon the fact that William Cuffay, an English worker of African origin, had become a leading figure in the Chartist movement (the popular workers' movement in England). The *Times* claimed that the Chartists in London were essentially an Irish movement led by a "half-nigger."[79] In the feverish imaginations of the Georgian upper class, the barbarians were not just at the gates but had breached them.

## Inventing the New Police

But what could be done? The problem for English officials was that they could not turn to the military for help. Sir Arthur Wellesley, the 1st Duke of Wellington, who later became the main sponsor of Peel's police bill, worried that the regular army was "overworked and untrained in the repression of 'domestic insurrection and disturbance.' "[80] Calling upon the army was also a provocative and unpopular act. Queen Caroline's funeral in 1821 had led to riots and violent affrays between demonstrators and the army, causing the English public to be wary of military might on England's streets. Two years earlier, at Peterloo outside Manchester, the army was summoned to contain a massive demonstration of workers—many of them Irish—but the army's intervention ended up killing fifteen civilians and injuring hundreds more.[81]

If the army could not be counted upon, neither could the existing array of constables and watchmen. This array had proven far too weak to manage mob violence, much less quiet the resistance posed by the fierce and purportedly savage Irish. Around the time of the 1798 insurrection, police forces consisting of Bow Street Runners and constables had raided Irish establishments in the St. Giles area and various other meeting places around London. This was most likely an effort to capture suspected Irish rebels and other dangerous "foreigners."[82] But the raids had ended badly. Amid their interventions, the constable forces faced angry crowds and even suffered fatal casualties.

Eventually, English authorities and police reformers came to the dawning realization that something new was needed to manage Irish violence and possible rebellion. Wellesley surveyed the issue and concluded that domestic disorder was "more properly the business of the civil government and of the police" rather than the military.[83] Peel also considered a force different from the army for the outlying rural districts where English Radicals and Irish workers had united to unsettle elite complacency. "I should not be surprised if it shall become necessary to organise some kind of local force in the manufacturing districts for the protection of property," he wrote his friend Sir John Hobhouse in 1826, during a period of worker-led turbulence, "something less cumbrous and expensive than yeomanry, but of a more permanent and efficient character than special constables."[84] One possible solution was to create something akin to the French-style gendarmerie.[85] But Peel, Wellesley, and their colleagues concluded that such a force would not sit well with the English public, any more than the repeated deployment of the British army on home soil. One investigative committee concluded that any Continental-style police force would be repulsive to the people and was "inconsistent with the traditions of English liberty."[86] Something else was needed.

The related dilemma was what to do about growing criminality ostensibly stemming from Irish migrants. The existing constable-watch system was proving to be insufficient. Colquhoun noticed this early on. After bemoaning the rise in criminality due to immigration, he concluded that English society was threatened by a "Corruption of Morals," which necessitated a "correct System of Police" to replace the constable-watch system.[87] Later Dr. James Kay picked up the theme. Kay had closely studied the Irish in and around Manchester. He reported that the Irish were prone to lawlessness, disorder, and crime and that, therefore, something needed to be done.[88] The system of poor relief had not worked. Neither had the constable-watch system. That system might have been fine for the English, Kay wrote, but for the Irish something different was necessary.[89] The issue was that those "importations from Ireland" had found themselves "placed under regulations devised for the government of one much more advanced in the social scale." In other words, Irish immigrants had been thrust into a policing context designed not for them but for the more "advanced" and presumably peaceful English. "[Ex]pedients," Kay continued, "which might be efficient in restraining vice and preventing crime among a purely English population, fail to produce these results in towns in which the Irish exist in great numbers, mixed with the native inhabitants."[90] He continued:

> The defective state of the *police* in the large provincial towns of England had not been found to produce any serious inconvenience on account of the habits of obedience to the law which the people have formed, and the mutual assistance

which, in emergencies, they afford to each other. But when large bodies of Irish, of less orderly habits, and far more prone to use violence in fits of intoxication, settled permanently in these towns, the existing police force, while sufficient to repress crime and disorders among a purely English population, has been found, under these altered circumstances inadequate to the regular enforcement of the law.[91]

Few disagreed. In London, committees to investigate changes in the existing constable-watch system were appointed in 1812, 1818, and 1828. These had been prompted by perceived rises in crime or highly publicized strings of criminal activity coded as Irish, such as the broadly publicized Ratcliff Highway murders, which were attributed to an Irishman, John Murphy (aka John Williams).[92] And they all admitted that the existing constable and watch system was ill-equipped for managing the Irish.

The new "civil police" was being hatched. The 1828 Select Committee on the Police of the Metropolis, originally formed by Peel himself, was seminal. Witnesses blamed Irish migrants for the growth of crime. They made references to the "Low Irish" who had been "swarming" their neighborhoods and the subsequent rise in crime and lawlessness. The "influx of Irish labourers into the Metropolis," declared one witness, "have increased . . . the probability of crime being committed." A magistrate from the fringes of London testified that the casual laborers in his district were Irish and were responsible for the rising crimes and various "petty depradations" there. A resident of Spitalfields declared that crime in his area had increased significantly, asserting that there were Irishmen "who go in a gang" and committed crimes and "very daring depredations" of all sorts. A solicitor complained that the Irish who were sometimes found in his otherwise "respectable district" of London tended to be vagrants or casual laborers who were responsible for violent "disorder" there, especially in the notorious Irish area known then as Calmel Buildings. "Dreadful affrays," he said, "where they half murder each other. It is quite appalling to see the state in which they are brought before one sometimes." This was an "evil," he testified, that required the help of extra constables and watchmen, and so additional ones had been typically summoned. Nonetheless, the problem persisted. "It is a standing evil that finds no alternation."[93] The implication was the same as Dr. Kay's conclusion: Irish-induced crime was a horrific problem that the existing constable-watch system could not handle.

After reading the select committee's report, Peel was emboldened to finally charge ahead with radical police reform. He had already been contemplating it, but the committee's report likely inspired him. In May 1829 he wrote to Wellesley to explain his plan for a new police in London that would "abolish gradually the existing watch establishments" and "substitute in their room a police force that shall act by night and day."[94] In justifying his plans for the new police, he referred to the select committee's report, noting its list of parishes that had no watchmen at all, such as Brentford. This was where, according to one witness, crime had risen due to unemployed vagrants and causal laborers like brickmakers—a typical Irish job at the time. Peel referred as well to districts such as Wapping, the site of the grim Ratcliff Highway murders; it was also where Irish dock laborers dominated and settled.[95] A new police force was especially needed in such areas because, according to Peel, "they collect together all the scum of society." Referring to the report in his letter to Wellesley, Peel concluded: "I really think I need trouble you with no further proof of the necessity of putting an end to such a state of things."[96]

This is what existing historiography obscures: when English officials called for a new police to fight crime and disorder, implicit was the claim that police reform was needed to discipline the Irish hordes seemingly overrunning the booming metropolis. Peel and his colleagues thus aimed to reform the existing policing system not in response to crime and disorder in general but rather as a response to its racialization.[97] To manage the "scum of society," as Peel put it, something other than the constable-watch system or the army was needed. The only question was what kind of police it should be.

## Formations of Colonial Coercion

While Peel and his colleagues agreed that some kind of new police was needed in response to the perceived Irish threat, they needed guidance. They needed a precedent or model to emulate, some kind of coercive organization that was neither the constable-watch system nor the army but that could deal with crime, disorder, and potential insurrection from presumably savage racial inferiors. Ultimately Peel and his colleagues found such an organizational form in the very spaces that had brought the racialized threat to their doors in the first place: the colonies.

Consider who designed the new police. They included Robert Peel, who got help from Charles Rowan and Richard Mayne (whom Peel appointed as police co-commissioners). Together they created the organizational components and policies of the new police. The Duke of Wellington, Sir Arthur Wellesley, a friend and political ally of Peel's, was another important player. Wellesley was the one who introduced the police bill in the House of Lords on behalf of Peel. What is notable about their backgrounds is that they all had experience with colonial Ireland. Both Charles Rowan and Richard Mayne had been born in Ireland. Mayne had been a young Irish barrister, the son of a judge of the King's Bench. Rowan had served in the British Army. He had been deployed to the Continent during the Napoleonic Wars, and in 1821 he served as a commanding officer in Dublin. Sir Arthur Wellesley had been aide-de-camp to the Irish viceroy, held the family seat of Trim in the Irish Parliament from 1790 to 1797, and, after commanding troops in India, became chief secretary of Ireland (1807–1809). Peel served as chief secretary for Ireland thereafter (1812–1818).

This colonial background, along with other colonial experiences, provided Wellesley, Peel, Rowan, and Mayne with knowledge of novel coercive forms. Ireland had been a central site for those forms. In the late eighteenth and early nineteenth centuries, the English colonial state's land-grabbing policies had fostered rising discontent from the Irish populace, generating what authorities called "disorder" and "degeneracy." The Rebellion of 1798, or in Irish, Éirí Amach 1798, had been particularly formative. Leaders of the United Irishmen, a group with some two hundred thousand members of different religious affiliations, mounted a revolt that summoned a massive English response, leading to up to thirty thousand fatalities. Meanwhile, what English authorities came to see as "criminal activity" had blazed across the colony. Rural "bandits," agrarian secret associations like the Whiteboys and Blackfeet, Protestant societies like the Orange Order, and roving bands challenged Anglo-Irish landlord power and English authorities.[98] In turn, the English colonial state had to continually improvise coercive responses, mustering its energy and assembling its forces into new organizational combinations, tactics, and strategies meant to squash both "crime" and insurgency at once (even as the lines between them were often unclear). These coalesced into a wide repertoire of counterinsurgency and policing models that constituted England's emerging colonial-military regime.

One part of that regime was the British Army's innovative deployment of light infantry for counterinsurgency campaigns. British forces had used light infantry in the Americas since the mid-eighteenth century, but at the century's end enterprising commanders in the colonies eventually devised new operations, tactics, and forms. Sir John Moore had been one such innovator. Later known as "the father of light infantry," Moore had "extensive experience in light infantry, raiding and counter insurgency in the mountains of Corsica and St. Lucia, the sands and deserts of Egypt, the woods in America, the marshland and beeches in Helder."[99] His new light infantry tactics turned the common soldier into "multipurpose soldiers, more adaptable to demands and more flexible in their drills and formations."[100] He developed the new approach in the West Indies in the 1790s as military governor of St. Lucia, where he transformed the West Indies light infantry into a colonial counterinsurgency group, dispatching them to chase brigands and insurgent slaves in the interior. These were campaigns that regular troop formations could not ably conduct.

After St. Lucia, Moore took the lessons to Ireland. His new light infantry tactics, along with the tactics developed by other military strategists, were codified in drills and training manuals, and they were used to subdue Irish nationalists during the 1798 uprising spearheaded by the Society of United Irishmen. Moore enjoyed a notable victory at Goff's Bridge, where his light infantry crushed a five-thousand-strong rebel force.[101] After Ireland, Moore took command of the Shorncliffe training camp, where the lessons were passed down to a new generation. Charles Rowan was a part of that generation. He trained under Sir John Moore at Shorncliffe and himself served in light infantry units during the Continental War under Moore's direct command.

The other part of the British colonial-military regime was colonial policing. While English colonial authorities in Ireland often turned to the British Army and militia to squash bouts of rebellion, they could not always rely upon them. Wars on the Continent threatened to siphon the British military away from the colonies, leaving English authorities in Dublin unprotected. The British colonial state soon experimented with new modalities of colonial coercion. Beginning in the late 1780s, in response to mob violence and continued threats of insurrection, English authorities in Dublin created a new armed force to police the Dublin Metropolitan District, then the second-largest city in the British Isles. The culmination of these efforts was legislation in 1799 and then the Dublin Police Act of 1808, prompted by Sir Arthur Wellesley, at the time chief secretary of Ireland. As a result of these efforts, Dublin had a uniformed, professionalized, heavily armed police inspired in part by France's gendarmerie. Subduing insurgency across the colony was the goal. As Wellesley's colleague explained, the new Dublin police would "suppress disturbance in the Capital, and as the Capital has always been the focus of Rebellion, it would also conduce much to keep things quiet in every part of the Island."[102]

Peel became chief secretary in 1812, inheriting control over the Dublin force. But he innovated further. The Dublin force had not had the predicted effect of quelling rural discontent, and Peel was appalled at the seeming lack of order in the rural districts. To manage crime in the countryside, there was only the ineffective baronial constable system; for public disorder, only the volunteer Irish Yeomanry and the small number of British troops stationed in the colony. This was not enough, in Peel's view. Peel's racialized views of the Irish, aided by a strong dose of anti-Catholicism, heightened his concerns. "Nothing could describe ... effectively the state of lawless society in Ireland," he wrote to a friend. "You have no idea of the moral depravation of the lower orders."[103]

Peel set out to fix the problem with his Peace Preservation Force, created in 1814. This was a regular police force that the English colonial state could deploy so that it did not have to rely upon the army. Rather than the London Metropolitan Police, these were the first "Peelers" and were colloquially called such. The mobile force was directed from Dublin Castle, dispatched to quell outbreaks of rural unrest. Its organizational structure included the novel position of a stipendiary magistrate, "a full-time police official with the powers of a magistrate" overseeing a body of special constables.[104] Later, as Peel's successors in Dublin Castle reckoned the need for more rural policing, the Peace Preservation Force was supplemented by the Irish County Constabulary. This sectioned Ireland into divisions, each of which had its own permanent body of constables at fixed stations. Officially it was created in 1822 under Chief Secretary Henry Goulburn, after Peel had left his post. But it was Peel's brainchild, sketched by him as early as 1816. He wrote of it in his journal as "an armed civil force under the order of chief magistrates."[105] In 1836, both the Peace Preservation Force and the County Constabulary were merged into the Irish Constabulary (later renamed the Royal Irish Constabulary).

The Dublin Police, the Peace Preservation Force, and the Irish Constabulary were different organs of the colonial state, but they nonetheless shared a number of important features pertinent to our story. First, these forces were meant to maintain alien rule over a people whom English authorities classified as inferior. These were colonial counterinsurgency forces in support of racialized rule. As Lord Lieutenant Whitworth had written of the Peace Preservation Force, colonial police was the best means by which "the lower orders can be kept down."[106] Second, these were heavily militarized forces. Organized hierarchically and centralized into the hands of a single authority (the colonial state), they typically drew upon the material, strategies, operations, and organizational forms of the British Army (including Moore's light brigades). The Dublin police was officially a civil force in the sense that it was not part of the army and it was under the command of civilian authorities in Dublin Castle, but it was nonetheless armed with "lanterns, poles, bayonets, carbines, blunderbusses and swords."[107] Peel's Peace Preservation Force was so named in a branding effort to win legitimacy, but in actuality it was a small army, living in barracks to be called upon at a moment's notice to squash Irish insubordination.[108] It is hardly surprising that Irish nationalists referred to it as a *gens d'armerie*; Peel had partly modeled it upon the French gendarmerie. Peel had also modeled it after Moore's light infantry. The force consisted of mobile "mounted patrols" dispatched to "suppress insurrectional and turbulent meetings" in the rural districts. In a nod to Moore's innovations that had begun in St. Lucia, Peel referred to the units as "light divisions."[109]

The Irish Constabulary was similarly militarized. Uniformed, heavily armed, and commanded by former army officers, it too was a colonial gendarmerie and was called such by Irish nationalist leaders.[110] In the summer of 1825, Sir Walter Scott toured Killinarney, Cork, and Dublin. He was struck by the Irish Constabulary's militarized features. He wrote to his friends in England that there is "a very strict police" in Ireland "which reminds me more of the gendarmerie of France than any other institution . . . This would seem a violent and unconstitutional proceeding in Britain, but in Ireland it works well."[111] Evidently, while the militarized colonial police was inimical to the sensibilities of Englishmen, it was perfectly fitting for a supposedly barbaric people like the Irish.

The final similarity across the different police forces is that they were all hybrid assemblages of power, merging components of the constable system and its mandate to manage crime with armed counterinsurgency military units. The colonial-military regime in Ireland was a professionalized, hierarchically organized coercive organization like an army but commanded by a civil authority and oriented toward the control of both crime and public disorder. In this sense, if the London Metropolitan Police was the very first modern police organization in England, these Irish precedents were among the first modern police organizations in the United Kingdom. It is telling that writers and officials would later point out that while the modern English sense of the word "police" originated in France, it was first used in the British Empire to refer to the police forces of Ireland. Sir Charles Warren, who was Metropolitan Police commissioner in 1886, even claimed that the path of importation of the police concept went not from Paris to London but through Ireland.[112] As Frederic Maitland wrote in 1885: "A full history of the new police would probably lay its first scene in Ireland, and begin with the Dublin Police Act."[113]

## The Boomerang and the New Police

Given this background, it should not be surprising that as Peel, Wellesley, Rowan, and other founders of the new police in London faced the rising racialized threat to order in England, and as they contemplated alternatives to the constable-watch system to meet it, they turned to Britain's existing colonial-military regime of coercion. Their official positions within the empire, in fact, compelled them to put England and Ireland into the same frame. When Peel was devising solutions for the London police system, his position as home secretary meant that he had also been overseeing the state's responses to labor agitation across the empire, including Ireland. And even as Peel advised English officials on questions of crime, insurgency, and policing, he was also advising Dublin on the Irish Constabulary. Throughout his writings and correspondence at the time, therefore, Peel reckoned that the problems of crime, disorder, and policing in England were not entirely distinct from those in Ireland. In 1829, Peel wrote from the Home Office to Lord Francis Gower, then chief secretary for Ireland, about the need for more police reform in Ireland and the use of repressive laws such as the Insurrection Act. He noted that laws akin to the Insurrection Act had been used in England in the not too distant past: "The circumstances of England at that period, and of many parts of Ireland at the present time, are in some respects similar."[114] In another discussion with Gower, Peel directly equated Ireland and England when discussing expenditures for policing. He urged Gower to ensure that the expense of "the administration of law" in Ireland would be paid for through taxes on Irish landlords, declaring: "Why should not Ireland from her own means make provision for the ordinary execution of the criminal law, for the preservation of life and property from all ordinary dangers, in the same way that every great town in England and Scotland does?"[115]

Peel, Wellesley, and Rowan thus found in Ireland a solution to the problem of policing in England. If they could not rely upon the existing constable and watch system to manage crime and disorder in England, and if they could not turn to the army to suppress disorder, they could do what they had already done in Ireland to address the same problems: create a new police under the command of civil authorities but with sufficient military capacities to manage crime and social unrest.[116] After all, if "the Irishman's natural predilection for outrage and a lawless life" (as Peel put it) was threatening England just as it had in Ireland, why not use the same tools in the metropolis that had been deployed in the colony?

Consider that the very structure of the London Metropolitan Police duplicated that of the militarized modalities of police power in Ireland. The Metropolitan Police Act centralized policing into a single organization, the Home Office. Overseeing everything from the top, the home secretary in the Home Office wielded ultimate control. This is exactly the same structure as in Ireland: the chief governor of Ireland in Dublin Castle was put in charge of the Dublin force and the constabulary. It meant, in fact, that Peel in the Home Office was now put in charge of the London police just as he had commanded the Irish colonial police forces when he was chief secretary of Ireland. Unsurprisingly, the language of the 1829 Metropolitan Police Act for London duplicated the language of the 1808 Dublin Act. Both laws began by declaring the need to improve the police. Both then specified boundaries of the new police district and divided the district into distinct "police divisions." And both laws empowered the chief governor/ home secretary to confirm the Crown's official appointments of the "justices" or magistrates of the divisions.[117]

The internal hierarchy of the London Met also duplicated the hierarchy of the colonial-military regime, drawing upon the army's and the Irish constabulary's systems in particular. Two commissioners, akin to magistrates, were to be in charge of the details and operations of the London force. For this, Peel appointed Richard Mayne and Charles Rowan. Beneath the co-commissioners were superintendents running the different divisions. The divisions consisted of inspectors, sergeants, and constables (or police officers); the title of sergeant (often spelled "serjeant") was taken directly from the army. They together constituted a "company," which was another army term. In all, the London Police was akin to Britain's army regiments, which also contained divisions and companies.[118] It is not inappropriate that Peel, when initially referring to the commissioners in his private correspondence, variously referred to them as "commissioners," "chief magistrates," and "military magistrates." He clearly had the military on his mind.[119]

Peel also had his own Peace Preservation Force in mind. His early plan for the Peace Preservation Force in Ireland was that it, like the light brigades upon which it was modeled, would be headquartered in central locations, to be dispatched to the farthest reaches of the colony as needed. Peel had initially planned for the London Metropolitan Police to act similarly. He had hoped for all of England's towns and districts to create a new civil police, but political practicalities meant he first had to focus on London. And until those forces were created, Peel planned for the London Metropolitan Police to be nimble enough to be sent to outlying areas of England in times of need. This actually happened as the decades wore on.[120]

Peel also drew directly from the colonial-military regime of Ireland to staff the new police. For the co-commissioners, Peel had expressly sought men with experience in Ireland or with military experience. He wrote to his friend in Ireland in 1829 as he was contemplating these appointments:

> It has occurred to me that if there were a military man conversant in the details of the police system of Ireland, he might possibly be very usefully employed here . . . tell me . . . whether you have any man now in Ireland who would exactly suit my purpose. There will be probably a force of between two and three thousand men ultimately under his command. With the Soldier I should unite a sensible lawyer as the other magistrate.[121]

Peel thus appointed Mayne, a barrister who had lived in Ireland, and Rowan, who, as noted, had been a commanding officer in Dublin. In turn, Peel, Rowan, and Mayne appeared to favor men with military backgrounds to serve in the role of superintendent. In the first decade or so, at least thirteen of the seventeen had been sergeant-majors in the army, just as the Irish Constabulary had been deliberately staffed at the top with military veterans.[122]

As for the rank and file, they were not overwhelmingly drawn from the army. According to some estimates, former soldiers made up only about 13 percent of the force in the early 1830s. Most had self-identified as "laborers." But the height, age, and literacy standards for recruiting the rank and file were nearly identical to those for the Irish Constabulary.[123] Furthermore, Peel and the commissioners applied to the London police a rule Peel had developed for his Peace Preservation Force in 1816. For the Peace Preservation Force, Peel believed that constables should come from outside the locality in which they served. The "less previous connection they have had with the county in which they are employed," Peel explained in a letter in 1814, "the more effectual will their exertions be."[124] The commissioners applied this rule to the London force: recruits were deliberately taken from the areas outside of London, and preferably from the rural districts, partly to prevent familiarity between the district residents and the police. Unmarried men on the force were quartered in section houses or small barracks, just like in Peel's Peace Preservation Force and the Irish Constabulary.[125] There was also an almost deliberate attempt to rid the police of Irishmen. Whereas the watch previously had seen enough Irish-born members to elicit complaints from English observers, the number of Irish in the London force declined over time, and this may have been due to the stringent entry requirements created by the commissioners. Not only did those requirements have to do with literacy and relative abstinence from alcohol—at a time when the Irish were seen as being il-literate and prone to drinking—they also prevented men from joining who had more than three children.[126]

The London police was uniformed, making them more like soldiers in the army and officers in the Irish police forces and providing—as Peel wrote to his wife—a "strong contrast to the old watchmen."[127] There was an important dif-ference, of course: the London Metropolitan Police did not wear red uniforms. This was seen by Peel to be too close to the army's uniform. But the fact that the new police were uniformed at all signaled the desire to replicate colonial-military power, and it is notable that the new police uniforms also happened to be the same color as the uniforms worn by the Dublin Metropolitan Police.[128] In fact, when Peel later tried to compel other English towns such as Manchester and Birmingham to replace their constable and watch system with a new police along the lines of the London Metropolitan Police, he told them that the precedent for such a civilian urban police lay not only in the London Metropolitan Police Act but also in the Dublin Police Act.[129]

The coloniality of the London force proceeded all the way down to its stra-tegic operations and tactics. Rowan divided the force into mobile patrols or "beats."[130] By this system, the policemen of each section were assigned a specified territory or "beat" that they were to survey. The beat system extended across the new districts; each beat was meant to be covered by foot in twenty minutes.[131] Today, the idea of a police beat is so common that we forget it had to have been invented at some point. But the origins of the beat system are colonial: a novel articulation of the plantation militia–slave patrols in the West Indies and planta-tion American South on the one hand and, on the other, the counterinsurgency light brigades that Moore had deployed against slave insurgents in St. Lucia and during the 1798 Irish rebellion.

To understand this, we must recognize that the other major sites of the British Empire besides Ireland in these years were the Caribbean and North America.

To meet the imperatives of the empire's plantation colonialism there, English settlers and authorities had forged a loosely organized formation of legal enforcement that included more than constables and watchmen. In the 1660s plantation owners in Barbados created a series of "slave codes" that regulated the behavior of slaves and made the local community, not just individual slave owners, responsible for them. The responsibility fell upon the local militia. As the governor of Virginia explained in 1723, a strong militia was meant to frighten "Slaves [and also appear] formidable to the Indians."[132] The militia became responsible for chasing down runaway slaves, inspecting slave dwellings, disrupting large gatherings, and ensuring order during festivals and funerals.[133] The Barbados slave code and the militia system to regulate slaves were spread across the Atlantic empire, resulting in the formation of militia-based slave patrols. South Carolina was among the first to adopt the system. There and elsewhere, the militia–slave patrols were tasked with stopping and questioning wandering slaves, demanding that they show permits given to them by their masters. They were also empowered to inspect the slaves' dwellings for arms or illicit goods, break up meetings, and in general keep the slaves in line upon pain of violence.[134]

Here is what is crucial for our purposes: to organize the militia–slave patrols, English settlers divided the territory into districts called "beats." The common (or "line") militias, in which the majority of the population served, compared to the more elite specialized militias, were organized around these districts. Service-age men living in the district, or beat, formed a line company; four line companies formed a battalion, two battalions formed a regiment, and multiple regiments in turn formed a brigade. The militia companies thereby became known as "beat companies." Serving as the "focal point for the registration and training of citizens," the beat companies were "strictly infantry units."[135] The earliest legislative references to "beats" in the state of South Carolina in the eighteenth century thus used the term "beat" interchangeably with "district" and slowly came to refer to them in terms of "beat companies."[136]

As militia took on slave patrol functions, beats became all the more important, for they specified the swaths of territory that slave patrols needed to survey and control. Knowledge of the land, dwellings, and slave populations in that area was crucial for the militia–slave patrols. The 1734 act in South Carolina stipulated that "every patrol shall go to and examine every plantation in their district once in a month at least, and oftener if the commissioners or the captain shall see occasion, and take up all slaves which they shall meet without the bounds of his master's lands who have not a ticket or permit."[137] The 1747 act clarified that these districts were to be based upon preexisting beats, and stipulated that the beats were for patrolling and surveying the male slave population: "Every master, mistress, owner, manager, attorney or trustee of or for any slaves in this Province, shall ... return to the captain or commanding officer of the respective companies of the militia, in whose beat or precinct such slaves do live or reside or are commonly used or employed, a true and faithful list" of the male slaves in that district. The typical district, or beat, was not to exceed fifteen miles.[138]

In devising police beats, Rowan drew upon this militia–slave patrol tradition and merged it with Moore's light infantry tactics. Those tactics had been an integral part of Rowan's experiences. Rowan had not only served in Ireland; he had trained at Shorncliffe in Moore's new programs and served as an officer in the 52nd (Oxfordshire) Foot, a light infantry regiment, and then the Light Brigade under Wellington. He applied this knowledge when organizing the beat system. In Rowan's plan, beat patrols covered their own swaths of territory but would also act like light infantry. They would be flexible and mutually supporting, coming to aid each other in times of need, just as light infantry units worked together in unison with rapid mobility. This would have been impossible under the old parish system. Each of the watches and constables had been isolated in their own parishes with little to no cooperation, coordination, or communication between them. But with the new centralized London force, each patrol was part of a larger centralized organization, working together as mobile infantry units within a light division.[139] It was entirely appropriate, therefore, that Rowan divided the Metropolitan District into eight "divisions" and each division into eight mobile beat patrols. Each police division was thus akin to the light division of the British Army: beat patrols were analogous to the light infantry units that chased down insurgents in St. Lucia and Ireland, while also akin to the militia–slave patrol companies that roamed Caribbean plantations.[140]

Rowan also brought military culture from the imperial-military regime to the London Met. Besides innovating light divisions, Rowan's mentor Moore had devised new leadership training programs. These were expressed in his plan for officer training, "Military Training and Moral Training," which was instituted at the Shorncliffe camp. Moore's goal had been to enhance troop discipline by enhancing troop morale. This became known as "the art of man-management."[141] In place of the traditionally brutal disciplinary methods that officers deployed, such as flogging, "man-management" required a more conciliary though nonetheless firm approach. "Discipline, imperative in any uniformed body of men, should proceed from a sense of duty, pride and mutual respect." Officers should "study and befriend the men under them, develop their personality, and induce their respect, approval and obedience" by teaching them the importance of cooperation.[142] This is the method that Rowan adopted as he attempted to create a professionalized London police force to replace the undisciplined watchmen. Rowan implemented training programs for the force, drilling them military style at Wellington Barracks, and applied army-level standards of conduct.[143] He sought out noncommissioned military officers to fill the ranks of the higher positions of the force and instructed them according to Moore's "man-management" principles. His first instructions to the superintendents called for them to became "well-acquainted, by frequent personal intercourse, with the Inspectors and Serjeants, and through them with the character and conduct of every Man in the Company under his orders: he will be firm and just, at the same time kind and conciliating towards them, in his behaviour, on all occasions." Instructions for sergeants required that "each Serjeant . . . will live much with them [the nine men under him], and is expected to make himself thoroughly acquainted with the character of every individual." These copied the orders for army officers in Moore's man-management system. Rowan thus conceived of his new police force as an army regiment, readied for the battle against Irish crime and disorder on London's streets.[144]

## Policing the Irish

If the civil policing model was birthed with the London Metropolitan Police, as so many scholars have suggested, it is more precise to say it was born from imperial feedback, modeled after and inspired by colonial-military forces.[145] This evinces the coloniality of the London Metropolitan Police: it was a boomerang effect of colonialism. Still, the Met's coloniality lies not just in its form but also its function: in its early years, the Met directed disproportionate attention to the Irish. Consider the first mass staging of the London Met's operations. In May 1833, the National Union of the Working Classes held a political convention in Cold Bath Fields in Islington. Among other things, the NUWC had been agitating to extend the franchise beyond the limited privileges afforded by the 1832 Reform Act to include more workers. Authorities were not pleased. The home secretary, Lord Melbourne, declared the gathering illegal and dispatched the recently formed London Met to break it up. Participants and bystanders stood amazed at the new police's militaristic appearance. Observing firsthand the results of the constables' military training at Wellington Barracks, witnesses described how the police lined up "15 or 16 abreast . . . like a regular file of soldiers." They "came on in military order, the same as a file of soldiers would do," responding to "military orders" from their officers like "quick march!" and "shoulders forward!" Protesters fought back; police responded by trapping the crowd and, reportedly, clubbing them with their truncheons. In the melée, a number of constables were injured and one was killed.

The NUWC, according to one historian, was a radical workers' organization that became "one of the most important working class political organisations of the pre-Chartist period."[146] Its membership did not consist of prototypical English laborers but included Irish migrant laborers, and it advanced Irish causes. It was an outgrowth of the Association for Civil and Political Liberty, which had been formed by Irish activists in London in 1828, and the London Irish for Catholic Emancipation, created in 1829. Manifesting the formidable connections between Irish anticolonialism and English Radicalism in this period, the NUWC was exactly the sort of threatening group that had prompted the formation of the new London police. Its connection to Irish immigrants and Irish causes made it part of the "Irish problem" that policing was meant to manage. It is fitting that authorities like Lord Melbourne were threatened by it and that they dispatched the Met to squash it.

The raid at Cold Bath Fields was not the London Metropolitan Police's first encounter with the Irish-led group. Before the Cold Bath Fields incident, members of the NUWC had petitioned Parliament to register a complaint against the new police. They alleged that a plainclothes police officer named William Popay had penetrated their organization under a false name to incite them to rebel, thereby provoking a strong police response. The NUWC members claimed that the police were acting as an illegitimate spy network and undermining citizens' liberties (not unlike the despised French police's spy network under the infamous chief of police Joseph Fouché). A select committee held hearings in 1833 and found that Sergeant Popay had indeed been instructed by his police superintendent to attend the political union meetings and report on what had transpired. It also concluded that this was perfectly legal and legitimate.[147]

That the London Met's policing of the NUWC extended to stealth surveillance is a testament to the Met's colonial provenance. In Ireland, English authorities in Dublin Castle had used spies to provide vital information on Irish anticolonial organizations such as the Society of United Irishmen in the 1790s. This had helped the English colonial state thwart rebellions.[148] Evidently, the London Metropolitan Police was now serving the same function, though in London rather than Dublin. It even used the same tactics as the English colonial state in Dublin, with a member of its force sent to infiltrate and inform on the targeted organization. The colonial panopticon was thus deployed both in the colony and in the metropole, against the very same populations.

Not only did the London Metropolitan Police use counterinsurgency tools of spying and riot control to subdue Irish organizations, it also disproportionately policed Irish residents amid its efforts to thwart crime. Data on the placement of the London Metropolitan Police in the 1830s and 1840s may enable us to explore this further. Table 1.1 shows the major police divisions and the number of officers there per capita. The limitation with this data is that the divisions do not correspond squarely with Irish neighborhoods. They typically included a variety of parishes and neighborhoods. For instance, the district of Holborn contained both the heavily Irish St. Giles neighborhood and a middle-class shopping area.[149] Some divisions had more homogenous demographics, but the picture remains

Table 1.1.  Distribution of London Metropolitan Police Force, 1830–1849

| Letter Division | Name Division | Number of Police per 1,000 Residents (1830) | Number of Police per 1,000 Residents (1849) | Robberies per 1,000 Residents (1849) | Value of Property Stolen (1849) |
|---|---|---|---|---|---|
| A | Whitehall | 19.2 | 15.6 | 8.1 | £322 |
| L | Lambeth | 4.2 | 3.6 | 5.3 | £1,521 |
| T | Kensington | 3.5 | 3.4 | 5.5 | £2,604 |
| N | Islington | 3.4 | 2.9 | 4.1 | £1,089 |
| P | Camberwell | 3.4 | 2.8 | 8.0 | £3,772 |
| B | Westminster | 3.3 | 2.4 | 2.1 | £1,340 |
| S | Hampstead | 3.1 | 2.2 | 7.9 | £3,115 |
| V | Wandsworth | 3.0 | 2.2 | 5.5 | £2,374 |
| R | Greenwich | 2.9 | 2.2 | 6.6 | £2,958 |
| F | Covent Garden | 2.7 | 2.1 | 4.6 | £1,913 |
| K | Stepney | 2.6 | 2.1 | 5.7 | £3,264 |
| M | Southwark | 2.4 | 2.1 | 6.8 | £3,087 |
| E | Holborn | 2.3 | 2.0 | 4.1 | £1,613 |
| G | Finsbury | 2.3 | 1.8 | 11.8 | £3,731 |
| D | Marylebone | 2.0 | 1.8 | 3.5 | £6,744 |
| C | St. James | 2.0 | 1.5 | 7.9 | £2,680 |
| H | Whitechapel | 1.7 | 1.4 | 3.3 | £2,007 |

Sources: Fletcher 1850; House of Commons 1830, 2.

complicated. Whitechapel was a poor district with many Irish residents, but it was among the *least* policed. The Southwark area was another poor working-class district with ample numbers of Irish residents, and while it had slightly more police per capita, middle-class residents there nonetheless complained that there were a lot of "disorderly and improperly characters" because "there is a great deal of Irish" and not enough police.[150] On the other hand, this apparent underpolicing of the Irish does not apply to other neighborhoods. Lambeth was a poor working-class district with Irish residents and, in 1830 at least, it had a significantly high number of police per capita. Furthermore, the tony, aristocratic district of St. James was among the least policed, along with Whitechapel.

Other evidence buttresses the claim that the police focused on Irish districts. Rowan and Mayne testified in 1834 that Irish districts such as St. Giles were patrolled more heavily than other districts that were "wealthy" and "peaceable" like St. James. Their implied argument was that by policing the poor districts, they were protecting the wealthier ones because they were preventing the criminals from penetrating the wealthier districts. "We look upon it that we are watching St. James's and other places while we are watching St. Giles's and bad places in general," explained Rowan.[151] The transition Rowan freely makes between the largely Irish area of St. Giles and "bad places in general" is indicative: the Irish-filled parts of the city were the "bad places" requiring policing. Relatedly, in the early 1860s one writer reflected on how the "semi-barbarians" of the "Irish district" of St. Giles in the 1820s had caused a horrific scene of violence, disorder, and criminality but that the new police of the 1830s stamped out the problem:

> The establishment of the police has done much to purify and pacify various Irish localities; still there is enough yet left, wherever this turbulent race congregates—and the Irish seldom completely amalgamate with people amongst whom they may cast their lot—to show what they must have been when there was no sufficient force conveniently at hand to overawe and overpower rioters.[152]

The remarks of Sir Edwin Chadwick further suggest that the London Met not only heavily patrolled Irish districts but also mimicked light infantry tactics, sometimes combining units to invade and swarm "bad areas" where the Irish predominated. A police reformer from Manchester who was part of the parliamentary commission to explore rural policing in the late 1830s, Chadwick alluded to how the London police were often rapidly mobilized to penetrate Irish districts. He maintained that the new police "are, as a rule . . . quick, and superior in the practice of military drill," while the army was "always slower to move"; as an example, he referred to how the London police sometimes "invaded" Irish neighborhoods. They typically did so to quell violent outbreaks that had erupted in the wake of process servers entering the area. "In London, at the time of the outset of the police force, there were Irish quarters in which no process could be served. The process-server was driven away; then ten policemen were sent, but a whoop was raised and the Irish assembled by the hundred; then a hundred of the police were sent and in conflict bested the shillelagh, and law and order were restored."[153]

The arrests that the London Metropolitan Police made in its early years further indicate that Irish individuals as well as Irish neighborhoods were overpoliced. Magistrates observing London's police houses in 1833 noticed that "the number of Irish that come to be passed, and the number of casual poor, take up a great deal time at the police-office."[154] Writers observing the London courts similarly remarked upon the fact that defendants tended to be Irish. One writer, George Hodder, concluded that Ireland must be peaceful now because all the "ruffian" Irishmen had evacuated Ireland and come to London.[155] Such anecdotal evidence is supported by official records. Commissioner Rowan boasted to a select parliamentary committee that the London Metropolitan Police in 1833 had apprehended 9,325 "vagrants" and that many of these were from Ireland.[156] Most of the other arrests made by police in the 1830s were likewise in categories that were identified as typically "Irish" offenses. From 1830 to 1833, around 65 percent of all people arrested by the Metropolitan Police were "drunk, drunk and disorderly characters, disorderly prostitutes, or vagrants." Through the rest of the decade the percentage of these arrests decreased slightly, but it nonetheless hovered at around half of all arrests or just over half. Public houses serving liquor were another target, no doubt aided by the passage of the 1834 Beer Act, which "allowed constables to enter public houses and beershops whenever they liked." Meanwhile, street offenses that were not typically associated with Irish, such as illicit Sunday trading at street markets or fairs, were left comparably unattended.[157]

In fact, some writers at the time did not hesitate to assert that the new police's main target was the Irish. In his pamphlet on the new police, one writer by the name of John Wade wrote that the London Met's purpose was to "protect the community from fraud, annoyance, violence and depredation" and expressly excluded the upper classes from the police's purview. The only crimes committed by the upper classes, he opined, were "mischiefs resulting from gaming" and these mischiefs were not "pernicious." The real targets of the police, Wade concluded, were "street nuisances and disorders; to licensed houses; to stage-coaches, carts, carriages and other vehicles; to counterfeit coin; frauds in weights and measures"; "female prostitution"; and in particular "mendicity," which made for a great "mass of wretchedness" in the metropolis. These were activities of the working class, and many involved the Irish in particular. Wade explicitly stated that the menace of mendicity was an Irish problem, with its cause in Irish immigration: "The chief source of mendicity in London, Manchester, Leeds and other large towns is the vast influx of lower Irish" with "their half-civilised habits."[158]

We can look at available arrest data more closely to explore the extent to which the new London police might have stopped and arrested Irish residents at higher rates than other groups. Records of the 1820s and 1830s from the London Metropolitan police's archives, such as the *Metropolitan Police Criminal Returns* and *Daily Reports*, provide arrest data starting from 1828 (just before the London Metropolitan Police was founded) through the 1830s. The data provide the names of those arrested and brief descriptions of incidents. These records do not provide information on the place of origin or ethnicity of the detained.

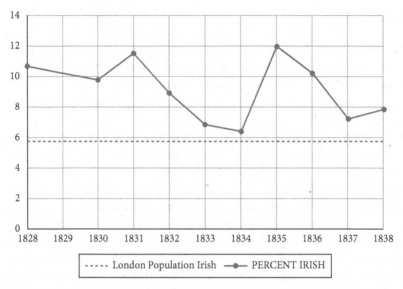

**Figure 1.1.** Percentage of Arrests of Irish-Born by the London Metropolitan Police, 1828–1838

However, the historian Adam Crymble has effectively developed a method of tracing ethnicity by surname. Using this method on a sample of arrests reveals that while the Irish-born and children of Irish-born immigrants made up about 5.75 percent of London's population by the 1830s (and likely less), the Irish made up over 10 percent of all arrests on average, and at times constituted up to 20 percent of all arrests (mostly for petty crimes like theft).[159] In other words, the Irish were arrested at nearly twice the rate as they would have been if they were not overpoliced (see Figure 1.1).[160] Given this, the new police indeed appear to have been functioning very much as a way to deal with "the so-called Irish difficulty" that traversed "Kerry or Limerick as in London," as the *Times* put it.[161] This further attests to the coloniality of modern policing. Militarized policing followed the trail blazed from colony to metropole by the very colonial subjects for whom it was initially designed.

## Performing the Civil Police

Finally we can address the puzzle that opens this chapter. On the one hand, Peel and the founders had hoped that the new police would be a "civil" police: an alternative to the army and the heavily militarized gendarmerie of the Continent. Even though they drew from the colonies to create it, the task was to forge a police force that could operate in the metropole and hence in the space where English citizens roamed—a civil police for a presumably civil society. This meant that Peel had to modulate the importation of a military form by crafting a force that did not *appear* to be too militaristic. Lest he be accused of French-style militarism, Peel had to win over the English public. He had to secure the support of upper-class and middle-class skeptics who may have feared that the new police would be turned on them.

All of this is to say that the so-called civil police had to be *performed*. Peel, Rowan, and Mayne had to portray the police as a nonmilitary force that would respect the liberties of the people. The instructions presumably given to the police force before it hit the streets conveys something of this. Sometimes referred to as "Peel's Principles" and recited today by police officials everywhere from London to Los Angeles, the instructions stated among other things that the "mission" of the police is "to prevent crime and disorder as an alternative to the repression of crime and disorder by military force"; that the police needed to gain "public approval" and "secure and maintain public respect"; and that it needed the "cooperation of the public," which "diminishes, proportionately, to the necessity for the use of physical force and compulsion in achieving police objectives."[162] Likewise, police commissioners Mayne and Rowan declared they hoped to win over "all respectable persons" in London—that is, earn their approval—and therefore instructed the new constables to proceed with caution.[163] They counseled restraint, reiterating another of Peel's principles: "police should use only the minimum degree of physical force which is necessary on any particular occasion for achieving a police objective." As the historian Wilbur Miller put it in his classic study, the new police had "to maintain order with minimal provocation and violence." They had to keep the military provenance of the new police "backstage."[164]

The brutality of the colonial-military regime overseas could not be transplanted to English soil wholesale. It had to be tempered for home consumption. This is why the founders of the new police chose blue as opposed to red uniforms: red uniforms had been worn by the British Army. If in the colonies the state's apparatus of violence is naked, in the metropole it had to be clothed. Furthermore, the first London police commissioners had to modulate some of the technologies and tools of the colonial-military regime. While the Dublin police carried bayonets, carbines, and blunderbusses, the London police had only truncheons. And they were instructed to keep them hidden from public view.[165]

To better perform civility, the new police had to improvise coercive devices, tactics, and techniques. For example, whereas colonial forces in Ireland and the British army at Peterloo controlled crowds with guns, the new police had to craft new methods for crowd control, born in the hybrid space between the exposed violence of colonial militarism and the restraint required for civil society.

Initially, to handle crowds, Rowan had directed his force to be defensive. Amid clashes between the police and crowds in October 1830, he instructed his men to stay on the sidelines. The police lined both sides of the street and defended themselves only when provoked.[166] But this tactic of defensive passivity in the face of mob violence was soon replaced with something entirely new: the baton charge. The tactic was developed by the London police upon a suggestion by the Chartist Francis Place. Place had suggested to his friend, a police inspector, that the police should not wait to be attacked by the rioters but should instead move into them and "thrash those who mob with their staves as long as any of them remained together."[167] The first reported use of this tactic came in November 1830 when "a huge mob" armed with pieces of wood came at the police from the Public Record Office building in Chancery Lane and toward Charing Cross. The crowd scattered as result.[168]

It is not, therefore, that the founders of the new police brought every single technology, organizational principle, or disposition from England's apparatus of colonial-military coercion overseas back home to be unleashed upon London's denizens. In the interest of performing the civil police and calling it into existence, modifications had to be made. This was a "civil" police in the sense that it was a *metropolitan* variant of *colonial* forces: a militarized organization whose coloniality and racialized imperiality had to be hidden from open view.

Yet performances sometimes fail; indeed, the coloniality and associated militarism of the London Metropolitan Police were noticed by astute observers soon enough. The military command-and-control structure of the new police, for instance, was not lost on a writer in the *Times* soon after the passage of the Metropolitan Police Act of 1829: "The metropolis is to be no longer protected by a constitutional constabulary force [i.e., the constable and watch system] but it is to be governed by a gendarmerie, taking orders from, and responsible only to, the Home Office."[169] The hierarchical structure and military training of the London police also became evident to keen observers. One critic wrote in 1838: "The latent object appears to have been that of placing at the disposal of the Home Secretary a body of well-trained, disciplined and armed men, competent to intimidate the public and to keep down the rising spirit of the population."[170] The *Weekly Dispatch* ironically referred to the new police as "these military protectors of our civil liberties" and called it "a gendarmerie." *Monthly Magazine* referred to Police Commissioner Rowan as "a Horseguard dependent" and a "military retainer of the Duke [of Wellington]."[171]

The charges leveled against the new police in its early years are also now legible. If the new police was accused of being the "Jenny Darbies," this was in no small part because its members were in fact *gens d'armes*: a heavily militarized force in form if not in function, a colonial-military unit in its organization and operations. The frosty reception, if not indignant ire, that the London Metropolitan

Police received from Irish residents thus makes sense. The Irish in the colonies had long criticized English colonial police forces such as the Irish Constabulary for their brutality, repressive function, and militarism. Now, having come to London, those same Irish migrants would have easily recognized the militarism of the London Metropolitan Police, not least because they were, in the 1830s, its targets.[172]

If recognizing the coloniality of the new police despite its performances of civility helps us cotton why the civil police was accused of being a gendarmerie, it also helps us understand something else: why, despite its auspicious beginnings, the London Metropolitan Police became less controversial over time to certain sectors of English society. Initially, the middle and upper classes had been hesitant to accept the new police, skeptical of any government arm that might introduce Napoleonic tyranny. But they increasingly became more accepting of the police as the 1830s and 1840s proceeded. The coloniality of the London Met offers an explanation: the middle and upper classes came to accept the new police because they slowly realized that the police was not aimed at *them*. Arresting Irish vagrants, raiding Irish communities, spying on workers' groups: none of this threatened the liberties of the "respectable persons" (in Rowan and Mayne's words). Rather than aimed at the upper and middle classes, the new police had been created to discipline and punish the racialized subproletariat who were seemingly upending their social order, the "scum of society" that Peel and others had in mind when they hatched the civil police.[173] The upper and middle classes could thus be assured that the new police was not to be feared. Its functional coloniality made it something to be praised.

# 2

# Cotton Colonialism and the New Police in the United States and England, 1830s–1850s

The civil police model that London birthed did not stay put. Within a decade, Liverpool (1836), Bristol (1836), and Manchester (1839) became the first English cities outside of London to create new police departments modeled after the London Met. Thereafter, nearly all other English towns, boroughs, and counties did the same. The London model sailed across the Atlantic too. In the United States, cities and towns had inherited the constable-watch systems from the English. In the South, they also had city guards, militias, and slave patrols. Then, in 1844, America's first civil police force was born in New York City. Replacing the prior constable-watch system, it was a "properly organised preventive police force, like that of London," as the press put it.[1] Other cities followed. In the North there was Chicago (1851), Cincinnati (1853), Philadelphia (1855), Baltimore (1857), and Boston (1854); in the South Savannah (1854), Charleston (1856), and New Orleans (1866). Cities and towns across the United States followed suit, all partly or wholly inspired by the London civil model.[2]

The civil police model was a transatlantic hit, the shiny new toy of the British-American imperial sphere. But questions arise here. We might wonder about *why* and *how* these forces emerged, and why they emerged *when* they did. What compelled these other cities outside London to create their own new civil police forces? What was happening during the decades of the 1830s through the 1850s in the transatlantic sphere that made the creation of new civil police forces so desirable at the time? As seen in the previous chapter, the London Metropolitan Police was a response to the perceived threat of barbarian Irish hordes overwhelming the capital. What about the new police in other cities? We might also wonder about the *organization* and *operations*, along with the *form* and *function*, of these new police forces. As seen in the previous chapter, the London Metropolitan Police was an effect of the colonial boomerang. Did the boomerang hit these other cities too?

This chapter explores the spread of the new civil police model across the transatlantic interimperial sphere in the formative years of the 1830s through the 1850s to address these questions. It is impossible to track the emergence of the

*Policing Empires*. Julian Go, Oxford University Press. © Oxford University Press 2024.
DOI: 10.1093/oso/9780197621653.003.0003

new police in every single town where it emerged. There are too many. We must therefore narrow our lens. Accordingly, this chapter looks at Manchester, which was the largest city outside of London to create a new civil police force, along with two other cities whose police departments were created by the same legislative act that created Manchester's new police: Birmingham and Bolton. This chapter also casts its eye upon New York City, since it was the first in the United States to adopt the London model. Finally, we will look at Savannah, Georgia, which created the largest and earliest civil police force in the American South, becoming a model for other southern cities alongside London's force. Savannah was a London of the South. Through this comparison we will find the reasons for the formation of the police of these cities, as well as variations across them—including variations in their colonial influences and armaments.

To begin, though, we need to consider something seemingly unrelated to the formation of the new police: the transatlantic interimperial relations of racialized state power and colonial capitalism that traversed the British-American cotton empires of the time. While this might seem like an odd detour, we will later realize that an understanding of these relations is paramount. The key to unlocking the puzzle of the formation and spread of the new police lies therein: in the relations of cotton colonialism whose dynamics and logics gave the new police its function and form.

## Networks of Cotton Colonialism

When reviewing the history of the birth of the new police in the transatlantic sphere, one question immediately arises: why did the new police spread and emerge as it did? Part of the story is emulation. Once London had the new police, other cities had to have one as well. It meant you were modern and important. Still, conventional histories would point to other factors besides this logic of emulation. They would suggest that the new police spread in the 1830s through the 1850s because in these years major cities in Britain and the United States experienced rapid economic growth, industrialization, and urbanization that generated troublesome levels of crime and disorder. This story is similar to the one told about the birth of the London Metropolitan Police: social changes such as urbanization generated new problems of crime and disorder that required new organizations including the civil police. The new police was created as an almost natural response.

This conventional story is on to something. But the wider transnational and interimperial network of cotton must be foregrounded. The economic growth, industrialization, and urbanization that historians point to as important for the formation of the new police had all been dependent upon cotton production and trade. Textiles had become England's most valuable industrial product by the 1830s and continued to be crucial for its economy. The vast majority of England's raw cotton came from America's southern slave plantations. While US cotton made up only 17 percent of all of Britain's cotton imports in 1800, that figure rose to 27.3 percent in 1810, 53.6 percent in 1820, and 76.5 percent in 1830. In 1860, Britain imported 88.5 percent of its cotton from the United States.[3] England's and America's financial centers, urban ports, and new zones of production were thereby tethered to America's settler-plantation colonialism, which in turn was predicated upon and concomitant with America's settler colonialism.

In the South, plantation production had required violent processes of dual dispossession: the seizure of land by the state and settlers and the seizure of Black bodies as slaves by white settler-plantation families. This system then fueled economic growth across the Atlantic. The number of slaves in the South grew markedly, from 1,191,362 in 1810 to 3,953,760 by 1860, and this growth facilitated the rapid rise in cotton exports to England.[4] As London financed, managed, and regulated cotton production and trade, Manchester's sprawling factories spun the raw cotton into textiles, earning it the name "cottonopolis" as the counterpoint to the "cotton kingdom" in the American South. Liverpool was the main entry and distribution point for that American cotton. In the years 1808 to 1809, only 653 ships entered Liverpool, but by 1827 the number of ships surpassed 2,000, and the number of bales of cotton imported grew proportionately. Some of America's leading cotton trading companies established branches in Liverpool.[5]

In the United States, plantation production helped fuel economic growth in major metropolises. New York had served as an important shipping port to England in the early 1800s. It was also an important nodal point for distributing southern cotton to the proliferating textile mills of America's Northeast and providing the financing and services for the cotton economy. Its "phenomenal" economic growth, along with the formation of a distinct New York City upper class, occurred exactly from 1820 to 1860. Meanwhile, New York City's population jumped from 123,706 in 1820 to 813,669 in 1860.[6] Down south, just as this was occurring, cities such as New Orleans and Savannah rose to prominence as new mercantile and shipping towns. Savannah in particular saw unprecedented growth by the 1850s. Aided by new railroad links, cotton accounted for four-fifths of the value of all exports from Savannah by that time. Savannah thus stored and shipped cotton from the region's plantations to Liverpool or New York (where it was redirected to points farther north) and became the third-largest cotton exporter behind New Orleans and Mobile. Known as "the New York of the South," and with prominent trading houses from the city establishing branches in Liverpool, Savannah was one of Liverpool's unofficial sister cities.[7]

Beyond the American South, the other important colonial site in the transimperial network was Ireland. English industrial development ensued at the expense of English agriculture in the early to mid-1800s. Ireland was ushered in as the new supplier of agricultural goods, literally feeding English industrialization. This meant that Ireland's burgeoning industries were replaced by a new colonial regime of commercialized agrarian monoculture, land concentration, and Anglo-Irish landlord power. In turn, displaced and dispossessed Irish were pushed to England to become the sailors, shipbuilders, dockworkers, drivers, warehousemen, and textile workers for England's cotton economy. Because many English workers—as employers complained—were not keen on this work, Irish labor filled the gaps. In Liverpool, the Irish were crucial for the growing port, providing the labor for loading and unloading ships or moving freight from the dockside to the warehouses. In Manchester, the Irish supplied not only the city's pool of warehousemen but also the entire region's factory workers for the ever-growing textile mills, where they occupied the lowest rungs of the labor hierarchy. "The rapid growth of the cotton manufacture has attracted hither operatives from every part of the kingdom and Ireland," wrote James Kay in his seminal study of the poor in Manchester, "[and] has poured forth the most destitute of her hordes to supply the constantly increasing demand for labor."[8] By 1851, 13.1 percent of Manchester's population had been born in Ireland. The only other city in England that had a larger per capita Irish population was Liverpool, where the Irish population grew by 25 percent between 1841 and 1851, by which time 22.3 percent of its population was Irish born.

The Irish went to the United States as well. Irish migration to the United States had begun before the Irish famine of the 1840s; the famine only exacerbated the trend. By the time New York created its new police in the mid-1840s, its foreign-born population—the majority of whom were Irish—had grown from 5,390 in 1820 to 235,733 by 1850, thereby making up 46 percent of the city's entire population.[9] Immigrants swiftly took up positions in the booming economy and, as in England, the positions were at the bottom of the pile. By 1855, Irish immigrants made up 87 percent of the city's unskilled laborers (while African Americans accounted for 3 percent).[10] The Irish also ended up in the South. With Savannah's rising prosperity came population growth (the number of souls rose from 13,573 in 1848 to 22,292 by 1860), and much of the growth was due to foreign-born immigrants, mostly Irish.[11] By 1860 the Irish in Savannah represented 14.1 percent of the city's population and 22.7 percent of its white population. This was the highest proportion in the entire South (see Table 2.1).[12] The Irish had been drawn to the new jobs attendant on Savannah's growing port-centered urbanism and the new railway that brought in the cotton. Most of the Irish men worked at the port, in the warehouses, on commercial and residential construction sites, or on the new railway, living tightly in neighborhoods with the city's bondsmen and free Black workers.[13] The Irish labored in the bottom rungs of the economy: 80 percent of the city's white laborers were Irish.[14]

**Table 2.1.** Irish and Black Populations in the Largest Southern Cities, 1860

| City | Irish as Percentage of White Population | Blacks (Freed and Slave) as Percentage of Total Population | Total Population |
| --- | --- | --- | --- |
| Memphis, TN | 22.2 | 17.2 | 22,623 |
| New Orleans, LA | 16.9 | 14.3 | 168,675 |
| Savannah, GA | 22.7 | 37.8 | 22,292 |
| Mobile, AL | 15.9 | 28.7 | 29,258 |
| Louisville, KY | 10.86 | 10.0 | 68,033 |
| Charleston, SC | 14.0 | 41.3 | 40,522 |

*Sources:* Gleeson 2001, 35; United States Bureau of the Census 1864, xxxi–xxxii.

In short, the transimperial network upon which England's economic growth had depended, and by which Savannah and New York's fortunes rose as well, was staffed by a transatlantic subproletariat performing the least desirable, least well paid, and most precarious labor. Doing the economy's dirty work, they were concentrated in cities, ports, plantations, or factory towns. They were also connected *across* these sites. Dispossessed Irish workers in Lancashire's factories spun raw cotton that had been cultivated and harvested by the hands of Black slaves in the American South. That cotton had been stored in and then shipped from Savannah by fellow Irish workers to Liverpool, where Irish dockworkers unloaded the white gold and sent it to Lancashire's factories, where it was spun by other Irish laborers. In effect, this was an "Irish Atlantic" that was layered onto the "Black Atlantic." It is not surprising that English officials saw Irish workers in England as homologous to slaves. George Cornewall Lewis's 1836 report announced that Irish immigration to England was a prime example "of a less civilized population spreading themselves as a kind of substratum, beneath a more civilized community; and, without excelling in any branch of industry, obtaining possession of all the lowest departments of manual labour." He continued: "So long as the institution of slavery was universal . . . such an emigration could not take place."[15]

## The Coercive Modalities of Transatlantic Cotton Colonialism

To understand the formation of the new police across the Atlantic, we must also reckon another key component of this sprawling network of plantation colonialism and industrial production: state coercion. One of the things that had enabled the creation and reproduction of transatlantic cotton coloni- alism was a wide array of modalities of colonial force and militarized violence. As seen in Chapter 1, English colonial rule in Ireland had required various colonial-military organizations there to maintain order. These forces were cru- cial for the transimperial network: they helped sustain the flow of agricultural exports from Ireland to feed English society while also dispossessing poor Irish laborers, "freeing" them to work in England's burgeoning ports and cities. Across the pond in the southern United States, cotton colonialism in the 1830s through the 1850s had been sustained through various coercive modalities as well. Foremost were militia-slave patrols inherited from Britain's plantation co- lonialism. Earlier, armed militias had been formed to defend against possible attacks from the Cherokee, Shawnee, or Creek. Later, following the precedent of English settlements in Barbados, these were charged with enforcing the slave codes. This system continued through the early nineteenth century, as did the system of militia-slave patrols organized around "beats" (see Chapter 1).[16] The militia-slave patrols stood alongside the constable-watch system, but they were complexified as plantation production expanded. In some states, such as Virginia and the Carolinas, the militia and patrols were pried apart and made relatively autonomous from each other. In some cities, the local watch or city guards were made responsible for enforcing the slave codes, such that city watchmen were in essence slave patrollers.[17]

In all these cases, the patrols were heavily militarized, with centralized hierarchies and an array of arms. The patrols in South Carolina consisted of one captain, commissioned by the governor, and four men for each district of the province. Each of the men was to "keep a good horse, one pistol, and a carbine or other gun, a cutlass, [and] a cartridge box with at least twelve cartridges in it."[18] By the 1850s, officials in South Carolina openly referred to the patrol as an "armed police."[19] In Mobile, Alabama, the watch-patrol members wore uni- form blue shirts and white pants and were armed with pistols, swords, muskets, and bayonets. After the Haitian Revolution of 1791 and the Gabriel plot of 1800, some city watches or guards essentially became counterinsurgency forces. In New Orleans in 1805, a new city guard was created in response to the threat of slave insurgency. It was literally a gendarmerie, named as such by city officials given the French legacy there (the gendarmerie had been created in France in 1790). It had an elaborate military hierarchy, including a captain, "lieutenant, sublieutenant, a sergeant and three corporals, down to the rank and file of thirty- two gendarmes."[20] Housed in barracks, they were armed with single-shot flint- lock pistols and swords. Militia-patrols throughout the South, both rural and urban, also sometimes carried whips along with their weapons to mete out pun- ishment to recalcitrant bondsmen.[21]

In the broader scheme, the militia-watch-patrol system for regulating slaves must be seen as distinct from the civil police of the northern United States and in England (which together constituted a single "London-northern" model born in London and spread to cities like New York). Historians of policing in the South such as Dennis Rousey refer to the distinct antebellum system of policing in the South as a "military style" or "martial style" of police that was more militarized than the later civil police in the northern United States.[22] But it might be more productive here to think of the militia-watch-patrol system not in opposition to the London-northern model of the civil police (or the earlier English constable-watch system) and instead as a variant of *colonial* police—a militarized form of policing designed to regulate, suppress, or otherwise discipline a racialized subject population. In other words, the militia-watch-patrol system that first emerged in the Caribbean and North America under the English was a variant of the colonial counterinsurgency police forces in Ireland, with the difference that the militia-watch-patrol system was developed to regulate slave labor, while the colonial counterinsurgency forces in Ireland were developed to control nominally "free" Irish populations. The militia-patrols constituted a colonial counterinsurgency force befitting a settler-plantation colony.[23]

Plantation colonialism also had to be protected from within and along the western frontiers and, ideally, expanded. The militia was initially meant to fulfill this role. South Carolina's seminal 1794 act empowered the militia to defend the realm while also serving as a slave patrol. But as the militia often proved insufficient to safeguard expanding settlements, and American settlers increasingly moved westward, the US Army stepped in. In the South the US Army helped finalize the removal of the Creeks from Georgia and the Seminoles from Florida. During the Mexican-American War (1846–1848), the army embarked upon its first protracted conflict in foreign territory, gaining new experience in occupying foreign countries and countering hostile insurgents.[24] The army was aided by the Texas Rangers, an armed, mounted, mobile unit known for its brutality. Enlisted into federal service, companies of the Texas Rangers helped with the invasion of Mexico in the 1840s, violently appropriating land from the Mexican population, and serving as important forces during the Mexican-American War. After the war, the Rangers were reconstituted by the state of Texas to help fight the Comanche, among other tribes.[25]

While this array of coercive forces had helped create and sustain cotton colonialism in its early stages, it soon faced limits given the cotton economy's growth and associated transformations across the transatlantic interimperial network of cotton. Prior modalities of coercion could not effectively handle the new perceived racialized threats to social order wrought by migration and urbanization. The path toward the civil police model was thus pried open. Let us look first at what happened in Manchester.

## The Colonial Boomerang in Manchester and Beyond

In 1839, ten years after the creation of the London Metropolitan Police, a new civil police force was officially created in Manchester. The bill that created it also created civil police departments in Birmingham and Bolton.[26] Key proponents of the London Metropolitan Police, including Peel and Rowan, had helped make this happen. Peel, in fact, had sat in the Parliament that oversaw the 1839 bill. He had long hoped to create new civil police forces all across England, not just in London, to match the topography of the perceived Irish threat, and the creation of the new police in Manchester was part of his larger plan. Local officials in Manchester shared that idea, disquieted by the same things that had bothered Peel: a growing Irish population and, with it, novel perceived threats to England's social fabric.

In Manchester the number of Irish immigrants had grown from about ten to fifteen thousand in 1804 to thirty-four thousand by 1841. This more or less kept pace with population growth in the city, but the growth was significant enough to make Manchester one of England's top five cities in terms of Irish per capita.[27] As noted earlier, the Irish had been drawn to Manchester's burgeoning manufacturing districts, particularly its cotton mills. Through direct employer prejudice and discrimination, Irish workers were sought after but then slotted into the worst-paid and most vulnerable employments, such as hand weaving.[28] Employers and cotton mill owners were blatant in admitting that they preferred the English to the Irish for the best jobs in their mills, decrying the Irish workers' "restless turbulent disposition."[29] Those who could not find work ended up reliant upon poor relief, a tendency that stirred up yet further derision because they appeared to be sucking up all of Manchester's funds. Official reports complained about the fact that Irish cases of poor relief increased fivefold from 5,902 to 30,156 between 1823 and 1833 alone, apparently proving that the Poor Laws were under stress.[30]

These social conditions contributed to a profound and stark racialization, with authorities and observers increasingly blaming the Irish for Manchester's ills—just as in London. Noting rising urban poverty and seeming degeneration, Manchester's elites associated it all with the Irish newcomers. Kay observed that the Irish districts of Manchester suffered from stark poverty, poor sanitation, and seeming chaos. Referring to these districts as "Little Ireland" or "Irish town," he claimed they represented the "worst" parts of Manchester.[31] He and others further claimed that the Irish were uncivilized, violent, and near-barbaric, insisting that even the English working class were of a better sort because of their relative passivity. This "turbulent population" of Irish workers, Kay explained, "has frequently committed daring assaults on the liberty of more peaceful portions of the working classes, and the most frightful devastations on the property of

their masters."[32] Worse still, according to Kay, the Irish threatened to culturally and morally infect the English population, teaching the latter their "barbarous habits."[33] "The colonization of savage tribes," declared Kay, "has ever been
attended with effects on civilization as fatal as those which have marked the
progress of the sand flood over the fertile plains of Egypt."[34]

The racialization of crime and disorder followed. The Irish districts, Kay
warned, were "frequently the haunt of hordes of thieves and desperados who
defied the law, and [are] always inhabited by a class resembling savages in their
appetites and habits." The Irish were responsible for the crime of the city, their
culture and habits doing little other than to "promote prevailing vice."[35] Kay was
not alone in these views. The deputy constable of the township of Manchester
testified before an 1836 commission on the status of the Irish poor and reiterated
the same points. The Irish, in his view, were responsible for Manchester's increase
in crime, much of it stemming from the children of Irish immigrants, who were
taught to lead "drunken, disorderly and dishonest lives."[36] One member of the
Manchester watch added that the Irish were dangerous rioters. He noted how on
Saturday evenings "parties of men come made drunk out of these places, armed
with pokers and staves, and patrol the streets in order to assault any person they
may meet."[37] A factory owner testified that the Irish "are the worst part of the population; usually the first to turn out, the first to commence riots, and, in fact, there
is no recklessness of conduct which they do not at times display."[38] Later, when
the 1839 parliamentary commission pondered the possibility of a rural constabulary force for all of England, it pointed to the "30,000 Irish" in Manchester who
have a "proneness to discontent, which must fit them as instruments from the
most serious disturbances."[39]

It did not help that the Irish were associated with the emerging threat of
Chartism. The Chartists were not a revolutionary group—they simply demanded
a series of political and economic reforms—but they led strikes and various
other actions that bothered local officials. And while conventional histories
note that police departments were created across England in response to fears of
Chartist agitation, they have not fully appreciated that the Irish were seen as key
agents. "Often they assemble by hundreds," reported a Manchester official about
Chartist meetings. "One of their number reads in a loud voice the Irish News, the
addresses of [Daniel] O'Connell or the circulars of the Repeal Association; and
afterwards the whole is commented upon without end and with great clamor.
They are so strictly organized that in the twinkling of an eye, one or two thousand can be collected at any given spot."[40]

Such worries about the Irish were not unfounded. The Irishman John Doherty
organized the first general union among the Lancashire cotton spinners.[41]
Feargus O'Connor, who traveled through Manchester in the late 1830s and
advocated land redistribution, was one of northern Chartism's most prominent

leaders. Known as the "Lion of Freedom" to his followers, he came from a well-known lineage of fiery Irish fighters: his family back in Cork had been part of the United Irishmen that led the 1798 uprisings in Ireland.[42] In September 1838, Feargus O'Connor spoke to a crowd of fifty thousand at Kersal Moor, just outside Manchester—the largest such meeting in Lancashire since Peterloo. Subsequently, "reports and rumors of arming, arson and military drilling" flooded into Home Office, and the government responded in turn by dispatching troops to the north and even sending men from the London Metropolitan Police to various towns, including Manchester.[43]

The fact that troops and police from London had to be sent to northern areas was indicative of the larger problem: outside of London, English towns and cities were ill-prepared for mass disorder and rising crime, having to rely upon troops, yeomanry, the constabulary, and watches. In Manchester the problem was increasingly palpable as labor agitation grew, seemingly sparked by the reckless Irish. In 1836, a report from city officials regretted a recent outbreak of social disorder, which, it declared, "easily might have been suppressed . . . had there been a sufficiently numerous and properly organized police force."[44] Peel received reports from outside observers that the constables and watch in Manchester "appear to have little or no authority without the Aid of the Military."[45]

Police officials and watchmen themselves knew their weakness, typically conjuring the Irish threat as they reckoned it. Before a committee on the status of the Irish poor in England, one Manchester watchman bemoaned that his force was not powerful enough to handle the "brutal and disorderly conduct" of the Irish in the town. The watchmen ended up in "fights and serious affrays," but "our men are beaten off and the prisoners with handcuffs are rescued." When they tried to issue warrants, constables were met with "bricks and stones," "brickbats and other missiles." He concluded in despair: "The laws cannot be enforced by the strength which we have." The superintendent of the Manchester watch testified to the same problem. It required "from ten to twenty, or even more" watchmen just to "apprehend an Irishman in the Irish part of town." The problem was that the Irish have a "lawless spirit . . . altogether alien to the native inhabitants" of Manchester, such that "the law, as it is administered, has no terrors for these people."[46]

As early as 1832, local authorities in Manchester petitioned the Home Office for help in creating a new police, writing that their existing system was "defective" and that a "Police somewhat resembling the Metropolitan [Police] should be adopted for Manchester and the adjoining townships."[47] Disputes over the transformation of Manchester from an unincorporated town to a borough (along with seemingly irresolvable differences between local Whigs, Tories, and Radicals over the substance of police reform) prevented substantial changes in the constable-watch system. But a city report in 1839 reiterated the request, referring to "instances of riot . . . that easily might have been suppressed in its origin by the civil power had there been a sufficiently numerous and properly organized police force."[48] In May 1839, Major General Sir Charles James Napier, commander of the Northern District, warned the Home Office that Manchester's politics were preventing police reform, which Manchester desperately needed. "The civil force here is quite inadequate," he wrote. "What are 500 Constables and Specials in a town which would turn out 50,000 people to see a dogfight! Manchester should, as you no doubt know better than I do, have a strong well-organized police of, at least, 1,000 men."[49] The 1839 parliamentary report pointed to the thousands of restless and disorderly Irish in Lancashire and concluded: "We cannot too strongly urge the increasing dangers of the continued omission on the part of the Government or the Legislature to provide the effectual means for creating and maintaining the public security in these excited districts."[50]

These views were shared by Kay, who criticized the fact that the military had to be summoned to manage the recalcitrant Irish laborers in Manchester: "The civic force of the town is totally inadequate to maintain the peace, and to defend property from the attacks of lawless depredators, and *a more efficient, and more numerous corps ought to be immediately organized*, to give power to the law, so often mocked by the daring front of sedition, and outraged by the frantic violence of an ignorant and deluded rabble. The police form, in fact, so weak a screen against the power of the mob, that popular violence is now . . . controled [sic] by the presence of a military force."[51] George Cornewall Lewis of the Poor Law Commission similarly argued for police reform, intimating that a new police system would best handle the Irish. "The violence to which the Irish are prone," he deduced, upon reviewing the tomes of evidence about the Irish in Manchester, "and the habit of disrespect for the law and resistance to its officers, which they had formed in their own country, are naturally increased when they find themselves under a feebler police and less rigorous administration of the law than they had hitherto been accustomed to." This problem was "particularly seen at Manchester, as well as in some other towns of Lancashire."[52] In other words, the problem of the "lawless" Irish was not so much a problem in Ireland because of the strong colonial police forces there. The militarized colonial police forces of Ireland could tame the presumed Irish disposition toward crime and violence. But it was a problem in England because the constable-watch system there was comparably "feeble," no match for the new barbarians in cities such as Manchester. Lewis thus deemed a new strong police imperative.

Change finally happened in 1839. By that time, Parliament had become impatient with the disorder in the northwest. Key MPs were especially concerned about industrial disputes and the unceasing rise of Chartist agitation led by Feargus O'Connor, whose rallies the year before must have been a turning point. Sir Robert Peel was among them. He was then a MP and leader of the opposition and proposed that Parliament step in to create a temporary transitional police force for two years in Manchester, Bolton, and Birmingham. Birmingham and Bolton were included in the plan because they were ostensibly facing new threats to law and order just like Manchester. Rising industrial cities fueled by Irish labor, each had earned a place in the list of the top twenty towns in Britain with the highest numbers of Irish, along with London and Manchester.[53] By 1839, fears of crime in the two cities had become seemingly unmanageable.[54] At the same time, Birmingham had become a center of Chartist organizing, with Feargus O'Connor launching campaigns that included a massive meeting at Holloway Head. The existing array of 170 watchmen had been no match for the agitators. Local authorities were also compelled to call upon the London Metropolitan Police to help face down an illegal Chartist meeting that drew two thousand attendees. Fifty London Metropolitan constables were dispatched, triggering a riot that eventually required intervention by the cavalry.[55] As in Manchester, the putatively Irish-led threat had become too much.

Peel's plan was to create temporary police forces in Manchester, Birmingham, and Bolton modeled after the London Metropolitan Police and controlled by the Home Office. The colonial-military structure was not lost on critics in Parliament, who cried foul. It would be "despotic" of the central government, they said, to impose a police force upon a town; that was something "every good Englishman must utterly abhor and abjure."[56] But Peel justified it by reference to Ireland, saying that the police force of Dublin, also a chartered borough under the control of the central government, had produced "universal satisfaction."[57] Peel even enjoyed support from the Irish parliamentarian Daniel O'Connell. O'Connell had been an ardent opponent of the 1798 and 1803 rebellions in Ireland and supported Peel's proposal by claiming that the Dublin police and Irish Constabulary were fine models for policing in Manchester, Bolton, and Birmingham. There could not be a better constabulary force in Ireland, O'Connell insisted, and he hoped to see one day an "Irish Constabulary force" established all across England too.[58]

The result was full-time, professional police forces in Manchester, Bolton, and Birmingham that inherited the colonial-military features of the London Metropolitan Police and its Irish precedent. Francis Burgess was tapped to head the Birmingham police. Burgess was a local barrister who had been among the local elite clamoring for a new police force. He was also a former officer in the army who had served at Waterloo.[59] He created a force of 260. His Police Instruction Book duplicated that of the London Metropolitan Police, which had been written by Peel, Rowan, and Mayne, and spoke of his police as if it was an occupying army.[60] After a year in office, Burgess claimed to have quelled the Chartist threat and so directed his attention to crime prevention. Adopting Rowan's beat patrol system, he instructed his patrol officers in a language reminiscent of the instructions given to the militia-slave patrols whose task it had been to obtain intimate knowledge of the slaves in their beats and closely inspect their dwellings. Each patrol officer, Burgess explained, had to "possess such knowledge of the inhabitants of each house, as will enable him to recognize their persons."[61] He dispatched more patrolmen to high-crime areas than he did to areas reputed to be of lesser danger. Men on the outskirts of town were allowed to wield cutlasses at night. Evidently, Irish residents did not take kindly to the new police in town. By the early 1860s, the Irish made up about 35 percent of all cases of assaults on police, though they constituted about 5 percent of the population.[62]

Manchester's police copied the London Metropolitan Police too, and its militarized character was no doubt aided by the fact that Sir Charles Shaw, a former military officer, was made the first chief commissioner. Shaw's junior officers included Colonel Gilbert Hogg, who had served in Ireland and would go on to lead police in Staffordshire County and the town of Wolverhampton.[63] Shaw and Hogg swiftly instituted military-style policies and programs. Local newspapers reported that the new police, 320 strong, were "drilled and disciplined like a military force with much attention paid to the minutia of discipline, drill and dress." They wore uniforms and had the air of a "paramilitary organization," "patrolling the slums" and deploying more "forthright tactics" than the previous watchmen.[64] The new police achieved a reputation for dispersing dangerous crowds. During an election-time affray in Salford involving "Irish rioters," the appearance of Shaw's force "was sufficient to cause [the mob] to flee in all directions."[65] Shaw also implemented colonial counterinsurgency tools, boasting to the Home Office in 1840 that he was successfully surveilling the Chartists in Manchester and monitoring the movements of Feargus O'Connor.

In Manchester as in Bolton and Birmingham, the initial police forces controlled by London were meant to be temporary, replaced in a few years by permanent forces under local direction. Accordingly, Shaw stepped down from his post in Manchester in 1842, and Manchester officials vowed to "take measures for the continuance of an efficient police force so that peace and good order shall not be endangered."[66] To replace Shaw, they appointed the city's first proper chief constable, Captain Edward Willis. But the militarization did not cease. Willis had served with the British Army in Ireland, Bermuda, and Jamaica before joining the recently formed Lancashire Constabulary as assistant commissioner. Once taking his post, he increased the ranks by 70 for a total of 390 men, making Manchester's the second-largest police force outside London in terms of ratio of police to population.[67] He also created new "preventive divisions," each with a superintendent, sergeants, and constables; introduced a special training officer for each division (a "non-commissioned officer in the army, to drill the officers and constables"); and borrowed London's recently adopted method of dressing constables in gloves and boots.[68] The transformation of Manchester's police into a military-colonial police force labeled "civil" was complete.[69]

Policing of the Irish subproletariat in Manchester followed. During Shaw's tenure, the police arrested 12,417 people in 1840 and then 13,345 in 1841. In 1842, when Willis began, the number was 12,147. While we do not know the breakdown of these arrests by ethnicity, we do know that the majority of the arrests were for offenses understood by contemporaries as "Irish" crimes (drunkenness, vagrancy, and prostitution). We also know that more than 80 percent of all arrests in this decade were in the "A" police division, which encompassed the Irish parts of town. Data on arrests by ethnicity is available beginning in 1844, and the trend is clear. In 1844, 10,702 persons were apprehended, and close to 3,000 of them were classified by the police as "Irish." The percentage of arrests that were of "Irish" persons, therefore, was over 21 percent, while the percentage of the population that was classified as "Irish" was just a little over 13 percent. This overrepresentation of the Irish in arrests continued over the next decades.[70] Evidently, the new police in Manchester adopted a military-colonial function as well as form.[71]

## The Birth of Police in New York City

In 1844, five years after new police forces were created in Manchester, Bolton, and Birmingham, New York City became among the first cities in the United States to create a centralized, uniformed, professional police force modeled on London's.[72] As in other cities, the new police was created partly in response to perceived increases in crime and disorder. We must stress the word "perceived" here. Reliable data on crime prior to the formation of the New York City police is not available, but extant data on criminal convictions suggests that crime rates per capita in New York City were roughly the same in the early 1800s as they were in 1830.[73] The *perception* among many New Yorkers, though, was that crime was on the rise. From 1820 to 1860, New York City's rising upper classes, mercantile segments, and associated professional fractions continually fretted over crime and street violence.[74] In the early 1830s, city government committees believed, erroneously or not, that population growth heralded a "corresponding increase of crime," contending that "higher and bolder grades of criminals" roamed about to "terrify the peaceful inhabitants, to set at naught the ordinary means of security, and to render dangerous the lives of prosperous citizens."[75] Newspapers contributed to the fear, complaining in 1840 about the "destructive rascality" that "stalks at large in our streets and public places."[76] The unsolved murder of a woman named Mary Rogers in 1841 received wide attention, with New York governor William Seward speaking of it in his annual address to signal the "appalling crime" in the city. The murder was surely notable: as recently as 1819, there had been only one case of homicide, and this was believed to be the first homicide the city had ever seen.[77] Critics connected these horrific developments with a general decrease in public morality and an attendant increase in vices like gambling, liquor, and prostitution.[78]

Public disorder was a worry too. The year 1834 was known as the "year of the riots" because of its multiple brawls and public affrays (including brawls between factions of political parties during the mayoral election), requiring intervention by the national guard.[79] In 1837 bread riots erupted; in 1840 there were at least nineteen riots.[80] Certain areas of the city become notorious as epicenters for such disorder. The Five Points district was labeled in 1828 as "a rendezvous for thieves and prostitutes," but it was also known for its public violence.[81] Gangs fought for territory and power within the district. "Under such appropriate banners as the 'Dead Rabbits,' 'Plug Uglies,' 'Roach Guards,' and the 'Shirt Tails,'" explained one historian of the area, "the denizens of the underworld would sally forth."[82] The weak constables and watches justifiably stayed clear of such areas.[83]

These concerns over crime and disorder were colored by race. New York's upper classes and officials did not see the incoming subproletariat fueling the city's growth in the most positive light. The class status of the newcomers surely did not help their image: most of the incoming Irish ended up in low-paid manual jobs. When they could not find work, they crowded the city's almshouse and hospitals. Many did not even speak English.[84] New York's elite soon blamed the influx of immigrants for the city's problems and sought to restrict immigration. The 1837 report on police reform by a select committee of city aldermen is indicative. The committee claimed that crime had increased in the city to unmanageable levels. It targeted liquor consumption as a leading cause. Adopting the moralistic rhetoric of Anglo-Protestant nativists of the time, the committee claimed that "many of the houses for the sale of spirituous liquors, and the gambling houses which are to be found in all parts of the city," have been "productive of very injurious effects on the morals of the community."[85] Most importantly, the committee blamed increased liquor consumption and the growth of crime more generally on immigration. New York had developed a "commerce that has no limit short of the globe, and an intercourse with almost every nation of the earth" along with a "growth . . . at a rate almost unexampled in the history of cities, by adding to its own population large numbers from the other States of the Union, as well as from all parts of Europe."[86]

The public and officials soon clamored for police reform. As a writer for the *New York Daily Herald* lamented: "There never was a period when the evidences of our total want of police were so numerous and so painful."[87] "When, O when!," cried one editorial among many complaining about crime, "shall we have a *real* Police Reform?"[88] In the early 1830s, government committees were appointed to explore police reorganization.[89] The 1837 select committee joined the demand. After blaming crime on immigration, it declared that the city needed to create "a system of Police as will be sufficient to protect the citizens in their persons and their property." It compared New York's situation with that of London and Liverpool and suggested that a "London-style" police would do the trick.[90] By the early 1840s, the chorus grew louder. The *New York Daily Herald* announced in 1843:

> We ought to have a reform in the Police. *All the ruffians and rogues of the whole Union, and part of Europe, are concentrated in New York.* They are the promoters and patronisers of the hells, houses of ill-fame, gambling places, faro banks and every other place of iniquity. They prowl about the city, day and night, in gangs, pairs, and singly. One portion are engaged in setting fire to buildings that contain valuable property, in order that they may plunder something in the melée. There is no end to the evils that may be inflicted on this city unless the Corporation reform and reorganize the Police system.[91]

The report from a committee on police reform in 1844 complained about rising crime and pointed to the "variety of people of all nations" who constituted the city's "floating population" as part of the problem. To support its claims, it listed the names and origins of prisoners held in the Blackwell's Island penitentiary. Of the 138 male court prisoners in 1843, 61 were foreign born (nearly all from Ireland) and 37 were Black. There were also 148 male "vagrants," 97 of whom were foreign born (mostly from Ireland) and 17 Black. The report then declared that the "inefficiency of the present Police system" had to be fixed.[92]

The racialization of crime and disorder in the 1830s and early 1840s, along with calls for police reform, was not consistent. It must be seen as part of a continuum. On the one end, some officials and the public called for police reform without reference to immigrants or race. They instead blamed the insufficiencies of the existing system.[93] In the middle of the continuum, officials highlighted a mismatch between the insufficiencies of the existing watch system and New York's changing demographic composition, pointing to the need for a new police due to the city's "heterogenous population."[94] In the early 1840s, the Democratic Party, led by Robert H. Morris (elected as mayor in 1841), typically shuffled between these two positions on the continuum, as did the Republican Party, which dominated state politics under Republican governor William Seward.

A more extreme end of the continuum openly racialized crime and disorder. This was the position of the main rival to the Democratic Party, the American Republican Party, sometimes known as the American Nativist Party (and later as the Know Nothing Party). As the leading anti-immigrant group of the time, the American Nativist–Republicans blended economic nationalism, xenophobia, and racism and blamed the city's ostensibly rising crime rates on the incoming laborers from overseas and other ethnic minorities in the city.[95] During the election of 1844, their newspapers warned of the presence of Germans and the "wandering Jews" who purportedly used "their shops as receptacles for stolen goods, encouraging thievery among our citizens."[96] While they were anti-German, anti-Polish, and anti-Jewish, the American Nativists were especially anti-Catholic and anti-Irish. They called Irish paupers and workers "thieves and vagabonds."[97] They noted that it was the "low-class" Irish, or the "bilge of Europe," who made up the criminal gangs and who mingled with African Americans in Five Points.[98] Inheriting and perpetuating long-standing Anglo-Protestant views of Catholics as pagans and barbarians, they classified Irish Catholics as prone to alcoholism and gambling, which in turn exacerbated crime and fomented street violence, rowdiness, and violence. "Intemperance," claimed James Harper, one of the American Nativists' New York leaders, is "the most fruitful parent of vice, poverty, crime and misery; and no lawful restraints upon it should be withheld."[99]

Unsurprisingly, the American Nativist–Republicans accused the British Empire of dumping their Irish refuse and job stealers onto America's shores, joining some nativist-minded workers in the city.[100] Meanwhile, they demanded that the Protestant King James Bible be read in public schools and sought to expel Catholicism from the public sphere. They advocated strict restrictions on immigration, naturalization, officeholding, and voting. Already New York had begun to restrict immigration, setting a bar that effectively impeded poor Catholic immigrants from entering, but the American Nativists wanted to prevent immigration altogether. They demanded that all foreign-born individuals convicted of crimes be deported and insisted that only native-born citizens hold governmental positions.[101]

A new police force was a fundamental part of the American Nativist–Republican anti-immigration platform. American Nativist alderman William Gale led the way in early 1844 when he blamed the city's crime on immigrants and proposed to create a new police system.[102]

While all political parties and leaders at the time sought police reform, only the American Nativists demanded that police officers had to be "native"-born Americans. Foreigners were not allowed.[103] Also, of all the parties' ideas for reform, the American Nativists' proposal was closest to the London model and the most militarized. The proposals from the Democratic Party, for example, did not call for uniformed police or officers to wear badges, nor did it call for officers to be armed with truncheons. The Democrats' plans also differed in terms of their entry requirements. Likely in an effort to use the police for political patronage, the Democrats' plan proposed that policemen be appointed by local ward leaders rather than city hall.[104] The American Nativists opposed the Democrats' policing bill, seeing it as a ruse for political patronage.[105] Their alternative police force was to be a full-time, hierarchical force appointed by the mayor's office, making it much closer to the centralized system of the English police and its colonial-military variants. It adopted the structure of the English police, with superintendents, captains, and sergeants, among others. The mayor was to prescribe either uniforms or badges, and eventually the London-style uniform was adopted, with single-breasted blue coats, white buttons, and standing collars.[106]

The American Nativists' plan won the day. Riding the rising tide of anti-immigrant sentiment, they won a majority in the city council in the 1844 elections and the mayoral office, with James Harper as their mayor. The American Nativists thus put into effect the city's first civil police force, firmly modeled upon the English precedent. Besides the London-style uniform, the new police force adopted a manual for patrolmen copied word for word from the Liverpool police. The press observed that the party had "selected the London system as it then existed as their model, even adopting the style of uniform," and that the patrolmen were called "the 'M.P.'s' from wearing those letters embroidered on their coat-collars."[107] The new police then hit the streets with bellicose zeal. Led by a superintendent who had served as an officer in the militia, and wearing their "blue coats and embroidered collars," observed the *New York Daily Herald*, the force had been trained in "military tactics" and marched across Washington Square bearing muskets.[108] The earlier proposal that only native-born Americans be appointed to the force was not codified in law but was put into practice nonetheless. No Irish or immigrants were to be found on the force.[109] Applicants to the force from the public fittingly made racialist appeals. "Pure blood runs in my veins," wrote one applicant to Mayor Harper.[110] Meanwhile, friends of Mayor Harper recommended for the new police force only those who are "entirely in favor of our native American principles."[111]

Harper's police did not endure the political weather. The Democrats swept into office, dismantled the Harper police, and created their own force in tune with their original proposal. The American Nativist Party diminished in importance, transmuting into the smaller Know Nothing Party, whose electoral influence waned. Still, the American Nativists' police force was seminal, setting a precedent for militarization that even the Democrats and subsequent political officials would not overturn. Initially, the new police emerging in 1845 under the Democratic mayor William Havemeyer had eschewed some of the militaristic features of its predecessor. While it retained the military hierarchy and beat system, its officers did not wear uniforms or carry badges.[112] Nor were they given firearms or even truncheons. This was most likely an attempt at legitimation. Harper's police had not been received well. The press and the public criticized its uniforms and took the new force as a threat to liberty. Some even declared that the uniforms represented a "degradation" of the officers and were a sign of submission to Great Britain.[113] Evidently, the Democrats did not want their new police force to be subject to the same charges.

In the 1850s, though, things took a remarkable turn. Beginning with legislation in 1853 and then proceeding with initiatives undertaken by Superintendent Charles Matsell under the auspices of Democratic mayor Fernando Wood, the New York City police was transformed into a force that looked much more like the London force than before and, by the same token, was more fully militarized. Matsell added a uniform that combined military influence with the flair of the London police: a blue cloth coat with a velvet collar, brass buttons (originally black buttons) adorning the front of the coat, gray pants with a black stripe on the side, and cloth caps. Observers noted how closely the New York police now resembled London "bobbies" and army units, with some even admiring their "soldierly" and "noble military appearance."[114] Matsell also put the force "under the command of lieutenants and sergeants, *a la militarie*," some of whom were veterans of the Mexican-American War.[115] Together he and Mayor Wood imposed new military-type discipline and strengthened the military-style hierarchy; the mayor was given unprecedented direct control over the police.[116] Finally, Matsell armed the new police force. Patrolmen were given the New York version of the truncheon: the "billy club" or "baton." This was a hard wooden stick, "not less than twenty-two inches long, and one inch and three quarters thick," capable of cracking skulls.[117] Newspapers now referred to the police as "soldiers with clubs."[118] One active reformer and proponent of these changes, J. W. Gerard, spoke admirably of the police in 1855 at a public meeting, boasting of how the new police was now equipped to properly fight crime and disorder:

No day passes in the policeman's life [without] the military drill—the drill under the tactics of Lieutenant-General Scott. The companies are formed into battalions. There are four battalions of two hundred and fifty men each, besides the officers, and when they are banded together they make as large and as striking a parade as a brigade of our own City uniform companies. They are drilled in the use of the club, and the effect is that a policeman now since 1853, under the knowledge of the club, is able to stand alone the attacks of four or five ruffians. Five hundred of these men, marching in solid column and under their club drill, with that little weapon could put to rout a mob of 5,000 men.[119]

As if to finalize militarization, patrolmen were armed with revolvers by the end of the 1850s, and Matsell hired drill instructors and firearms experts from the military to train the force.[120]

What began as a muted and hesitant militarization soon became self-conscious and adamant. Mayor Wood, a Democrat, announced unequivocally in his annual message that the New York police was becoming much more like a military unit. Referring to the uniforms and military drills, he noted that the "military spirit . . . to some extent has been introduced" and that the changes were among those that had "added to the efficiency of the whole corps." "To procure efficiency there must be discipline, and to preserve discipline there must be military rule."[121]

Several forces had served to unleash this renewed militarization of the New York City police under the rule of the Democratic Party in the 1850s. One was the continued perception that social disorder was still a pressing problem; the new police had not been able to quell such events as the 1849 Astor Place Riots.[122] At the same time, crime continued to rise and newspapers continued to discuss it.[123] Just as important was the seemingly relentless invasion of New York's shores by foreigners. Immigration from Ireland and Europe skyrocketed during the late 1840s and into the early 1850s. In 1845, the foreign-born population was only 30 percent of the total population of New York City. By 1855 it had jumped to 50 percent, with the Irish alone making up half of that amount.[124] In 1853, Frederick Douglass noted how the Irish immigrants continued to take up the low-paid jobs that African Americans had been forced to take previously: "If they cannot rise to the dignity of white men, they show that they can fall to the degradation of black men."[125]

This continued influx of abject immigrants served to generalize the xenophobic racism that had once been largely restricted to the American Nativists.[126] In fact, both the Democrats and the Whigs adopted anti-immigrant rhetoric and policies in the 1850s. Democratic Party newspapers fretted about the crime-ridden Fourth and Sixth Wards, where "whites, negroes and mongrels," including Irish women and Chinese men, readily intermingled.[127] They also blamed crime and disorder on immigration. In his annual address in 1852, Judge Beebe presented statistics to show that immigration led to the "prevalence, within the last year, of the crime and murder and assaults with intent to kill." New York's port was constantly "receiving in its boom many of the most hardened criminals of the Old World," such that "a large majority of criminals brought before the court for trial [are] of foreign birth."[128] Another city judge remarked in 1855 that while native-born Americans might commit forgeries or petty theft, the Irish committed all of the "murders, riots and violent assaults" of the city.[129] Gerard, who supported the Democratic Party, similarly blamed immigrants for "the mighty flood of crime which is sweeping over our city with tremendous annual increase." He pointed to statistics to claim that most prisoners were "foreigners," concluding that the horrific acts of violence and offense against persons "are done by foreigners recently come here, and not by our citizens."[130] In 1856, Mayor Fernando Wood reiterated these very same views, asserting that foreign governments had been sending to New York their "criminal and indigent population," the "outcast of a people who, themselves in the aggregate are far below the moral standard of this nation."[131]

To the press, reformers, and officials, transforming the police to make it more like the militarized London police was now the solution to the apparently relentless crime and disorder brought on by the immigrant invasion.[132] Gerard's influential writings are indicative of the broader trend. Throughout his public writings, he blamed rising crime and disorder on "the passions and criminal instincts of foreigners," insisting that a militarized police like that in Europe and London was the solution. New York's immigrants had "passions and criminal instincts," Gerard wrote, but these had been restrained in their homelands because they faced powerful police forces there. By contrast, the New York police was too weak. It lacked "moral power." "Why do not these foreigners commit these acts of violence in their own countries? Why do they commit them when they come here, in this land of liberty? . . . The answer is obvious, and found in the weakness of our police." The solution followed: "If New York, Baltimore, and Philadelphia will only take a few practical hints from the experience of London, they will soon give moral power to their police."[133] Gerard further noted that London had more police per capita than New York, and he suggested that the New York police should increase its numbers. He was also impressed by the martial style of London's police, manifest in their drill, discipline, and uniforms, and saw it as a key component of the police's success. The London police, he wrote with awe,

> are placed under military instruction; they are drilled to walk in regular and compact bodies, with the lock-step; to march and counter-march, in platoons, companies and large bodies; to exercise with the broad-sword, so that, in case of public commotions, they may exchange their short club (which is never visible) for the sword, and be as effectual as the military in suppressing riots . . . You may see them in London any hour of the day, being detailed on duty, in squads of six to a dozen, marching in silence with their lock-step, and by their quiet demeanor, and simple, neat uniform, inspiring respect.[134]

The New York police, Gerard concluded, should likewise be instilled with military discipline and "should all be required to wear a *distinguishing costume*" similar to that of the London police. The police, he insisted, "must be clothed in a costume that shall have a *moral* power upon the mass of *foreigners*" in New York City.[135]

Mayor Wood, who oversaw the intense militarization of the New York City police, heeded these calls. He had already been converted to the nativist cause, accepting a position on the executive committee of the Know Nothings in 1854. He swiftly adopted their rhetoric, joining in the calls for the federal government to restrict immigration.[136] He then adopted the nativists' support of militarized policing. He countered criticisms that uniformed police threatened liberty and that the uniform itself was a "badge of servitude" and "degradation" by retorting: "There is no degradation in the uniform of a policeman, more than there is in the epaulette of an officer in the regular army; no greater badge of servitude in the *star* than there is in the *button* so highly prized by the Navy." He likened his new police to "an army on the field of battle" and insisted that he needed to directly control the force, just as militaries needed strict centralized control. In a parade in 1855 addressing the force, he referred to himself as the policemen's "commanding officer" and "Commanding General"—the "head of an army" fighting crime.[137]

A year later, in his annual message, Wood further decried the criminality of immigrants and praised the fact that the New York police was becoming much more like London's in its militarized orientation. The New York police force was now "based upon that of London," he boasted, "with many improvements, rendering it more applicable to the people of this country ... The police are to become thoroughly imbued with its [London's] advantages and its requirements. As before stated, the nearer we approach military discipline in the organization, personnel and control of the police, the nearer we approximate to its true character." Wood maintained that the New York police "shall soon equal any similar corps in the world not strictly military."[138]

The Democrats' decision to arm the new police followed the same logic. For instance, while the turn to the "baton," or the New York version of the truncheon, was partly an attempt to blindly imitate the London police, it also emerged from the practical need to police putatively unruly and violent Irish immigrants. In 1853, police captain George W. Walling was put in charge of policing the Irish tenement districts of the Fourth and Eighteenth Wards but faced rowdy resistance. To better police the area, Walling formed patrol units of three men and provided them with clubs made of hard wood, thereby emulating the London truncheon. Thus armed, Walling led a squad, which he called the "Strong Arm Squad," in charges against various Irish "gangs," such as a "notorious party of ruffians" that he said was known as the "Honeymoon Gang." He and his men tracked the gang members and beat them with their new clubs, hunting them similarly for days until they completely disbanded. Thereafter, Walling and his "Strong Arm Squad" attacked other gangs in the tenements. In the same year, the entire New York police force adopted the "billy club."[139]

Arrest patterns suggest that the new police was indeed intent on controlling the perceived immigrant threat. We do not have arrest data that provides the ethnic background of those detained in the 1840s and 1850s, but the types of crimes are suggestive. From 1848 to 1853, the number of people arrested by the police for "drunkenness" and "disorderly conduct" rose by 278 percent. These were the offenses for which poor immigrants, and particularly the Catholic Irish, were known to be arrested.[140] "Drunkenness" and "disorderly conduct" also constituted the vast majority of arrests from 1845 to 1853.[141]

Data on arrests for 1864 and 1865 does offer "nativity" of the individuals, and it is revealing. There were 19,482 arrests in that time, and more than half were of individuals of Irish nativity.[142] Furthermore, the police tended to more heavily occupy the city wards with the most immigrants (see Table 2.2). In 1855, the First, Fourth, and Sixth Wards had the largest Irish-born populations (in terms

Table 2.2. Distribution of the New York City Metropolitan Police, 1855

| Ward | Percentage Irish | Number of Police Officers | Police per 1,000 Residents |
|------|------------------|---------------------------|-----------------------------|
| 1 | 46.0 | 63 | 4.7 |
| 4 | 45.6 | 57 | 2.5 |
| 6 | 42.4 | 60 | 2.3 |
| 18 | 37.2 | 50 | 1.3 |
| 14 | 36.2 | 50 | 2.0 |
| 2 | 35.8 | 45 | 13.9 |
| 19 | 35.4 | 59 | 3.3 |
| 7 | 34.2 | 62 | 1.8 |
| 12 | 33.0 | 32 | 1.8 |
| 16 | 29.8 | 55 | 1.4 |
| 21 | 29.7 | 47 | 1.7 |
| 3 | 28.9 | 43 | 5.4 |
| 20 | 27.3 | 56 | 1.2 |
| 15 | 26.1 | 45 | 1.9 |
| 22 | 25.4 | 42 | 1.9 |
| 17 | 24.9 | 54 | .91 |
| 5 | 22.5 | 56 | 2.6 |
| 8 | 21.2 | 53 | 1.6 |
| 9 | 20.2 | 53 | 1.4 |
| 13 | 18.7 | 48 | 1.9 |
| 11 | 17.5 | 48 | .91 |
| 10 | 13.0 | 22 | .83 |

Sources: New York Secretary of State 1855; Valentine 1855; Miller 1977, 153.

of percentage of population). In the First, Irish-born made up 46 percent; in the Fourth, they made up 46 percent; and in the Sixth, they made up 42 percent. The Sixth Ward contained the infamous Five Points neighborhood. These were also the wards that had the highest number of police officers per capita. In the First there were almost five police officers for every thousand residents; in the Fourth and Sixth there were more than two police officers for every thousand residents. By contrast, the two districts with the fewest Irish-born were the Eleventh and Tenth Wards, and they were much less policed, with fewer than one policeman per thousand residents. In New York as in England, policing the Irish was apparently a major concern.[143]

## Policing the "New York of the South"

While the New York City Police Department represents the birth of the militarized civil police in the northern United States, the Savannah Police Department (SPD) represents the birth of the same in the South. Created in 1854, the SPD had a striking resemblance to the military-style civil police forces that London birthed and that were being created in northern cities: a full-time, uniformed, centralized police replacing the constable-watch system.[144] But the SPD was also unique in certain respects, garnering the attention of officials in other southern cities who sought to emulate it. Charleston officials in 1857 referred to the "Savannah Plan" as a "successful . . . system of police which seemed to commend it to all" and proceeded to model its police force after it.[145]

Before examining the unique features of the SPD, let us consider the reasons for its formation. The story is not unlike that of other cities: population growth, economic development, and urbanization facilitated by cotton colonialism laid the conditions for a perceived racialized rise in crime and disorder.[146] Officials and the city's upper classes blamed two groups. The first was Black Americans, who migrated to the city in droves. Slaves served as domestic laborers in the grand houses of the rising merchant and upper classes. Slaves were also brought into the city as temporary hires, loading goods onto ships or unloading them from warehouses, building roads and railroads, or laying bricks.[147] From 1850 to 1860 the number of slaves in the city jumped from 6,231 to 7,712, constituting almost 35 percent of the city's population. Freed Blacks were also present, filling the demand for domestics and other unskilled work. Their numbers in the city grew along with the growth in the number of slaves.[148]

The growth of hired slaves and freed Black individuals in the city exacerbated the anxieties among the white establishment. The Savannah planter John Stoddard complained that "many owners cannot tell where their servants are, or what they are doing."[149] Another resident complained that "there are . . . hundreds of negroes in this City who never see their masters except at pay day." Said another resident: "This want of supervision gives them the opportunity to brew mischief."[150] To the white establishment, the city's Black population seemed more brazen in their tactics of resistance, with white residents complaining of their increasing, boisterous, and almost defiant presence in traditionally white public spaces. Further, the town watch discovered that the Black community sometimes created temporary camps in the outskirts of town where the freed men and slaves would gather, dance, and make merry, often while hiding runaways—all of it outside the gaze of the government's surveying eye. To city officials, this was not good.[151]

The other targeted group was immigrants who arrived in huge numbers to become carpenters, bricklayers, wagon drivers, porters, draymen, stevedores, and longshoremen for the city's new railroad, central station, warehouses, wharves, docks, hotels, and stores. The Irish-born population of Savannah doubled from 1850 to 1860, making up close to 30 percent of the city's white population.[152] They labored in the bottom rungs of the booming economy. Many loaded cotton, picked by Black slaves, onto vessels that would make their way to Liverpool to be unloaded by their fellow Irish and then hauled north to Lancashire to be processed into textiles by yet more of their Irish countrymen.[153]

The Irish of Savannah were thus deeply connected to the transatlantic imperial cotton network. But they fared differently than their counterparts in New York. The presence of slaves in Savannah meant that the Irish there, because they were free, were not at the very bottom of the hierarchy. But this relative advantage did not mean that the Irish enjoyed privileges of whiteness. They were still racialized as lesser.[154] The standard stereotypes applied. The Irish were thought of as ignorant, uncivilized, and prone to lawlessness. They were sometimes referred to as "n——s turned inside out," while African Americans were sometimes referred to as "smoked Irish."[155] One plantation owner claimed that the Irish were just the same as Blacks, and "instanced their subserviency, their flattering, their lying, and pilfering, as traits common to the characters of both peoples.'"[156] The Irish were thus consigned to live like and with the city's Black population, ending up in the suburbs that housed 75 percent of the city's laborers. The largest was Oglethorpe Ward.[157] This was triple the size of the city's next-largest ward. With its 1,000 whites (most of whom were Irish), 1,046 slaves, and 281 free African Americans living in overcrowded wood dwellings, it rivaled New York's tenement districts and Manchester's Victorian slums. Outsiders from the North referred to it "low, dingy, dirty [and] squalid," standing in stark contrast to the bustling downtown, which "exhibits unmistakable signs of enterprise, refinement and wealth" with "spacious and elegant" homes.[158]

Many of Savannah's white residents were not happy about the influx of more African Americans and Irish, even as their labor was necessary for the new economy. They soon perceived racialized threats to law and order. Those residents included members of the anti-immigrant Know Nothing Party. Known in Savannah as the American and Order Party (but essentially a continuation of the Know Nothing Party), it enjoyed some success at the polls, thus solidifying anti-immigrant sentiment. They joined with officials and wealthy white residents to decry the racial mingling and mixing that the port economy encouraged. Slaves cavorted freely with freed Blacks, and both were putatively being corrupted by their Irish counterparts. The new "grog shops" or "dram stores" where Irish and Blacks mixed posed a special affront. As the number of these "spirit-shops" swelled from 125 in the 1840s to over 200 by 1855, the city's white residents complained that the shops "corrupt our negroes terribly" and were sites of drunkenness, gambling, prostitution, and illicit trade in goods stolen by slaves from masters' residences and warehouses.[159] City representatives and commercial elites saw rises in crime and blamed the liquor shops, declaring that intoxication was "an inducement to theft" among the slave population.[160] The city's leading businessmen blamed crime on the "growing evil" of the shops, contending that "three-fourths of the indictments are for crimes committed or originating in dram shops, from petty larceny to murder," and pressed the city council to pass new ordinances to stop it.[161]

Meanwhile, authorities lamented the "mixed" districts where the Irish and Black laborers lived. These were the districts of the "often lawless class . . . where the dissipated and the vicious congregate."[162] Reporting on the city's reputation for crime and disorder, the *Daily Georgian* in 1854 listed "Negro insubordination and riot" as one of the culprits resulting in that reputation and referred to an incident where a group of "about one-hundred negros" had gathered in a sawmill and rioted in response to an officer's attempt to break it up.[163] Authorities also worried over runaway slaves in the city. Because Savannah was a port town, sending ships all the way to Boston and Liverpool, slaves from around the region flooded into the city in hopes of sneaking aboard one of the vessels. Given the city's large "mixed" population, they could easily blend into the urban fabric, hiding in open view.[164]

It soon dawned upon city authorities and upper-class representatives that the city's existing system of watchmen was not sufficient to handle this new racialized threat to order.[165] In the 1850s, Savannah had twice as many wards as it had had in the previous decade, and nearly twice as many people, but the constable and watch system remained the same meager size as before. Five constables, the city marshal, and fewer than ten watchmen guarded by day, while the rest of the hundred watchmen operated only at night.[166] Furthermore, of all the watch patrols in the South, Savannah's was probably among the least disciplined. They were paid too little to care and were sometimes found sleeping on the job. They were also the least martial, despite their origins in the city's long-standing militia.[167] Calls for a new police became more frequent and loud. When a string of burglaries occurred in 1851, the captions in the dailies were "Watch! Watch!," criticizing the watchmen. One paper claimed that there was no "such a thing as a police force in this city . . . A 'watch' in Savannah! Capital joke."[168] A reporter witnessing Black residents flout the ordinances against drinking on Sundays in 1853 wondered: "Where is the Marshal—where the Captain of the City Watch . . . Will they not act before it is too late, and before public indignation breaks from its pent up bounds and overwhelms them in ruin?"[169]

Savannah's leaders looked for solutions. The earliest attempts were piecemeal, such as increasing the watch's numbers in the hopes that simply adding bodies would thwart the terror.[170] But the city's elite aimed for more drastic changes. In 1850, one resident, former mayor and plantation owner Dr. W. C. Daniell, wrote to Congressman Howell Cobb to ask that a company of "flying artillery" be sent to Savannah. "Such a company here," he wrote, "will have a very desirable influence on our slave population . . . which is becoming very licentious & give occasional indications of insubordination which tell badly of the future."[171] Flying artillery had been successfully deployed during the Mexican-American War as part of a series of tactical innovations by Major Samuel Ringgold. Daniell's letter reveals not only that the planter class was anxious about the seemingly rising obstinance of their bondsmen, but also that they were searching for solutions from colonial scenes of power.

The artillery was never sent. Instead, officials looked to England. Considering Savannah's place in the network of cotton colonialism, the turn to England is not surprising. Wealthy merchants and city officials traveled there. Newspapers carried stories about the London Metropolitan Police.[172] In 1854, the first steps toward creating a London-style system were taken. Mayor John Ward, who had previously been a commander in a militia company, demanded an "immediate re-organization" of the city watch.[173] His successor, Mayor Edward C. Anderson, finally instituted the changes under the purview of the new captain, Joseph Bryan. The constable-watch system was replaced with a new hierarchical structure with a captain, lieutenants, sergeants, and privates organized into two divisions that were "at all times at the command and in the service of the city." The men were paid higher salaries, and officers as well as privates were expressly forbidden from holding other jobs. Mayor Anderson later explained that professionalizing the force in this way would help create the proper "spirit du corps."[174] The measly uniform of the watch, which had been little beyond a white belt, was replaced with militarized attire that was close to the northern and London attire but even more martial: gray pants with a "dark stripe an inch down the outer seam of the leg," blue single-breasted frock coats with a standing collar and silver buttons with the words "Savannah Police" on each button; and caps and badges with a silver-plated star, the coat of arms of the city, and the individual's rank engraved below.[175] Mayor Anderson later boasted that uniforms enabled the force to "present a highly officer-like and respectable appearance."[176]

Captain Bryan imposed a strict martial order for the new force.[177] Newspapers wrote approvingly that Bryan "understands the importance of thorough discipline and rigid accountability among subordinates." Overall, the city's residents appeared impressed. "The police paraded in a body, yesterday afternoon," observed the *Republican*, "in their new uniform, under command of their energetic Chief, Capt. Bryan. . . . [T]he Police have been brought to a state of great efficiency, and their appearance on parade yesterday, was such as to inspire the public with confidence and respect." The police also had a rattle, evidently to be used as an alarm, about which one reporter noted: "The rattle used by the watchmen in Savannah is the same, it is said, as that which has been used in London. . . . It differs, moreover, from that in use in nearly all the other cities in this country."[178]

Savannah's police thus appeared similar to the London-northern variant of the civil police, but its roots in southern plantation colonialism gave it some distinctive accents. One distinction had to do with weaponry: the Savannah police was armed with guns from the outset. Unlike the English police or the New York police in its early years, the Savannah force was permitted to be "armed in such manner as the captain of the said police . . . may from time to time direct." Bryan subsequently armed the force with "pistols and batons."[179] This was a direct legacy of the heavily armed militia-slave patrols and watches. The city watch, which had served as a slave patrol and anti-insurgency force to respond to slave insurrections, had wielded firearms.[180]

Another of the important novelties was the mounted patrol established by Captain Bryan. Beginning in 1854, the watchmen were replaced by a mounted patrol of twenty men. By 1856 there were twenty-four mounted privates distributed into squads of eight privates and one sergeant.[181] While the rest of the privates formed the foot police, the mounted police formed an elite corps of sorts, with higher pay and special badges.[182] One of the advantages was that patrols could "move with great rapidity from point to point" to cover all areas, as the mayor noted.[183] The Charleston officials who investigated Savannah's force added that the mounted patrols "can go over a larger beat—are more on the alert, and fresher after pursuit for any necessary encounter."[184]

Relative to the London-northern model, this mounted force was an innovation. Cities in the Northeast would not have mounted patrols until later in the century. In England, there had been mounted guards and patrols before the formation of the London Metropolitan Police, such as the Bow Street Mounted Patrol (incorporated into the London Metropolitan Police in 1836 as the Horse Patrol). But these mounted forces had mostly been deployed to patrol the roads outside London and manage the threat of highway robberies. The London mounted patrol would not become a regular feature of London policing until later in the century.[185] By contrast, Savannah's mounted unit formed an integral part of the police force from early on. Unique for its urban orientation, it was referred to by the Charleston investigators as "the most striking feature in the Savannah system and is the principal cause of its efficiency."[186]

The provenance of this mounted feature of the Savannah police lay in the coercive modalities of settler-plantation colonialism. Mounted military forces had been the key to Moore's light brigades in St. Lucia. Mounted militia or regular army forces had also been deployed in Florida and Texas, in the latter taking the form of the Texas Rangers. Captain Bryan as well as Mayor Anderson would have been familiar with the Rangers, as both had served in the Mexican-American War, and Anderson had served in Florida in the campaigns against the Seminoles. The early beat companies in rural areas had been mounted too. Mounted slave patrols had been especially useful for covering extended territory in plantation country, with beats as large as twelve miles. The creation of Savannah's mounted unit thus represented a creative transposition of the militarized counterinsurgency regime of plantation colonialism to the urban context.[187]

If these innovations, and the intensified militarization in the South more generally, reflected traditions of militia-slave patrols and settler colonial regimes of coercion on the frontier, they were also the product of the same conditions that had generated those patrols and regimes in the first place: an ostensibly threatening population of racialized workers who seemingly required coercive discipline to stay in line. City officials in Charleston readily recognized the racialized functionality of Savannah's mounted unit. The committee investigating Savannah's police reported that not only did the mounted unit "have a most salutary effect . . . in keeping evil-doers in check," it was also of "great value" given "the growing custom of negros assembling by night on farms out of the city proper but within the corporate limits, [which] requires imperatively to be looked after."[188] The Charleston committee further praised Savannah's police as a model to emulate not only because it "has a high reputation for efficiency" but also because Savannah had "a mixed population similar to our own." Given that both cities had "mixed" populations, both required forms of policing different from "the Police system which prevails at the North—and more especially in New York . . . [which] is not unlike that which exists in England." Among the key differences was that in "the North . . . [there is] no such mixed population as we have, composed of two races—superior and inferior." Given this difference, the northern cities did not require a pronounced militarization. Without this "mixed population . . . composed of two races—superior and inferior," then "anything martial about their police is uncalled for and would be out of place." The committee continued:

But with our institutions at the South we ought to have a military feature a little more prominent in our police system. It has a salutary effect upon our slave population, who are very much impressed by external forms and ceremonies, and peculiarly susceptible to the influence of military display.

The difference in the racial composition of the police's targets, concluded the committee, "implies somewhat more of a military organization than is found in the police systems of England and . . . the Northern States of the Union."[189] The complexified and more pronounced racial threat in the South generated not only colonial feedback—with a police organization modeled upon the coercive forms of plantation and settler colonialism—but also a more pronounced militarization.

The coloniality of the Savannah police was soon seen in its early activities. The very ordinances that served to reorganize the police force in theory prescribed racist policing in practice. One of the new founding ordinances called upon the police to take into custody "all felons and rioters, all disorderly or suspect persons, who may be found misbehaving themselves, or in any manner disturbing the public peace or quiet." In particular, "all slaves and free persons of color who may be found out of his or her house or enclosure, or his or her owner or employers house or enclose, after the ringing of the guard house bell at night, unless the said slave or free person of color be accompanied by a white person over the age of ten years, or be provided with an open written ticket" were to be arrested and detained at the guard house.[190] This ordinance further specified that a white person disturbing the peace was to be fined $100 or sentenced to thirty days in jail, while a "Negro, free or slave," arrested for the same violation would be subject not only to the same fine and jail time but also to corporal punishment.[191] As the Charleston committee recognized, the new Savannah police was to become the new slave patrol.

Still, the SPD did not only target the slave population. The city's elite also worried about the freed Blacks and the Irish who appeared to be influencing them and who posed threats of their own. It is fitting that two of the main proponents and creators of the new police were Mayor Anderson and Captain Bryan, both of whom were nativists with ties to the Know Nothings in the American and Order Party (and one of whom, Bryan, would go on to have a short stint as a slave trader, just before the war). In fact, Anderson had run for mayor on the ticket of that party, whose platform demanded a cessation in the arrival to the city of the "serfs and outcasts of starving and despotic Europe."[192] He and Bryan thus directed the police toward the city's racialized subproletariat, including the Irish. They hoped that the new police would thwart "the keepers of two hundred rum-holes in the city, the pirates who infest the river, and the heterogeneous mass."[193] In one of his first reports as chief of police, Bryan accordingly boasted that he was directing his force's energies toward the districts of town that had "the worst elements." He clarified that the eastern periphery and the western district that included Oglethorpe Ward—the two main "mixed" areas where freed Blacks, bondsmen, and Irish lived and where the various grog shops operated—required the "special attention" of a "strong and well maintained police force." With the precision of a military operation, Bryan surveyed these areas and the abutted districts and advocated for the construction of new police stations placed in such a way that they could serve as a "barrier between the disturbers on the east, and the quieter population" in the tonier parts of the city, where the upper- and middle-class whites could be found.[194]

The available data on arrests, however limited, offer further evidence that the new police directed attention primarily toward African Americans and the Irish. Slaves were slightly overrepresented among those arrested: a sample of jail records for the years 1855 to 1858 shows that of 1,292 total individuals, 505, or 38 percent, were slaves (the slave population was around 35 percent of the population).[195] As for the 62 percent in Savannah who were classified as "white," their birthplaces are not known, so it is unclear how many were Irish. However, there was a general trend across the South of Irish overrepresentation in the region's jails. According to Edward Ayers's analysis of court records for Savannah, the Irish made up about 14 percent of the city's population but at least 31 percent of defendants in superior court.[196] Given that this is an underestimate of arrest rates (because it represents only the Irish who were arrested and whose cases went all the way up to the county superior court), we can safely estimate that the Irish were arrested at least two times more frequently than they should have been if arrests were proportionate to population. As in other cities within the transatlantic network of cotton colonialism, militarized policing in Savannah followed the trail blazed from colony to metropole and from rural to urban areas by the very colonial subjects for whom it was initially designed.

## The New Police in Perspective

The reasons the civil police proliferated across England and the Atlantic beginning in the late 1820s and continuing through the 1850s are now intelligible. Rather than an arbitrary outcome of chaotic forces, the formation and spread of the new police in the Anglo-American sphere was patterned by the interimperial networks of trade, labor, and production within the transatlantic cotton empires. The flows of labor and material commodities in this network generated upheaval and perceived threats, restaging in Manchester, New York, and Savannah the story that had unfolded in London earlier. The new racialized subproletariat became the repository of residents' fears about the social changes wrought by

empire, prompting officials to summon the colonial boomerang and create ostensibly "civil" police forces that were militarized from the start.

There are variations worth nothing. In London, veterans of the imperial-
military regime such as Peel and Rowan drew directly from colonial models and
methods as they forged the London Metropolitan Police. This is not exactly true
for all subsequent cases. In Manchester the first police officials had significant
colonial-military experience. In Savannah and New York too, some of the high
officials had experience in America's colonial-military regime (especially in the
Mexican-American War or the Indian Wars). But not all of the proponents of
police reform had colonial-military experience. In New York, mayors Fernando
Wood and James Harper, who led police militarization, had been civilians.
Militarization thus happened even without the leadership of military-imperial
veterans.

Another difference has to do with intentionality. While creators of the first
new police in England and the United States drew upon the London model, they
were not always conscious of the coloniality of that force and so did not intend
to emulate colonial forces. An article in the *New York Daily Herald* in 1843, titled
"The London Police System," reviewed the features of the London Metropolitan
Police and urged the city to enact a similar police force, but failed to register its
colonial origins or even mention the Irish Constabulary.[197] Another writer came
closer to the colonial provenance in 1845, suggesting that in New York "an adequate and properly organised preventive police force, like that of London, Dublin
or Glasgow," be instituted.[198] Even then, the writer did not refer to Peel, the Peace
Preservation Force, the rural Irish Constabulary, or Sir John Moore's counterinsurgency operations, which had provided so much inspiration for the London
Metropolitan Police's operations.[199] In the United States, militarized police
forces were created, but their coloniality was often unrecognized and unstated.

Another variation is this: while the so-called civil police in Manchester, other
English counties, New York, and Savannah were partly modeled after the London
Metropolitan Police, they had an array of other distinct influences. In New York,
the frontier militia that had been so crucial for settler colonialism was influential, and veterans of the Mexican-American War played a role in militarizing
the police. The same is true for Savannah. And with Savannah, the influence of
slave patrols and coercive forms of settler colonialism was direct and palpable,
evidenced in the heavily armed and mounted features of the SPD. For the formation of police in the United States, the London influence was matched if not
surpassed by local varieties of the boomerang effect.

Hence the final crucial difference to note as the London model spread across
the Atlantic: weaponry and operational forms. Due to its particular colonial
influences, the Savannah police was the only police to have both mounted units
and fully armed officers with guns in its earliest years (and entirely without

controversy). Alternatively, except for the short-lived police force under Mayor Harper, which wielded muskets like the militia had, the New York City police was neither mounted nor routinely weaponized with firearms until 1857. This latter weaponization was part of a second moment of militarization in the city, likely sparked by the proliferation of violent attacks against lone policemen and the fear, as the press put it, that "every ruffian carries a concealed weapon of destruction."[200] It was also likely triggered by the looming threat of riots and violent gangs. In 1857, two Irish gangs overwhelmed the police and the militia had to be called. This was also the year when riots involving German immigrants erupted and the militia was the only recourse.[201] Still, the transition to firearms in New York City was unofficial, a contingent decision made by captains. And it was initially denied by commissioners, suggesting that arming the police was controversial and that the commissioners were initially intent on performing civility.[202]

Conversely, the police in England's cities abjured firearms more or less completely. As the historian Wilbur Miller explains, Rowan and Mayne of the London Met permitted some constables to wield cutlasses, but only those constables who patrolled the highways on the outskirts (on the grounds that those·remote districts were besieged by violent robbers). They also allowed some inspectors to carry pocket pistols, particularly those on dangerous assignments, "such as ferreting out notorious criminals from their slum hideouts."[203] But the general rule was that constables would only routinely carry truncheons and, as part of the performance of civility, even their truncheons were to be shielded from public view. As discussed in the previous chapter, the London bobbies were worried about looking too much like a French gendarmerie or the British Army. The same was true for Manchester's force and the county police. Officials were especially concerned that the county police would look too much like the Irish police and so decreed that only small cutlasses, not firearms, could be held.[204] All of this despite the fact that the public could carry firearms at the time, making the police likely "less well protected than some members of the public."[205]

Why did both Savannah and New York provide their police with firearms (albeit at different times), while England did not? An easy answer is that the right to bear arms in the United States, codified in the Second Amendment, led to a more armed public, and so the police naturally had to bear arms too. But does this explain the difference? While there is surely something to this explanation, it is incomplete. A full explanation would have to acknowledge varieties of colonialism and racialized threats.

First, we must remember that the right to bear arms in the United States was itself a product of America's distinct pattern of settler colonialism and slavery. American settler colonialism had long required armed militias to subdue Indigenous peoples and expropriate their land. In the South, plantation colonialism required armed slave patrols and urban forces to put down slave rebellions. Adam Smith, the founder of neoclassical economic thought, recognized this clearly. Firearms gave an advantage to the "opulent and civilized over a poor and barbarous nation," enabling the "extension of civilization" over barbarous lands and permitting its "permanency."[206] In this sense, the Second Amendment was partially meant to ensure that armed citizens could effectively conquer and control colonized peoples.[207]

England did not have this kind of frontier on its own turf; it was not a settler empire on home soil. Therefore, armed militias to protect against armed colonized insurgents were not deemed necessary. The armed work of colonial expansion and control happened outside the metropole, in Londonderry, Dublin, Jamaica, and St. Lucia. This made firearms less common in the homes and streets of Britain. Further, and relatedly, it was not just the availability of firearms that mattered, but *who* wielded them. In England, hunting required firearms, but this was an aristocratic tradition, a practice of the upper classes. There is little to suggest that Irish immigrants in London, Manchester, or the countryside carried firearms. They were a threat, but not an *armed* threat. In the United States, alternatively, the history of expansion and expropriation made guns more widely available to all classes. In the streets of New York, Irish gangs and other "ruffians" (as the press called them) were more likely to carry pistols and other dangerous weapons.[208] It was thus the *racialized* armed threat that made it more likely for the civil police in the United States to end up with firearms.[209]

\* \* \*

What happened in other cities and towns not discussed in this chapter? Certainly in some places, similar logics of racialization and militarization in the making of the new police applied. These cases would be the English counties, Liverpool, Bristol, and Wolverhampton in Britain, as well as the city of Chicago in the United States.[210] On the other hand, the formation of the new police in other cities and spaces after the initial emergence of the first civil police forces did not all follow these exact same logics. In some cases, the connection with the cotton empires mattered still, but in circuitous ways. In the port towns of Bristol and Boston, the incoming presence of the Irish and heated affrays over the slavery question were likely key factors leading to the formation of militarized civil police departments. Riots over racial issues sparked by cotton colonialism revealed the need for new police.[211] In other cities, imitation or emulation was the rule. The London-northern form was modular, capable of being created for one purpose but redeployed for others, and so authorities later adopted it to keep up with the times or in response to threats that might not have been thoroughly racialized.[212]

In any case, the story of the birth of the police in the cities discussed in this chapter is clear. The racialization of crime and disorder, prefaced by the arrival in metropolitan spaces of the colonial subproletariat, gave birth to militarized police labeled as "civil," and cotton colonialism's modalities of coercion—extending from the Caribbean to Ireland—provided the templates, tactics, operations, and organizational structures of the new police. Once this logic birthed the new civil police, it produced a model for other cities and towns to emulate, even if racialized threats did not always provide the initial impetus. The civil police across Britain and the US retained a hidden unconscious coloniality.

# PART II
# THE NEW IMPERIALISM
# AT HOME

# 3

# Police "Reform" and the Colonial Boomerang in the United States, 1890s–1930s[*]

I cannot think of anything that has produced more disrespect for government in general than policemen in this country. For their old brutal, crude and grafting methods, the police departments are to blame. The responsibility is not on the shoulders of the individual officers; it is the system.

—August Vollmer, address to Berkeley Police Department, July 8, 1927[1]

Killing a man is no easy task and I know exactly how you feel. These are some of the unhappy duties that are imposed upon police officers.

—August Vollmer to Willard Smith, January 3, 1930[2]

A policeman who shoots a bandit is serving his city exactly as a soldier when firing at his country's enemies.

—Smedley D. Butler, war veteran and head of Philadelphia Department of Public Safety, January 19, 1924[3]

The birth of the new civil police in the United States in the nineteenth century marked a significant development in the history of policing. The constable-watch system, militias, and slave patrols were replaced by new centralized uniformed police departments modeled after colonial-military forces. But the early years were rocky. Though donning military-like attire and organized as soldiers, the new police forces were weak and disorganized. Patrolmen could be found drinking at local pubs rather than dutifully patrolling their beats, police departments were sometimes tools of local political machines and politicians, and their capacity to squash crime and disorder was limited. In form and

[*] Parts of this chapter have been previously published in Go 2021b

Policing Empires. Julian Go, Oxford University Press. © Oxford University Press 2024.
DOI: 10.1093/oso/9780197621653.003.0004

function, policing had been militarized from the outset, but the police of the nineteenth century was not always an effective and efficient domestic army.

Things began to change in the late nineteenth and early twentieth centuries. Historians refer to it as the "reform era" of policing, or the age of "moderniza-tion" and "professionalization." In these reforms, which typically were initiated by middle-class Progressive reformers and their political allies, police departments were centralized, rationalized, and disciplined. Police chiefs were made autonomous from local political machines, clearer chains of command were created, and distinct jurisdictions were enforced. New standards and stricter criteria for entry were es-tablished. Discipline was imposed upon the ground troops. Rigorous training was implemented; new police academies and schools popped up across the country. Compared to its founding phase, policing became less personalized, less corrupt, and less politicized. Police forces also become more powerful. They enlarged their ranks and increased their abilities to penetrate society and attack crime. They be-came more adept at conducting raids, identifying criminals, and hunting offenders. In a sense, police departments finally became the powerful, professionalized, and capable modern police organizations we know them as today.[4]

Still, something strange was going on. While this was the period when police were supposedly disciplined and further professionalized, the police did not al-ways behave accordingly. In the South, police were known to indiscriminately murder African Americans. "The killing of colored men by policemen," wrote the African American journal *The Crisis* (edited by W.E.B. Du Bois) in 1912, "still goes on [and without] the slightest justification." In northern cities such as New York, the NAACP found cases where police repeatedly beat or brutalized African American men.[5] These were also the years when police carried out "the third degree." The Wickersham Commission, a special committee investigating law enforcement in the United States in the late 1920s, defined the "third degree" as "the use of physical brutality, or other forms of cruelty, to obtain involuntary confessions or admissions." The commission found such methods to be "wide-spread" among police and prison officials.[6]

A particularly gruesome form of the third degree was "the water cure." By this method, confessions were extracted by inserting a hose running a "high pressure of water" into the prisoner's mouth until the prisoner experienced a sense of drowning. The pressure would be removed and then applied over and over again as deemed necessary. A variant was where the prisoner was simply held under water. According to the description of the practice as conducted in Jefferson City, Missouri, one prisoner was stripped naked "to the skin," his arms "strapped to his sides and his ankles pinioned." Officers then filled a bathtub with freezing water, and while "one man seize[d] the victim by the ankles," the other "plunge[d] his head under the water." The "ducking" was repeated multiple times.[7] Chicago police used this water cure as early as 1907. Officials in police departments and prisons in states such as Texas and Mississippi also used it. The victims were typically African American. In one case in Mississippi, a "Negro charged with murdering a white man" gave a confession to police only after he was held "down upon the floor, tied . . . on his back" as the police slowly poured water into his nostrils "until he nearly strangled."[8] Illinois state house representative B.M. Chiperfield claimed in 1907 that this practice and others were common: "Methods as brutal and cruel as this are used almost daily on prisoners who are taken to police stations and subjected to all manner of brutalities."[9]

Some sense needs to be made of this. How could the police in the early twentieth century at once become "reformed," "professionalized," and "disciplined" and at the same time be found to be administering the water cure to suspects, beating them, or, as in a case in Texas, laying a naked suspect across a log and whipping him into making a confession?[10]

One explanation is that such abuses were tragic exceptions, instances of individual police officers who somehow escaped discipline and professionalization. According to this view, the brutal methods represent an incomplete modernization process—cracks in an otherwise seamless and inevitable process of discipline, professionalization, and reform. But there is another explanation. We will see in this chapter that police brutality on the one hand and the so-called professionalization-reform movement on the other were not contradictory currents. They were two sides of the same wave of militarization that overtook policing in the early twentieth century. The torture of suspects, the violence meted out by police, instances of racist brutality—rather than perversities of police professionalization, these were merely its darkest expressions. We will see, in short, that both the water cure and the police "reform" movement had the very same origins: American empire. They were the effects of the colonial boomerang triggered by perceived racialized threats, making another wave of militarization in US policing history.

## Professionalization and the "Reform Era"

To begin, it will help to first provide an overview of what the so-called modernization or professionalization-reform of policing in the early twentieth century entailed. When historians speak of the "reform era" of the police, they refer to changes in policing initiated by Progressive-era officials, police officers, and various middle- and upper-class groups. These police reformers had become disappointed in, dismayed by, or otherwise disgusted with the new police departments that had been birthed a few decades earlier. In their view, the new police were too corrupt to be effective enforcers of law. They pointed out how police officers could be easily bribed to turn a blind eye to gambling, prostitution, or other "vices" that bothered so many among the Puritan upper and middle classes. They also disliked the weakness, inefficiencies, and politics of the police. While the early police wore uniforms, marched like soldiers, wielded guns, and were organized into loose military hierarchies, they lacked professional discipline and power. They were underpaid and untrained, and they lacked clear qualifications. Promotions were based on personal loyalty or bribes; professional standards were absent.[11] Too often, the rank and file were subjected to "paternalistic domination by chiefs" and political machines. Patrolmen declared loyalty to the ward boss or chief who hired them rather than to the police force and its ideals. They were often used as political tools to intimidate voters during elections or, at the behest of local capitalists, to suppress labor strikes.[12] The police were thus not only corrupt but also inept, incapable of doing much about crime. Many departments ended up serving as social service organizations, chasing after lost children in their respective neighborhoods, housing vagrants in their rudimentary station houses, or arresting vagrants to little positive effect. If their initial mission was to stop crime and crush social disorder, they were not doing a good job.[13]

The professionalization-reform movement was a response to these perceived deficiencies. Reformers called for police departments to be centralized and for police chiefs to have more autonomy so that they might be sheltered from political machines. They sought to create more distinct jurisdictions within departments and called for patrolmen to be more strictly supervised.[14] They sought to increase pay, create new standards and criteria for employment, and impose discipline through a series of incentives and rewards. They pushed departments to institute new entry tests and create new training programs.[15] Police academies become common, and departments sometimes worked with universities to create policing and criminology programs to train new recruits.[16]

Along with these reforms came the enhanced power and capabilities of urban police forces. One part of this was sheer growth in personnel, with most city police forces doubling their size from 1865 to 1905.[17] There were also important increases in strategic and tactical capabilities in an effort to better manage crime and disorder, thereby reinvigorating the police's purported mission. Police officials created various specialized "squads" to better deal with distinct areas of criminality (e.g., the "vice squad" or, later, "Red Squads"). Police reformers created new intelligence and detection units, along with new filing and record-keeping systems for tracking and predicting crime.[18] With the new data, officers began "tactical crime analysis" involving pin mapping: using maps to identify the areas with the most crime, called "hot spots," and distributing patrols accordingly.[19] Police tested and adopted new surveillance and detection methods. To identify criminals, they began using the modus operandi system, the Bertillon system, and eventually fingerprinting. The International Association of Chiefs of Police (IACP) was founded in 1893 and facilitated the dissemination of these technologies and techniques.

Police departments also enhanced their capacities to monitor, control, and regulate territory. Most patrolmen in the nineteenth century operated parochially, each covering a small beat on foot.[20] Only in the South, as seen in the previous chapter, were patrols mounted, a practice inherited from slave patrols. But the reforms of the early twentieth century served to extend the ranks of mounted police officers: police departments increasingly used horses, bicycles, wagons, and later motorcycles, electric wagons, and eventually automobiles.[21] Mounting officers enabled police to cover larger swaths of territory than before, reach into previously unregulated spaces on the outskirts of metropoles, and rapidly deploy, with swifter response times. "We must be able to move men rapidly from one scene of action to another," declared August Vollmer, police chief in Berkeley, California, and a prominent police reformer.[22] Richard Sylvester, police reformer, police chief in Washington, DC, and one of the first presidents of the IACP, stressed that mounted police finally enabled police officers "to respond promptly to calls in widely separated sections of the city."[23] Mounting policemen also enhanced the ability of police to control crowds, rioters, and strikers.[24]

New communication systems enhanced these police capacities. In the nineteenth century, "the patrolman . . . was almost completely isolated on his beat," wrote Vollmer. He was isolated and difficult to reach for rapid mobilization.[25] But a range of new technologies radically changed this. Signal boxes, telephone kiosks, and later two-way radios—along with the proliferation of police stations scattered around the cities—enabled information and commands to spread quickly from one beat to another.[26] These enabled the police "to act in unison."[27]

A final development was the creation of new layers of policing covering previously unpoliced territory. Much of the professionalization-reform movement focused on reforming urban police forces, but state police forces also emerged in this period. These forces were meant to regulate and control rural districts. They were new for their time. The Massachusetts District Police (established 1865) and the Connecticut police (established 1903) had already existed, but they concentrated mostly on criminal detection. And they were exceptions. In 1905, Pennsylvania innovated by creating the Pennsylvania State Police (which was also referred to as a state "constabulary"). Placed under the control of the governor of Pennsylvania, its force of over two hundred armed and mounted policemen was deployed to suppress strikes and put down mobs, demonstrations, and riots. It served as a model for other state police forces around the country, influencing the creation of the New York State Police in 1917, the Michigan State Constabulary in 1917, and the Rhode Island State Police in 1925, among many others.

The spread of these changes across police departments in the United States was uneven. Some cities were early adopters, leading the way before the First World War, while others emulated them later, in the 1920s and 1930s.[28] At any rate, the changes were profound. Through the reform movement, policing was professionalized, transformed, developed, and expanded as never before. In this sense, it is with good reason that existing historical scholarship refers to these years in the early twentieth century as the moment of modernization and reform. The only thing missing from this scholarship is the recognition that these so-called reforms had imperial origins.

## Coercion and Control in the Making of US Empire, 1880s–1910s

Like policing, America's imperial-military formation underwent significant changes around the turn of the twentieth century. Most of the changes began in the late nineteenth century, preceding the professionalization-reform movement. As seen in the previous chapter, America's empire had already been expanding westward over the course of the nineteenth century. The tactics, techniques, and forms of that conquest informed the making of the first police departments. But the 1890s marked a turn. After subduing fierce resistance from the Sioux, Comanches, Apaches, and Cheyennes in the Plains to finalize its conquest of the West, the American state looked farther afield to construct an overseas colonial empire. In this, the American empire joined the "new imperialism" of the period, whereby European and Asian powers embarked upon new colonial conquests. America's subsequent empire consisted of a panoply of territories and zones of influence. The United States seized Hawaii in 1893. It took the Philippines, Guam, and Puerto Rico from Spain as a result of the Spanish-American War of 1898. The United States then acquired Samoa, the Panama Canal Zone, and the Virgin Islands. By 1940, the American formal empire—referring to the territories it declared sovereignty over and which were unequally incorporated into the American polity—ruled nineteen million subjects overseas. But American empire also entailed a range of military occupations and interventions falling short of colonial acquisition. The United States occupied Cuba multiple times, as well as Haiti, Nicaragua, the Dominican Republic, and other, smaller countries.[29]

America's military was the leading agent of America's new global position. The US Army had been the main mechanism of America's westward expansion in the early part of the nineteenth century. Vital for settler colonialism, its primary function had been fighting Indians and suppressing Native resistance, and the army continued in this role in the late nineteenth century.[30] Through the 1870s and 1880s, the US Army engaged in more than one thousand combat actions.[31] But with the new overseas commitments at the end of the nineteenth century, the US military took on even greater importance. In the Philippines beginning in 1899, the army had to subdue the resistance to American sovereignty from the anticolonial nationalist movement housed in central Luzon, leading to the Philippine-American War. Ending officially in 1902, this was America's first guerrilla war and its largest protracted overseas war up to that time. It cost some half a million Filipino lives and five thousand American lives.[32] The US military also acted as a governing power. After defeating Spain in 1898, the military took the reins of government in Cuba from 1898 to 1903 (and then again from 1906 to 1909), in Puerto Rico from 1898 to 1900, and in the Philippines from 1898 to 1902. The navy acted as the sole government of Guam and Samoa for decades. And as the US military repeatedly intervened in countries in Central America and the Caribbean, it ended up serving as the occupying government in Haiti (1915–1934), Nicaragua (1912–1913), and the Dominican Republic (1916–1924), among other countries. Furthermore, because the American state did not have a proper "colonial office," administration of the colonies and western territories was put into the hands of the United States War Department, the overseer of America's armed forces.[33]

Through these experiences, America's imperial-military formation underwent important changes. In fact, as late as 1898, the United States did not yet have an "army" in "any operational sense of that word." While the army had indeed been successful in conquering the frontier and quelling Native rebellion, it was merely "a large collection of companies, battalions, regiments and batteries" without proper training, equipment, and centralized structure.[34] The Spanish-American War made these limitations clear as never before, and US officials vowed to fix things to fit the country for its new global role. The US military, said one strategist, had to be "prepared to go even to the ends of the earth, not only with ships but with powerful armies."[35]

A series of reforms led by Elihu Root at the War Department followed. Root worked on the reforms just as he was administering the colonies in his formal capacity as secretary of war. Among these changes, known as the "Root Reforms," was centralization. Previously, the military lacked central coordination. The War Department consisted of relatively autonomous bureaus with overlapping and sometimes conflicting roles. Root changed this with the Army Reorganization Act of 1901, which reduced the autonomy of bureau chiefs and led, in 1903, to the creation of the position of chief of staff and the General Staff Corps. A second change was professionalization. After the Civil War, the military had already created educational programs, training schools, and a new military science—which eventually found a home in 1881 in the School of Application for Infantry and Cavalry at Fort Leavenworth, Kansas. But the inability of some officers during the Spanish-American War to mobilize forces and adapt to organizational exigencies showed the limits of this training. To fix things, Root assisted in reforming the Military Academy in 1901 and the military school at Fort Leavenworth. He also created the Army War College, which taught military science along with strategy and tactics, launching a novel scientific orientation in military leadership. Root also helped to heighten standards of recruitment, improve training, and increase pay, privileges, and benefits for officers and the rank and file. Root helped professionalize the military as never before.[36]

The experiences of empire also yielded innovations in military operations and tactics on the ground, generating a new science and practice of counterinsurgency. Before this time, the military had already seen some advances in military science and strategy, not least through the publication of the "Leavenworth Board manuals" in 1891. These were the army's manuals devoted to combat arms, providing officers with lessons in tactics for the first time.[37] But America's imperial experiences in the late nineteenth and early twentieth centuries generated further innovations, not least "open order" operations (sometimes also called "extended order" or "loose order" operations). These involved small mobile units led by company captains operating on their own individual initiative with relative autonomy from central command posts. The wars with the Plains and Southwest Indians in the latter part of the nineteenth century had been formative for these operations. As the Sioux, Kiowa, Arapaho, Comanche, Cheyenne, and Apache forces had been mounted on horses, the army had to devise ways to move columns through rugged terrain and operate deftly, swiftly, and flexibly. Small open order mounted units were the solution.[38] Other forces such as the Texas Rangers had operated similarly: they were armed and mounted mobile patrols.[39]

It was during the Philippine-American War that the US Army expanded and perfected open order mobile units as never before.[40] In the Philippines, the army faced insurgent guerrilla forces who moved swiftly through a complex terrain of rivers, jungles, and mountain villages. In this context, large-scale cordon-and-sweep campaigns and close order formations were useless. The US Army had to divide into small mobile units, mounted on horses or in boats along rivers, to move through foreign terrain, gather intelligence, and deploy rapidly. This essentially amounted to what is known as the "hike," combining what later became more commonly known as "reconnaissance-in-force" and "search-and-destroy" missions. These enabled the American forces "to match the mobility of the *insurrectos* [insurgents]."[41] Open order mobile units often deployed under the cover of night, launching long-distance expeditions to surround and surprise enemy encampments. Such tactics thus required an unprecedented reliance upon cavalry units and "special detachments of mounted infantry and scouts"—that is, elite forces that "bore the brunt of the counterguerrilla war, acting in reconnaissance, strike, and mobile reserve capacities, functions in which they quickly developed an expertise."[42] The army in the Philippines increasingly relied upon such elite units as the war raged on.[43]

Other innovations had to do with intelligence gathering. The Philippine-American War was among the United States' first protracted overseas campaigns. The army found itself in a foreign land consisting of thousands of islands and peoples about which most Americans knew nothing. To fill the gap, the army formed a new counterintelligence unit known as the Division of Military Information (DMI), the very "first field intelligence unit in [the army's] hundred-year history," according to the historian Alfred McCoy.[44] In turn, the division devised novel record-keeping and information-gathering techniques. For instance, it created a new mapping section utilizing telegraph lines recently constructed across rural and urban territories. The mapping section merged reports from the army's field officers with data from local officials and police forces. The division also used "identity cards" to profile insurgent leaders.[45] All of this information proved vital for the Americans' counterinsurgency campaign, which had become dependent upon mobile elite units. As rapid deployment required up-to-date information, "the DMI's field units proved agile in tracking rebel movements and identifying their locations for timely raids" by the army's new elite units.[46]

The developments in the Philippines influenced military operations across the empire. The Americans in Cuba under the control of General James Franklin Bell (1906–1909) used similar counterinsurgency tactics and technologies. They created a Military Intelligence Division, sent mobile units on intelligence-gathering missions, and established files on Cuban insurgents.[47] The US military also deployed mobile units and related tactics to defeat insurgents in Haiti, Nicaragua, and the Dominican Republic. During the US military occupation of Haiti beginning in 1915, the military government responded to the rising Caco insurgency by establishing small mobile units that saturated suspected insurgent areas of the country for one to two weeks to suppress rebel activity. These forces later worked with the newly revamped Gendarmerie of Haiti, an American-led constabulary, and were aided by an intelligence branch that mapped out swaths of enemy territory for saturation missions.[48]

The exigencies of empire thus led to the formation of an "army for empire": an imperial-military regime that learned how to repress and regulate populations deemed racially inferior, a regime that could conquer foreign land and more readily suppress native revolts, riots, and insurgencies.[49] The influence of America's early experiences in the overseas empire on the US military cannot be overestimated. As one historian notes: "Virtually every officer in the Army served in either Cuba, Puerto Rico, or the Philippines between 1898 and 1902 and the experiences they gained in nation building, pacification, and, in the case of the Philippines, counterguerrilla warfare, became the models on which the Army would base its approach to these issues for the next forty years."[50]

Colonial policing was also a part of this emerging imperial-military regime. Colonial police organizations dotted America's new expansive "imperial archipelago" of some seven million inhabitants spanning from the Caribbean to the Pacific.[51] In the Philippines, as the army eventually wound down its activities, the void was filled by the Philippine Constabulary. Designed to cover the remote outlying areas of the countryside that served as a "refuge and base of operation" for "lawless men" (as US colonial officials phrased it), the constabulary was "an effective and mobile force . . . adequate at all times to meet any emergency that might arise."[52] The earliest officers of the constabulary were from the US Army, many of whom had served previously on the Indian frontier, and the constabulary incorporated the mounted emphasis of the US Army's new operational orientation.[53] The mapping systems and telegraph lines established during the early days of the Philippine-American War served the constabulary well. Swaths of territory could "be divided . . . into checkerboard squares" for detachments of the constabulary to comb, probe, and attack (as one constabulary officer recalled), all directed by US officials sitting at their desks in Manila.[54]

The Philippine Constabulary was one part of a three-tiered structure of colonial counterinsurgency and coercion in the Philippines. The system borrowed from the British Empire and particularly the Irish colonial system. The Philippine Constabulary was structured like the Royal Irish Constabulary (RIC) and functioned similarly to it. Like the RIC, it was heavily armed and mobile, and it was meant "to prevent and suppress brigandage, insurrection, unlawful assemblies, and breaches of the peace" in the rural districts.[55] Meanwhile, other police units covered the urban districts. The Manila Metropolitan Police regulated the bustling colonial capital, just as the Dublin Metropolitan Police monitored Ireland's capital. The towns were covered by a series of smaller but nonetheless armed municipal police forces that consisted mainly of local Filipinos. The American governor-general of the Philippines had the power to place the municipal police forces under the direct control of a senior officer of the constabulary, thereby creating a tight command-and-control hierarchy.[56]

Puerto Rico had a population of almost one million in 1899, consisting of "whites," "mestizos," "negroes," and a small number of Chinese (according to US Census categories).[57] In 1900, the newly formed colonial state replaced the US military as the island's authoritative power. It swiftly created a two-tiered police force consisting of the Insular Police and the Municipal Police. The Municipal Police covered the towns. The Insular Police covered rural areas and some urban areas except for the largest cities, like San Juan. It chased down so-called criminals and brigands and fashioned itself the benevolent hand of law and order in the island.[58] In his 1901 report, the chief of the Insular Police, Frank Techner, boasted that his force had been successful in providing "protection to lives and property, preventing serious crimes from being committed, and maintaining the public order at all times."[59] This was characteristic rhetoric of the civil police elsewhere, but it covered up the martial coloniality of the force. A former army lieutenant, Techner led his force as if it were a national gendarmerie like the RIC and the Philippine Constabulary. It was mounted, "uniformed in khaki, drilled, regulated in military routine and armed with carbines."[60] He boasted that while previously the island had been "overrun by brigands," in its first year his force had "cleared them out, killing four and imprisoning 200 others."[61] Later, in the 1930s, the Insular Police would launch the Ponce Massacre, firing upon peaceful anticolonial protesters and killing at least nineteen civilians, plus injuring more than two hundred others. In Puerto Rico as in the Philippines, and elsewhere in America's new colonial empire, violence was at the core of the police power.

Still, the novel tools, tactics, and technologies of America's newly global imperial-military regime did not only circulate throughout the peripheries of empire. They also came home. Here is where we can better understand the provenance of the so-called professionalization-reform of policing in the United States. It was actually an effect of the colonial boomerang.

## Vollmer's War

To see one of the ways in which the boomerang returned, consider August Vollmer, the police chief (his title was "marshal") of the Berkeley Police Department in the first decade of the twentieth century (see Figure 3.1). Vollmer became a widely influential police reformer, rightly praised in criminology textbooks and the popular press for the advances he promoted. At Berkeley and then throughout his varied career, he innovated and implemented most of the policies, programs, and changes associated with the professionalization-reform movement. He is accordingly known as "the father of American policing."[62] In Berkeley, for example, Vollmer mounted the entire police force, putting his men on bicycles (1905), on motorcycles (1910), and then in patrol cars (1914). When he first put his force on bicycles, he "drew laughs from the press, the public and other police officials," but he was vindicated later by the spread of mobile units across the country.[63] Vollmer also innovated methods of filing and record-keeping that became standard for police departments. He insisted upon precise data collection and the regular review of police reports to better coordinate and direct policing activities. Vollmer was also among the first police chiefs to implement the modus operandi system of criminal identification, along with the Bertillon system and fingerprinting techniques to solve crimes.[64] Merging these systems with his record-keeping and data collection methods, Vollmer helped inaugurate what later became known as "scientific" policing or "criminal science."[65]

Vollmer also created the first police intelligence divisions, whereby intelligence officers developed algorithms for maximizing the use of beat patrols,

**Figure 3.1.** August Vollmer, Berkeley Police Department
*Source:* August Vollmer Portrait Collection, BANC PIC 1957.018--PIC, The Bancroft Library, University of California, Berkeley

basing the spatial distribution of patrol officers on anticipated emergency calls and crime volume. This was connected to the tactic of pin mapping or crime mapping, which Vollmer is known to have invented.[66] He later explained that the spatial data and the practice of pin mapping were for locating "the time of attack, the place of attack, and the type of crime committed," which in turn helped police find the "infested sections" of the city that police should patrol.[67] Vollmer led the way in professionalization too. He created a youth police program called Junior Police to attract kids to police service. He inaugurated the first police school in 1908 at the University of California at Berkeley with classes on "criminal psychology," "police organization and administration," "police micro-analysis," "special police drills and exercises," and many other topics.[68] A part of this school was his "college cops" program to train college students to be police officers. He later taught the first classes on criminology and policing at the University of Chicago.[69]

Already by the 1910s, Vollmer and his department's innovations had become so influential that police departments around the country from Los Angeles to Chicago and Detroit brought him in as a consultant or as temporary chief. His protegés, such as O.W. Wilson, became some of the most important figures in criminology and police reform at midcentury, as well as police chiefs in their own right, typically deploying the lessons they learned from him. His officer training programs spread like wildfire across the country.[70] Vollmer was named president of the International Association of Chiefs of Police, the new professional association that brought together law enforcement personnel from around the country and beyond. In 1935, the National Academy of Sciences awarded Vollmer its medal for "the most distinguished contribution to the public welfare of the nation."[71]

But this is crucial: before he became police chief, Vollmer had served in America's imperial-military regime. When he was a young man in Berkeley, the Spanish-American War broke out, and Vollmer eagerly enlisted. He joined the Eighth Army Corps and was sent to the Philippines to fight the Spanish forces there. After Spain was defeated, Vollmer stayed in the Philippines as part of the army's occupying force in Manila. He was among the few soldiers charged with policing the city during military occupation, filling the vacuum left behind by the Spanish Guardia Civil. While he was carrying out his policing duties in Manila, Filipino insurgents in central Luzon took up arms against the Americans, led by General Emilio Aguinaldo, and so began the Philippine-American War. Vollmer was then handpicked to join one of the army's new elite mobile units. Embodying the new open order tactics and counterinsurgency approach, these units were tasked with penetrating the country's interior from the waterways. Some of those missions involved the use of small catamarans disguised as trading boats and sent into the depths of Luzon to hunt rebels and launch raids on insurgent camps. Vollmer later explained: "We captured quite a few towns, conveyed troops, shelled insurgent nests, kept the Pasig river open and tried to make things as unpleasant as possible for Aguinaldo's men."[72] He later reminisced with his old war buddy about "the old days on the Passig [sic] river," when they would spend their time "doing a little sharpshooting at . . . Insurrectos."[73] In all, Vollmer participated in twenty-five engagements with insurgents.

Vollmer finished his service in August 1899 and returned to Berkeley.[74] In 1905, after serving as a postman, he became town marshal, aka chief of police. He drew directly upon his experiences in the Philippines as he launched his police reforms. For instance, soon after becoming town marshal, he instituted a new record-keeping system for the department. Previously, officers had not kept records of incidents. Vollmer devised the department's first system to do so. The system was taken from his time policing colonial Manila. As a patrolman in Manila, he and the rest of his unit were required to keep records of their daily activities and report them to the desk sergeant in the garrison. The desk sergeant in turn logged all of the activities, generating a comprehensive set of records. This was the system Vollmer adopted for Berkeley and which other police departments later emulated.[75] The police scholar Felix Fuld later noted the connection between these records systems and those of the military: "The reports and records which the police are required to make and keep . . . are of considerable importance. . . . The police is essentially an army, which is constantly at war with crime and criminals, and in order that this army may be properly directed, it is essential that the central office be kept accurately informed of the progress of the fight."[76]

Many of Vollmer's other innovations were taken from his colonial counterinsurgency experience in the Philippines. One of the problems he faced at Berkeley, and later in Los Angeles when he served as temporary police chief there, was an expansive territory, just like in the Philippines. At Berkeley, Vollmer had only a small force of men to cover wide swaths of land. This is partly why he mounted his force, despite the initial mockery from the press and the public. He explained to a colleague that with mounted police, "mobility is greatly enhanced," "time is saved in all emergencies in responding" to crises, and "a tremendous amount of force may be exerted."[77] Mounted police thus followed the military principle of "getting there the fastest with the mostest men" and the "military rule" that "rapid concentration of force at the critical point is the secret of victory."[78] As one newspaper story on Vollmer in 1923 explained with admiration: "Vollmer put into effect some of the methods he'd used in chasing elusive river pirates on the Pasig and bushwhackers in the steaming wild jungles. He added mobility to his force. He mounted his patrolmen on bicycles—this was before the days of motorcycles."[79]

In 1923 Vollmer came down from Berkeley to run the Los Angeles Police Department (LAPD). Corruption and inefficiency had beset the LAPD. Crime overwhelmed the town. Vollmer took up the new post with zeal. The LAPD had been unable to form a "close and mobile organization necessary to combat criminals," he explained to his friends back home, and then announced that one of his first steps would be to create a new mobile force.[80] "One of the things I will establish," he told the media, "is a mobile squad of at least 100 picked men for use at any point in the city." The unit, which became known as the "Crime Crushers," would be able to show up in areas of high crime "almost instantly on the spot" and form a "concentrated force for handling whatever . . . problem" might arise.[81] This new mobile unit was guided by the same military idea behind his mounted force in Berkeley. "We must have good tactics, deploy men to take the best advance of the situation," he explained to the officers. "We must be able to move men rapidly from one scene of action to another. Concentration of force is supremely important in military science, and it will be important to the task we have at hand."[82] "He reiterated to them that one of the key "military rules" for policing was "rapid concentration of force."[83]

For his mobile unit in Los Angeles, Vollmer added other innovations taken from the colonial-military regime. He drew upon the military distinction between "strategy" and "tactics" when discussing ideal police operations. "We are using the military term strategy," he explained to L.V. Jenkins, police chief in Portland, Oregon, "which may be briefly defined as making war on the map, or, in other words, a group of men in the police department estimate where, when, and what kinds of crime are being committed."[84] Here lies the origins of pin mapping (what is today called "crime mapping," "predictive" policing, or "hot spot" policing).[85] As Vollmer explained later, "Information obtained from the officers' reports" is "transferred to the tabulating cards" and pinned on a map, with the cards specifying "the time of attack, the place of attack, and the type of crime committed."[86] In the Philippines, this had been the task of the army's Military Intelligence Division, which used identification cards on insurgents and pins to map insurgent movements, strikes, and camps.[87] Vollmer took the same approach in Berkeley and then later in Los Angeles, effactually equating criminals with Filipino insurgents and crimes with insurgent strikes. In Los Angeles, he created an intelligence division or Statistical Bureau that drew upon data from the Record Division to do the work. He employed a "statistical expert" to locate the "crime centers of the city."[88] "Use of an intelligence division," he stated, "may be as necessary in a police department as in the state department of a government. It is the only way to find out what your enemy is doing, and the end in this case, which is the protection of society, justifies the means."[89]

Vollmer used this "strategy," or "making war on the map," to guide his "tactics." Police forces would be directed to those areas where the most crimes occurred, just as the army's mounted open order units like his own had been directed to the areas where the insurgents operated or rested. This was where the mobile units, or what Vollmer sometimes called "Reserve Units," would be deployed.[90] "When it is found that the same offense [located on the map] is occurring with great regularity in the same area and at about the same hour, special details of police are organized and placed on duty in these infested sections during the hours that the crooks are operating. Needless to say the results are disastrous to the crooks."[91] The tactic would also be helpful for patrolling "areas of high delinquency," which were "the breeding places of gangs that later terrorize communities with desperate crimes."[92] Vollmer explained this strategy further to his men: "We are going to use this force where it is most needed and we are going to know where and when it is most needed from the statistical bureau of our record division."[93] The movements of the mobile force, sometimes armed with shotguns, would be known only by Vollmer and his high-level officials, with all the air of military secrecy, and would "concentrate wherever crime concentrates."[94] He explained to his officers: "We are up against a tough fight against organized criminal enemies. To make the most of the forces at our command, we will have to operate according to the principles of military science."[95] Subsequently Vollmer's "Crime Crushers," two hundred strong, made 396 arrests in Los Angeles in the three weeks after the unit's establishment in 1923—five times as many arrests as before it debuted. By 1924 it was making close to fifteen hundred arrests a month.[96] Shootouts between the Crime Crushers and criminals sometimes erupted on LA's streets, leading newspapers to refer to the city as a "battlefield."[97] Vollmer was unapologetic. "We're conducting a war," he told his fellow police officers as president of the IACP, "a war against the enemies of society and we must never forget that."[98]

Vollmer's other initiatives, such as Berkeley's police school and rigorous testing of police officers for entry to the force, were also informed by his military-colonial experience. As he wrote to a friend, he envisioned

> a new profession in which the very best manhood in our nation will be happy to serve in the future. Why should not the cream of the nation be perfectly willing to devote their lives to the cause of service providing that service is dignified, socialized and professionalized. Surely the Army offers no such opportunity for contributing to the welfare of the nation and yet men unhesitatingly spend their lives preparing for army service.[99]

Accordingly, just as the Root Reforms had instituted higher standards for recruitment, new training programs, and schools to train army officers and soldiers, Vollmer created training programs where no such programs had existed before. Those programs had military inspiration as well as military content. Vollmer told reporters about his "junior police" school: "We began drilling them [the students] right away in military tactics, to teach them discipline and order." When Vollmer devised courses for police officers, he insisted that one of the core classes be "military science" alongside other more traditional courses like economics and political science.[100] After acquiring .22-caliber revolvers for his force in Berkeley, Vollmer offered "highly specialized training" in use of the weapons, instituted regular target practice, and (using army practice as a model) gave medals to his best pistol shooters.[101]

His entire grandiose vision of creating a professional force was guided by the military analogy. Praising both the military and colonial police models (such as the police in Cuba he so admired), he was a leading advocate of standardized testing of police officers for entry and used army standards for entry to his police programs.[102] He enlisted the help of psychologists who had devised the army's Alpha test and used a version of the army's tests to choose aspiring police officers.[103] "Examining and testing large bodies of men," said Vollmer when announcing his plan for professionalizing policemen through schools and testing, "has been standardized by the army," adding that "the army plan of selecting men can be successfully applied to the selection of policemen." While heading the LAPD, Vollmer further instituted a rating system based on the system used by the army. To impose effective discipline and maximize individuals' capacities for policing, each police officer "below the rank of Chief" was "rated by his immediate superior" based on "physical qualities," "intelligence," "leadership," "personal qualities," and "general value to the service." The system, Vollmer explained, "is practically the same as the United States Army rating school."[104]

## Spreading the Boomerang

Vollmer was not alone. Across America's cities and towns, police departments adopted tactics, tools, policies, and programs similar to those that Vollmer promoted. They too were influenced by America's imperial-military regime. This is partly seen in the language of police at the time. After the Spanish-American War, officials at the annual meetings of the IACP increasingly used military analogies or metaphors. They referred to the police as the "uniformed army of our cities," "municipal soldiers," "the uniformed army of our cities," or "the great army that is the bulwark of public safety."[105] Police also spoke of criminals as "enemies" who sometimes formed their own "armies" and of homeless "hobos" as an "army of lawless bums."[106] They evoked policing as "warfare against crime and disorder."[107] Richard Sylvester, chief of police in Washington, DC, added: "If it is a patriotic and honorable profession to break down by force the foreign enemies of the state, why should it not be equally so to subdue the domestic invaders of property and destroyers of lives who are continually engaged in criminal warfare?"[108]

This was not just wordplay. So-called police reformers were indeed turning to the imperial-military regime for inspiration. For example, when they pushed for more centralized command structures in police departments to increase discipline, they looked to the new centralized system created under Elihu Root.[109] Under the Root Reforms, military personnel had been subordinated to the army chief of staff, appointed by the US president. Police reformers proposed the same idea for police departments, suggesting that police chiefs be appointed by the mayor and given full command. Notably, Root himself advised police reform committees, such as the New York Committee on Police Problems. Henry Baldwin of that committee aptly referred to the Root Reforms when arguing for reform. Mayors, he said, should appoint police chiefs just as the president appointed the chief of staff in "our new General Staff Bill."[110] The rest of the commission added: "The police hold the same relation to the city government as the army does to the nation."[111] Another committee member advocated for longer tenure for police chiefs by referring to the army: "If you have an army whose commanders change every two years, the discipline of the army will before long be worth nothing, and the army itself will be worth nothing. . . . The same can be said of our police force."[112]

Police reformers likewise turned to America's imperial-military regime as they aimed to discipline and professionalize their forces with increased pay, higher entry standards, and new police training.[113] In Jersey City, New Jersey, chief of police Benjamin Murphy pushed for new promotion standards and training programs while referring to the army's training program and its Leavenworth manuals. Police, he said, "should be drilled in the school of the soldier" and the "school of the company and battalion," and police patrols should act as "pickets of an army during war."[114] After taking office as chief of police in Philadelphia in 1912, James T. Robinson created a new daily training regimen for his force that also drew from the army's Leavenworth manuals. As he reported, "All the patrolmen appointed during the past year have been instructed in the 'school of the soldier' and the importance of military courtesy."[115] New York City's police not only incorporated the "school of the soldier" from the army's training program into its exercises and drills but also created new regulation uniforms that incorporated US army leggings and the double-breasted British army box coat.[116]

These measures were sometimes framed as a matter of preventing police corruption by instilling discipline, but they were also a way to increase the power capabilities of the force. "One company of well-drilled police officers," exclaimed the chief of police of Cincinnati, Ohio, in 1899, "can do more with a mob than a whole battalion of undrilled policemen."[117] "We want to make a solider of him in efficiency when his services are required," explained Richard Sylvester.[118] In Savannah, various reforms adopted there were meant to turn the rank-and-file policeman into a "well-disciplined soldier" and to generally increase the "military and soldierly bearing and discipline of the force."[119] In 1910, the *Seattle Times* published a story titled "The Metamorphosis of the Cop" that noted the trend: "The ideal is to have every [police] force be a Varangian Guard in soldierly activity and strength."[120]

From Savannah to Cincinnati to Berkeley, other departments instituted new regular drills modeled after military training. Referring to the army's training regime, police officials insisted upon daily weapons training and target practice. They issued .38 pistols or Winchester shotguns for their forces on the grounds that those weapons were used by the US Army.[121] Police departments also collaborated with the National Rifle Association, which was in turn tied to the US military.[122] In Los Angeles, after Vollmer departed, Chief James Davis reported that more than eight hundred members of the LAPD had joined the National Rifle Association, under the direction of the United States War Department, and "are practicing assiduously to attain skill in marksmanship," training in revolvers as well as rifles.[123] Police reformers were unequivocal about the military provenance and links of these programs. The pro-reform writer Raymond Fosdick reported that the "methods of training in use in West Point" were being used in police schools "with excellent results."[124] In 1930, Vollmer wrote to a friend praising New York City's new "Police Academy" and a similar academy in Ohio that had direct ties to the army's Camp Perry. The school was "designed for the purpose of instructing police officers in the use of the pistol, rifle, tear gas, smoke bomb, and specialized weapons."[125]

Following Vollmer's lead in adopting operational forms and tactics of the imperial-military regime, police forces created mounted units and intelligence divisions, and they used pin mapping to distribute and concentrate police forces. Vollmer noted the military origins of these tactics. Police chiefs, he wrote, "learned the necessity of concentrating the force when and where it is most needed" from the military. He added that nearly all of the other new developments were taken from the military. In a retrospective discussion of the changes of the reform era, he remarked that "principles of military science, including those of strategy, tactics, logistics, communications, and others, were adopted by the police and applied to the problem of reducing crime and protecting the community."[126]

The imperial boomerang thus inspired the professionalization-reform movement, but it also shaped the formation of the new state police forces. The Pennsylvania State Police was inspired by the Royal Irish Constabulary, the Canadian Mounted Police (itself inspired by the RIC), the Philippine Constabulary, the Texas Rangers, and the United States Cavalry. Unsurprisingly, it looked just like these colonial forces. Armed with pistols, riot batons, and carbines (of the kind previously used by the cavalry and the Philippine Constabulary), it was called upon to handle emergencies at a moment's notice. The state policemen lived in barracks like the men of the RIC; single males were preferred. They rode ponies brought up from Texas carrying "the regulation black McClellan army saddle bags and black leather bridle with the Prussian cavalry bit."[127] They underwent strict inspections and followed the drill formation of the US Cavalry.

The Pennsylvania State Police was also manned by veterans. John C. Groome, the first superintendent, had served in Puerto Rico during the Spanish-American War. He staffed the force almost exclusively with military veterans. Of the 225 men in the first Pennsylvania State Police force, 223 had had military experience. The top officers included men like Frank Hershey, who had served in the 9th US Infantry and the Marines from the Philippines to China to Panama; Timothy Kelleher, who had fought in the Boer army in the Transvaal War before joining the US Cavalry and serving in the Philippines; Joseph L. Reese, who served in the Spanish-American War and the Philippines; George Lumb, who served in China and the Philippines; and Jesse Garwood, who served in the

Philippine Constabulary "with a record of having acted gallantly in a number of engagements with the insurgents upon the Island of Luzon," according to the press.[128] State policemen thus wielded skills befitting colonial constabularies. As newspapers reported: "Every man [knows] how to make a camp for the night, to cross streams where there are no bridges, to tap telephone and telegraph wires and to do many unusual things that do not come within the understanding of city police officers." They had "the kind of horsemanship that is demanded in the United States Cavalry."[129] The mainstream press was laudatory, praising the fact that most of the troopers were "soldiers with brilliant records" and predicting that "it is only a question of time when a force like this, the first of its kind in the United States, will attain fame as world wide as that of the Canadian police or the constabulary of the Cape Colony."[130]

The Pennsylvania State Police resembled colonial constabularies in function as well as in form and content. It was essentially a colonial counterinsurgency force developed in response to rural workers' agitation, particularly the workers in the coal mines and their environs. The first four divisions were placed squarely in the four most important mining districts known for "disorder," in the words of Groome. The New York Times called the new force "special troopers for riots."[131] Another newspaper was awed by the force's mobility: "The presence of the coal mines in Pennsylvania, where large numbers of men are employed, and frequent outbursts occasioned by strikes and other labor troubles, first suggested the need of a body of state police that could be readily mobilized, and moved to any point where trouble threatened."[132] Workers' periodicals unsurprisingly complained that the Pennsylvania State Police not only looked but also behaved like the Royal Irish Constabulary, operating on a "strictly military basis."[133]

## Imperial Importers

What historians have called the "modernization," "professionalization," or "re-form" era of policing actually refers to a militarization that was an effect of the imperial boomerang.[134] Still, we might wonder: why did the boomerang return? Why did police officials and reformers import military-colonial models to re-form policing? Part of the answer lies in the background of those officials and reformers. Many were military veterans.[135] Existing data suggests that while military veterans did not predominate in the rank and file, veterans did serve as police chiefs (or "superintendents," "heads," or "directors").[136] Of all police chiefs in the largest 112 US cities from 1890 to 1915, close to 40 percent were veterans.[137]

New York City is one example among many. New York had a long string of police chiefs with experience in America's imperial-military regime. In 1898, John McCullagh, who had been police chief in the city, was dispatched to Havana to help reorganize the Cuban police force under American occupation.[138] Major General Francis V. Greene was his commanding officer in Cuba. Greene had also served in the Philippines. Greene then became New York's police commissioner in 1903.[139] In 1906, Rhinelander Waldo became deputy commissioner of the New York City Police, and in 1911 he rose to commissioner. Waldo had served in the army in the Philippines, commanding the Philippine Scouts (a counterinsurgency Filipino infantry integrated into the US Army) while "putting down the Philippine insurrection" (as his fellow police head Richard Sylvester boasted of him).[140]

Veterans served as police department heads or chiefs in smaller cities too. The chief of police of Allentown, Pennsylvania, from 1902 to 1905 was Harry H. Eastman, a veteran of the Spanish-American War. In Indianapolis, the chief was George V. Coffin, who, like Vollmer, had served in the army in the Philippines. Coffin also served during the Boxer Rebellion in China. In Yonkers, New York, Daniel Wolff became police chief in 1908. He had served as a captain in the army during the Spanish-American War. In some of these cases, Progressive reformers and political officials expressly sought out veterans to lead their departments. When reformers in Evansville, Indiana, called for a new police chief, they sought out a "military man" who "could obtain better discipline in the department than anyone else."[141] When John F. O'Connor became chief of the Columbus Police Department in Ohio, the local community praised him for his prior military experience: "In the far West, on the great wide plains, on the frontier of civilization, the present Chief of Police had the training that has been of great practical value to him in his present position." That training presumably taught him the "value of discipline," which "expects the same of subordinates."[142] Meanwhile, in Milwaukee, Wisconsin, municipal officials not only hoped to appoint a veteran of the army for the position of police chief but stated that they preferred someone who had served under one of the two leading military officials from the imperial campaigns of 1898: Colonial Theodore Roosevelt and General John J. Pershing.[143]

Not all of these veteran police chiefs were as innovative as Vollmer, but many nonetheless drew upon their imperial-military experience to militarize their forces. Consider Savannah. As seen in the previous chapter, the police force there had been created prior to the Civil War. After the war, it was reconstructed under the aegis of northern occupation. Throughout, it retained its militarized character, drawing upon influences from the North, England, and militia-slave patrols. Like other police departments, it was soon plagued by corruption and inefficiencies. Even the mayor's office and other residents complained about the lack of "discipline" of the police force.[144]

In 1907, William G. Austin took over as superintendent (aka chief) of police in Savannah with the aim of fixing things. Austin had served in the 7th Cavalry

Regiment of the Arm and fought in the Battle of Wounded Knee in 1890, for which he was awarded the Medal of Honor. He later commanded Company A of the Savannah Volunteer Guards, which was mobilized during the Spanish-American War. Upon taking up his new post as police chief (or superintendent, as he was called at the time), he lamented the "deterioration" and "inefficiency" of the existing police force, explaining that he was determined to "take the police force out of politics."[145] He wanted to "insure effective discipline" and put the department "on a military basis."[146] He subsequently restructured the promotion and pay structure according to that which "prevails in the United States army."[147]

Austin adopted some of the lessons from America's counterinsurgency operations. He reorganized the existing mounted patrols to create a new mounted force. While the previous mounted police unit in Savannah had been modeled upon militia-slave patrols and were used primarily for beat patrol, Austin's new mounted force carried the influence of the army's recent counterinsurgency mounted units deployed overseas. Consisting of a "body of well drilled men," it was meant to survey the "outlying areas of the city" in particular and, "in case of an emergency . . . be quickly assembled and moved rapidly from point to point."[148] Ultimately, he explained, the new force would not only reduce crime but also manage "disorder."[149]

Another example is the Philadelphia police under Superintendent James T. Robinson. Robinson had served with the Third Regiment of the Pennsylvania Volunteer Infantry during the Spanish-American and Philippine-American Wars. After the war he remained in the army as a captain, and his regiment trained, drilled, paraded, and engaged in sham battles at Camp Gregg and Camp Hastings in Pennsylvania alongside other veterans from the Philippine, Cuban, and Puerto Rican campaigns. He won prizes for his marksmanship.[150] In one of those practice battles he and his fellow soldiers—armed with Krags, as in the Philippines—engaged the troops of Major John C. Groome (who, as noted above, had served in Puerto Rico and helped militarize Pennsylvania's first state police).[151]

In 1912, Robinson was brought in to serve the police force under the aegis of a Progressive reformist movement led by the new mayor, Rudolph Blankenburg. Blankenburg was among the first to try to rid the force and the entire city government of its putative corruption.[152] Progressive reformism and militarism soon converged. Robinson, with his remit to reform the police, swiftly applied his military experience and training to the unruly police force. He began his tenure by instituting military drills, instructing his policemen in the "school of the squadron" taken from his army experience and the 1891 Leavenworth manuals. Robinson even created a new manual for patrolmen that closely resembled the recently issued army manuals for soldiers.[153] Robinson also helped create a police academy, developed a new signal system for rapid communication between beat patrols and headquarters, and adopted the three-platoon system for patrolmen. He expanded the police's mounted force, nearly doubling the percentage of the force that was mounted. "Military methods have been adopted and military discipline enforced," he boasted in his annual report. The militarized measures, he explained, had "raised the efficiency of the police to a point second to no city . . . No city can show a police force of more military appearance or higher efficiency, or better uniformed men than the force of this City."[154]

We could multiply examples of these imperial importers. As noted earlier, the first superintendent of the Pennsylvania State Police was the veteran John Groome. In helping create the new state police, he was inspired by colonial models. Upon being chosen to help breathe life into it, Groome studied the Texas Rangers and the Canadian Mounties, and he traveled to Europe to study police organizations there.[155] He was particularly enamored of the Royal Irish Constabulary. He stayed in the barracks with the RIC to "get their ideas and their rules and regulations," as he later explained to a legislative committee.[156] Similarly, after becoming commissioner of the New York Metropolitan Police in 1911, the veteran Rhinelander Waldo adopted the three-platoon system for his men, created a motorcycle squad and anti-vice squads, and insisted that they receive a pension, giving policemen the same consideration from the municipal government as "the soldier is entitled to from the federal government."[157] In Yonkers, Spanish-American War veteran Daniel Wolff became head of police in 1908 and subsequently "put the department on a military basis."[158]

In Philadelphia, Smedley Butler took over as police chief in 1924, by which time the Philadelphia police had been renamed the Department of Public Safety. Butler was named director. A veteran of the Spanish-American and Philippine-American Wars, Butler had also served in American-occupied Puerto Rico, Nicaragua, and Haiti. In Haiti, he helped establish and lead the Haitian police force, the Gendarmerie de Haiti, which acquired a reputation for its brutality.[159] Butler had also been part of the American occupying force in Veracruz, Mexico. Back in Philadelphia, Butler instituted more militarized forms and tactics, adding yet another layer to the already existing militaristic formation. He created a new unit called the "gunnery squad" and armed it with revolvers, sawed-off shotguns, and rifles. He put new armored cars with spinning rear seats "like an artillery limber" on the streets and mapped out a string of checkpoints around the city to capture fleeing "bandits," modeling the system upon the Marine outposts with which he was so familiar from Haiti.[160] Butler's methods earned criticism from some civilians who saw them as *too* militaristic. "Military tactics which might do in Mexico and other places," wrote one critic to the United States Secretary of the Navy, "has no place in the administration of civil affairs."[161] But his methods were evidently effective for their purpose. In one series of missions lasting only forty-eight hours, his forces conducted as many as seven hundred raids and arrested 1,045 persons.[162]

In short, veterans of the imperial-military regime played an important role in spreading the colonial boomerang. This is similar to how the militarization of policing happened in earlier years (as discussed in earlier chapters). But veterans were not the only reason police departments brought the boomerang home to militarize. There were more police chiefs who were *not* military veterans than there were veterans, and yet even in those cases police chiefs militarized their forces.

This is the story of Richard Sylvester, the superintendent of the Metropolitan Police of Washington, DC, Sylvester ran the police from 1898 to 1915 and later became president of the IACP. He was not a military veteran. He had been a journalist and disbursing officer of the Ute Indian Commission. Nonetheless, he aggressively militarized the Washington, DC, police. He instituted military drills, created a police academy (called the School of Instruction), and advocated the use of the .38-caliber pistol on the grounds that the army used it.[163] He also expanded the city's bicycle patrol and appointed a veteran to lead the new patrol: Lieutenant G.H. Williams, who had fought the Apache Indians under Geronimo in New Mexico.[164] As president of the IACP, Sylvester also promoted the adoption of "uniform insignia of rank for the officers commanding police organizations in the United States. as well as subordinate members of forces," as he told his fellow officers. This, he insisted, would be in "keeping with propriety for a citizen soldiery."[165] He was later known by historians as the man who turned the Washington, DC police into a "paramilitary" force. And, advocating harsh interrogation of subjects, Sylvester is credited with inventing the term "the third degree."[166]

The case of Sylvester suggests that police militarization during the reform era was not the sole product of military veterans. Something else was going on.[167]

## The New Migration and Racialized Menace

What other factors explain the return of the boomerang? One possible factor was the need to subdue the industrial working class. As noted, the formation of the Pennsylvania State Police in 1905 was a response to the threat of worker agitation.[168] Relatedly, the rise of anarchists, socialists, the Industrial Workers of the World (Wobblies), and the American Federation of Labor frightened authorities, who strengthened the police in order to repress those groups. It is not surprising that police violently put down strikes and used so-called vagrancy acts to arrest labor organizers and union members. And in the 1920s, police departments began stocking early forms of what later became known as tear gas, a weapon used by the European armies during the First World War and then later in Britain's colonies. This was driven exactly by the fear of worker revolt.[169] Furthermore, in the 1930s, police created specialized units called "Red Squads" as key modalities for repressing worker militancy.[170]

Still, the boomerang was brought back not only because of the menace of industrial workers. Police officials such as Vollmer in Berkeley, Austin in Savannah, and Sylvester in Washington, DC, had different groups on their minds when they militarized their departments. If they were concerned about white workers, they were just as concerned with racialized minorities, if not more so. Here is the missing key for unlocking why police militarization through imperial feedback happened in this period: *the racialization of crime and disorder.*

Racialization had played a key role in the founding of police departments decades earlier (as seen in Chapter 2). But the turn of the twentieth century brought new bouts of racialized discourses, a veritable explosion of claims about biological differences among people. American empire was the platform for many of these new racial discourses. As scholars, scientists, and officials scrambled to make sense of the seemingly infinite racial heterogeneity of the inhabitants of Puerto Rico, the Philippine archipelago, Samoa, Guam, Hawaii, and everywhere in between that American empire touched, they relied upon emergent forms of scientific racism, including social evolution and eugenics. These forms helped colonial officials and administrators determine what imperial and colonial policies would best suit the "natives."[171] Despite differences within this sprawling new discourse that took pains to differentiate the true essence of the "Tagalogs" from the "Moros" or "Negroes" of Puerto Rico, overriding it all was a process of alterization by which Filipinos, Puerto Ricans, and other overseas groups were seen as racially inferior, undeveloped, ignorant, unfit for self-rule, morally corrupt, and prone to all kinds of evils due to their biology and blood.[172] It was exactly this classification that justified American empire. The colonized's inferiority required America's "strong and guiding hand" in the form of colonial control.[173] And when the natives became recalcitrant and violent, they required coercive intervention by America's counterinsurgency regime. A popular mantra at the time about the war against the rebellious Filipinos was that American soldiers would "civilize them with a Krag" (a reference to the army's new gun).[174] The assumption was that colonized peoples could only understand the language of violence. From Puerto Rico, General George Davis reported in 1899 that the inhabitants of the colony had not learned "the ordinary requirements of organized society." "Obedience to law" was "incomprehensible" to the natives; they did not understand the law "without display or constant exercise of force." The creation of the Insular Police and the local municipal police forces in Puerto Rico followed these claims.[175]

Such racism also applied to populations in the imperial metropole, prompted by a new wave of immigration and internal migration. More than nine million immigrants arrived between 1900 and 1910. Most ended up in America's booming cities.[176] While this wave of immigration continued earlier patterns of migration from Europe, it was nonetheless a colossal development. In the West, while anti-Asian sentiment had already led to the Chinese Exclusion Act in 1882, illegal Chinese immigration continued, leading to the use of Angel Island outside San Francisco as a detention center wherein 70 percent of the detained immigrants were Chinese. There was also internal migration to bustling cities. In Berkeley and Oakland, the Chinese population more than quadrupled from 1900 to 1910.[177] Meanwhile, Japanese immigration continued unabated: in California, the number of Japanese quadrupled between 1900 and 1910 (from 10,151 to 41,356). By the 1920s, Filipinos were increasingly brought to California to work in the agricultural sector, culminating in horrific race riots and violence led by disgruntled white men jealous of the immigrants' flirtations with white women.[178] In Los Angeles, the Mexican population swelled by 1,000 percent between 1900 and 1920 to number around fifty thousand (a rate of growth double that of the population as a whole).[179]

The respatialization of production in this period also compelled African Americans to move. The so-called Great Migration northward was not yet in full swing in the first years of the twentieth century, but there was significant movement nonetheless. From 1880 to 1910, New York City's Black population grew threefold, to 90,000; over half came from the South.[180] In Philadelphia, the Black population grew from 3.7 percent of the total population in 1860 to 4.8 percent by 1900.[181] In the South, migration from the rural areas to cities heightened. In Savannah, Georgia, the growth rate of the Black population in 1880 was 9 percent, but by 1890 it was 41 percent. By 1900 it fell back down to 26 percent, but through 1920 it was never under 20 percent. In many other cities of the South, the Black population grew at faster rates than the total white population.[182]

This new movement of people had important correlates. Not least was the further "whitening" of some immigrant groups. By this time, the Irish had already started to overcome prior stigmas to become more "white."[183] This was related to their increasing assimilation into the workers' movement and mainstream society. The Irish had even been incorporated into northern police forces. In New York City, the Irish became an important basis of patronage for political bosses. Irish and European immigrants made up the majority of police officers across northern cities.[184] This whitening happened at the expense of other groups who became "darkened," increasingly stigmatized and criminalized. In the industrial cities of the North, political leaders, "Anglo-Saxon" middle and upper classes, supposed crime experts, and government officials became faithful adherents to the same sort of scientific racism that justified imperialism overseas while proclaiming "the assimilability of the Irish . . . by explicit contrast to the Negro" (as the historian Khalil Muhammad has shown).[185] With the publication of the 1890 census, they seized upon prison statistics suggesting that "Negroes" were inherently prone to crime. Along with northern authorities and the public from Philadelphia to New York, self-described "scientists" denounced Black migrants as a "distinct and dangerous criminal population"—the "cause, not the victims, of the social ills plaguing the city."[186] Meanwhile, in the South, the elite class continued to link Blackness and crime but added new accents. Black Americans, they claimed, were racially unfit for city life, and uprooting them from their rural habitats would exacerbate their unruly proclivities and criminal tendencies. Increased migration to cities thus resuscitated long-standing racialized fears of urban Blackness that had prompted the formation of southern police departments in the first place.[187]

Asians constituted comparably smaller proportions of the population, but they too were racialized as a threat to law and order. Officials and white publics in western cities feared that the Japanese and Chinese—or "Orientals," as they were called—were not just job stealers but criminals as well. Matching the discourse in the East and South about the presumed criminal tendencies of Black Americans, the popular press and experts propagated new folk theories of "Oriental" criminality.[188] Urban elites in California were especially appalled if not panicked by Chinese urban dwellers whom they blamed for running "vice dens" and "opium dens" where drugs, prostitution, and gambling ran rampant and white women were drawn into "white slavery." One doctor in San Francisco reported on "the sickening sight of young white girls from sixteen to twenty years of age lying half-undressed on the floor or couches smoking with their 'lovers.'" He wrote with detectable disgust of how "men and women, Chinese and white people, mix indiscriminately in Chinatown smoking houses."[189] Starting in 1905, these same periodicals carried similar horror stories of opium dens in the Philippines, where colonial authorities passed new legislation prohibiting opium use.[190]

Police themselves joined the racializing chorus. They had long espoused racist constructs of crime and disorder, but in the early twentieth century police officials proclaimed that there were new racialized threats. Some policemen were proven to be members of the Ku Klux Klan (KKK); in California, about 10 percent of police in almost every city were members of the KKK in the 1920s and 1930s.[191] Regardless, many police officials often spoke of immigrants and racial minorities in the same evolutionary language that marked colonial discourse, blaming perceived rising crime rates on everyone from the "Orientals" to Black Americans to dark Italians. Chief W.J. Petersen of Oakland, California, at the 1913 annual meeting of the IACP, decried: "We have thousands of Greeks, Italians, Chinese, Japanese, Jews, many of them of the lower order of humanity." He complained about the rise in crime in California's cities, particularly "sexual crimes," and blamed it on the "floating population" of "Italians, Chinese and many other foreigners."[192]

Police officials across the country espoused the same ideas. Chief William Gunn of Hartford told his fellow police chiefs at the 1908 IACP meetings that, just as "immigration is another cause of crime," the "negro factor is one of the most important and serious to be dealt with."[193] The chief of police of Louisville complained in 1899 about the pressing issues faced by his police department, and he pinpointed the rising "negro factor" due to migration from the country-side. "Louisville police have a great deal of trouble with negroes, having a negro population of over 50,000 . . . and where you find a dozen law abiding negroes, there are a hundred as vicious rascals as police ever had to contend with." He added how difficult it was to manage racially diverse cities: "The larger the city and the more varied her population, the harder it is to police."[194] According to Fosdick, it was exactly these sorts of new racial threats that differentiated police problems in the United States from those in Europe. The police in the United States was unique in having to confront "Negroes" and other "unassimilated or poorly assimilated races" who had "criminal propensities," poised to foment urban "disorder."[195]

The racialization of America's new overseas imperial subjects was thus matched at home by the racialization of crime and disorder. Analogies were made. Parallels were constructed. The Chinese were seen as a threat to morality in San Francisco, just as "Orientals" were seen as a threat overseas, just as the growing presence of African Americans in northern and southern cities was constructed as a threat. Unsurprisingly, a popular term used by soldiers to refer to Filipinos during the Philippine-American War was "n——r."[196] Overseas colonialism and migration within the United States constituted a transnational and transcolonial field of racialized discourse that constructed all racialized populations as not only inferior but also inherently violent, disorderly, and criminal—a threat to both the white order in America's cities and the white order of global domination.

## The Boomerang Returns, from City to Country

Warranted by this racial analogization, the imperial boomerang was brought home. Reformers, city officials, and the police saw policing as the primary modality for managing the new racialized threat to law and order.[197] To the white establishment in cities and towns across the country, the new migrants became intimate enemies whose bodies had to be controlled, contained, and coerced if necessary. "One of the problems in connection with government on these shores," said John B. Jenkins, chairman of the Norfolk Civil Service Commission of Virginia, at the 1907 IACP convention, "has been that of municipal control. How to control the lawless elements that are attracted to the centers of wealth and population has opened a problem. One of the most efficient and effective ways in which peace and security is guaranteed is by the efficient, brave, and loyal police forces all over this country." He continued:

> Not very long ago in the City of New York I remarked to one of their citizens gracious me, I wonder as I walk through these streets and see this population that you have, how in the world do you get along? Yes, he said, we have a great many foreign people. We have more Germans than any city in the world except Berlin; more Italians than any city in the world except Rome and Milan; more Jews than there are in Palestine. I said, How in the world do you keep order, peace, and public security amidst all this mixed population? He said, The New Yorker relies on one thing . . . We have an army of men in our city who are sworn to do their duty in any event in keeping peace and order, and as lawless as New York has been, and the riots that have been started, our police always rise to the emergency and we feel perfectly secure as long as we have an army of bluecoats to cope with any mob that refuses to listen to its leader.[198]

But if the police were to help manage the continued racialized threat, they required reform to better meet the task. And as the new racialized threats were analogous to those of the periphery, policing could best be reformed by turning to the imperial-military regime for templates and tactics. This was the view of Chief M.J. Donahue of Des Moines, Iowa. At the IACP convention he noted that the urban admixture of races due to migration and immigration was what differentiated the United States from Europe and thereby made policing a distinct problem. The problems of policing in the United States, he said, "are much greater than in Europe, with especial reference to crime, for the reason that *our worst criminals are seldom local but come from every nation on earth* and may move freely from State to State without . . . hinderance [*sic*]." How, then, to deal with this problem? "Modern Bertillon methods, finger print systems, arranging of shifts for efficient work, the proper handling of mobs during strikes and riots, the keeping of our force in close touch with other police departments and the latest and best methods of suppressing crime and apprehending criminals." To address "the problem of the police in the United States," new methods were needed.[199]

Others had the same idea. In Cincinnati, Chief Phil Deitsch instituted military drills and formations for his police force partly because "every means in our power must be used to suppress the criminal class of our country, and every police department should use its utmost endeavor to accomplish this."[200] He added that "the criminal element of this country must be run down" and that a "well disciplined police department" with "well drilled police officers" can help realize the task.[201] In 1903, soon after the Philippine-American War officially ended, Chief Benjamin Murphy of Jersey City urged his fellow police chiefs to drill their forces "in the school of the soldier" and the "school of the company and battalion so that when it becomes necessary to assemble large bodies of police the commanding officers can manuever them so as to be able to control orderly or riotous crowds effectively."[202] Murphy also promoted the idea of a national database of criminals that local police departments could use. The database would use new methods of identification like fingerprinting and modus operandi, thereby making it akin to the data collected by the army's Division of Military Information in the Philippines, which collected personal data on Filipino insurgents. He urged his colleagues to do this because "no army is successful is in war unless well armed and equipped to meet the enemy. No police force is efficient unless thoroughly fitted with all that is required to meet and defeat the enemies of society, the criminal classes. The most efficient ammunition that can be used is . . . knowledge."[203]

We can see these logics of analogization and the boomerang effect more clearly by taking a closer look at Vollmer's early career. Prior to his election as chief, the Berkeley community had been lamenting the influx of Chinese from other parts of the state and complained about "the ruinous effect the presence of the Chinese has upon the vicinity."[204] This was part of a bigger chorus. As noted earlier, Progressive reformers in the region feared that the new "Oriental" migrants were creating a culture where, "crooks, gamblers [and] opium addicts" reigned.[205] It was in this context that Vollmer was urged by his friends in city hall to take the job upon returning from the Philippines. Reminding him of the trouble posed by the Asian invasion, they told him: "It will be a fighting job for whoever takes it. That's why we want you, Gus. You were a pretty good fighting man when you went up against those gugus over in the islands" ("gugus" was the American soldiers' racist name for Filipinos during the Philippine-American War).[206] Notably, soon after his appointment, the *Oakland Post-Enquirer* described Vollmer's "resourcefulness and courage," which "had been proved in the Philippines," where he had been "fighting the insurgents in the island jungles" and chased an "army of concealed enemies up and down dark tropical rivers."[207] Because the white community at home faced racialized threats akin to racialized threats overseas from colonial subjects, it turned to someone who had already put down the latter: August Vollmer.

It is therefore fitting that after Vollmer took office and began militarizing the Berkeley police, he mounted an attack on the perceived Oriental threat. Data on arrests in Berkeley by race are not available, but we do know that one of Vollmer's first major campaigns as police chief was to lead his force on raids of "Chinese gambling and opium dens" in Berkeley.[208] Those dens were guarded by "yellow hatchet men," according to one newspaper account, leading Vollmer to easily equate them and "the little brown men with curved knives and spitting rifles in the swamps along the Pasig river" that Vollmer had encountered in the Philippines.[209] The press referred to it as Vollmer's "crusade against Chinese lottery games," with one headline reading: "Marshal Vollmer Descends Upon Chinese Horde."[210] Vollmer thus matched his targets with his tactics, using his military experience with the "gugus" abroad to police the "gugus" in his city. After these efforts, the Berkeley Central Improvement Club praised Vollmer for his "recent raids upon opium dens and gambling houses in this vicinity."[211] Newspapers from neighboring Oakland claimed that Vollmer's campaign should serve as a model for other police departments facing the "reign of crooks."[212]

Vollmer's campaign against the Chinese dens fit his racialized understandings of criminality. Later in his career, Vollmer would emphasize the rehabilitative aspects of policing, insinuating that criminals could be disciplined into civility. But he meant this primarily for whites who had gone astray rather than racialized minorities. To be sure, Vollmer bought into the eugenicist thinking of the time, which saw race, hereditary, and criminality as tightly threaded together. His police academy offered courses to police officers on different "racial types" and the links between "heredity" and "race degeneration."[213] He had his officers in the Berkeley Police Department create criminal identification cards for fingerprints sorted by racial type. White cards were for "Caucasians," yellow cards "for Mongols, light chocolate for Negros, and light salmon for the red races," as he later explained.[214] Vollmer even fashioned himself a race expert. He corresponded closely with police officials in Cuba, including Israel Castellanos, director of Cuba's National Bureau for Identification. Beginning in 1913, Castellanos had led the way in fingerprinting prisoners in Cuba to compare fingerprints in an attempt to locate biological differences among "whites," "negroes born in Cuba," and Haitians and Jamaicans.[215] Vollmer was taken by this research and conducted his own, concluding among other things that the "Oriental fingerprint pattern" was different from that of "Caucasians."[216] By the 1920s, Vollmer had joined the American Eugenics Society.[217]

Vollmer was not unique. While not all chiefs were chosen because of their imperial experience, many militarized their forces to strengthen presumably weak police in the face of new racialized threats. Let us return to Savannah. As seen in the previous chapter, the Savannah police had been created in response to a perceived threat to law and order from the Irish and Black subproletariat. By the early twentieth century, the Irish threat had subsided. But the city's Black population rose by close to 20 percent each year from 1900 to 1910 to constitute almost 50 percent of the total population of Savannah.[218] Chief Austin took office in 1907 and complained immediately about the "lawless element" in the outlying, largely Black districts of town—the very districts that had grown due to the new migration.[219] After adding new layers of militarized power to the police force, Austin deployed his newly strengthened force accordingly. He directed his reorganized mounted force to "keep down disorder" in the Black areas and ordered his police force to arrest vagrants, primarily targeting African Americans.[220] Notably, before Austin's tenure, African Americans had made up 60 percent of total arrests. However, after Austin took up his post, that rate increased to 77 percent, far disproportionate to their share of the population.[221] African American churches in 1916 complained to newspapers about the "whole scale arrests of negroes because they are negroes—arrests that would not be made if they were white under similar circumstances."[222] Sympathetic city officials agreed, decrying the "police repression" of African Americans in the city.[223]

A similar logic of racialized militarization and policing unfolded in Philadelphia, but with added complexities. Of all the cities in the Northeast, Philadelphia had the largest African American population, with the percentage of nonwhites nearly doubling from 1890 to 1910. Political officials readily equated the city's rising Black population with crime and disorder.[224] In response, Chief Robinson did as Vollmer in Berkeley and Austin in Savannah had done: he drew upon his imperial experience to militarize his force and deploy it against the ostensible threat to the city. Robinson initiated an almost religious mission to attack perceived moral decline, spurred on by the mayor and religious Progressive-era reformers. He set his sights on quelling prostitution and other "vices" in the working-class districts of the city such as the Tenderloin, where "Orientals" owned vice dens and where Black and other populations mixed and mingled. Robinson's campaign led to the closure of hundreds of "bawdy houses" within the first years of his tenure and high arrest rates that Robinson boasted were the product of his militarized methods.[225] The total number of arrests in the city went from 87,557 in 1911, before Robinson's administration, to 103,673 in 1913 and 100,629 in 1914, after Robinson instituted his militarized measures.[226]

Moralism and militarism in Philadelphia thus went hand in hand. Together they marched to the beat of white supremacy. Robinson's anti-vice campaigns had an unmistakable racialized character. Policing "vices" implied controlling Black residents because they were seen to be corruptors of white virtue and were assumed to play a "supporting role" in the degeneracy of white morality.[227] Furthermore, the racial admixture in dens of sin presumably led to "instances where whites became victims of black lusts." This was a clear instance where gendered policing was articulated with racial and moral militarism: police patrolled the color line to protect white girls and Black men from crossing it.[228] Hence, when Robinson's newly militarized force directed their attention to Black men or Black districts, they often did so brutally, eliciting righteous complaints from Black residents.[229] In his 1899 book *The Philadelphia Negro*, W. E. B. Du Bois described his neighborhood in the Seventh Ward as a place where the "police were our government." And when Black Americans ventured too far out of their neighborhoods, they were swiftly monitored and typically arrested. In 1911, before Robinson's administration, Black arrests made up 10.7 percent of all arrests, but after Robinson was named to his post that percentage slowly rose, reaching 12.5 percent in 1916 and 14.6 percent in 1917 and 1918. By the 1920s, a rare survey of "crime among Negros in Philadelphia" reported that the police considered Black residents "easy prey" for illegal arrests. It likely did not help that the Philadelphia police consisted of large numbers of Irishmen, who in the nineteenth century might have been the targets of police themselves but by this point had become notoriously antagonistic toward the Black population.[230]

The dark underside of the so-called professionalization-reform movement is here revealed. Not only was the movement a form of militarization through imperial feedback, but it was also partly a racial project. Militarized innovations were adopted to strengthen presumably weak police in the face of perceived racialized threats. This helps explain why police chiefs without military experience ended up militarizing their police forces just as veterans did.

The case of Richard Sylvester in Washington, DC, is suggestive here. In the early years of the twentieth century, the District of Columbia had the largest population of African Americans in the nation (attracted to the city's federal jobs) and a swelling population of Chinese. In 1910, close to 27 percent of DC residents were nonwhite, a higher percentage than in Philadelphia and New York. City officials noticed this trend as they fretted over an apparent uptick in crime rates and potential social upheaval.[231] Sylvester attributed rising crime to racial minorities, reporting statistics purporting to show that Blacks committed crimes at higher rates than whites.[232] After militarizing his force, Sylvester launched what newspapers called "an active warfare on crime."[233] His main targets were racialized minorities. Sylvester mobilized his force to raid Chinese gambling dens and African American pool halls and drinking establishments.[234] "All of the 'speak-easies' in Washington are not colored," decried an editorial in a Black newspaper, but "all those that suffer from raids happen to be colored."[235]

The formation of rural state police forces also followed a racialized logic. The only difference was the racialized group that constituted the perceived threat. As noted above, the formation of the Pennsylvania State Police was a response to labor troubles in the rural mining districts of the state. Yet the recalcitrant workers were neither fully white nor fully nonwhite; they were recent immigrants from Eastern Europe and Ireland. This marked an instance in the early twentieth century where the threat thought to be posed by Irish and European workers had not fully dissipated. The earlier racialization had given way to ethnoracialization that was nonetheless as derisive as its predecessor. Observers noted that most of "the mine laborers came from Ireland"; others were "Slavs and Italians." They saw the Irish miners as particularly dangerous, having sprung from "that unspeakable society of murderers, the 'Molly Maguires.'" But they also saw *all* the immigrant miners as a threat. They had not yet learned to heel to "authority and law." "Liberty . . . they knew not how to use, money that they knew neither how to spend nor save," instead exercising "license, greed, drunkenness, and through drunkenness all brutalities let loose." It is not coincidental that the motto of the all-American state troopers was "One American can lick a hundred foreigners."[236]

Pennsylvania governor Samuel Pennypacker in his 1903 inaugural address had alluded to immigrants when he announced the creation of the new state police force. "Conflicts between capital and . . . labor are of frequent occurrence" in Pennsylvania, he stated, and "occur more frequently here than elsewhere" because Pennsylvania's industries required "the employment of masses of men, many of them born in other lands, and some of them uneducated, unfamiliar with our language and indifferent to our institutions." He then suggested the creation of "a constabulary of sufficient force . . . to be used wherever needed in the State in the suppression of disorder."[237] John Groome, one of the first officers who helped design the force, likewise betrayed racialized motivations. Groome had found the Royal Irish Constabulary to be a particularly appealing model for the police because of equivalences he perceived between the unruly colonial subjects in Ireland and the recalcitrant Irish miners in Pennsylvania. He told a legislative committee that he had looked at various potential models for the state police, including the Texas Rangers and the Canadian Northwest Mounties. But the Royal Irish Constabulary, Groome insisted, was especially useful because "I came to the conclusion that the conditions in Ireland were more similar to those in Pennsylvania, so far as the industrial and agricultural conditions and the character of the population were concerned."[238] Like August Vollmer and other police officials at the time, Groome summoned back the imperial boomerang, detecting racialized equivalences between metropole and colony. Targets were matched with tactics to be used against them.

Colonial-military style bellicosity toward the immigrant mine workers followed. In one of its first major operations, in 1906, the Pennsylvania state troopers faced down hundreds of striking miners near Mt. Carmel. They "blazed . . . deadly fire into the crowd," which the press characterized as consisting of "mobs of riotous foreigners." They hit seventeen miners, killing four and leaving two more in critical condition.[239] Another 1906 mission was led by Sergeant Jesse Garwood, fresh from his stint in the Philippine Constabulary. He and his men descended upon a crowd of Italian workers at the local colliery near Wilkes-Barre. Reportedly, the "idle" Italian workers had been "amusing themselves with a little gun practice," aiming at the mine owners' property (and putatively at other workers). Garwood's men were called out, forcibly entering the miners' homes and seizing their guns. The press praised them later for thwarting "the homicidal tendencies of the Italians," claiming that "not a hint of trouble or a spark of rebellion has been observable in that colony since."[240]

The use of the word "colony" here is precise: workers' periodicals at the time complained that the Pennsylvania state troopers' violent treatment of immigrant miners duplicated the Royal Irish Constabulary's vicious suppression of Irish insurgents across the Atlantic. The Pennsylvania State Police, claimed *Bridgemen's Magazine*, "appears to assume in taking the field in connection with a strike that the strikers are its enemies and the enemies of the State, and that a campaign should be waged against them as such."[241]

\* \* \*

By 1927, the professionalization-reform movement that August Vollmer had helped spark had been in full swing for two decades or more. In that year, he gave an address in which he referred to that movement while registering caution. He decried that "methods are still in effect in some of our cities where [police officers] take a fellow and beat him within an inch of his life" to get him to "admit that he is guilty where he is not."[242] Vollmer saw this brutality as the exception that proved the rule. Colleagues such as Richard Sylvester thought similarly. According to Sylvester, acts of police brutality were "exceptions" to the usual "humane treatment" that police gave to prisoners. In most cases, officers follow the "principles of police" and "strive for a "higher standard . . . in order to better unfortunate humanity."[243] The American police, he insisted, were among the "leading civil defenders of the world."[244]

We can now see that these explanations of police brutality are misleading at best. By treating brutality as exceptional, they portray the professionalization-reform movement as a benign development that had little to do with racist militarized policing. But as seen in this chapter, the so-called reform era of policing was merely a domestic variant of America's imperial and colonial projects overseas. Police brutality was not the exception to the professionalization-reform movement but rather its logical underside.

Note, then, the torture method called the "water cure," which, as remarked earlier, was used by police in California, Kansas, Missouri, Mississippi, and Illinois (and these were only the known instances). It was typically meted out to African American detainees. What is important is that this form of torture was not an invention of the police; it was an imperial one. Purportedly, the water cure was used by US Marines and Butler's gendarmerie during the US occupation of Haiti.[245] Newspapers justified its use on the grounds that Haitians were like "Mexican irregulars and Apache Indians, governed by no code of decency," and so deserved it.[246] Even earlier than this, US forces used it in the Philippines, where it originated. There, the US Army had used the water cure to extract information from Filipino insurgents during the Philippine-American War. As one US soldier later described it:

> A man is thrown down on his back and three or four men sit or stand on his arms and legs and hold him down; and either a gun barrel or a rifle barrel or a carbine barrel or a stick as big as a belaying pin . . . is simply thrust into his jaws and his jaws are thrust back, and, if possible, a wooden log or stone is put under his head or neck, so he can be held more firmly. . . . He is simply held down and then water is poured onto his face down his throat and nose from a jar; and that is kept up until the man gives some sign or becomes unconscious. And, when he becomes unconscious, he is simply rolled aside and he is allowed to come to. . . . A man suffers tremendously, there is no doubt about it. His sufferings must be that of a man who is drowning, but cannot drown.[247]

The connection between the police use of the water cure in the United States and the army's earlier use of it in the Philippines was not lost on astute journalists. The "water cure" used in Jefferson City, Missouri, wrote one journalist, was "once practiced in the Philippines, in which luckless Moros were pinned to the ground and water poured down their throats with a hose."[248]

In short, the water cure torture was a colonial counterinsurgency tactic. It was used by the very same imperial-military forces that also used innovations like mapping to track insurgents, small mobile units to conduct search-and-destroy missions, and new training programs to create disciplined soldiers and informed officers. Imperial-military forces used the water cure alongside and in tandem with these methods, not in opposition to them. The police in the early twentieth-century United States did the same. Just as they borrowed practices and programs like mapping, mounted units, and military training from America's rising imperial-military regime to manage crime and disorder on America's streets, so did police borrow methods of brutal torture from the imperial-military regime to interrogate racialized suspects. The use of the water cure by police was not an aberration; it was just another effect of the colonial boomerang.

The police use of the water cure tells us something about what was really going on with the transformations in policing that historians have told us about. Rather than indexing benign processes of "modernization," "professionalization," or "reform," those transformations were forms of militarization brought about through imperial feedback triggered by racialized fear. Just as the US military was the arm of the colonial state overseas to enforce the racialized order of colonialism abroad, urban police departments across America were strengthened with the boomerang to become the coercive arm of governance within America's traditional domestic borders—"reformed" and "professionalized" to put down perceived racial threats within. Central Luzon, Santo Domingo, and San Juan, Jefferson City, Berkeley, Chicago, New York, and Los Angeles: these were not distinct or separate urban zones of militarized policing but nodal points in a larger imperial circuit of militarized power by which the global color line of empire was being drawn and defended. Violently.

# 4

# "Our Problems ... Are Not So Difficult"

## Militarization and Its Limits in Britain, 1850s–1930s

Splashed across the front page of the *Illustrated London News* on May 1, 1886, was the bold image of a stern middle-aged gentleman sporting a long, thick handlebar mustache. The man was Sir Charles Warren, KCMG. As the newspaper explained, Warren was a man of the empire, having "seen a great deal of service in various parts of the world."[1] He had joined the British Army's Royal Engineers in 1857 and then embarked upon surveying expeditions with the Palestine Exploration Fund in "the Holy Land, Syria and Arabia." He rose to the ranks of colonel and served as a special commissioner to settle the boundary line of the Orange Free State and Griqualand West. Later he commanded British forces to suppress the Kaffir outbreak in 1877–1888 and the Griqua rising in 1878–1879 before leading an expedition into Arabia Petraea during the Anglo-Egyptian War of 1882, for which he was later made a Knight Commander of the Order of St. Michael and St. George.

But Warren did not make the cover of the newspaper for his imperial service alone. Rather, Warren had just been appointed to take charge of the first and largest police department in all of Britain. The caption read: "Sir Charles Warren, K.C.M.G., the New Chief Commissioner of Metropolitan Police." Evidently, policing was big news.

Warren represents two trends during the period from the 1870s through the early 1900s. The first is Britain's imperial expansion. In the mid-nineteenth century, the empire had been relatively small, controlling small islands in the Caribbean along with Ireland. But from the 1870s onward, the British state launched new overseas campaigns that generated an unprecedented territorial expansion. As the empire shifted its attention away from the transatlantic slave economy, its attention likewise drifted away from the Americas and toward the East, conquering new territories at an unparalleled scope and pace to eventually become the largest empire in the world. By the early twentieth century, Britain ruled imperial territory 125 times its own size, covering almost a fourth of the livable surface of the planet and exerting sovereignty over four hundred million colonial subjects.[2] The British military in which Warren had served had been a vital organization for creating and maintaining this expanded empire.

*Policing Empires*. Julian Go, Oxford University Press. © Oxford University Press 2024.
DOI: 10.1093/oso/9780197621653.003.0005

The second trend represented by Warren is the growth of the British police and its continued reliance upon veterans of the imperial-military regime. Starting in the mid-nineteenth century, county constabularies and borough police forces were created and expanded, while the urban police departments that had been founded earlier grew in number and strength. The number of police in London grew from 3,000 to 15,000 from 1831 to 1892. The ranks of the Manchester police swelled from 328 in 1841 to 989 in 1901. During the same period, Liverpool's force expanded from 615 to 1,802.[3] To lead these departments, new men were needed. Many of the highest police officials of the police forces were like Warren: they came from Britain's imperial-military regime.[4] Of the ten largest city forces between 1905 and 1935, close to 80 percent of chief constables were either military veterans or former colonial police officers.[5] In London, before Warren and after him until 1945, every commissioner had military or colonial experience; other high officers in the Met had similar backgrounds.[6] As one MP put it during a parliamentary debate in 1928, the police were "from the Army; they have been drawn from the Royal Irish Constabulary; and they have been drawn from the Indian Police or administrative services and, perhaps, here and there, from Rhodesia, Nyasaland, or places of that kind.'"[7]

These entanglements of empire and policing in Britain's mid- to late Victorian era invite us to wonder about their effects on militarized policing. We have seen in previous chapters how Britain's early imperial experiences launched a process of imperial feedback and police militarization: veterans of empire served in colonial theaters abroad and brought home the lessons they had learned overseas. We might therefore predict that Warren and other veterans of Britain's imperial-military regime likewise drew upon their imperial experiences to inaugurate a renewed round of police militarization in this era. The British Empire was the largest in the world. How could that *not* impact policing at home?

On the other hand, the existing historiography of British policing suggests that the opposite happened. According to extant histories, police forces grew in personnel during this era but did not change much in forms, functionalities, or practices. Furthermore, existing scholarship suggests that the English public would have resisted any attempts to bring back the tools and tactics of despotic colonialism abroad.[8] The working classes continued to fear that the London Metropolitan Police was too militarized. Meanwhile, the English middle and upper classes remained jealous of their liberties, never faltering in their fretting over how the state, including the police, might upend them. Their determination to fight against state intrusion, coupled with their liberal values, would have likely militated against any further militarization of policing. According to the historian Bernard Porter, even the threat of serious foreign subversion in this period did not compel the English public to call for increased state power. In the face of foreign danger, English residents were nonchalant. While anticolonial rebels in India or elsewhere in the empire were being violently crushed by Britain's imperial-military regime, "at home Britain's way with subversion was to try to kill it with kindness."[9] English devotion to liberal values was presumably too strong to permit much else.

The question remains: was British policing further militarized through imperial feedback in the late nineteenth and early twentieth centuries? For an answer, we can begin our investigation with London. It was the capital of the empire and the country's largest city. All of London's police commissioners through the mid- to late Victorian era had colonial-military backgrounds, and crime and sociopolitical turbulence persisted. If militarization through imperial feedback was going to happen at all in Britain, it would have most likely happened there. Still, as we will see in this chapter, the story of the militarization of London's police in this period is a multifaceted one. While Britain's expanded empire had made new coercive tools, tactics, and technologies available for use at home, this availability did not lead directly to importation. Instead, specific configurations of local forces affected *when* and *what* veterans of empire brought back home for policing, as well as the *depth* and *limits* of imperial militarization. From the late nineteenth century through the early twentieth, there was a colonial boomerang effect indeed, adding yet more layers of militarized power to the already militarized civil police of Britain. But its effects and extent were modulated by peculiar logics of racialization in the imperial metropolis.

## Britain's New Imperial-Military Regime

One thing is certain: police officials had a multitude of new military tactics, tools, and templates upon which to draw if they wanted to. The expansion of the British Empire was not just a matter of expanding its size and scale. It also required transformations in its imperial-military regime that led to a significant expansion of its repertoire of coercion.[10]

Take the British Army, which had become increasingly important alongside the Royal Navy for imperial campaigns. On the one hand, from the Napoleonic Wars through the mid-nineteenth century, the army's organization and tactical templates remained largely unchanged. Stasis was the norm. On the other hand, a series of transformations unfolded after the Crimean War, the so-called Indian Mutiny of 1857, and the new colonial conquests beginning in the 1870s. Paramount among them was the development of mounted infantry.[11] As in the US empire, imperial expansion led to the British Army's increasing reliance upon mounted infantry. Nearly every military expedition and conquest, in fact, depended upon mounted forces of some sort or another.[12] The earliest mounted infantry units gained prominence in the Cape in the 1830s. Mounted rifle units had been vital in Australia in the 1850s, where they were initially conceived as a colonial gendarmerie, and over subsequent decades the mounted infantry was further developed. The Anglo-Zulu War of 1879, the First Anglo-Boer War of 1881, Egypt in the early 1880s, the Sudan and Nile expeditions of 1884–1885, and the Boer War of 1899 all served as sites for innovation.[13] The British Army's mounted infantry ended up as one of the most important developments of the late Victorian and Edwardian armies.[14] Recognizing this increased importance of mounted infantry, reformers such as E. T. H. Hutton in the 1880s (who had served in the mounted infantry in Egypt) began theorizing ways of perfecting their use in the colonies, including the use of reserve units to act as "rapidly moving infantry, for service on colonial expeditions, campaigns in uncivilized countries, or otherwise" to better manage the "savages."[15]

New firearms were also part of the empire's expanded repertoire. From the 1850s to the 1860s, Lieutenant Frederick Beaumont of the British Royal Engineers led developments in the Adams revolver, which became the preferred tool of British officers.[16] The Irish colonial theater also proved generative. The Webley firearms company would become world famous later, but it gained prominence in Ireland in the 1860s, when Philip Webley designed a new revolver for use by the Royal Irish Constabulary. This "RIC model revolver" was later picked up across the empire.[17] By the end of the nineteenth century, a variety of other new weapons—from the Snider-Enfield or Lee-Metford rifle to shorter swords for mounted units—had also emerged, part and parcel of the expanding industrial production of weaponry.[18]

These new means, mechanisms, and modalities of violence came with emergent doctrines of war and nascent counterinsurgency thought, which were rife with rising racialized constructions. Imperial conquests and colonial coercion conjured new military thinking about how "uncivilized" peoples required different tools and tactics of violence. By the 1870s, British explorers, soldiers, and officials from the African theater were giving lectures on the particularities of "savage warfare." Much of this thinking was consolidated in Colonel C. E. Callwell's famous early work on colonial counterinsurgency and conquest, *Small Wars: Their Principles and Practice*, originally published in 1896. Callwell conceptualized "small wars" as distinct from "regular warfare" not in terms of scale but in terms of civilizational difference. Small wars, he wrote, were a "heritage of extended empire, a certain epilogue to encroachment into lands beyond the confines of existing civilization." They were campaigns "against savages and semi-civilised races by disciplined soldiers," and required distinct modalities of violence.[19]

Colonial policing was expanded in the new empire as well. In older colonies, existing assemblages of slave patrols, armed guards, watches, and constables were all eventually replaced with more centralized police departments, along with new criminal justice systems and prisons. Under the control of the Colonial Office, they constituted "the largest criminal justice system ever organized in the history of the world."[20] From India and British Columbia to Trinidad and Tobago, many of these new colonial police forces looked like and were modeled upon their predecessors in Ireland. The influence of the RIC was often direct: RIC officers fanned out across the empire to help establish and train new forces, and officers of colonial police forces traveled to Ireland for training at the RIC training site in Dublin. Hence most colonial police were typically militarized constabulary forces meant to keep colonized peoples in line, with little to distinguish them from military units.[21]

As seen in Chapter 1, the London Metropolitan Police and subsequent departments in Britain had also been influenced by Irish colonial policing, but the new colonial forces sprouting up across the empire were different from their metropolitan variants, generating a deepening gap between metropolitan and colonial police. The transparent and aggressive use of deadly weapons was one such difference. While the London police mostly wielded batons, the new colonial police forces were more heavily armed, wielding not only batons but also sabers and firearms. To take just one example, the Ceylon police, formed in the 1840s, were armed from the beginning with rifles and carbines because, as Ceylon's inspector general of police in the 1920s explained, "occasion may arise when the only method of preserving law and order is by means of an armed force" and "the prompt arrival of a body of armed police on the scene of a threatened disturbance frequently has the effect of preventing a riot."[22] Another distinct feature was colonial policing's insulation from local populations. Police lacked accountability to colonized populations; their loyalty lay with colonial authorities and settlers, and upholding the law was less important than maintaining colonial rule.[23] Their approach to "crime" followed. Operating from racialized assumptions about the inherent criminality of the natives, and constantly fretting over possible uprisings, colonial police operated from an automatic and endemic "criminalization of the colonized," and criminal activity—exactly because it was an affront to colonial authority—was seen as a menacing prelude to rebellion.[24]

A final important difference between metropolitan and colonial modalities of coercion has to do with innovation. The racialized structure and function of colonial policing, as well as the imperatives of colonial conquest and maintaining rule at the untamed frontiers of empire, birthed novel policing tools and coercive capacities. Consider intelligence gathering. In England, most citizens had long been fearful of state spying; this was one of their major concerns about the London Met.[25] But the colonial theater offered a different stage. Persistent worries about anticolonial insurgency invited the use of the very sort of state intelligence in the colonies that Londoners despised. Freed from concerns over public legitimacy, colonialism served as a breeding ground for expansive and intensified surveillance.

Ireland served as an early laboratory. The British imperial state had spied on Irish anticolonialists since the 1790s. In the next century the spying continued, with the police leading the way. The Dublin Metropolitan Police did the bulk of the work, providing Whitehall with detailed information on the movements and activities of Irish nationalists, "secret societies," and their leaders.[26] British India was ripe too. From the beginning of the East India Company's rule, British officials had developed an elaborate network of Indian spies and informants (grafted upon Hindu and Mughal predecessors). After the uprisings of 1857–1858, British officials elaborated the system, with district superintendents of police creating their own local networks of informers and spies.[27] In India too the British perfected modes of identification that could be used for surveillance purposes. Fingerprinting, to be discussed later in this chapter, was among the most important ones. Furthermore, as the historian Daniel Brückenhaus reveals, in the early twentieth century British colonial officials worked closely with metropolitan officials at home and in other empires to monitor emerging anticolonial networks extending from India to Ireland. Nationalists moved across and through different empires, and so British intelligence officers and colonial police collaborated with French officials, synchronizing their efforts to create new transnational and transimperial systems of surveillance and intelligence gathering.[28]

The imperatives in the peripheral zones of the British Empire thus unleashed a range of new colonial tools, tactics, and technologies. The question is whether the civil police in Britain's imperial metropole had reason to adopt them, thereby closing the emerging gap between metropolitan and colonial policing.

## From the Irish to the "Criminal Class"

In previous chapters we have seen that the availability of new coercive means and methods is not in itself sufficient to bring the boomerang home. Perceived racial threats are also required. In Britain, those perceived threats had come from Irish immigrants. But things were different through the late Victorian period. While there remained the general sense that the Irish were prone to crime, the racialization of crime was less common.[29] The Irish might have been associated with crime, but crime became slowly "de-Irishized"—no longer seen as an exclusively Irish phenomenon.

A number of developments made this happen. One was the decline in the number of Irish migrants to England. Irish immigration peaked from 1841 to 1861, with the number of Irish-born in England and Wales rising from 289,404 to 601,634 to constitute 3 percent of the total population. But the numbers declined to 566,540 in 1871 (reducing the share of the population to 2.5 percent) and 375,325 by 1911 (only 1 percent of the population).[30] At the same time, the Irish were slowly dissociated from vagrancy (which had been previously equated with criminality). Over most of the entire Victorian period, between 50 and 70 percent of all vagrants were of English origin; the Irish proportion reached but 40 percent. While this was still a large proportion of Irish relative to population, the numbers made it harder to assume all vagrants were Irish (and vice versa).[31] Furthermore, the Irish took up more diverse and conventional occupations, and some were upwardly mobile as never before. "Our people," announced John Denvir, an Irishman in Lancashire, "are rising on the social scale."[32] More and more Irish even joined police forces, and the Irish were fully integrated into the political system, with the Irish vote becoming a factor that MPs had to consider.[33]

Many Irish immigrants still suffered from discrimination in the late nineteenth century. The Irish poor continued to concentrate in certain urban districts. Racist imagery of the Irish persisted (as we will see shortly), and the Irish remained overrepresented in the criminal justice system.[34] But integration lessened if not slowly eroded the "Irishization" of crime. If the Irish were still associated with crime, crime was much less likely to be racialized as *exclusively* Irish, and racialized panics about the Irish and crime were the exception rather than the rule.

Consider influential texts on poverty and urban issues. As seen in previous chapters, various reports and writings offered extensive lamentations about the Irish threat to law and order. But beginning in the 1860s, the discourse began to change. Henry Mayhew, who wrote infamous tracts about crime, observed that the Irish constituted a part of London's criminal population, but he restricted this to the more impoverished Irish, attributing criminality to class rather than race. The high representation of the Irish in criminal statistics, he wrote, showed not "that the Irish are naturally more criminal than our race, but simply that they are poorer."[35] By the time Charles Booth published his influential texts on the London poor in the 1880s and 1890s, the "de-Irishization" of crime that Mayhew's text indexed was nearly complete. Despite his extensive analysis of crime and poverty in London, Booth made almost no mention of the Irish. This intimates that Irish were no longer seen as a racialized class of invading criminals wreaking havoc on English order. As one scholar puts it, the "immigrant Irish, though known by national stereotype," were no longer "seen as exotics." The "condition [of the Irish], if less than satisfactory, was settled and familiar."[36]

Rather than a continued association of crime with the Irish, what emerged instead was the idea of a "criminal class" of "habitual criminals": a distinct group of people, mostly men, living off English society through habitual and lifelong criminal activity, often through repeated offenses.[37] The Habitual Criminals Act of 1869 was one result of the new classification. It required that anyone who was convicted of a felony and not sentenced to penal servitude (hence not shipped off to Australia) was subject to police supervision for seven years. The Prevention of Crimes Act of 1871 required that these criminals be tracked closely.[38] Some observers made analogies between this "criminal class" and colonized peoples, seeing the latter as having inherent biological tendencies toward crime. Mayhew was one of those with that belief, along with a range of psychiatrists, medical doctors, and some officials.[39]

Yet even this "criminal class" did not generate a racialized threat to law and order. To be sure, some writers saw the criminal class as society's new enemy. But the class did not map onto existing ethnic or racialized groups. It was seen as consisting of English as well as Irish and Scots. Furthermore, while some observers classified the criminal class as a separate race, most did not. Prominent officials in the London Metropolitan Police, such as Sir Robert Anderson, rejected biological explanations. Although biological theories of the "criminal class" circulated, they were typically restricted to a handful of protoscientific experts.[40]

Most importantly, neither the Irish nor the "criminal class" was seen as posing a serious threat to law and order. In the 1810s and 1820s, the rising numbers of Irish immigrants had coincided with worrisome crime rates. However, official estimates of the numbers constituting the "criminal class" in the mid- to late Victorian period suggest a decline in the presence of the class over time. While the estimated numbers remain controversial, the statistics consulted by officials and the press reveal that the ranks of the so-called criminal class in England fell from almost 78,000 in 1869 and 1870 to 31,000 in 1889 and 1890.[41] And this happened as crime appeared to decline or at least stabilize across the country.[42]

Of course, we know that perceptions are as important as actual crime rates, if not more so. But in this case, perceptions correlated with the numbers. Whereas the earlier decades of the century had brought about extensive periods of concern if not panic over perceived rising crime rates, the late Victorians were relatively calm. In 1839, Dr. W. C. Taylor wrote of crime in London:

> That crime has thus proportionately decreased is undeniable. There never was a period when persons and property were more secure in England. Who now sleeps with pistols beneath his pillow or hangs a blunderbuss within reach of his bolster? How many Londoners deem it necessary to spend a mortal half hour every night in bolting, barring, and chaining doors and windows?[43]

In 1876, one of the first serious historians of crime in Britain, L. O. Pike, wrote that compared to the earlier decades, "the sense of security is almost everywhere diffused."[44] Even Booth, who spent so much time observing London's poor neighborhoods, declared, "The hordes of barbarians of whom we have heard, who, issuing from their slums, will one day overwhelm civilization, do not exist. There are barbarians but they are a handful; a small and decreasing percentage: a disgrace but not a danger."[45] A "criminal class" emerged, but it barely touched a nerve.[46]

Government officials were not bothered either. Everyone from the criminal registrar in the Home Office to the director of criminal investigation and Sir Robert Anderson of the London Met noted England's relative safety and security—with Anderson asserting that the real problem was not criminality but the "barbarous" treatment of criminals in London's jails.[47] These claims were attendant on assertions that the London Metropolitan Police was doing its job effectively. If crime was no longer a major threat, it was because the police was efficiently repressing it.[48] The *London Quarterly Review*, to take just one example among others, asserted this exactly. One editorial classified the "criminal classes" as "enemies of society . . . in a state of constant war" against civilization but opined that the London police were managing it just fine: While "the lawless classes arrayed against society are weak, the constabulary forces arrayed in defence of society are strong." There was no need to militarize the force; even the constable's baton was a more than sufficient tool. "Armed with it alone, the constable will usually be found ready . . . to face any mob, or brave any danger." The article continued:

> It is in this conscious weakness and disorganization of the criminal classes on the one hand, and this conscious strength and organization of the defenders of law on the other, that the chief security of civilised society consists. A comparatively small number of honest, steady, active men—compact and well organized,—acting under the direction of skilled and experienced officers, will always have an immense advantage over the heterogeneous mass of roughs, thieves, and desperate characters which constitute the scoundrelism of great cities. And such a body London unquestionably possesses in its Metropolitan Police Force . . . [A] more carefully-selected, well-conducted and efficient body of men, than the Metropolitan . . . Police, probably does not exist in any country.[49]

We can thereby see that, without the imagined menace of invading subhumans seeking to overturn the English social order, there was no reason to initiate a new round of militarization as the nineteenth century wore on, no need for new coercive policing tools drawn from overseas. Even when minor bouts of panic did seem to occur—such as in the late 1860s, when there was a "garroting" scare and fears about the "ticket-of-leave" men, or in 1919, when there was fresh concern about crime but no moral panic—militarization did not follow. These were instances where the criminals were seen as "white" and "English."[50] At most, officials adjusted the legal apparatus and tried to improve the prisons to make them more humane. The racialized logic was impeccable: because the criminals were perceived as equal citizens, they deserved empathy and rehabilitation.[51]

There were exceptions. But even in these cases, militarization faced limits.[52]

## Exceptional Disorders, Irish Terror

If crime did not constitute a major problem triggering the search for colonial tactics or a militarized transformation in policing methods, this says nothing about other racialized threats to social order. So what happened from the 1850s through the early 1900s? While the Chartist movement subsided by the 1850s— by which time "the general social order of Victorian England did not seem under threat," as one historian puts it—there was indeed social turbulence thereafter.[53] In 1866, the Hyde Park riots were of such magnitude that the army had to step in, marking the first time after the founding of the new police that officials had to call upon the military for help. In the 1880s, other major demonstrations and riots erupted. By the turn of the century, officials were fretting over anarchist terrorism, various socialist movements, and strikes led by the rising trade union movement, including large-scale colliery stoppages in 1893 and the London dock strikes of 1911 and 1912.[54] From the 1910s onward, as one historian notes, "the country was racked by a series of major strikes—miners, dockers, railwaymen, even East End tailors."[55]

Some of these events appeared to push English society to the brink of chaos. Others were threatening but less perceptibly worrisome. But of all of them, only two were significant enough to trigger the addition of new imperial-military components to the already existing assemblage of police power in the metropolis.

The first happened in 1867. On December 13 of that year, a loud explosion unsettled the working-class district of Clerkenwell, London. The blast, "which seemed to shake every house in the vicinity," according to onlookers, broke "every pane of glass for several hundred yards" on each side of Bowling-Green Lane and shattered the houses in the area, blowing one of them "to pieces."[56] In all, twelve died, and 120 were injured. The cause? A cask of gunpowder planted by members of the Irish Republican Brotherhood, otherwise known as the Fenian Brotherhood.

The brotherhood had been founded in 1858 by exiles in the United States. It was a secret Irish republican organization that traced itself back to the 1790s rebellion. Proclaiming themselves the true inheritors of Daniel O'Connell's earlier repeal movement, the brotherhood turned to violence after the failure of the Young Irelanders' armed rebellions in Ireland in 1848 and 1849. It mounted unsuccessful attempts to seize British outposts in Canada and incite full-scale rebellion in Ireland in 1866.[57] Fenians also launched a failed attempt to steal thousands of rifles from Chester Castle. The explosion at Clerkenwell was part of the brotherhood's plan to free two of their members, Ricard O'Sullivan Burke and Joseph Casey, from prison. It was thought of by some as the first "terrorist" attack in Britain since the Guy Fawkes gunpowder plot against Parliament in the seventeenth century. The press called the Clerkenwell incident a "crime of unexampled atrocity."[58]

The Clerkenwell explosion highlights that even if Irish criminality was no longer shocking, Irish anticolonial nationalism remained an issue. To be sure, the Fenian Brotherhood's bold campaigns, occurring in the wake of the so-called Indian Mutiny and Black revolt in Jamaica (which Governor Edward John Eyre had to subdue with a violent heavy hand), incited the public and officials.[59] Long-standing racialized discourses of the barbaric Irish race resurfaced. In newspaper cartoons, Irish terrorists were portrayed as "the offspring of a liaison between a gorilla father and a prognathous Irish mother."[60] The "Fenian Paddy" was portrayed as an "ape-like monster" that "dared to defy British authority." One cartoon in *Punch*, published soon after the Clerkenwell explosion, was titled "The Fenian Guy Fawkes" and showed a simian-like creature dressed in "Paddy" clothing sitting atop a barrel of gunpowder, fireworks in hand ready to light (see Figure 4.1). The London *Weekly Dispatch* equated Fenians with common criminals and then equated both with colonized subjects in Africa: "Adventurers as worthless and consciousless [*sic*] as highwaymen are the best of these revolutionists . . . as inhuman as the lowest Africans."[61] Lord James of Hereford described the Fenian plotters as "enemies of the human race, the lowest and most degraded of beings, unfit to be regarded as belonging to the human community."[62] Common crime was slowly being disarticulated from its exclusively Irish provenance in this period, but social disorder in the wake of the so-called Fenian disturbances was not.

These "Fenian disturbances" shattered the police's image as the effective agent of social control. After the Clerkenwell explosion, a member of the Dublin police force quipped: "They [the London Metropolitan Police] know as little how to discharge duty in connection with Fenianism as I do about translating Hebrew."[63] The public and official reaction to the Clerkenwell explosion was thus similar to the reaction to Irish insurgency in the 1820s and 1830s. Alongside calls for bloody revenge, the public and the press demanded stronger police. Soon after the Clerkenwell explosion, an editorial in the *Weekly Standard* cried:

> If the British were schoolboys, as the Irish are by nature we should cudgel the rascals that . . . brave the law and incite revolt, out of the streets . . . how dare they insult us in our homes? . . . There must be an end of this style of demonstration.

**Figure 4.1.** The Fenian Guy Fawkes (John Tenniel, artist, and Swain, engraver)
*Source:* Image capture and text by George P. Landow from the webpage "The Victorian Web," *Hathi Trust Library*, University of California, orig. *Punch*, vol. 53, 28 Dec. 1867

In spite of all foes, internal and external, we must vindicate our own laws and customs. The wretched minority—wretched in power and in means as well as numbers—must be driven to their dens. . . . [T]he police [must] be made quite sufficient, fairly supported by the respectable citizenhood. The Government, we trust, is at its post, and will do its duty.[64]

Suggestions for how the police should be strengthened poured forth. One was to militarize personnel. Some called for more ex-military or ex-colonial officers in top policing positions. Others called for the further professionalization of the police by copying the recent reforms in the British Army offering pensions and easier promotions.[65] Another suggestion was for the police to more directly copy the British Army's hierarchy by creating a new layer of officers between the chief commissioner at the top and lower-level officials and constables at the bottom. "The case of the police," wrote the *Saturday Review*, "is analogous to that of a brigade of five thousand men commanded by a general, two brigadiers, and a large staff of sergeant-majors, colour-sergeants, and sergeants. No British army could be so commanded without losing difficulty and efficiency."[66]

The racialized threat posed by Hibernian terror thus tempered long-standing fears of militarized policing. While the public and officials had earlier claimed that armed police was "un-English," some began calling for the police to be armed.[67] "The frequent repetition of murderous attacks on the Police in these days of Fenian fury," asserted the *Illustrated London News*, "makes it expedient that the civil guardians of our peace should be taught how to use more formidable weapons than the truncheon, in case of need, for the purpose of self-defence."[68] The *Times* added: "It may, perhaps, be necessary for the public safety to arm them [the police] with greater powers."[69] The *Saturday Review* noted that arming the police might be a "constitutional anomaly," but it was warranted given the new danger posed by the putatively barbaric Fenians. Reproaching those who were raising objections to an armed police on constitutional grounds, it said:

> Such folks should wait to see how effective a charge a score of well-drilled and disciplined policemen can make upon a phalanx of excited roughs ten times their own number. . . . Why the police should be without the means of catching that *spirit de corps* which is the cheapest substitute for numbers must be left for explanation to the transcendental logic of Vestry orators. If these gentlemen think that drill and knowledge of arms are indefensible on general principles, they may ask themselves how they expect London to be defended from the next Fenian conspiracy.[70]

Even police constables agreed, with some suggesting that the London police should be armed like the French gendarmerie or the Royal Irish Constabulary.[71]

Three significant changes followed. First, soon after the Clerkenwell explosion in 1867, the entire London Metropolitan Police force held its first firearms course and underwent regular cutlass training. The training became routine.[72] This was followed by the regular supply of firearms to the police: in August 1868, the secretary of state, upon recommendation by Commissioner Mayne, authorized the supply of Adams breech-loading revolvers (.450 caliber) to the Met. Some 622 revolvers were given to the force, with most going to officers patrolling the working-class Irish districts of the East End.[73] The 1868 *Manual of Drill,*

*Prepared for the Use of the County and District Constables*, based on the Drill of the Army and revised from the 1861 version, included a new section on the use of these pistols.[74] More than manifesting just another round of militarization, this new supply of arms was another boomerang effect. The Adams revolver had military-imperial origins and had been used in various colonial theaters.[75] Later, in the early 1880s, in response to more Fenian threats, the Met adopted the Royal Irish Constabulary revolver, the Webley Mark IV. 455. Though constables would not carry them routinely, they were to be stored and made available for use when required.[76] The emerging gap between metropolitan and colonial policing was being reduced.

Second, the police tightened its command-and-control structure to look more like the military's. After the Clerkenwell explosion, the Home Office established a departmental committee to look into questions of security and policing. The committee suggested that the metropolis be reorganized into four districts, each under a district superintendent. It also made a series of other related changes. The new system came into force through the Police Orders for February 27, 1869.[77] Though the police did not institute all the committee's suggestions, the changes marked a significant militarization. Fittingly, two of the four new superintendents had come directly from the military-imperial regime: A. C. Howard, from the Bengal Constabulary, and Lieutenant Colonel R. Pearson, of the Grenadier Guards.[78]

A third change involved political surveillance. After Clerkenwell, the Home Office noted that the London Met's existing small Detective Department could not "cope with conspiracies and secret combinations."[79] Dublin officers observing from afar asserted that the violence at Clerkenwell would have been thwarted if the London Metropolitan had had a "competent Intelligence Department."[80] After all, it had been the Dublin Metropolitan Police, not the English police, that had notified the London Met about the Fenian plot at Clerkenwell. In response to these criticisms, the Home Office in the 1870s assisted in the creation of the Criminal Investigation Department (CID) within the London Metropolitan Police. The CID was tasked with detecting conventional crime, but its remit implied that it was also to track political insurgents and terrorists.[81]

Subsequently, the London Met took yet more steps to strengthen surveillance. This was in response to continued threats from Irish anticolonialists. In the 1880s, the Fenian Brotherhood reemerged as the Irish Republican Brotherhood and joined hands with Clan na Gael to hatch new plots—including one that used dynamite, a frightful new weapon of the time, which killed civilians and two policemen.[82] In 1883, the Home Office responded by creating a new intelligence unit within the CID of the London Metropolitan Police: the Special Irish Branch, sometimes called simply the Irish Brigade. The officers of the new branch had prior experience in Ireland.[83] At least thirteen RIC officers were sent from

Ireland to London on loan to help.[84] Its earliest incarnation was led by Sir Charles Edward Howard Vincent, an army officer who had served in Ireland before becoming head of the CID.[85] In form and function, the new Special Irish Branch copied the intelligence unit of the Dublin Metropolitan Police and other colonial police forces. Its job was to monitor and gather intelligence on Irish nationalists. The branch worked closely with officers of the Royal Irish Constabulary and intelligence officers in Dublin (and elsewhere across the empire).[86] Later, by 1887, the Irish Special Branch had become known simply as the Special Branch, charged with handling all threats to internal security.

Like arming the police, this too marked a significant change. Londoners had previously loathed spying. Their concerns over police surveillance had fed their initial fears that the London Met would be like Paris's tyrannical police under the notorious Joseph Fouché. But because of the threat from Irish anticolonialists, Londoners presented little opposition to the creation of their own English version of a secret police: the Special Branch. Domestic spying by the police was thus firmly and officially established, but only due to the fear of insurgents within.[87]

## The Rise of Warren

The other major public order event that triggered changes in the London police was the rioting at Pall Mall in 1886, an event sometimes known as "Black Monday." The first major public disturbance in London in decades, it began in Trafalgar Square, which had become a gathering site for unemployed workers, vagrants, and rival political groups seeking to mobilize the masses. On February 8, political demonstrations brought close to twenty thousand workers to the square, eager to express their anger at the economic depression and mass layoffs plaguing the country. After fiery speeches, arguing, and debating, an estimated ten thousand of the demonstrators turned toward Hyde Park, and then some five thousand of them broke off to terrorize Pall Mall and St. James's. They smashed windows, looted shops, attacked the Carlton Club (a classic Tory establishment), and intimidated upper-class citizens in their carriages. The rioting lasted several hours and caused up to £60,000 worth of damage.[88]

The public outcry in the wake of the riots was loud and clear. The *Globe* of London called it "the most alarming and destructive riot that has taken place in London for many years."[89] The press and officials called the rioters a "wild and lawless mob" that consisted of nothing but "loafers and thieves," equating many of them with the "criminal classes."[90] Others saw it as a portent of more widespread recalcitrance, pointing out that the groups seemingly involved in the riots included the Social Democratic Federation, Irish nationalists, and anarchists.[91] The *Times* referred approvingly to a letter by police reformer Edwin

Chadwick, who painted a worrisome picture not only of mob rule but also of "future revolution . . . openly promised by Socialist leaders" and the "hostile Irish." He claimed that "recent events . . . have displayed to revolutionists the weakness of the present conditions of disintegration and the temptations and facilities it gives to their enterprises." He asserted that cities "appear to be now exposed to greater danger from internal enemies than the dangers from external enemies."[92] Meanwhile, the press and the public castigated the police—and especially the police commissioner, Colonel Sir Edmund Henderson—for being too weak and incapable of handling mass disorder, just as it had been ineffective in facing down the Fenian threat.[93]

The stage was set for a new round of militarization. Soon after the riots, the home secretary created a committee of inquiry to look into the "disturbances" and ended up appointing one of the members, Sir Charles Warren, to replace Henderson as commissioner of the London Met.[94] The press and the public roundly praised the appointment. Though Warren was known to be "abrasive" and a "strict military disciplinarian," his "imperious military attitude" was just what was needed to steel the police against further public disturbances.[95] "If we are to have a soldier as Chief Commissioner of Police," declared the *Times*, "no better choice could have been of a man of the wide and varied experience which Sir Charles Warren has gone through."[96] Warren thus entered office "determined to bring about reforms."[97] He swiftly put his military experience to work.

Warren's reforms were not uniquely innovative, but they served to hasten and deepen the militarization of the London Met. He first carried through on earlier suggestions to match the London Met's hierarchy with that of the army, creating a line of new officers of superior rank between the commissioner and the superintendent. For these posts, he preferred officers from the army.[98] Warren also reinvigorated squad drill, which, he claimed, had been halted. The new drill meant that up to thirty-five hundred men trained at Wellington barracks at the same time.[99] Warren explained that the drill was meant to enable constables "to march in file from one street to another, to form up quickly in times of procession and fête days in order to line the streets."[100] Accordingly, Warren distributed copies of the army's *Field Exercise and Evolutions of Infantry* to all inspectors. He also revised the existing drill manual to incorporate other elements of the army's exercises.[101]

Warren increased the overall number of constables, adding more inspectors and sergeants. This was a move that the press praised widely, claiming that London constables are "soldier[s] of the street" in a city (London) that "is equal [in size and population] to that of some our Crown colonies."[102] In addition, Warren strengthened the Mounted Branch of the Met.[103] He was likely inspired by the successful use of mounted infantry during his celebrated campaigns in Egypt and the increasing reliance on mounted forces around the empire. Warren expanded the numbers of the Mounted Branch, put it under the supervision of one of the new assistant chief constables from the army, and gave it new riot training.[104] The *Saturday Review* took note: "Organized as a purely civil force, our constabulary has of late metamorphosed into a semi-military body.... Our mounted patrols ... are not unlike the horse police or gendarmerie of Berlin and St. Petersburg."[105]

Warren went further, bringing an army-like culture to the Met. He gave his constables new boots and stronger truncheons and imposed strict if not excessive discipline.[106] He endeavored to free himself from all civilian control, seeking full autonomy from the Home Office (and other officials at Scotland Yard). This likely reflected his own experiences as a military commander and colonial official operating with discretionary powers on the ground, far away from London. As historian Victor Bailey explains, Warren "considered that his relationship with the Home Secretary should resemble the one which existed between the Secretary of State for War and the commanding officer of an overseas expedition," where the officer acted as a "high-handed military campaigner in the outskirts of Empire."[107]

Warren was finally able to display his freshly remilitarized force in October 1887 in response to another bout of demonstrations in Trafalgar Square. The demonstrations were led by the Social Democratic Federation and Irish nationalists. Warren met them with martial vigor. Observers described the police tactics against the crowd as a kind of "guerrilla warfare" using "military methods." Squads of police "were moved about, breaking up knots of people," and charged into the crowd using truncheons (and reportedly revolvers). Mounted constables entered affrays from on high to disperse rioters.[108] The press was astounded at "the striking change which has come over the Metropolitan Police within the last ten or twelve years. Organized as a purely civil force, our constabulary has of late been metamorphosed into a semi-military body, with certain points of resemblance to the police of Germany and Russia."[109]

Then came "Bloody Sunday" in Trafalgar Square in November 1887. In hopes of subduing any future rioting, Warren unilaterally banned all organized processions, banners, and placards from the square.[110] On November 13, incensed by Warren's ban, close to twenty thousand angry demonstrators defied police cordons. Warren had learned of the rally the day before and mobilized four thousand officers, including his new force of three hundred mounted constables. The mounted unit was organized into "military formation," according to one observer, with three hundred Grenadier Guards and three hundred Life Guards in reserve.[111] Violent clashes ensued. Police reportedly charged into crowds while "striking indiscriminately." Blood "was flowing freely." About two hundred civilians ended up in the hospital, and three died from their injuries.[112]

According to historians, it was "the most serious public confrontation which the Metropolitan Police had faced in the sixty years of its existence."[113]

Warren's militarized approach to Bloody Sunday was not only conditioned by his remit and his imperial-military orientation but also imperial analogization. Warren took great racialist pride in the British Empire, giving speeches at society events with titles like "The English as Rulers of Other Races."[114] He classified the demonstrators as enemies akin to foreign subversives or irrational colonized peoples, placing the blame for the Trafalgar Square unrest on the leaders of the Social Democratic Federation and the Irish National League.[115] Some of his colleagues pointed to the "foreign element" at Trafalgar Square, referring to Russian anarchists supposedly present.[116] Warren also claimed that the "criminal classes" were at the demonstrations, referring to them as the "rough and criminal element."[117] In private correspondence with the Home Office, Warren did not hesitate to refer to them as the "veriest scum of the population."[118] His militarized response followed. As the historian David Ascoli remarks, "So far as he [Warren] was concerned, where discipline was involved, there was not much difference between the natives of Bechuanaland and the natives of Bethnal Green."[119] In regards to his heavy-handed militaristic response in the square in November 1887, the *Times* observed: "Sir Charles Warren must have imagined himself to have been campaigning in Africa."[120]

## The Limits to Militarization

Warren's militarization, though, did not go much further. In fact, it generated a backlash that would last for decades. Unsurprisingly, workers' groups were especially vocal in their opposition. The Social Democratic Federation called Warren the "military Chief Constable of a military police" and decried how the London police had become a "gens-d'armes."[121] Such comments continued the criticisms of the "Jenny Darbies" that workers in London had articulated since the beginning of the Met, but disapproval also emerged from other sectors. While many of Warren's peers initially supported his efforts to clamp down on the "mobs," they did not embrace Warren's attempt to make the police fully autonomous from civilian control and criticized Warren accordingly (Warren and the Home Office soon clashed).[122] The press turned on Warren too. The *Pall Mall Gazette* had initially supported Warren's appointment as commissioner, but its editor, W. T. Stead, was incensed at what he and his circle took to be an affront to the right of public assembly.[123] His newspaper soon leveled a litany of criticisms. It called Warren a "soldier in jackboots" who was infringing upon "the rights and liberties enjoyed from time immemorial by every inhabitant of the metropole."

It complained about Warren's "police cavalry" and his "troops with ball cartridge ready to massacre an unarmed populace."[124]

Members of Parliament were also displeased. MP Charles Bradlaugh of Northampton decried that "Trafalgar Square was occupied virtually in a military manner."[125] MP William Harcourt, in the House of Commons, accused Warren of turning the London Met from "a civil force into a body of *gendarmes*."[126] MP Harry Lawson called the police repression at Trafalgar Square part of a larger "deliberate attempt to drive the police force back into a military and anti-popular groove." Lawson referred to how the London Metropolitan Police had originally been run by Rowan and Mayne, one a "military man" and the other a civilian, but Warren had filled the new offices of chief constable and assistant chief constables with army veterans. "The civil element" of the police was now "conspicuous by its absence" because of Warren.[127]

These criticisms indicate the broader problem that Warren's militarism faced: while the majority of officials and elites obviously wanted to repress mob violence, they did not see a serious threat to social order—at least not to the extent that Warren portrayed. By 1888, the initial trauma of the Pall Mall riots of 1886 had subsided. Some officials even felt that its danger had been overblown. Prime Minister William Gladstone insinuated that such threats to order would readily pass and that "any great alteration in the metropolitan police as a consequence of the West End Riots" would not be needed.[128] Neither he nor the press seemed swayed by Warren's justifications for militarization. Few if any bought into Warren's insistence that London had been repeatedly besieged by riotous mobs, subjecting the metropolis to a "reign of abject terror."[129] The press found such claims "absurd" and assessed the "disorderly element" in London as "weak" at best.[130]

To be sure, the Social Democratic Federation was hardly an insurgent group. While some "foreigners" had been part of it, the anarchists had left by Warren's time, and the federation was more closely associated with upper-class Tory socialists and middle-class English radicals such as William Morris and Annie Besant (both of whom had been present at Bloody Sunday). Its platform was influenced by the Chartists but proclaimed neither criminal nor revolutionary intent.[131] And by this time it would have become increasingly difficult to assume that Irish nationalists in London were a significant threat. The Fenian violence had been squashed; at worst there was a handful of nationalistic Irishmen located in the United States (as officials and the press noted). The Irish National League had taken over the mantle of Irish nationalism, and the League, enjoying the support of Gladstone and the Liberal Party, sought constitutional change through electoral politics rather than revolt.[132]

Perhaps for these reasons, most Londoners rejected Warren's analogies between the demonstrators at home and enemy barbarians. In their critiques of Warren's heavy militarized hand at Trafalgar Square, the press spoke of the protestors as "citizens" deserving of civil treatment rather than colonized subjects requiring forcible compliance. "Sir Charles Warren," cried the *Pall Mall Gazette*, "has taken upon himself to deny to the *citizens* of London the right to hold public meetings in Trafalgar Square." And if the demonstrators were citizens rather than foreign enemies or colonial subjects, militaristic and violent tactics taken from the edges of empire were inappropriate. The *Pall Mall Gazette* condemned Warren for acting like a colonial ruler in Ireland and turning the Met into a colonial police force. "It is a new experience for Englishmen to see peaceful citizens ridden down at the gallop by police cavalry," it announced. "A few more days like yesterday and there will be as much bad blood between the masses of London and the metropolitan police as there is between the Royal Irish Constabulary and the bulk of the Irish people."[133] Other periodicals concluded that Warren was not fit to lead the London Met because "he is, *par excellence,* a soldier ... his only administrative experience has been in dealing with barbarians, not ... the police and inhabitants of London."[134] The press and public drew lines between "barbarians" and the protesting Londoners, and found militarized policing to be inappropriate for the latter but fit for the former.

In the end, Warren was forced to resign. As one historian put it, his tenure marked "a signal instance of the failure of a military administration of the Metropolitan police."[135] In fact, after his resignation, Warren continued to receive criticism from parliamentarians for his excessively militaristic approach, with some, including MP Lawson, vowing to ensure that it would not be repeated. Lawson bemoaned the fact that Warren had appointed military men "who had received their training in most instances ... in the far East, in our Indian possessions or in South Africa, where they were hardly likely to have acquired that delicate touch and appreciation which enabled them to deal with the wants of the London population." Lawson then demanded that the future police commissioner be a civilian. Rather than a military man, the Met needed a "civil head who would put a stop at once to the militarizing tendencies which had characterized the administration of the last few years."[136]

Lawson's suggestion was taken to heart. After Warren resigned, he was replaced by James Monro. Monro had been assistant commissioner in charge of the Criminal Investigation Department. Prior to that, he had been an inspector general of the Bengal Police. Though he had a colonial background, he was not a military man of Warren's cloth. The lesson was clear: Warren had gone too far, and his militarism was not matched by the threats posed. Future commissioners of police would have to take heed. They could not get away with excessive militarization.

Over the next three decades at least, no police commissioners would militarize the London police in the way Warren did. In fact, Sir Robert Anderson, who became assistant commissioner of the Met in 1888 to replace Monro, explicitly rejected the idea that police should be like an army. In 1902 he wrote an editorial in which he declared: "Military conceptions of organization and discipline are generally harmful in the sphere of police."[137] The most violent tools of the boomerang were thus kept at bay, even as other tools—as we will now see—were snuck in.

## From India to London

The London police were not militarized any further in the late nineteenth and early twentieth century, but the influence of colonialism upon policing did not completely wane. After Warren, there was one more important change in policing that derived from Britain's imperial-military regime. This was not a form of violent militarization domesticating tactics and forms from warfare. It was rather an appropriation of colonial surveillance technologies. It reveals that, in the wake of Warren's failures, while police commissioners might not have been able to boldly and publicly draw from the army to transform London policing, they were still able to draw upon colonial governmentalities. And like other forms of imperial feedback, this too was conditioned by a racialized threat—however, of a sort different from what England had seen before.

The transformation was manifest in 1901, when Edward Henry replaced Sir Robert Anderson as head of the Criminal Investigation Department of the London Metropolitan Police. Almost immediately Henry created a fingerprint branch of the CID, later known as the Metropolitan Fingerprint Bureau. The purpose was to collect, organize, and maintain records on criminals based on their fingerprints. By 1903, the bureau had 70,000 fingerprint records on file, with around 350 records added every week. That same year, the London Metropolitan Police used fingerprints to make more than 2,000 identifications.[138] Henry's fingerprint bureau, recalled Melville Macnaghten (Henry's successor at the CID), was a "clear and unbroken success."[139]

Fingerprinting was a new policing device. For years, the police and courts had relied upon "personal recognition" to identify criminals, deploying face-to-face recognition by police or prison officials. Other methods such as photographs had also been employed. By the 1890s the London police were experimenting with the criminal identification system developed by the French police clerk Alphonse Bertillon. Bertillon had been fascinated with identification issues and eventually implemented an anthropometric system that used various physical measures of the body to identify individuals. Fingerprinting followed the same principle but focused on the imprints of fingers only. It was eventually adopted as the superior method for identification, replacing the Bertillon methods.[140]

The story of how fingerprinting was developed and came to replace the Bertillon system is multifaceted, but any variant of the story must reckon with British colonialism in India. Before being anointed head of the CID, Henry had been inspector-general of police in Bengal, where he and other British officials had been groping for reliable methods to identify, track, and surveil their colonial subjects. The need for such methods arose from the imperatives of colonial rule. The British state had to manage vast amounts of foreign territory and control foreign peoples with a small corps of civil servants. The police, in the historian David Arnold's words, had to serve as a "repressive force" but also as the "eyes and ears" of an alien state ruling a diverse and seemingly inscrutable population.[141] This required surveillance aided by identification methods. The need for sufficient identification methods had also arisen in India due to legal issues. In the wake of the Sepoy Mutiny of 1857, the British government took over from the East India Company, and William Herschel, chief administrator of the Hooghly district of Bengal, faced the problem of "litigation and fraud; forgery and perjury" from locals whom officials did not know personally.[142] How could they tell that an individual was actually who they said they were? In English eyes, the Brown natives of India all looked the same, and as most Indians were illiterate, authorities could not rely upon written signatures. Personal testimony was likewise useless. Using their racialized lens, the British thought of Indians as natural-born liars.[143] The *Home News for India, China and the Colonies* summarized it all in 1893: "In India the rarity of any native being able to write, the proneness of the Oriental to fraud, and the difficulty which Europeans have in distinguishing one black face from another" meant that the identification methods used in Europe were "useless" in India.[144]

Identification problems became even more acute after 1871, when the Criminal Tribes Act called for the "registration, surveillance, and control of certain criminal tribes" and authorized local governments to report "any tribe, gang or class of persons addicted to the systematic commission of non-bailable offenses."[145] The notion of "criminal tribes" was the Indian version of the English "criminal classes": British officials assumed that certain ethnoracial groups had a hereditary disposition toward criminality. But identifying, registering, and surveilling members of such tribes required individual identification.[146] Local registries were of no help, as some tribe members moved from district to district, and criminals took advantage of the new railroad to move across the colony.

These are the reasons British officials in Bengal searched for a reliable method of identification. Eventually they hired Edgar Thurston, curator of the Madras Government Museum, to advise them. Thurston had been using Bertillon-like anthropometry to ascertain the physical bases of caste differentiation, and soon afterward the Bengal police implemented the Bertillon system.[147] The problem was that even the Bertillon system did not work well for the Indian situation.

The system was partially based upon identification by eye color, but Indians all appeared to have the same color eyes.

As inspector-general of the Bengal Police, Henry eventually landed upon a possible solution in Sir Francis Galton's recent work on fingerprinting. Galton, a prominent eugenicist scientist, had learned about the identification problems of the British colonial state from officials in the Indian Staff Corps and earnestly studied them. Galton concluded that fingerprinting would be useful for identifying not only Indians but Chinese coolies as well, whom he thought were even more difficult to individuate.[148] Influenced by Galton, Henry began collecting thumb impressions and used the data collected by Herschel.[149] He soon created his own system for organizing and classifying fingerprint data. His system facilitated easy retrieval and identification, and by 1894 the Bengal Police was using it to identify habitual criminals. The "means now at the disposal of the Bengal Police for dealing with recidivists," Henry boasted, "are more complete than are possessed by the police either in England or in any English colony."[150] He trained subinspectors in his methods at the police training school and the method spread among police forces across India.

Henry also wrote a monograph, *Classification and Uses of Fingerprints* (1897), to be used as a manual of sorts. He provided evidence to parliamentary committees on identification issues and addressed the British Association for the Advancement of Science. Just before being appointed to head the CID in London, he had been dispatched to South Africa, where he organized the civil police forces of Johannesburg and Pretoria. There he set up a documentation system for native, Arab, and Chinese laborers who were subject to arrest without warrant if they could not produce identification. The system relied upon fingerprints, much to the protestations of a young lawyer named Mahatma Gandhi (who declared that Henry's identification system treated all Asians as criminals). Henry then came to London to take up his new position in the Met's CID. To help staff his new Fingerprint Branch, he brought some of his own men from India. An internal police report later conveyed that fingerprinting was adopted by the London Metropolitan Police after it "had been adopted by the Government of India as a complete success."[151]

Why was fingerprinting eventually adopted in London and not just India and South Africa? On its face, it might appear inevitable. Fingerprinting was a novel method with apparent scientific validity that had been tried and tested overseas. But the eventual adoption of fingerprinting by the London Metropolitan Police cannot be seen as a foregone conclusion. For one thing, fingerprinting was costly, especially in terms of time and labor. Countless prints had to be collected for the system to work. For another, fingerprinting affronted late Victorian liberalism. Strict surveillance of citizens' identity by police had been anathema to Londoners, conjuring associations with the despotic secret police of Paris (not least since Bertillon's anthropometric methods were already being used by the Prefecture of Police in Paris). Unsurprisingly, some of the English public were not happy when fingerprinting was introduced in London. They saw it as suspending "the ideal of English liberty," according to the historian Chandak Sengoopta.[152] It was difficult and politically risky to implement fingerprinting in England. The question is what made the risk worth taking.

## Racialization and Identification

In India, the need for fingerprinting arose because of the putatively criminal, inscrutable, and deceitful character of Indian colonial subjects. In England, the need for fingerprinting arose for the same reasons, just that the people to be monitored were not Indian. One group was the "criminal class." Logically speaking, there is no immediate need for police to use fingerprinting methods or even any identification method. Identification is only necessary if police think that criminals are habitual and hence repeat offenders. If those arrested, accused, or convicted are not seen as predisposed to crime, and thus to repetitive criminality, the arduous process of maintaining registers to identify individuals would be neither necessary nor prudent. Therefore, it was only with the emergence of a perceived "criminal class" of habitual offenders that the need for identification became potent.

Still, the need to monitor and identify the "criminal class" in England took on added importance because of the emergence of a particular segment of the class that garnered increasing attention in the latter decades of the century. This group was what CID head Sir Robert Anderson called the "master" and "skilled" criminal (or, alternatively, the polished "professional criminal"). These were not street thieves or vagrants, nor were they violent drunkards and brawlers or menacing political insurgents. They were "able and skillful," "resourceful" and "clever," pulling off such criminal feats as fraud, diamond theft, and embezzlement.[153] Some were lower-level operatives conducting petty fraud and theft through complex deceitful schemes. Others operated at higher and more sinister levels. One famous criminal was Henry J. Raymond, who stole £90,000 worth of diamonds. Raymond had used disguise and impersonation to pull off his heist. In his discussion of the new criminal type, Anderson referred to Raymond as a paradigmatic "master criminal."[154]

This new skilled and crafty "master criminal" captured the late Victorian imagination. The figure was most starkly represented in popular detective fiction by characters such as Sherlock Holmes's nemesis James Moriarty (who was loosely based on Raymond).[155] In turn, capturing such criminals required intellectual capital rather than militarized weaponry. Solving crimes, as Martin

J. Wiener puts it, became an "intellectual puzzle" and a "scientific and administrative problem"—again represented in fiction by the Sherlock Holmes mysteries.[156] Identifying individuals and criminals was a scientific and intellectual pursuit; it thus had natural affinities with this new kind of police work. But there was a problem with the old methods of identification. The Troupe Committee, which had been created to investigate criminal identification methods, noted that "professional criminals" could not be identified through "personal recognition" because, unlike other criminals, they were not local. Because they traveled across the country, they were not known by police personally.[157] Photography did not work either. The new type of criminal was far too clever for this. They could manipulate their appearance and impersonate others. As contemporaries complained, they could even change their facial expression enough to make photographic identification impossible.[158] Fingerprinting was the solution.

The other emergent figure besides master criminals whose presence contributed to the need for fingerprint identification was the immigrant. Many of the highest-profile professional criminals were English, but by the 1880s, some immigrants and traveling foreigners became identified as part of the class. Here is where a new racial threat finally emerged in Britain. For as Irish migration waned, a spate of new incomers entered. Most came from Eastern Europe. The Jewish population was the largest. Fleeing persecution and economic downturns in Poland, Russia, and Germany in the 1880s, Jewish immigrants came to Britain at astonishing rates. By the end of the 1890s their numbers had swelled to 150,000 (in a city of 5 million, excluding the greater metropolitan area), and by 1914 their ranks grew to 400,000.[159] Most of them crowded into London's East End with Germans, Italians, and other poor immigrants.[160] Their poverty, putative uncleanliness, and appalling housing conditions were discussed in periodicals and books like Booth's *Life and Labor of the People in London*.[161] Detective Inspector John Sweeney referred to the area in the East End where they lived as a Jewish "colony."[162] William Evans-Gordon in his account of a visit to East London noted that "the Hebrew Colony . . . unlike any other alien colony in the land, forms a solid and permanent distinct block—a race apart, as it were, in an enduring island of extraneous thought and custom."[163]

The ostensible invasion by Eastern European immigrants generated governmental responses reminiscent of when Irish immigrants had flowed into England in the early 1800s. In 1888, the House of Commons created a select committee to investigate the new "alien" question. It was chaired by Howard Vincent, who had been part of the Special Irish Branch of the London Met. These and many other hearings established publicly what many already believed privately: Jewish immigrants were prone to criminality. "We are importing a criminal Jewish population," testified Arnold White, author of the anti-Semitic *The Modern Jew* (1899).[164] The Royal Commission, beginning its work in 1902, summarized the larger view: many of the "Alien Immigrants" were "criminals, anarchists, prostitutes, and persons of bad character." Officially, the term "alien" included other immigrants besides Jewish immigrants, but the two became almost synonymous.[165] "Alien," notes Knepper, "meant 'Jew'" and with it, the assumption of guilt.[166] Robert Anderson of the London Metropolitan Police spoke sympathetically of English criminals, but when he spoke of the new European immigrants, his tone was transformed, becoming foreboding and fearful. "The aliens question claims notice in any treatise upon crime. . . . In the past this country has been an asylum for the oppressed of every land: it is now becoming the common cesspool of Christendom."[167]

Anderson and others classified the criminality of the new "aliens" differently than that of the Irish before them. Rather than insurgents, drunken brawlers, or petty street criminals, Jewish immigrants were perceived as a variant of the newer professional criminal class that operated by stealth and deceit, aided by the dark cunning assumed to be inherent to the race. "If the Irish were accused of being roughs and drunkards," notes one historian, "the Jews tended to be charged with more sinister transgressions."[168] Detective Inspector John Sweeney wrote that the new immigrant Jews were "shrewd and clever" with a "regard for truth" that "is not too strict," much like the Indians in Bengal who had frustrated British officials with their presumed propensity for lying.[169] The fact that the immigrants spoke Yiddish worsened the matter. It enabled them to hide their crimes more easily and speak about them in plain sight—a concern that compelled the London Met to try to persuade patrollers of the East End to learn Yiddish.[170]

According to conspiracy theorists, the Jewish proclivity for clever deception enabled some of them to spin large-scale international webs of control and power. According to police officials like Sweeney, however, their stealth and smarts birthed localized crimes. In their view, the Jews engaged in a "more scientific class of crime": fraud, forgery, shady business dealings that enabled them to unduly profit from their gambling houses, or burglaries involving special tools and knowledge.[171] The racial logic was extensive enough to encapsulate activity that, on its face, lacked affinity with the presumed Jewish traits. Jewish immigrants were seen as anarchists or peddlers of prostitutes when not prostitutes themselves.[172] They were also accused of spectacularly violent crimes. Without proof, the police and the public believed that the Whitechapel murders, also known as the Jack the Ripper cases, were committed by a Jewish immigrant. Under the assumption that no Englishman could have committed the crime, they thought that "Jack" must have been of the "low-class Polish Jews," as CID head Sir Robert Anderson put it. In their view, Jack was a bloody and brutal maniac, but he was also calculating, clever, and deceitful. Anderson even accused the entire Jewish community of hiding the Ripper's identity, insinuating that their deceptive character and communal bonds were to blame: "People of that class in the East End will not give up one of their number to Gentile Justice."[173]

This was a new racialized threat akin to the prior Irish threats that had prompted earlier militarization. But the methods to address it had to be different, given that the *character* of the racialized threat was thought to be different. As the new immigrants were not allying with strikers, marching in the streets, laying dynamite, stoking mass brawls, or upending social order through large-scale violence, militarized tactics and forms from the army would not work. Instead, in the 1890s, parliamentary committees began entertaining restrictions on immigration, just as they had during the earlier influx of Irish immigrants. The result was the 1905 Aliens Act, which introduced immigration controls in England for the first time. The act dictated that foreigners arriving in Britain had to be assessed for their worthiness, and it gave immigration officials the right to exclude "undesirable" aliens. This meant that the police had to monitor immigrant populations, and fingerprinting was to be a vital tool in that effort. Its adoption by the London police was in this sense racialized.

While it would be misleading to claim that all of the importers of fingerprinting technology were reacting to the new immigration of the 1880s and 1890s, it is the case that advocates of the technique typically had "aliens" and "foreigners" on their mind. When British officials first began seeking out new methods of identification to replace personal identification, they were initially inspired by Bertillon's anthropometric system, but Bertillon himself had developed the methods to manage not just the "criminal classes" of Paris but also colonial subjects and immigrants in French Algeria.[174] An article in the *London Quarterly Review* about the London police noted how detectives were necessary to help handle "the influx into London of foreign criminals" who were "very dangerous men—of desperate and subtle character—who need constant surveillance."[175] Fingerprinting was to help.

This racialized importation of fingerprinting is further evidenced in the work of E. R. Spearman, one of the most prominent English promoters of fingerprinting. He had been enamored of the Bertillon methods in Paris and helped popularize them among British officials.[176] In 1890, two years after the first of the Whitechapel murders and as foreign immigration to London was mounting, Spearman wrote that police should use anthropometric methods instead of personal recognition to handle cases of mistaken identity and to track "professional criminals," particularly foreigners. He claimed that "many hundreds" or more of foreign criminals were already in English prisons. The problem, in his view, was that foreign criminals could not be identified by "our present system" of personal identification or even photography because they were too deceptive. "If a foreign criminal is a good linguist," Spearman opined, "he can easily pass as an Englishman; the police have no means of disproving the assertion."[177] Because "identity is the important business of the policeman," a better method was needed—hence fingerprinting.[178]

Newspaper editorials made similar calls for a new system of identification beyond the old methods, and they too pointed to immigrants. The *Times* announced an urgent need for better identification technologies than the photograph because of the "numerous and crafty disguises" of the "habitual offenders." Its example was a "German girl" who was a "most notorious offender" arrested by the London Metropolitan Police. Scotland Yard could not identify her. The police had "sixty" photographs of the same girl, but investigators presumed they were of different girls, because the "offender" had been able to craftily change her look for each one.[179] Police officials also acknowledged the difficulty in identifying immigrants. In his memoirs, Detective Inspector John Sweeney discussed the criminal tendencies of immigrants in London, especially the Jewish community and their deceitful proclivities. One of the problems of policing them, he suggested, was the inability to know their criminal past, and "the difficulty of establishing the fact that an alien convicted here was a criminal in the place whence he comes." They lied and did not carry documentation of their status in their home countries.[180]

The very origins of fingerprinting betray its racialized character. One of the innovators was Sir Francis Galton, who undoubtedly had racial populations in mind. As part of his interest in connecting behavior and heredity, and especially in discerning the particular traits of Jews, he had worked tirelessly in advancing fingerprint data and technology. His book on fingerprinting was published in 1892. He worked closely with Edward Henry and other British officials to promote it, and they in turn referred to his work and expertise.[181] When the press in London first caught wind of Galton's techniques, some writers noted how they would solve important cases involving disputed identity, like the famous Tichborne case, but some also noted the racial dimension. "The practical applications of such a method of identity are endless," wrote the *St. James Gazette*, "and are useful for such varied company as deserters, previously convicted prisoners, Malay coolies, Chinese and other classes of human beings whose similarity of feature makes it difficult for Europeans to distinguish them."[182]

The official committees in England that led to the adoption of fingerprinting techniques also connected the need for identification with racialized immigrants. The 1893 committee, chaired by Charles Troup, investigated Bertillon's methods and conducted interviews with multiple officials and experts. Some of the witnesses reiterated the notion that crime was increasing due to foreign immigrants; they thus suggested that an efficient and reliable system of criminal identification was needed.[183] In turn, the committee's report offered statistics presumably connecting crime with immigrants and agreed that new methods of identification were needed.[184] Existing "English methods" such as personal identification (whereby police already knew the suspect) were not useful, according to the committee, because so many of the "professional criminals" were "foreigners" unknown to local police. This was especially so for the London Metropolitan Police. London had become the "centre for the criminal classes." London "is the chief if not the only resort in England for the most bold and cunning criminals of foreign countries."[185]

Edward Henry also saw the potential of his new technology for tracking aliens and immigrants. Fingerprinting was "particularly well suited to the requirements of a country where the mass of the people are uneducated, and where false personation is an evil which even the penalties provided by the penal laws are powerless to control."[186] Henry was referring to India, but he could have just as well been referring to late Victorian London with its rising immigrant population. Henry's testimony to the Royal Commission on Alien Immigration reveals this. The commission took testimony on the "alien question" from a variety of officials and businessmen, many of whom connected crime to immigration and raised problems of identity. One businessman working in textiles complained about the "aliens—principally Jews" who operated "houses of ill-fame" that are "centres of every possible form of vice and crime" but who could not be properly identified "because these people have gone under so many aliases that in our district has been almost impossible to trace them." Another testified that "with regard to Jews [it] would be a very good plan" if they had some form of personal identification that would attest that they were not "a criminal," like a photograph, certificate, or sheet of fingerprints signed by a rabbi.[187]

Henry was also brought before the committee and asked about how to deal with "aliens who are criminals." Henry's answer was to expel them as "undesirable aliens." He noted that there were legal precedents for this (including the Prevention of Crimes Act of 1882, which originated in Ireland) but that in order for them to work, the police would have to identify and register all criminal immigrants. Fingerprinting, Henry concluded, was the best method for the police to do this work.[188]

Fittingly, in 1906, a year after the Aliens Act was first passed, the government decreed that any alien ordered to be expelled under the Aliens Act of 1905 was to be "measured in the same way as a criminal prisoner," using photographs and fingerprints. That same month, Henry, as assistant commissioner of the London Metropolitan Police, wrote to the Home Office that he had made arrangements "at this Office for the reception and classification of the fingerprints and records of expelled Aliens separately from the existing criminal records."[189] Both the London Metropolitan Police and the Special Branch were soon busy policing the immigrant districts.

We can now see why the London police adopted fingerprinting techniques for home use rather than keeping them in the colonies. They deemed it necessary in the face of new racialized threats to law: fingerprinting was useful for the war on the "criminal classes" presumed to have a biological disposition toward criminality and on the cunning immigrants and "aliens" who needed to be captured and contained. But we can also speculate why the English public, though initially fearful of fingerprinting as a threat to their liberty, eventually came around to it. As with previous rounds of militarization, the English public began to see that the new police powers were not meant for them. They were meant for those deemed other and inferior: the racialized "criminal classes" and "aliens" who were not seen as deserving of the rights and freedom of citizens. The colonial boomerang returned, but only because it was aimed at those racialized populations.

## Waves of Militarization and Their Limits

In summary, the period of the late nineteenth century through the first decade of the twentieth century saw some militarization, but it was shaped and limited by local conditions. Unlike the first wave of militarization in England, the racialization of crime was minimal. The Irish threat diminished. While the criminal classes and new immigrants raised some concern, the character of the perceived threat led only to the importation of fingerprint techniques—a tool of surveillance rather than bloody violence. At the same time, the racialization of disorder did lead to significant changes. The Fenian threat led to firearms training and storage. Warren's perception of threat from Trafalgar Square protestors led him to import new crowd control techniques and mounted forces from the imperial-military regime. But these were limited too. Both threats were fleeting, and not all members of the public or officials agreed with Warren. Warren's initial moves were stopped short.

Is there a pattern to all of this? Before coming to conclusions, let us consider one more moment of militarization. In 1931, Prime Minister Ramsay MacDonald appointed Lord Hugh Trenchard to be the new commissioner of the London Metropolitan Police. Trenchard was a military man. He had fought in the Boer War, commanded the Southern Nigeria Regiment, and then served as a high-level officer in the Royal Air Force (RAF) during the First World War. His background was not unlike that of Sir Charles Warren. And like Warren, Trenchard embarked upon a campaign of militarization, couching his efforts as "changes and reforms." The goal, he said, was to create a "much more enlightened" police. The military inspiration was clear. Trenchard vowed to create in the police "a higher degree of organization" such as that "recognized in the Defence Forces."[190] Trenchard then hatched a plan to fill the roads with "Q-cars": secret unmarked police vehicles, some carrying armed police officers, based upon the operations of the "Q-ships" that the Royal Navy deployed during the First World War.[191] He also created a police Information Room and an adjacent Map Room to receive emergency calls, map police movements, and dispatch police in response.[192] This complemented the Q-car scheme, and while it had clear similarities with August Vollmer's pin mapping schemes and mobile units (as seen in Chapter 3), Trenchard most likely based it upon the Royal Air Force command-and-control system that he had advocated for during his prior service. Both the RAF's system and Trenchard's Information Room and Map Room, as Williams explains, "used grid maps, coloured counters moved by plotters, a strict demarcation of tasks, centralisation of information, and a senior officer able to cut into his subordinates' lines."[193]

Trenchard was also the main force behind the Metropolitan Police College at Hendon, a new training school intended to create a "police officer corps." The plan was described by the secretary of state as "revolutionary."[194] In Trenchard's vision, this was to produce an elite corps of police officials for England's police and for colonial police forces: an officer training school for the entire empire.[195] Trenchard had made similar educational reforms in the Royal Air Force. His proposal for Hendon College came partly from that experience and partly from similar programs at the Royal Military College at Sandhurst.[196] Meanwhile, Trenchard staffed the top positions in the London Metropolitan Police with former military officers.[197] Throughout, the Royal Air Force was a key source of ideas and personnel, but Trenchard also found inspiration in colonial police forces. Trenchard had interacted with colonial police officers in India and Iraq where he was in the RAF. His idea of creating an elite officer corps for the police was taken not only from the military—with its posh high-level officers—but also from those colonial police forces, particularly India's police, which had its own elite officer corps and recruiting system. Some of Trenchard's other reforms were also taken from colonial police forces. He assigned former military officials to new additional posts of chief inspector and instructed them to act as "criminal intelligence officers." This was a deviation from the tradition of gathering intelligence through the CID and the Special Branch. It likely was inspired by the Indian colonial police, which had a similar organizational array for collecting intelligence.[198]

Trenchard's program is telling because it hints at the cyclical dynamics of imperial militarization. Before Trenchard's wave, Charles Warren's reforms in the 1880s had been the last major one. After that, as noted above, his militarization faced resistance, and over the next few decades little happened in the way of police militarization. The only police appropriation from Britain's colonial-military regime was fingerprinting—a technical tool rather than a tool of violence. Trenchard's program was a return of sorts, marking a new wave of imperial militarization that once again appropriated a variety of tools, tactics, and techniques from Britain's imperial-military apparatus after decades of near-deliberate rejection of them.

But Trenchard's militarizing moves also met barriers. Unlike other waves of militarization, Trenchard's program was not triggered by a racialized panic. His plan for Q-cars appears to have been directed at the London neighborhood of Kilburn, populated by large numbers of Irish and Jewish immigrants, but it was likewise a response to "motor bandits" plaguing the highways in and around the metropolis.[199] His other plans were meant to strengthen the internal discipline of the force in the wake of low morale and controversies earlier in the 1920s. Some of these had to do with the new policemen's union, the Police Federation. The federation had been agitating for better conditions and was seen by some as dangerously flirting with radicals. Officials like Trenchard barely tolerated it.[200] Trenchard's reforms, therefore—not least his new educational schemes and his imposition of disciplinary measures—make sense as a response to white working-class recalcitrance rather than as a racialized panic over crime and order. This underscores the multivocality and modularity of imperial-military tools, tactics, and templates: colonial tools and tactics can be used on white populations too.

Yet exactly because Trenchard's program was triggered in the absence of a racialized panic over crime and disorder, it only went so far. We have seen how Warren's changes were swiftly rebuked—that is, once it was clear that Warren's militarism was not directed at racialized alters but rather against those perceived to be good citizens. Trenchard faced a similar problem. From the beginning of his appointment, various sectors registered concerns. George Lansbury of the Liberal Party worried that Trenchard might create a political police that would, like Warren's police decades earlier, repress public demonstrations. Registering his reservations about "the militarisation of the London Police Force," he noted the difference between Trenchard and Sir Edward Henry, who had previously served as commissioner:

> Everyone who had any experience of Sir Edward Henry when he was Commissioner of Police will say that there was less fault finding with him and his administration than there is at the present time, with regard to demonstrations, meetings, discussions and so on. I think the reason was that Sir Edward Henry had another view of the duties of a Police Commissioner. I do not think we want a semi military force as a Police Force. We do not need all this regimentation and drilling and so on. We need a Police Force for quite other purposes than those for which we need a military force.[201]

Even the home secretary who appointed Trenchard, Sir Herbert Samuel, recognized the danger of Trenchard's militarization. Though he defended

Trenchard against charges of excessive militarization, he nonetheless warned against any further "steps which would in any way result in the militarization of our police forces" and advised against many more military appointments to the police.[202]

During his administration, Trenchard continued to suffer criticisms. In the police journal called *The Police Chronicle*, an anonymous writer responded to Trenchard's program to offer new training in small firearms by writing: "The idea savours very strongly of Chicago or the militarization of the police force, and we are confident that neither the police of this country nor the general public are desirous of such a state of affairs. We consider that Lord Trenchard's project will be liable to cause unnecessary alarm in the country."[203] Others in the police rank and file, represented by their new union, also rebuked his plan to create a corps of elite police officials, claiming that this was a scheme to "alter the whole police force in the country by militarising it."[204] Members of the Labour Party asserted that the scheme was intended to "militarise and Hitlerise the police force." An editorial in the workers' journal *The People* decried: "I cannot distinguish the new Trenchardism from militarization."[205] Trenchard's attempt to enhance firearms training thus raised concerns. Rumors floated that he was trying to arm the entire police, and loud opposition came from the press as well from inside the police.[206]

We can now see the pattern. Militarization often happens through the work of imperial-military veterans, but its degree and the limits it faces are conditioned by varying local conditions. In Britain, the *targets* of police militarization shape its fate. From the beginning of the London Metropolitan Police, initial moments of imperial militarization were driven by racialized panics, with the idea that the enhanced powers of the police would be aimed at racialized others. But when militarization under Warren and Trenchard appeared to the public or to other officials and police constables to be aimed at *them* rather than at colonial subjects or racialized enemies, their resistance to imperial militarization was loud and pronounced. Evidently, so long as the imperial militarization of the British police was triggered by threats from racialized enemies, and so long as the appropriated coercive tools were applied to those racialized alters, imperial militarization could proceed with vigor. Otherwise, it was less likely to happen. Or if it did happen, as with Warren and Trenchard, it was halted in its tracks.

To conclude, consider one other example where militarization via the imperial boomerang was stopped short.[207] At stake was weaponized gas. As the historian Erik Linstrum tells us, beginning in 1919 British officials in the military and in colonial regimes began advocating for the use of weaponized gas on insurgent populations in the colonial periphery. One of the early advocates was Winston Churchill, who as war secretary in 1919 advocated the use of tear gas against Iraqi rebels and insurgent tribes on the North-West Frontier of India. In the 1930s, British officials finally used it. After fitting colonial police forces with tear gas equipment, the British deployed gas against a crowd in Burma in 1939. This set a precedent for its use in other colonies during the war, from the West Indies to India and Africa, to put down strikes and protests.

While tear gas made its way to the colonies, British authorities barely contemplated its use on English crowds. In 1933, a Home Office bureaucrat claimed that the "conditions in India are so vastly different from those obtaining here" that the police would never use it. In 1935, Home Secretary John Simon noted that "*our* problems are as a rule not so difficult [as those faced by officials in the colonies]" as to warrant the use of tear gas on home soil. As Linstrum points out, the difference was race: British officials came to the conclusion that tear gas was fine for racial inferiors, but taboo for English citizens.[208] This attests to the larger point: the colonial boomerang is most likely to return home only when it is aimed at those racialized peoples deemed deserving of it. The imperial militarization of the civil police sometimes reaches limits marked by the color line.

# PART III
# INFORMAL EMPIRE AND URBAN INSURGENCY

# 5

# Tactical Imperialism in the United States, 1950s–1970s

It is now accepted by most scholars that a new wave of police militarization was initiated after August 1965, when the neighborhood of Watts in Los Angeles erupted into flames. A violent encounter between police and a Black family started it all. The encounter attracted hundreds of observers, and the crowds soon swelled. Eventually, up to thirty-five thousand residents and their neighbors took to the streets. They threatened police command posts, shot at officers, threw Molotov cocktails, and laid waste to white-owned businesses. Authorities responded with a campaign of staggering proportions. It involved the National Guard, tanks, helicopters, tear gas, and a series of surprise raids on residents' homes. There were one thousand injuries, almost four thousand arrests, and thirty-four dead. It was the biggest urban uprising the nation had yet seen. But it was not the only one. In its wake, Black communities across America's cities— Detroit, Michigan; Dayton, Ohio; Atlanta, Georgia; Philadelphia, Pennsylvania; and Newark, New Jersey, among many others—rose up with indignation and defiance.

Two responses to the Watts uprising and the later "ghetto riots" constituted the wave of militarization that followed. One response was from the federal government. After Watts erupted, and as many other cities also saw similar uprisings, members of the public, leading politicians, and frightened officials clamored for "law and order." In response, President Lyndon Johnson and his allies in Congress stepped up the "war on crime" that Johnson had previously announced by creating the Office of Law Enforcement Assistance (OLEA). The OLEA program gave funding to local police departments to thwart future revolts and urban crime. As the historian Elizabeth Hinton details, the funds provided by the OLEA went to "military-grade rifles, tanks, riot gear, walkie-talkies, helicopters, and bulletproof vests" and the training of police departments on the "proper use of new, cutting-edge military technologies." This set the precedent for later legislative moves, such as the 1968 Omnibus Crime Control and Safe Streets Act, which further facilitated the transfer of military technologies and techniques to local police departments through the newly created Law Enforcement Assistance Administration (LEAA). The federal attempt to restore order through militarized policing in the aftermath of Watts continued thereafter, as the "war

*Policing Empires*. Julian Go, Oxford University Press. © Oxford University Press 2024.
DOI: 10.1093/oso/9780197621653.003.0006

on crime" transmuted into the "war on drugs."[1] After Watts, noted one police officer, "domestic counter insurgency has become a growth industry."[2]

The local-level response to the Watts uprisings was just as seminal: the formation of the Special Weapons and Tactics (SWAT) unit within the Los Angeles Police Department (LAPD). Two LAPD officers, John Nelson and Daryl Gates, conceived of SWAT in the aftermath of the uprisings. Gates had been serving in the LAPD, and Watts proved to him that the police "were not equipped to deal with the situation at all." As Gates later recalled: "Watts was hugely different from what we had been taught to encounter." Accordingly, Gates and his colleagues, including fellow officer Nelson, created a new tactical force within the LAPD called the Special Weapons and Attack Team, later renamed Special Weapons and Tactics. This was a small, elite militarized group within the LAPD. Trained in counterinsurgency tactics and formations, arrayed in battle-ready gear, wielding military-grade weaponry and anti-riot tools like CS gas (a form of tear gas), the LAPD SWAT unit was born. Its first major operation was an assault on the headquarters of the Black Panther Party. Armed with "sawed-off shotguns, semi-automatic rifles and tear gas," the twenty-seven-man unit used them all as they laid siege to the building in which eleven Panthers huddled for safety.[3] Soon enough, the unit became notorious for its heavy-handed approach to Black ghettos. It also served as a model for other police departments to emulate. Johnson's federal programs helped fund their formation across the country. By the 1980s nearly all police departments had their own version of it. Today, the American Civil Liberties Union, among many other organizations, sees SWAT teams as prime examples of "excessive militarization."[4]

Still, as the present chapter will show, the story of police militarization in the late 1960s is bigger than this, reaching far beyond what happened in Watts. For one thing, the story extends into America's imperial peripheries. We must not forget that Lyndon Johnson's crime management program, which gave cities funding to create their own SWAT-like units, was concomitant with America's war in Vietnam (in his 1967 State of the Union Address, the Vietnam War was the only topic that received more attention than his "war on crime" initiative). This underlines the fact that the same US military that offered knowledge, expertise, and weaponry to local police departments through the OLEA program was simultaneously engaged in an imperialistic war overseas.

In fact, both Gates and Nelson had been in the military before creating SWAT. Nelson had a wealth of knowledge to draw upon: he had served in elite units, such as "force recon" units, which in Vietnam were helping squash anti-imperialist guerrillas in the jungle. Watts was "guerilla warfare," Gates explained in his memoir, and so in response he and Nelson searched for better approaches. "We began reading everything we could get our hands on concerning guerilla warfare," Gates explained. "We watched with interest what was happening in

Vietnam. We looked at military training, and in particular we studied what a group of marines, based at the Naval Armory in Chavez Ravine, were doing. They shared with us their knowledge of counter insurgency and guerilla warfare."[5] SWAT was thus born from the ashes of imperial war overseas. Not co-incidentally, most of the SWAT members were veterans of either the Vietnam War or the Korean War.[6] The origins of militarization in the 1960s lie as much in Vietnam as in Watts.

The story also goes further back than 1964. To identify presumed subversives and danger zones during the Watts uprising, the LAPD used a tactic that was being used in counterinsurgency campaigns in Vietnamese villages: painting numbers on the roofs of public housing domiciles to facilitate helicopter surveillance.[7] This suggests that the LAPD had gone into Watts with an existing militarized mindset. Even before the Watts uprising, the police had already had the tools of imperial counterinsurgency in their repertoire. We are led to speculate that the wave of militarization that putatively began after the Watts uprising had been under way *before* Watts. Perhaps it was exactly this prior militarization that contributed to the uprising in Watts in the first place.

This chapter situates the wave of militarization in the aftermath of Watts within this broader frame. The chapter will look beyond Watts and even beyond Vietnam to consider other parts of the American empire, along with various other points of the Anglo-American interimperial network of postwar power. That network extended from the Philippines to Puerto Rico and Nicaragua, and from Shanghai and Singapore to Malabar and the Dominican Republic, among other places. Tracing that network will also take us to rural Vermont, where a veteran named Merritt Edson in the 1950s was charged with heading up its new state police force. In addition, the chapter stretches back in time from the 1920s through the 1950s. We will see that, indeed, the boomerang had returned home to militarize policing even before Watts, and that this prior round of militarization set the conditions for the Watts uprisings in the first place. It also set the stage for an entire wave of insurgencies that exploded across America's cities in the 1960s. Counterinsurgency tools used by the police in the 1950s and early 1960s bred the very horrors they were ostensibly meant to quell.

But it makes sense to begin the story in Harlem, one year before Watts erupted.

## "Special Operations" and the Rise of Tactical Policing

On July 18, 1964, the mostly Black residents of Harlem in New York City marched to the Harlem police station demanding the resignation of police lieutenant Thomas Gilligan, a war veteran. Two days earlier, Gilligan had shot and killed a fifteen-year-old boy named James Powell after a neighborhood altercation between a white apartment superintendent and local kids. Protestors chanted, "Murder, murder, murder." Their numbers grew to more than a thousand. The protest spread to Brooklyn. A series of subsequent violent confrontations with the police lasted almost a week. Newspapers called it "one of the most violent weekends in that Negro area's history."[8] It was Watts's precursor.

What is most salient for our purposes is not the protest itself but the police response. According to newspaper reports, the New York Police Department (NYPD) had a "carefully prepared battle plan" that included the deployment of three hundred cops along with a unit of the police known as the Tactical Patrol Force (TPF). The New York TPF was a specialized and heavily militarized squad. Created in 1959, it was led by a military veteran and consisted of men who were "all judo-trained riot-control experts." The men "wore hard hats of plastic or steel to ward off missiles—bottles, garbage can lids, broken pieces of pipe, beer cans—thrown from roofs and windows and to protect them from blasts of the Molotov cocktails."[9] The TPF had arrived in their own bus and, according to one local reverend, came into Harlem "swinging their clubs . . . as though they were on a rabbit hunt."[10] Eventually, authorities had to extract the TPF from the Brooklyn neighborhood of Bedford-Stuyvesant because their presence had been too provocative. "TPF men, all husky 6-footers trained in the roughest combat techniques," noted the press, were "particularly feared and hated in slum areas."[11]

If the Harlem uprising of 1964 reminds us that Watts was not the first such urban uprising in the United States, the NYPD's response to the Harlem uprising tells us that the LAPD's SWAT team was not the first heavily militarized police unit in the country. In fact, neither NYC's TPF nor LAPD's SWAT team was especially unique. They were variants of a new postwar form of policing that was spreading around the country: special units within police departments variously labeled "tactical units," "tactical forces," "reserve units," "shock troops," "task forces," "flexible units," "mobile reserve forces," or "mobile strike forces." By the mid-1960s, most large US cities had them. President Lyndon Johnson's Presidential Commission on Law Enforcement noticed the trend in 1967: "The concept of a mobile striking force or task force has been growing in importance in recent years."[12] *Newsweek* magazine took notice too, observing in 1966: "New York calls its shock troops the Tactical Patrol Force, Chicago the Task Force, Detroit the Tactical Mobile Unit."[13] In 1968, P. D. Knights, a constable from England, toured twenty-three states and talked to representations of thirty-four police agencies, finding that nearly all had a tactical unit.[14]

The spread of tactical units had been partly facilitated by President Johnson's Crime Control Act of 1967, which directed funding to "the cost of training new tactical units . . . so they can become weapons in the war on crime."[15] But it is noteworthy that the first of these tactical forces was born in the 1950s, well before the tumult of the early 1960s that would later lead to the birth of SWAT in Los

Angeles. If we had to identify a new wave of police militarization after the Second World War and before Watts, this is where to look: the rise of tactical policing in the late 1950s.

What were these new postwar tactical units? V. A. Leonard, a former police officer in Berkeley, California, and Fort Worth, Texas, was prescient in his 1951 textbook *Police Organization and Management*. Drawing upon his teacher Vollmer's ideas, he made one of the first references to tactical units in the published policing literature. He distinguished between the "general operations" and "special operations" of police. The former encompassed "the normal daily problems associated with crime, vice, traffic and miscellaneous activities," while special operations encompassed "the attack upon specific problems and emerging situations" and required "an overwhelming concentration of striking power at a particular time and place to meet a specific problem."[16] The tactical unit was one modality for carrying out these special operations. Unlike routine patrols and their strategically oriented beats, tactical units stood ready to be dispatched on command. Tactical units embodied "the mobile power of the department which can be concentrated in any quarter of the city and at whatever hour or hours the circumstances may dictate."[17] Or as the President's Commission later explained: "Mobile striking forces" were "designed to operate as a compact, mobile, effective, operational striking force in given locations at times where the record indicates the need for a special concentration of enforcement pressure."[18]

Tactical units specialized in two areas. One was crowd control during strikes, demonstrations, protests, and "riots," as O. W. Wilson noted in his reference to tactical units in his 1963 textbook.[19] Tactical units were riot squads. As noted already, the LAPD's SWAT team was created exactly to control urban uprisings. In Oak Park, Michigan, one of the fastest-growing communities in the country in the 1950s and home to major auto factories, fears about workers' strikes led to the creation of its tactical unit, which was "trained not only in the techniques of reducing civil disorders but also in handling other civil emergencies.[20] Anne Arundel County in Maryland did not experience any major strikes, demonstrations, or riots, but the county police nonetheless created a tactical unit in anticipation of the sort of unrest that had erupted in nearby Baltimore and Washington, DC.[21] The city of Delano, California, created its tactical unit in response to the grape workers' strike. The LAPD's SWAT unit, according to its creators, was partly inspired by Delano's tactical unit.

The other main task area of tactical units was the suppression of neighborhood-level, spatially delimited crime. New York's TPF began as a unit aimed primarily at crime control, as did Chicago's Task Force (1956), St. Louis's Mobile Reserve Division (1958), New Orleans's Tactical Unit (1959), and Tucson's Tactical Squad (1960), among others.[22] Some units were formed initially for crime control but later shifted toward order maintenance, and vice versa. New York's TPF began primarily as a crime-fighting unit, but as the 1960s progressed it shifted its attention to riots, strikes, and demonstrations (including but not restricted to the Harlem riots of 1964). Detroit created its own Commando Squad in 1956, inspired by New York's TPF, meant to "quell riots or tumultuous assemblies," but it was also redirected to crime prevention and other policing tasks.[23]

The tactical units' approach to crime was saturation. Whereas police patrols operated according to their regular beats, tactical units were deployed to areas of the city where there was a perceived (or recorded) spike in criminal activity, or where criminal activity was projected to be high. They would occupy the area for short or extended periods of time in the hopes of subduing the specified criminal activity. This was a temporary territoriality marked by heightened concentrations of force.

This approach differed significantly from conventional beat patrols and nearly all prior models of policing. In the idealized image of Anglo-American civil policing, patrolmen were tied to their beats and thus known to the communities they covered. This is the image of the "bobby on the beat" in England (or, in the film *West Side Story*, Officer Krupke, the local patrolman whom New York's juvenile gangs taunted). But the mobility and territorial temporality of tactical units changed things. According to policing scholar Albert Reiss Jr., tactical units exemplified a different emergent form of policing, which he called "reactive."[24] Rather than routinely patrol an area, units would be dispatched as the situation demanded, swooping in to manage outbreaks of social disorder or crime, and then swiftly exit. They "moved rapidly from one point to another," as Leonard explained, with no connections to the neighborhoods upon which they descended, nor familiarity with the populations they policed.[25] In this regard, the labels "mobile striking force" and "tactical unit" are especially appropriate, as they captured the flexibility and movement of coercive forms lacking any roots or sustained interactions with their targets. The historian Simon Balto accordingly notes that Chicago's mobile strike force, known as the Task Force, marked a "fundamental shift in policing methods, and represented a transformed relationship between police and community." The task force had "no acclimation period to a neighborhood and no intimate knowledge of the people and place, instead policing citizens with whom they had no relationships whatsoever."[26]

The elite nature of tactical units also marked them as distinct from regular patrols. Tactical units typically consisted of a select subset of the larger police force chosen for their special qualities, characterized by V. A. Leonard as "moral courage, together with physical courage and endurance of a high order."[27] They were young, eager, and aggressive. The members of the New York TPF were described in 1962 by Commissioner Michael J. Murphy as "less than 30 [years of age], more than six feet, and with an I.Q. of 110 or higher." Murphy explained that the most important characteristics "are desirable attitude, top potential in physical characteristics, [and] aggressiveness tempered by common sense and intelligence."[28] A former New York TPF member described his force as "cops all over six feet tall who had shown their capacity for tough policing. These were cops who liked being cops, liked being active, and liked making arrests."[29] In accordance with their elite status within the force, they typically received extra training in specialized tactics and operations such as riot control. The New York TPF trained in the Police Academy but also underwent extra training in riot management, the use of tear gas, sniper-level marksmanship, and academic topics including sociology and law.

Many members of tactical forces were selected because they had military backgrounds. The preference for veterans to man police forces was part of a larger trend during the period. Due to shortages in police personnel, some police chiefs expressly sought out veterans to join their departments. But tactical units stood out for the military experience of their members. The head of New York's TPF in 1968 stated that he selected men "with some military experience . . . because we work more like a highly mobile Army unit than like traditional policemen."[30] McCarthy himself was a military veteran. St. Louis's tactical unit, the Mobile Reserve Division, was also led by a veteran of the Second World War, Lieutenant Robert Matteson, who had served in the Marines and participated in the Saipan, Tinian, and Okinawa campaigns.[31] Similarly, every one of the members of LAPD's first SWAT unit had military experience.[32]

Fittingly, tactical units were often seen as akin to highly disciplined and specialized elite units of the military rather than regular forces. Gates described SWAT teams as "essentially infantry type units."[33] The chief of police in St. Louis declared that his mobile reserve unit functions like "military reinforcements during a battle."[34] In its analysis of various mobile strike forces in the early 1960s, *Newsweek* magazine referred to tactical units as "shock troops" akin to "green berets."[35] The writer William Turner noted in 1968 that New York's Tactical Patrol Force were men "imbued with a 'gung-ho' spirit reminiscent of the Army's Green Berets."[36] A member of New York's TPF scaled up the comparison, classifying the TPF as "the police equivalent of the Marine Corps" as opposed to the regular army.[37]

Tactical units were equipped like elite military forces. They used the latest technologies (such as automobiles or special vans and two-way radios) and intelligence just as elite reconnaissance forces did. They tracked enemies, generated spot maps, and calculated enemy movements.[38] Tactical forces typically wielded military-grade weaponry. Detroit's Commando Squad was "drilled in riot control" and was "equipped with the latest in special arms, rifles with bayonets, tommy guns, extra size night sticks, tear gas, steel helmets and other special equipment," as Detroit commissioner Edward S. Piggins explained in 1956.[39]

The squad also had a modified M-8 armored car: "a battlefield vehicle with a battering ram prow given by the army to use in breaking up riots and flushing barricaded gunmen out of buildings." Its crew was armed with "tear gas guns, submachine guns, shotguns and pistols."[40] In the 1960s, in the aftermath of the Watts uprisings—and not least through President Johnson's "war on crime"— many more police officers and departments would have access to this militarized training, weaponry, and equipment. But the mobile strike forces, crime task forces, and tactical units emerging in the late 1950s and early 1960s led the way.

All of this begs the question: where did these units come from? The military influence is already clear, but the imperial-military inspiration needs to be considered too.

## Tactical Imperialism from the Philippines and Haiti to Shanghai

The creation and proliferation of tactical police units in the late 1950s through the 1960s were shaped by important transformations in imperial repertoires of power. For example, the Americans' campaign against Axis forces in both the European and Asian theaters during the Second World War had relied upon small tactical units and elite forces. US Army strategists thus praised the "tactical mobility" of elite units as vital for victory. "Our forces must be able to concentrate with great speed, fight to a quick decision, and then disperse rapidly," declared Major General Haydon Boatner, provost marshal general of the army, in 1958 to the IACP.[41] This sounds very much like the way police officials described their new policing tactical units. It is not coincidental that many of the military veterans who manned the new tactical forces had cut their teeth during the Second World War or the Korean War.[42]

Still, even these elite tactical units in the military had not dropped from the sky. They were part of a longer history of war, counterinsurgency, and colonial policing that not only predated but influenced the army's creation of small elite units during the Second World War. This is a history of America's rising overseas empire and its expanding global role in the early twentieth century.

One key component of America's earlier imperial formation had been the division between territorially based power and more fluid tactical interventions. This is exactly the sort of division that tactical policing later generated when it emerged in the 1950s: that is, between regular fixed patrols on the one hand (or what Leonard had called "general operations") and specialized and mobile tactical forces (or "special operations") on the other. This division was embedded in the new structure of American empire in the early decades of the century. On the one hand, America's overseas possessions such as the Philippines, Puerto

Rico, Guam, Samoa, and the Virgin Islands required enduring institutions that extended America's direct colonial control—near-permanent colonial states with persistent, repeated, and routine administration. On the other hand, as the early twentieth century proceeded, America's imperial repertoire included other modalities that might be characterized as "informal imperialism" or, more appropriately, *tactical imperialism*. This is a form of imperialism that fell just short of direct colonial rule. Rather than declare sovereignty over a territory and create a lasting colonial state and associated juridical, economic, and other social systems, the United States created a more flexible imperial network of power whereby it would invade a society and subject it to overwhelming military power. It would temporarily occupy that society, creating nominally independent national institutions in the country and installing a friendly regime before exiting to control matters from afar. Such was the preferred mode of intervention in Latin America, Central America, and the Caribbean in the first decades of the twentieth century, as the United States sent its military to invade and temporarily occupy Cuba, Haiti, the Dominican Republic, and Nicaragua, among many other countries.[43]

Tactical imperialism, as opposed to colonial empire, thereby entailed temporary territoriality and required flexible interventions, mobile units, and concentrated force rather than fully fledged colonial states. It involved the same practice of saturation that tactical police forces launched, just at the level of a foreign nation rather than a neighborhood. As the US imperial-military apparatus served as a regional (and then global) policeman, tactical imperialism was the way for the US to saturate foreign countries with military force, oust unfriendly regimes, establish military governments, and squash insurgencies. America's occupying military forces thereby acted as mobile strike forces or tactical units on a global scale, ready to suppress "crimes" against American interests (such as rebellions or foreign regimes defying America's authority). If the United States rose to power to become the "world's policeman," it did so through a form of global policing that operated through tactical deployments rather than fixed territorial patrols (i.e., colonial control). President Eisenhower intimated this in his speech on America's role in the Korean conflict. America's military, he declared in 1952, must "be the great mobile reserve of the free world . . . to provide air and sea support where ever and whenever needed."[44] American force, the press noted in response, was being reconfigured into a "mobile reserve" to be sent to "trouble spots" around the globe.[45]

The emergence of tactical imperialism as a dominant modality of empire in the early twentieth century alongside colonial rule was concomitant with new forms of military organization. As the army nestled into its new regional and global imperial role in the wake of the Spanish-American War, military strategists recognized the need to construct new systems to better defend "the nation and its modest insular possessions."[46] In 1912, Brigadier General Clarence R. Edwards, chief of the Bureau of Insular Affairs, in charge of America's overseas colonies, accordingly suggested the army bifurcate "into tactical as distinct from territorial divisions," which would permit greater flexibility, mobility, and reach.[47] The term "tactical unit" was subsequently used and applied more regularly in the military thereafter. It was also used by the British: in the 1930s, the Royal Air Force had its own special "tactical units" for home defense.[48]

Tactical imperialism was scalar. On the global scale, tactical imperialism meant sending military forces to international trouble spots, saturating foreign countries through temporary military occupation. But on a national-level scale, it meant the deployment of small tactical units during occupation, dispatching elite units from the military government's base in the capital to insurgent areas in the jungles and mountains. This goes back to August Vollmer's experience in the Philippines: the US Army's elite mobile units in which Vollmer had served were perfected and deployed during the Philippine-American War before transmuting into the Philippine Constabulary (see Chapter 3). It is hardly coincidental that V. A. Leonard, who first discussed tactical units and mobile "strike forces," took the distinction between "general operations" and "special operations" from Vollmer.[49]

After the early deployments of small mobile forces in the Philippines, US military manuals on counterinsurgency tactics slowly incorporated the lessons learned. The 1908 Field Service Regulations offered the newly emerging idea that elite mobile patrols "could be specially formed to combat other small units" rather than just serving reconnaissance functions.[50] Small mobile units, in the form of either military units or colonial police forces, subsequently proliferated from the 1910s through the 1930s. The US military in Haiti created them to face down the Caco insurgency. The Gendarmerie of Haiti, led by Smedley Butler, was a kind of tactical unit. Mobile units also emerged in the form of the "Coco patrols" during the Marines' counterinsurgency efforts against Augusto Sandino's uprising in nearby Nicaragua during the 1920s.[51] The small units created during the Second World War simply copied these early forces. By the time of America's war in Vietnam, small mobile units deployed to saturate and temporarily patrol territory were the basis for the entire invasion. The US Army's "tactical doctrine" dictated that mobile units be sent to areas of the jungle for "saturation patrolling," in the words of military strategists.[52]

The British Empire also served as a space for the development of tactical units and mobile strike forces, first emerging in Madras, India, in the 1920s and then spreading through the empire in various guises. These forces included anti-riot units to supplement regular police forces (see Chapter 6). There were also developments within the shared imperial space of Shanghai in the 1920s and 1930s. The Shanghai International Settlement was a large and diverse urban port in Shanghai that, by the 1920s, had become a nodal point in America's and Britain's imperial networks: a form of "transnational colonialism," as the historian Isabella Jackson characterizes it. Since 1854 it had been run by an administration called the Shanghai Municipal Council (SMC), which was putatively international in membership but was controlled mainly by British agents and US interests (in the 1920s it had five members, British, American, Chinese, and Japanese, but the British and Americans together outnumbered the latter two). The SMC behaved like an "aggressive and militarized city-state," protecting the interests of transnational capital against the mixed population.[53] It had created the Shanghai Municipal Police (SMP), whose senior officials were all British (at least before the Second World War). This was an Asian-styled Royal Irish Constabulary, with former members of the RIC filling senior posts.[54]

The SMP also had its own tactical unit: the Shanghai Reserve Unit (SRU). This was modeled partly upon India's anti-riot units and mobile strike forces, but it was modified for the particularly urban and cosmopolitan terrain of Shanghai.[55] It was created in 1925 by British assistant commissioner William E. Fairbairn in response to recurrent rounds of worker-led strikes, riots, nationalist protests, and criminal gang activity. Separate from regular SMP patrols, the SRU was meant to deal with emergencies and outbreaks requiring concentrated skilled force. Of particular concern were riots, demonstrations, and strikes staged by the growing population of seemingly recalcitrant workers, as well as by anti-imperialist nationalist groups (such as those affiliated with Sun Yat-Sen's Guomindang before it took power in 1927 and which the SMP labeled "criminal").[56] As R. M. J. Martin of the SMP noted, the SRU was referred to by the press as Shanghai's "Riot Squad."[57] The unit was also available to conduct raids on gambling dens, track criminals in the subterranean spaces of the city, and perform urban counterterrorism operations.[58]

The SRU had its own special tactical vehicle, called the "Red Mariam," containing special searchlights, sirens, a "Thompson sub-machine gun on a detachable roof mounting, a .12 gauge riot-gun; a riot flag and gas-masks; ladders, axes, crowbars, bolt-cutters and hand-cuffs; knotted ropes for climbing; ropes for barricades; spare batons; bullet-proof shields; reserve ammunition and a medical chest."[59] The SRU also wielded tear gas, advancing upon unruly crowds and would-be rioters while bearing banners that warned crowds that gas might be deployed against them should they disobey. The unit consisted of about eighty men divided into fourteen-man squads; its members were Sikh, Chinese, Japanese, and European and were led by Fairbairn and his largely British team. The men were trained in a variety of combat techniques. Fairbairn became renowned for teaching the Reserve Unit hand-to-hand combat techniques from the East, such as jiu-jitsu and judo, along with small arms training, sniper training, and other specialized combat skills.[60]

Some historians refer to the Shanghai Reserve Unit as the "world's first S.W.A.T. team."[61] This is likely an exaggeration, though it is true that Fairbairn's SRU was influential. It influenced the US Marines and its riot-control methods, combat techniques, and special forces. During the Second World War, Fairbairn's book on close combat training received so much popular attention that he was asked by the US military to compose a training curriculum on "commando" techniques like jiu-jitsu and "Chinese boxing." His curriculum was instituted as part of regular army training.[62]

The turn to Fairbairn by the US military was natural. Marines had been stationed in Shanghai in the 1920s and 1930s, working with the SRU and developing their own riot company similar to it. At times the Marines' unit was even called in to support the SRU.[63] An array of prominent US military strategists and officers learned from the SRU. They included future generals like Clifton Cates, Wallace Greene, Robert Hogaboom, Victor Krulak, Herman Nickerson, and Robert Williams.[64] One Marine who worked with the SRU in Shanghai, Evans Carlson, drew upon his Shanghai experience and combined it with his previous experience with small mobile units in Nicaragua (the Guardia Nacional) to become a leading figure in creating America's Special Operations Forces during the Second World War and after.[65] If America's small "commando" units during the Second World War inspired tactical police units in the 1950s, their origins lie in the peripheries of empire.

## Circuits of Influence

Through various circuits and networks, the mobile strike forces, police reserve units, and "riot squads" like the SRU would become well known to police officials in the mainland United States. Police officials across the nation were likely introduced to the Shanghai Reserve Unit and Britain's repertoire of colonial police units through the new International Police Conferences or meetings of the International Association of Chiefs of Police, where police chiefs from around the world—ranging from Cuba and the Philippines to India, Canada, countries in Africa, and other Asian countries—mingled and exchanged ideas. These interactions represented a larger internationalization of policing in the 1920s and the 1930s. Some officials like Vollmer, who served as president of the IACP in this period, corresponded with British police officials and visited British colonies to observe their policing systems. In turn, Vollmer was among police officials in the United States who hosted visits and inspections of US police agencies by British colonial police officials.[66] Fairbairn of the SRU came to the United States from Shanghai to give lectures on his police force. While in Chicago Fairbairn was quoted as saying: "We in China can't understand why Chicago police have so much trouble with gangsters. We don't allow our criminal element to organize in Shanghai."[67]

There were also straight lines from America's imperial-military regime to US policing. Police chiefs like Vollmer and Smedley Butler (discussed in Chapter 3) had had direct experience with mobile counterinsurgency units. Butler had even gone to Shanghai.[68] Others included Merritt A. Edson, who served in the "Coco patrols" in Nicaragua. In 1929, he returned to the United States to train soldiers. He then went to Shanghai, worked alongside the Shanghai SRU, and served in the Second World War. After the war, he became the first commissioner of the Vermont State Police.

Still, police chiefs were not the only veterans with knowledge of mobile units, as military veterans flowed into the lower ranks of US policing as well. In Los Angeles, Chief William Parker reported in 1951 that 72 percent of the police force were "veterans of military service."[69] In 1946, the NYPD "appointed 2,000 new police officers, all of them recently discharged veterans."[70] Some of these military veterans acted as imperial importers by advising or training police. Rex Applegate joined the US military police in 1939, trained in England with British commandos, and fought with them in the European campaign during the Second World War. Back in the States, he also worked with Fairbairn of the SRU to train soldiers in Fairbairn's close combat methods, earning a reputation as one of "the most lucid proponents of the Shanghai methods of Fairbairn and Sykes [Fairbairn's colleague in Shanghai]."[71] He advised riot squads in Mexico City and counseled the military and police officials alike on riot control techniques. He published books on close combat and riot control, one of which, *Crowd and Riot Control*, was reportedly used by law enforcement agencies all around the world.[72] In that work, Applegate devoted a long chapter to the "professional riot control unit," which drew from his experience of colonial policing and counterinsurgency units overseas to discuss various anti-riot gear, techniques, and formations—many of which had been innovated by the Shanghai Reserve Unit.[73]

Through these and other channels, the tactical forces of the American imperial-military regime came to influence policing. The LAPD was a nodal point. As seen in Chapter 3, Vollmer had innovated mobile police tactics. He mounted his entire force in Berkeley and later established a special mobile unit in Los Angeles in the 1920s, the Crime Crushers, modeled upon counterinsurgency army units. While Vollmer's unit was short-lived (due to internal politics, Vollmer was ousted and his Crime Crushers unit was dismantled), the precedent was nonetheless set, opening the door for further elaboration. Vollmer's successors created their own versions of the Crime Crushers under different labels. In 1933, Chief James E. Davis created the LAPD's Reserve Unit, consisting of a lieutenant, a sergeant, and thirty-nine men, and subsumed it under his new Metropolitan Division.[74] The nominal similarity to Fairbairn's Shanghai Reserve

Unit was probably not coincidental. By 1933, Fairbairn and the Shanghai police were well known. Fairbairn passed through Los Angeles in 1930 on his lecture tour.[75] Chief Davis himself must have been familiar with the SRU and its colonial variants, for he, like Vollmer, had served in the army in the Philippines.[76] Davis's Reserve Unit subsequently expanded on Vollmer's Crime Crushers by taking on the same dual functions as the SRU. As Davis explained in his report, the Reserve Unit was meant to saturate areas of high crime and where "criminals often congregate" but also "to suppress riots and to police demonstrations."[77] Vollmer's tactical unit had only been tasked with crime control, not public order events. Davis's Reserve Unit was thus a perfect amalgam of Vollmer's Crime Crushers and the SRU.[78]

In the 1950s, the Metropolitan Division of the LAPD took over the functions of Davis's Reserve Unit. Newspapers noted that the Metropolitan Division was a direct descendant not just of the Reserve Unit but also of Vollmer's Crime Crushers. It was an elite unit that served as the "mobile reserve" to be sent to "areas of high crime frequency" and also police "riots, strikes and public events."[79] Consisting of seventy officers, two lieutenants, and eight sergeants, the Metropolitan Division, sometimes called the Metropolitan Squad, Metropolitan Unit, or Metro, was described by one journalist in 1958 as "the small, tough, mobile force of super-specialists," moving "all over the place, geographically and procedurally," that excelled in everything from "shotgun handling" to "riot work."[80]

It is significant that the chief of the LAPD responsible for the Metro was William Parker. Parker was a military veteran who had also served under O. W. Wilson (a protégé of Vollmer's) to help rebuild the German police department after the Second World War. During his tenure, Parker studied Vollmer's writings and restructured the LAPD into a tight military hierarchy. He wore four stars on his uniform, referred to his deputy chiefs as "the general staff," and issued directives that were known as "general orders."[81] He revamped the intelligence section he had inherited from the Vollmer years, referring to it using the military nomenclature "G2" and employing it to guide the Metro Division's movements.[82] Under him, the Metro Division became known as the "commando cops." Parker boasted in 1961 that the Metro Division was responsible for reducing crime, for freeing Los Angeles from any major "crowd control incidents," and for being "the most effective mobile police force in the nation," one that other cities studied and copied.[83] Vollmer's influence, and with it the influence of America's imperial-military regime, thus persisted long after Vollmer.

The LAPD, in short, served as a laboratory by which tactical policing was imported into the domestic field from the imperial field in the 1920s through the 1950s. Vollmer's Crime Crushers, Davis's Reserve Unit, and Parker's Metro were all precursors to tactical units like SWAT. Later, LAPD's SWAT would take credit for being the first tactical unit, even though it was created within and was *part* of the Metro Division (the difference being that it was focused exclusively on crowd control). SWAT did not represent much that was new, therefore; it was merely a revamped and more specialized version of prior tactical units in LA that had been brought to the metropole from imperial peripheries.

In any case, the influence of LA's tactical units was wide. Vollmer's Crime Crushers and Parker's Metro Division were popularized in police administration texts and training programs. In 1954, Chief Parker wrote about the LAPD's Metropolitan Division in a textbook used by the Institute for Training in Municipal Administration.[84] One of Vollmer's students had been V. A. Leonard, and he discussed the LAPD's tactical units in his 1951 text and subsequent editions. This is the book in which Leonard, borrowing from Vollmer, introduces the distinction between general operations and special operations, specifying the tactical unit as the main component of the latter. Notably, when Leonard named the influences upon and precedents for tactical police units, he referred to mobile forces in the British Empire, the Texas Rangers, and the LAPD's units that Vollmer had begun. Leonard later recalled that it was Vollmer who "conceived and created the first tactical unit, the mobile task force."[85]

O. W. Wilson was another of Vollmer's students who helped popularize tactical units. He had served as police chief in Fullerton, California, and Wichita, Kansas, before becoming provost marshal for the US Army during the Second World War, after which he helped reconstitute the German police force. Parker had been one of his protégés. Wilson ran Chicago's police department from 1960 to 1967, but before that he had published *Police Administration* (1951, 1963), which extolled the virtues of the "mobile reserve unit or task force" and the "use of Tactical Forces."[86] By the time the LEAA under President Johnson provided funding for tactical units in 1968, its main reference point was Wilson's analysis and his positive assessment of tactical police units.[87]

Through Vollmer's descendants, the LAPD, and various other circuits, the idea of mobile tactical police units to supplement regular police patrols became an integral part of America's policing repertoire well before the 1960s.[88] After Los Angeles, the earliest known tactical police units included Chicago's Task Force (1956), St. Louis's Mobile Reserve Division (1958), New Orleans's Tactical Unit (1959), and New York's Tactical Patrol Force. These were all fashioned after colonial police units and mobile counterinsurgency forces and employed their tactics.

The saturation campaigns of these units to quell crime, for example, used spot maps of crime areas from statistical and analytic bureaus, just as Vollmer's mobile unit in the Philippines, Edson's Coco patrols in Nicaragua, and Butler's Marines in Haiti used mapping of insurgent movements and strikes to determine how to distribute their patrols. In his discussion of tactical units, Leonard stressed in his textbook that maps and statistics from the Record Division for special operations should be used "according to tested combat principles," and he referred to Vollmer's use of pin maps as an example.[89] The NYPD's TPF was one among many that picked up the trend. It had its own "analytic section" that, as Commissioner Murphy reported in 1961, "has the function of examining departmental crime statistics to determine the most fertile areas for future operations" and thereby enhance the force's "striking power."[90] By the end of the 1960s the NYPD used an IBM "crime index" to predict hot spots so that the TPF could "saturate a precinct and at the same time work as a reserve force," as TPF commander Michael J. Codd explained.[91] In 1960, in Pontiac, Michigan, the Flexible Unit used data on suspects and crime to generate "standard and special spot maps" to see where there was "a need for force."[92] New Orleans's tactical unit moved in patrol cars "following color coded maps" created by intelligence officers for its "all-out attack against criminals, vagrants, and floaters in the city."[93] San Francisco's tactical unit collected information through its saturation efforts and created identification cards on suspects and residents, like those used in the Philippine-American War.[94] This was a practice adopted as well by St. Louis's Mobile Reserve Division, which used pin maps to guide its saturation efforts. The Mobile Reserve Division routinely stopped and questioned "suspicious persons at night," collecting information using "interrogation cards" and storing the information for future use. In the first six months of 1959, the division conducted 976 "field interrogations" (as they were called by the division, using a term also employed by the military).[95]

The high mobility, tactical nature, and secrecy of some police tactical units also mirrored the operations of counterinsurgency forces. Chicago's Task Force emulated the precision and surprise of army units, keeping its movements secret until the moment of its deployment.[96] The *Chicago Sunday Tribune* described the Task Force as "Chicago's unique police commandos, the latest weapon against the war of law versus crime," noting: "As if the assignment were to take a Normandy beachhead, each skirmish is stamped secret. Neither day nor night shift knows where it is going until minutes before departure time."[97] In Philadelphia, in response to the ongoing uprisings of the latter part of the 1960s, Commissioner Frank Rizzo had his force placed in "air-conditioned buses at strategic points around the city, ready to move quickly to any area where a massive show of police manpower might nip an incipient riot in the bud."[98] To guide its riot control activities, New York's Tactical Patrol Force mapped out the city as though it were foreign terrain, using "riot maps" that showed "topography, access and escape routes, possible police mobilization points and all liquor stores, bars, clubs, sewer lines, Con Ed tunnels and gun stores" to "supply all the necessary information" for controlling riots once they erupted.[99] All of this was conceptualized in military terms. Commissioner Edward Piggins of Detroit's police said that his tactical unit met riots with the principle of "getting there first with the most."[100] This was exactly Vollmer's "military principle" of "getting there the fastest with the mostest men." The same phrase was used by observers to describe Chicago's Task Force.[101]

Police units were trained accordingly. Leonard opined that tactical units should be trained by the military in riot control methods. "The services of commanding officers in the United States Army and in the National Guard, who are usually available in nearby military installations, should be engaged as instructors in such a training program. Their training and experience will prove indispensable to the success of police plans and operations in this phase of the departmental program."[102] Most if not all units, from New York and Chicago to San Francisco and Hawaii, copied the Shanghai Reserve Unit directly by training their men in jiu-jitsu, judo, or other forms of hand-to-hand combat that had been popularized by Fairbairn and Applegate (see Figure 5.1).[103]

It is clear, therefore, that the new tactical units of the late 1950s and 1960s had imperial origins. Tactical policing from Los Angeles to Chicago to New York—and places in between—was an effect of the imperial boomerang. The remaining question is this: what exactly drew the boomerang home? *Why* were the modalities of force used in the Philippines, India, Shanghai, Haiti, and elsewhere imported for domestic use?

**Figure 5.1.** Hand-to-Hand Combat Training, Honolulu Police, Circa 1939
Source: August Vollmer Portrait Collection, BANC PIC 1957.018--PIC, The Bancroft Library, University of California, Berkeley

## Racialization and New Urban Threats

The availability of tactical units by the 1950s did not immediately lead to their swift proliferation across America's cities and towns. Instead, tactical police forces first cropped up in certain vanguard departments. After the seminal experimentation in Los Angeles under Vollmer and his successors in the 1920s and 1930s, the earliest and most prominent forms of tactical policing emerged in Chicago and New York. In Chicago in 1956, after some fleeting and minor experiments with "special squads" in the immediate postwar years under Police Commissioner Prendergast, the notorious Task Force was born under Commissioner Timothy O'Connor.[104] In New York, the Tactical Patrol Force was created in 1959 under Commissioner Stephen P. Kennedy. Both tactical forces are notable because of their comparably early formation; they were among the first to pick up the tradition of imperial importation that Vollmer and Davies had initiated in Los Angeles. They are also notable because they engendered emulation by other departments. Examining the reasons they were formed might tell us something about why the imperial boomerang returned in the late 1950s and early 1960s.

One possible explanation for the creation of tactical units is the military experience of the police chiefs. In Los Angeles, Vollmer, Davis, and Parker were all veterans. But the police commissioners in Chicago and New York who created the seminal tactical units were not military veterans; O'Connor in Chicago and Kennedy in New York had begun their careers as patrolmen. The converse also applies. In the 1950s, some police departments were led by veterans, many of whom would have had experience with elite specialized units in the army or Marines. But not all of these departments led the way in creating tactical units or mobile strike forces.

Merritt A. Edson of the Vermont State Police is a case in point. In 1947, Edson was appointed the commissioner of Vermont's new state police department (also called the Department of Public Safety). Given his wide discretionary power to shape the department, Edson had every opportunity to militarize the new force and create a dual system of patrols and tactical units.[105] The department, manned by fifty-five troopers, had been created in response to public demands for a statewide system to repress criminal activity and manage emergencies. The public might have welcomed a militaristic tactical force. Existing models of state police, like the Pennsylvania State Police, had already set the precedent for militarized state police agencies (as seen in Chapter 3).[106] And Edson had experience with America's tactical counterinsurgency regime, perhaps even more than Vollmer had. He had served along the Mexican border in 1916 and in France and occupied Germany during the First World War. In the 1920s, he served in the US colony of Guam and then went to Nicaragua to lead an elite counterinsurgency Marine unit, the Coco River Patrol, which was deployed to saturate insurgent areas. He later served with the 4th Marines in Shanghai, working with Fairbairn's Shanghai police, and then led a unit known as Edson's Raiders against the Japanese in the Pacific.[107] If anyone would have imported small, elite, martial tactical units to American policing in this period, it would have been Edson.

Edson did create a militarized form of police that extended the London Metropolitan model to the entire state of Vermont. He made the force a professionalized and full-time body of men who wore uniforms modeled after the Marine Corps in which Edson had served. He also divided up the state as police officials had divided up London, New York, and other cities, creating geographic districts (District A, District B, etc.), each with its own headquarters and patrols, equipping them with cars, radios, and .38 revolvers.[108] But Edson did not overlay this system of general operations with special operations units consisting of mobile strike forces or tactical units. He stuck to regular patrols. Was this because the police force was meant only to deal with traffic? In fact, Edson was determined that his force would attend to crime and disorder, not just traffic violations, so that the public "will come to look to the state police as their first source in case of necessity," as Edson put it.[109] Did Edson fail to create a tactical unit because there was no crime? To the contrary, the state police had been created precisely in response to perceived increases in crime. And in its first years of operation, Edson's police attended to cattle thefts, shootings involving hunters, cases of hit-and-run, thefts from homes and automobiles, and gambling dens. In 1950, the department made 843 arrests relating to such crimes (that is, not involving motor vehicle violations).[110] Still, Edson did not follow the LAPD model or draw upon his military experience to create a tactical unit.[111] Why not?

Vermont, of course, was not Los Angeles, Chicago, or New York. It was largely rural, and Edson expressly noted that he wished his police to be the go-to police force for rural Vermont (even as his force had the authority to intervene in Vermont's urban areas too). This is likely one reason Edson did not bother creating a tactical unit or mobile strike force. After all, police officials across the country had been discussing differences between policing in "rural" and "urban" zones; most agreed that the "urban core" of America required much more complex policing systems, operations, and strategies than the rural environs.[112] Was this why Edson failed to create a tactical unit—because he was operating in a rural rather than urban zone?

To answer, we must consider what "rural" and "urban" signified at the time. Here this much is clear: when police officials and the public wrote about the difference between urban and rural in the 1950s, *race* was at the core of the distinction. The postwar period in the United States was exactly a time when "urban" increasingly signified "nonwhite" and especially "Black." In the North, there was indeed a "whitening" of the rural and a "darkening" of the urban, largely a result of the second wave of the Great Migration. Mechanization in southern agricultural industries pushed more and more African Americans to northern cities. And many cities saw an "exodus of white families and manufacturing jobs" alongside the influx of nonwhite working-class families.[113] Chicago's white population decreased by 13 percent from 1950 to 1960, while its African American population increased by 65 percent.[114] Similar trends were seen in the West. In San Francisco, the African American population swelled, notably exceeding the city's Asian population, while young white families headed to the suburbs. The nonwhite population grew by 67 percent from 1950 to 1960, while its white population decreased by 13 percent.[115] Los Angeles saw an even larger growth in its African American population, taking in more southern Black migrants in the 1950s than all other cities. Adding to the city's constantly growing Latino/a population, the African American population in Los Angeles Country rose from 63,744 to 763,000 between 1940 and 1970.[116] By 1960, every major city in the United States except Houston had seen negative changes in the percentage of whites in their populations and positive changes in the percentage of nonwhites. As Los Angeles's nonwhite population grew by 97 percent from 1950 to 1960, Detroit's and Boston's grew by 60 percent, and Buffalo's by 95 percent—just to name some of the cities.[117] Social scientists stood astonished, with some seeing it as a "nonwhite population surge" in major cities and classifying the surge as "one of the outstanding sociological phenomena of our time."[118] Others added that America was fast becoming the world's most urban country due to the growth in the urban population, noting with a tinge of alarm that the nonwhite population of cities had ballooned by 3.3 million from 1940 to 1950.[119]

At the same time, police officials and politicians across the country feared rising crime levels, with the inauguration of national-level data collection on crime serving to heighten the concern. The Federal Bureau of Investigation deployed the new data to warn that crime increased from 1940 to 1960 at four times the rate of population growth.[120] O. W. Wilson similarly fretted about the seemingly "abrupt increase" in crime.[121] Parker gave a speech to the IACP in 1957, warning his colleagues about the "ever-increasing depredations of the criminal army" whereby "order is replaced by disorder, security by insecurity," marking nothing less than the entire "disintegration" of society.[122]

Underlying these fears of rising crime was race. In the eyes of police and the public alike, urbanization and nonwhiteness went hand in hand, and criminality went with both. Crime was color-coded, and spatial location served as its grid.[123] A representative from the Eastman Kodak Company tried to sell new color cameras to police departments precisely on the grounds that crime was nonwhite. He told police officials at the 1956 meeting of the International Association of Chiefs of Police that traditional black-and-white photos were useless because they did not always capture "Negro skin." "If a dark colored Negro is printed in a black-and-white print so that he looks too light, or a light skinned Negro so he looks too dark, it's difficult to make a positive identification from the photograph." This, he insisted, was a problem in cities because most criminals were Black.[124]

Arrest rates and related statistics—increasingly collected, collated, and catalogued by sociologists, political agencies, and of course police departments' statistical bureaus—perpetuated these views while acting as a cover for racial bias. Articles in police magazines typically referred to crime statistics to demonstrate that "Negroes" made up 25 to 30 percent of arrests but only one-tenth of the population. Articles in those magazines lamented that "colored editors" in major cities "have concealed" the extent of this "Negro crime."[125] Amid such talk, it was not often recognized that arrest rates, which purportedly captured crime rates, might have reflected prior racial assumptions about who should be arrested in the first place. Nor was it ever mentioned that police chiefs sometimes distributed patrols in racially disproportionate ways that in turn generated more racialized arrest rates.[126]

The racialization of urban crime also unfolded through more subtle discourse where race was a silent referent but a referent nonetheless. "Criminality is a complex social illness," O. W. Wilson declared in his widely read text on police administration. "Crime has been stimulated by immigration and migration, with their problems of assimilation," and "by blighted slum areas resulting from rapid urban population increases, concentrations, and movements."[127] The implication? Crime happened in urban spaces wherein roamed poor migrants and immigrants swelling the "blighted slum areas" of the city. There was no explicit reference to race in this formulation, no statement connecting crime with African Americans, Mexicans, or Asians. But at a time when the majority of poor migrants living in "blighted slum areas" were nonwhite, such a direct and explicit reference was not needed.

William Parker in Los Angeles made similar references. He contrasted the "relatively stable patterns of rural life" with the "turmoil of the larger cities," where there were "so many people of varied beliefs . . . national origins, and diverse cultures." This was when the Mexican population of Los Angeles was continually growing and African Americans were entering the city at unprecedented rates.[128] Parker did not need to openly state to his fellow Angelenos which groups of "diverse cultures" were generating the "turmoil of the larger cities." Nor did he have to mention race when he declared: "Of the people that migrate to a city, a percentage may be expected to have criminal tendencies."[129] When Parker famously spoke about how the police functioned as the "thin blue line" between civilization and savagery, the undertone was the equation between "civilization" and suburban whiteness on the one hand and "savagery" and urban blackness (or, in Los Angeles especially, Mexican-ness) on the other. At other times, Parker did openly racialize the threat of crime and disorder, not least to justify strong policing. Following the Watts uprisings, Parker warned white residents that by 1970, "45 percent of the population will be Negro. . . . If you want any protection for your home and family, you're going . . . to have to get in and support a strong police department. If you don't do that, come 1970, God help you!"[130]

In short, the racialization of crime meant that policing cities was different from the task of policing white rural and suburban areas. The latter meant managing traffic violations on highways and minor instances of cattle theft. This is what state police officials like Merritt Edson focused on. Urban policing was a different matter. In the face of perceived racial threats, policing the city meant targeting, regulating, and repressing the rising numbers of nonwhites. This in turn required new police measures and modalities. Many police departments thus expanded their personnel and expenditures in this period. In 1940, cities in the United States employed 1.7 police officers per 1,000 population, a ratio that had remained more or less stable since the early twentieth century. However, by 1955, there were 1.9 police officers per 1,000 population, and by 1965, the figure rose to 2.3. This was largely a response to perceived racial threats. The cities that showed the largest growth in police officers in the 1950s also were the cities that had the largest nonwhite populations and the highest property crime rates (but not the largest rates for crimes against persons).[131]

Another police response was targeted patrols—that is, increasing patrol officers in nonwhite neighborhoods. In New York City in 1954, years before he became police chief and created the Tactical Patrol Force, Kennedy, in his role as chief inspector, heightened patrol numbers in the 25th Precinct of Manhattan, which mostly encompassed nonwhite Harlem.[132] This was an early instantiation of predictive policing, which was itself a reiteration of Vollmer's earlier tactics of guiding patrols based upon pin mapping—a spatially determined form of racial profiling. Officials easily justified it in statistical terms. Chief Parker beefed up patrols in LA's nonwhite areas and defended it by saying: "[Police] deployment is often heaviest in so-called minority sections of the city. The reason is statistical—it is a fact that certain racial groups, at the present time, commit a disproportionate share of the total crime."[133] Parker famously argued that while race was a "fiction," it was nonetheless a "useful fiction" for policing.[134] Similarly, in 1961, when community activists charged the Detroit Police Department with racist overpolicing of Black neighborhoods, police officers justified it by saying that "65 percent of the crimes are being committed by this 26 percent [Black] minority." They were simply focusing on the places where the crimes were committed.[135]

Besides expanding personnel and redistributing patrols, the other major response to the perceived racial threat was to create tactical police units. On the one hand, manpower shortage was a persistent problem in these years; even as departments grew, police officials felt they still needed more officers on the ground. Transforming patrolmen into members of tactical units was one way of dealing with this perceived problem. Rather than committing hundreds of officers to persistent patrols across the city, officials could take a small number of them and create units that went into and out of targeted areas as needed. On the other hand, the manpower problem was exacerbated by the new racialized threats. Absent those threats, there was a less pressing need for more officers. Therefore, police chiefs often created tactical units to at once manage the manpower issue and strengthen the city's metaphorical walls against the presumed criminal barbarians—the nonwhite "criminal army," in O. W. Wilson's words.[136] This is why military veterans were not the only ones who created tactical units. It is also why veterans did not always create tactical units even when they could. What mattered was not whether the police chief was a veteran but whether there was a perceived racial threat.

## The Racial Logics of Importation: New York's Tactical Patrol Force

To more clearly see how racialized threats led to the creation of tactical units, we can look at the formation of New York's infamous Tactical Patrol Force, which followed this path exactly. The TPF first hit the pavement in December 1959, and it became notorious for its heavy-handed approach to crime control in poor Black sections of the city. The man responsible was Police Commissioner Stephen Kennedy (accordingly, the unit was first referred to as "Kennedy's Commandos" in the press). But there was little about Kennedy that would have suggested that he would take such a militarized turn. Kennedy was not a military veteran, nor did he have direct experience with America's imperial-military apparatus. Furthermore, during the summer preceding the formation of the TPF, Kennedy had initially rejected calls to take tougher measures on crime in nonwhite areas of the city. He instead supported what critics called a "too lenient policy" by supporting social programs to alleviate problems.[137]

But pressures mounted on Kennedy. He became commissioner in 1955, a time when the NYPD had suffered accusations of corruption and inefficacy, and when new challenges from the city's racialized minorities emerged. As the emerging civil rights movement in the South was riveting the nation's attention, the NAACP in New York mobilized local groups to criticize police brutality.[138] The city's African American Islamic community joined the criticisms. Their leader, Malcolm X, rose in status, becoming known as the "idol of many of Harlem's youths." In August 1959, the press reported that Malcolm X returned from a tour to Egypt and Africa and led a rally of up to "10,000 Muslims and guests" at St. Nicholas Arena. The press and the public sounded the alarm. Referring to Malcolm X and his followers as militant "black nationalists," they blamed racialized minorities for expressing "anti-white sentiment" and elevating racial tensions in the city.[139] A national telecast of a documentary by Mike Wallace on the Muslim Brotherhood accused Malcolm X, Elijah Muhammad, and "the Black Nationalists" of "preaching hate of the white man and his eventual destruction."[140]

New York's Black leaders were showing their power, while local authorities seemed weak. A series of events in 1957 and 1959 manifested the power imbalance. In April 1957, Malcolm X led a protest against the beating of Johnson X. Hinton, a member of the Nation of Islam, Temple No. 7, in Harlem. The number of protesters swelled to the thousands. As the press observed, the police were helpless; they were outnumbered and underprepared. Only Malcolm X could tame the crowd.[141] A similar protest in July 1959—before Kennedy created the TPF—forced the police to call in the boxing champion Sugar Ray Robinson to help quell the passions of five hundred protesters outside the police station. The only thing Kennedy could do was assign eighty-eight extra patrolmen to the besieged Harlem police station while making bold but ultimately empty statements against "mob violence" and the potential for a "race riot."[142] Kennedy's leadership was being tested, as was the power of the police.

Around the same time, local politicians, the press, and the public were pressuring Kennedy to clamp down on criminal activity. Crime had seen a steep rise since the beginning of Kennedy's tenure, precipitating something close to a moral panic. It was predictably racialized.[143] In the eyes of the press and the public, the crime wave was due to African American and Puerto Rican youths who gathered in groups of two, three, four, or more. The press called them "gangs."[144] Meanwhile, high crime rates in nonwhite districts confirmed to the white imagination that crime was due to nonwhite youths (and their putatively lazy parents who did not provide sufficient supervision). Newspapers reported that the first seven months of 1959 alone had seen a rapid increase in juvenile crime, outpacing national levels.[145]

Things worsened in the summer of 1959, as prominent cases of street murders and attacks seized the public's attention. In response to the case of a Puerto Rican youth murdering two middle-class white teens, the public chanted, "Kill the spics."[146] One NAACP official decried the racism: "If one were to believe much of today's literary output of delinquency, one would conclude . . . that Negroes and Puerto Ricans are responsible for its appearance in our midst."[147] The association between crime and race was so widespread that one judge asked city officials to halt migration from Puerto Rico and the American South on the grounds that such a move alone would stop crime. Meanwhile, sociologists and social workers did not question whether Puerto Ricans committed more crime than whites but only debated the causes, and police in other cities with large Puerto Rican populations gathered to discuss the "problems arising from Puerto Rican migration."[148] In September 1959, an editorial in the *Daily News* suggested that the alarming crime problem in the city could be solved by more police and more jails.[149] New York's newspapers also reported on high crime rates in Washington, DC, that were purportedly caused by the city's nonwhite population. They wrote that officials in DC had ignored the problem of the "juvenile Wolf Packs" for too long and that the situation was out of control. They suggested that New York's officials were following suit. The "Wolf Packs" of dark youths were rising everywhere, yet the police were doing nothing.[150]

The press and the public not only racialized the so-called gang crime problem in New York but classified it using terms that resonated with long-standing colonial discourses. Earlier in the century, America's occupation of Puerto Rico had been justified by references to Puerto Ricans as "children" who required a firm hand from their white imperial masters. Continued US control over the colony in the 1950s was legitimated through further discourses about the colony's primitiveness, backwardness, and putatively violent character. The latter view was validated by the fact that Puerto Rican nationalists had recently, in 1954, fired shots onto the floor of the US Congress—an act denounced as "savage" even by the "civilized" Puerto Rican leader Luis Muñoz Marín.[151]

When New York City officials and the press decried the crimes of nonwhite youths in the summer of 1959, they drew upon the same colonial vocabulary. They claimed that the "streets and playgrounds of a great city" had "become peril-haunted concrete jungles" overrun by an "unruly element."[152] After a Puerto Rican youth killed two white teens, the priest at the memorial Mass denounced the city's "gangs and marauders" and called for more jails to house them. "After all," he stated, "we cage wild animals because we are afraid they might destroy or maim us."[153] A *Daily News* editorial was more direct in its equation between New York and Puerto Rico, suggesting that New York officials seek advice from colonial officials in Puerto Rico on how juvenile delinquency in Puerto Rico was dealt with—an unabashed hunt for colonial policing tactics.[154]

The press and the public soon decried Commissioner Kennedy's reluctance to get tough. Kennedy had been supporting social programs to curb juvenile crime, but the priest at the memorial Mass in 1959 for the two white teens demanded that the police "be allowed to fight force with force—the only language the juvenile criminals who are taking over the city understand." The "coddling theory has been tried and failed," he continued, and "the only thing these juvenile gangs understand is force. . . . We are at war."[155] An editorial in the *New York Age* similarly called for a tougher approach, announcing, "These gangs have declared war on society . . . we in turn must 'go to war.'" They urged Kennedy to act.[156] The rank and file under Kennedy, along with some of his top officials, murmured complaints about their chief's "too-lenient policy on youthful crime" and restrictions on their ability to employ "judicious use of the nightstick and the toe of the boot" on juveniles. One longtime officer told reporters: "Just a tap on the rump with a billy and the effect will be better than all the do-gooding sociology you can think of."[157] The *Daily News* similarly criticized Kennedy's costly social programs that did nothing to stop the "mobs." It suggested that the police should instead "handle it with a nightstick," noting that nightsticks only cost $1.35 but the city's social programs cost $60 million. The same paper asked random citizens, "Should the police be allowed to use their clubs against teen-age gangs?" One man, a white food and beverage manager, answered, "The police should have been given this authority a long time ago. The lawless elements that have migrated here have gotten out of hand and the police are losing the war against crime and violence. It's like a jungle inhabited by wild animals." Another man replied: "I'd go a lot farther than the mere use of clubs. . . . Let's treat them as the Insular Police treats them in Puerto Rico. These punks wouldn't get away with it in their native land."[158] Colonial discourse had classified Puerto Ricans and Filipinos as savage animals, putting them on the other side of the abyssal line, thus justifying the violence police used against them. The new discourse of Puerto Rican criminality in New York City did the same.[159]

In the face of this pressure, the mayor and Governor Nelson Rockefeller conferred with Commissioner Kennedy and other officials. Eventually, Kennedy's critics won. Kennedy withdrew his support of social programs for the city's youths, confessing that he believed that the social agencies "had done as much as they could." Vowing to get tough, he diverted funds from social programs into more patrolmen, increasing his force to 24,508 strong. As the new recruits would not be deployable until the subsequent year, he redirected 1,400 members of his existing force to patrol the more "troubled areas."[160] Then Kennedy announced another step, in line with the man on the street's suggestion to call upon the Insular Police of Puerto Rico. He announced the formation of a new unit, initially known as "Kennedy's Commandos" but soon called the Tactical Patrol Force. Kennedy explained that the new force, consisting of seventy-five men who would "roll in paddy wagons," was to be deployed for any "danger area" of the city, such as "areas where a teen-age gang rumble develops."[161] Kennedy instructed the new "platoon" that they "had a duty to use such force as . . . necessary."[162] The *Daily News*, which had been clamoring for a hardened line on the nonwhite youth gangs of the city, praised the move. "Considering that major crimes increased 7.5% in New York City during 1959's first nine months . . . Commissioner Kennedy's Tactical Patrol Force is a most timely experiment."[163]

As in New York, so too in Chicago. Chicago's Task Force—variously referred to as a "crime fighting tactical unit" and "mobile task force"—was created by

Chief Timothy O'Connor, who, like Kennedy in New York City, lacked military experience.[164] O'Connor created the Task Force as part of a larger "punitive turn" meant to discipline the city's growing Black population, whose movements into parts of the city beyond the South Side threatened the city's racially segregated order. The threat was so menacing that some white residents responded to Black interlopers with mob violence. Other white residents organized community groups that pressured city officials to get tough on crime, insinuating that Black residents were responsible for rising crime rates. One of those groups, the Greater Lawndale Conservation Commission (GLCC), took credit for convincing O'Connor to create the Task Force.[165] The story is thus familiar: a perceived racialized threat prompted the return of the colonial boomerang—in this case in the form of a tactical police unit. Is it so surprising that Kennedy in New York City and O'Connor in Chicago created tactical police units while Merritt Edson in Vermont did not?

If the wave of militarization marked by tactical units in the late 1950s had colonial and racialized origins, it likewise had pernicious effects. Here, finally, we can force into visibility the secret of the Watts uprisings and the other uprisings of the 1960s: they were the perverse outcome of tactical policing.

## Making Insurgency

In 1966, *Newsweek* magazine published an article on policing in America, taking special notice of the new tactical units that so many law enforcement agencies had created. It noticed how tactical units were known for "cruising the ghettos" and "challenging anyone who seems in any way suspicious."[166] The article hit the nail on the head. In Chicago, the Task Force almost immediately targeted Black communities. In its first year of operation, the Task Force visited the city's communities 799 times, made 1,122 arrests, issued 48,961 traffic violation tickets, and confiscated 511 concealed weapons. Its activities increased in the next two years. As the African American press pointed out, Black districts received visits from the Task Force twenty to twenty-eight times more often than white areas.[167]

In New York, too, the TPF's first assignments were racially disproportionate: the TPF first saturated the Lower East Side ("scene of recent muggings and youth gang wars"), the Greenwich Village area ("where dope pushing and racial tensions have increased recently"), and the Clinton Hill area of Brooklyn (which had purportedly been in a "state of siege" because of the "influx of an unruly element").[168] Thereafter, racialized policing continued unabated. Using "departmental crime statistics" scrutinized by its "analytic section," the majority-white TPF was dispatched to areas of high crime. By the magic of statistical discrimination, this ultimately meant that the TPF was primarily dispatched to Black and Puerto Rican neighborhoods.[169] In these neighborhoods, as newspapers reported, it was common "to see as many as four members of the judo-trained Tactical Patrol Force deployed on a single street corner."[170]

The New York TPF was also deployed to manage protesters (so-called mobs and rioters), for which the TPF was rumored to be trained "to inflict maximum pain while leaving the least outward bruises and scars."[171] Most of the "mobs" and "rioters" were nonwhite; the TPF was deployed, for instance, to quell the 1964 protests in the wake of the murder of James Powell (mentioned earlier in this chapter) and the 1967 protests in Spanish Harlem against the police killing of Renaldo Rodriguez.[172] The TPF was later sent to Columbia University to squash student protests in 1968. And while most of the students were white, this was an exception that proved the rule. One member of the TPF recalled: "Looking back, Columbia was basically no different than any other mob confrontation we had. The only real difference became apparent in hindsight. It was one of the few times this kind of force was used on a white crowd."[173]

These early saturation campaigns and heavy-handed militarized policing practices of tactical units in turn contributed to further racial tensions, resentment, and disorder. This is part of what the historian Elizabeth Hinton calls the "cycle" of police violence and Black rebellion: one begets the other, which perpetuates the first. To be sure, in New York, the continued racialized deployment of New York's Tactical Patrol Force did nothing to quell the racial tensions it was purportedly meant to manage. If anything, it contributed to them. Sometimes the mere presence of the force summoned indignation and derision from African American and Puerto Rican communities. This is why, during the 1964 protests against the murder of James Powell, police officials deployed the TPF but then changed their minds and pulled it out. The TPF's reputation preceded it, and it was not a good one.[174] But even this recall was fruitless, because the damage had long since been done. In the wake of those protests, a gang called the Blood Brothers formed in central Harlem to protect themselves against police brutality. According to news reports, the Blood Brothers had a "hatred of precinct patrolmen" and "an even more intense hatred of the Tactical Patrol Force officers."[175] If the New York TPF created the conditions for the very racial uprisings and disturbances it was meant to suppress, its racially disproportionate deployment reproduced the problem.

In Chicago, the racialized distribution of the Task Force's saturation campaigns was equally if not more inciteful, especially as the force typically relied on early versions of stop-and-search discretionary powers. A Chicago attorney in 1958 claimed that the Task Force's treatment of African American residents constituted a "definite violation of basic civil rights" because the Task Force officers "stop cars, many times without reason, and search the vehicle and the driver." During its campaigns, "as many as 10 patrolmen are to be seen in one two block stretch, stopping all vehicles, frisking the occupants and searching the cars." African American residents responded with official complaints against the Task Force, ranging from "illegal search and seizure to outright police brutality."[176] Simon Balto concludes that the task force "was the laboratory in which police administrators germinated aggressive and repressive police policies such as stop-and-frisk, arrest quotas, and neighborhood saturation during the late 1950s."[177]

We can now consider how tactical policing generated the conditions for uprisings in Los Angeles. In the 1920s and 1930s, one of the LAPD's main targets had been Latino neighborhoods, but as the African American population grew in the 1940s and early 1950s, the police added Black neighborhoods to their maps. By the 1950s, LAPD's tactical unit, the Metropolitan Division, was sent regularly to saturate "areas of high crime frequency," according to LAPD reports. By Chief Parker's own admission, this meant Black and Latino neighborhoods. The "saturated" neighborhoods of Los Angeles thereby became occupied territories. As one investigative journalist observed in 1967: "Convinced as they are that Parker's statements accurately describe reality, the patrol officers drive into the Negro or Mexican American neighborhoods as if into occupied territories in which almost everybody is likely to be either a criminal or willing to protect criminals from apprehension by the police."[178]

Racially disproportionate arrests followed.[179] In 1959, the Black population of Los Angeles was just over 7 percent but accounted for about 30 percent of all arrests (see Table 5.1).[180] During a two-year period around the same time, about twelve thousand African Americans were arrested for gambling, while only twelve hundred whites were arrested for the same reason. These figures were

Table 5.1. Arrests by Los Angeles Police Department, Various Years

| Year | Blacks | | Mexicans[1] | |
|---|---|---|---|---|
| | Percentage of all arrests | As percentage of total population | Percentage of all arrests | As percentage of total population |
| 1940 | 9.7 | 2.7 | — | — |
| 1949 | 20.6 | 5.25[2] | 15.9 | — |
| 1959 | 29.9 | 7.64[3] | 15.1 | — |

[1] 1959 category in LAPD is "Latin"; 1949 category is "Red Mexican."

[2] Population based on 1950.

[3] Population based on 1960.

Source: Los Angeles Police Department, annual reports.

well known at the time. A judge criticizing Parker inquired why the LAPD was policing African American neighborhoods rather than white ones.[181] Parker responded: "The main source of Los Angeles crime just happens to be areas populated heavily by the Negroes and the Negroes just happen to be figuring in most of the city's crime. I don't say this from opinion. This comes from the record."[182]

By the early 1960s, the LAPD under Parker had become renowned for its racial profiling, excessive force, and brutality, even as Parker boasted that his force was thoroughly disciplined and professionalized.[183] Civil rights hearings in 1960 revealed that the LAPD's policing of Black citizens ranged from humiliating and seemingly random stops and searches to outright police violence, especially in the areas of East and South Central Los Angeles. An ACLU official explained that this reflected a belief "that the effective control of crime in the Negro and Mexican-American communities requires periodic deliberate public shows of force."[184] In 1961, Roy Wilkins, executive secretary of the NAACP, referred to LAPD officers as "next to those in Birmingham" for the way they treated African American citizens.[185] Observers and investigative commissions, including the McCone Commission, which offered up its assessment of the Watts uprising in 1965, noted the LAPD's harsh treatment of Los Angeles's minorities.[186] Months before the Watts uprising, California assistant attorney general Howard Jewell penned a report predicting an imminent violent event due to the LAPD's treatment of the Black community.[187] Later, the McCone Commission admitted that long-standing criticisms of the LAPD and the perception of its brutality contributed to the Watts uprisings.[188] The historian Max Felker-Kantor and others agree with the McCone Commission's assessment of the causes of the Watts uprising of 1965. They offer only one qualification: it was not just the *perception* of police brutality in African American communities that mattered but the police's *actual* racist practices. "Racist policing," Felker-Kantor summarizes, "was ultimately the uprising's trigger."[189]

Tactical units were not solely responsible for the racialized practices of the LAPD in the years preceding the Watts revolt. Patrolmen and other units were culpable as well. It is telling that regular patrol officers assigned to the 77th Street precinct called their nightsticks "n——r-knockers": regular patrols, not just elite mobile units like the Metropolitan Squad, were part of the problem too.[190] On the other hand, the aggressive and militaristic approach of tactical policing cannot be underestimated. Civil rights lawyers critical of the LEAA's funding of tactical policing rightly noted that tactical units' saturation campaigns in nonwhite urban areas most typically led to an "increase in community tensions."[191] One of the main journals of the Black Power movement likewise criticized President Johnson's 1965 crime bill and its program to expand tactical units. The program, noted an editorial in *The Movement*, would solve nothing: "It will only create more rebellion against the oppression which [President Johnson] calls law and order."[192] If, as Felker-Kantor argues, the Watts "uprising was ultimately a demand for an end to police practices that maintained white authority, control and order in black spaces," those practices surely included the saturation campaigns of the LAPD's Metropolitan Squad under Parker and birthed initially by Vollmer.[193]

The irony should be clear already: tactical units were modeled upon counterinsurgency forces in the colonial and postcolonial world, but their domestic deployment fomented the very sort of insurgency from colonized peoples that those units were initially meant to suppress.

## The Post-Watts Boomerang: Into the 1970s

We have now seen that the Watts uprising of 1965, subsequent demonstrations in the mid-1960s, the formation of SWAT in the LAPD, and Johnson's war on crime in the mid-1960s did not mark a new wave of police militarization; rather, they trailed the emergence of tactical policing in the late 1950s and early 1960s. Still, the events of the 1960s did have an important impact on police militarization. While they did not create an entirely new wave of militarization, they amplified and extended the existing wave, summoning the imperial boomerang yet again. Not surprisingly, racialized analogies permeated the process. As officials confronted the urban uprisings in Watts, Newark, and elsewhere, they perceived them as akin to anticolonial insurgencies, rebellions, and movements occurring across Asia, the Caribbean, and Africa at the time.[194] Major General William P. Yarborough reportedly told his staff during the Detroit riots: "Men, get out your counter insurgency manuals. We have an insurgency on our hands."[195] In the heat of Watts in 1965, Chief Parker saw the rioters as akin to the "Viet Cong."[196] Robert B. Rigg, a retired army intelligence officer, popularized the analogies through his writings in military journals and the press. He warned of "urban guerillas" in the United States, equating them with guerrillas overseas: "Man has constructed out of steel and concrete a much better 'jungle' than nature has created in Vietnam." He added:

> Rooftops, windows, rooms high up, streets low down, and back alleys nearby could become a virtual jungle for patrolling police or military forces at night when hidden snipers could abound, as they often do against U.S. and allied forces in Vietnam in daylight. . . . Could local police or National Guard units carry out such search-and-destroy campaigns in the cement-block jungles of high-rise buildings?[197]

Given these analogies, police and government officials across the country turned yet again to America's military-colonial forces for inspiration and guidance.

One result was the creation and spread of more tactical units, though now those units increasingly focused on crowd control. LAPD's SWAT team, in this sense, was both new and not new. It was not new because it was just another reserve unit like the Metropolitan Squad or Vollmer's Crime Crushers. But it *was* new in that it specialized in crowd control and counterinsurgency. And to do so, it consciously emulated imperial-military forces. As Daryl Gates recounts it, the Los Angeles police had been woefully unprepared to quell the uprising in Watts in 1965. To meet future uprisings, he and his colleagues created SWAT and enlisted colonial counterinsurgency materials and modalities. They attended sessions on "guerilla warfare" and other tactics offered by the military at the Naval Armory in Chavez Ravine.[198]

As concern over urban insurgency grew in the wake of Watts and further rebellions of the decade, more and more police departments did the same thing, creating new tactical units aimed specifically at crowd control (or repurposing their existing ones). Even law enforcement agencies that had not seen uprisings created tactical units structured as counterinsurgency units, anxiously anticipating future revolt. President Johnson's "war on crime" helped fund the process. In 1965, the federal government gave $10 million to local police agencies. The subsequent Safe Streets Act of 1968 continued the funding with an initial budget of $63 million that expanded to $850 million by 1973.[199] The imperial boomerang thus spread beyond major cities like Los Angeles, New York, and Chicago.

A related result was the retraining and retooling of entire police departments, not just elite tactical units. Up until the 1960s, police training in crowd control— or "riot control"—had been spotty and tentative. As President Johnson's Katzenbach Crime Commission of 1965 noticed, some larger cities and police agencies with tactical units had benefitted from training in crowd control methods. But other cities and agencies, especially smaller ones, lacked such programs.[200] In 1965, in the wake of the Watts uprising, a report by the Defense Research Corporation lamented the police's inadequate preparation for "urban insurgency": "The preventive or responsive measures available to handle routine riots and occasional terrorism, the broader concept of a whole program of counterinsurgency is hardly even discussed among police here or abroad."[201]

The uprisings of the 1960s, and especially after the summer of 1967, triggered new training programs to fill the perceived holes, with the federal government playing a key role. In July 1967, as the streets of Detroit were still on fire, President Johnson established the Kerner Commission (named after its chair, Governor Otto Kerner of Illinois) to explore the causes of and cures for the recent urban insurrections. Noting again that the police and the military were sorely prepared for riots, it recommended new training programs, often involving input from military or ex-military personnel. The LEAA adopted many of these recommendations. One result was a "civil disturbance orientation course," aka SEADOC, which began in 1968 at the United States Army Military Police School. Taught by military or ex-military personnel, the course was described by one former military police officer in Vietnam as "the best and most complete course available in civil disturbance planning."[202] In its first year it trained 4,186 students; by the early 1970s, the course had trained at least ten thousand police administrators, officers, and other public officials.[203]

The topic of the SEADOC courses varied, but many of the lessons were inspired by the Kerner Commission's recommendations and incorporated principles and tactics of crowd control from the colonies and ex-colonial world. The Kerner Commission had already looked at those colonial principles and tactics with approval, taking special notice of riot control efforts in British Hong Kong. There, the British had long innovated a series of sophisticated approaches to crowd control, building upon its early tactical police units in Shanghai and colonies such as Ireland and India. A series of riots in the late 1950s and through the 1960s had sparked the innovations, resulting in the creation of the Hong Kong Police Tactical Unit (HKPTU). The effective suppression of the 1966 Kowloon riots and of the 1967 worker-led insurrection by the HKPTU earned the Hong Kong Police a reputation for being a "'class one' colonial constabulary."[204] Attendant on the development of these colonial-military forces was an emergent counterinsurgency principle known later as the "doctrine of minimum force." In the British Empire, this had been developed by General Sir Charles Gwynn, and later it became an important part of the repertoire of British counterinsurgency theory. As a doctrine, it formalized what many tactical units and colonial forces in the British Empire had already been practicing (though to varying degrees).[205] The idea was to prevent the escalation of violence and obtain crowd compliance without bloodshed. Military-style equipment and weaponry were necessary for protection or for intimidation, and they were to be available as a last resort, but the goal was to obtain crowd compliance through a series of tactics and tools that fell short of bloodshed. If violence was to be used at all, it was to be used carefully and strategically. As one British writer noted in 1952 about colonial riot control methods, the theory was that "a very little amount of force will prevent a riotous situation getting out of hand if the force is applied at the right moment."[206]

The doctrine of minimum force was one of the key doctrines of colonial counterinsurgency theory in the British Empire that Byron Engle, head of the United States Office of Public Safety, touted in his testimony to the Kerner Commission.[207] He sold it as a part of a larger package of suggestions that essentially imported colonial police tactics from the British Empire, including the formation of tactical units (or in his words "emergency police units" devoted to riot control rather than just crime, and the development of intelligence-gathering capabilities). Ultimately, the Kerner Commission adopted the principle as its own. The commission suggested to police that riot control methods should not involve an unthinking use of military-grade weapons, strongly advising against using "mass destruction weapons of modern warfare" such as "flame throwers, recoilless rifles and artillery" or the army bayonet.[208] Instead, police should draw on the tactics and tools developed by colonial police in the British Empire. This included the use of rubber bullets and CS gas, which had been employed by the British in the colonies. Both weapons were seen as useful nonlethal tools for realizing the doctrine of minimum force. The Kerner Commission also advised US military and police forces to copy the Hong Kong Police's use of nonlethal crowd control technologies (such as the "wooden peg," a sort of wooden bullet to be used in place of live ammunition) and tactics (such as "psychological techniques to ventilate hostility and lessen tension in riot control").[209] The SEADOC courses likewise adopted the principle.[210]

The post-Watts boomerang also brought a new wave of military equipment, weapons, and technologies to police. The tactical units of the 1950s had emulated military forms, but they had not mobilized massive amounts of military ware. The Omnibus Crime Control and Safe Streets Act's LEAA fixed this by facilitating transfers of military technologies and weaponry to local police. The shiny new tools included technologies and weaponry that had been used or developed in Vietnam. As Elizabeth Hinton explains, they included everything from surveillance and communications technologies to armored troop carriers and helicopters. In June 1966, the Los Angeles Sheriff's Department received $200,000 for Project Sky Knight, an air-surveillance program. Over the next four years the federal government granted helicopters to police departments in at least fifty other cities.[211] Even the press took notice, reporting that local police departments were acquiring "helicopters and armor-plated trucks which can be used to transport police quickly into riot areas," "scope-equipped rifles" for countering sniper fire and other "high-powered rifles," tear gas, armored vests, and helmets.[212] Much of this equipment had been seen previously by officials as inappropriate for domestic use, but in the post-Watts era of heightened white fright and colonial fear, military equipment was seen as legitimate and indeed necessary. In the event, urban policing across the country became "increasingly militarized," as Judith Kohler-Hausmann summarizes, "and the new firepower was aimed directly at inner-city communities."[213]

While these were state-sanctioned projects that served to bring the imperial boomerang back home, more nefarious projects were also part of this wave of militarization. Beginning in the early 1970s, a Chicago police officer named Jon Burge led a group of other officers, known as the Midnight Crew, on a horrific campaign of torture at a police facility in Homan Square, Chicago. Burge's team detained and tortured more than one hundred people to extract confessions, all but one of them Black. As seen in Chapter 3, earlier in the century Chicago police had tortured Black detainees too, using the "water cure" adopted from colonial forces in the Philippines. Burge's methods were different but just as brutal, if not more so. They included Russian roulette, beatings, shackling for extended periods, mock executions, and shocks on the victims' genitals, anus, ears, or fingers. Many of these techniques had been used in Vietnam by US forces interrogating presumed or proven members of the Viet Cong. The shock technique was referred to by Burge and his team as the "Vietnam special."[214]

The source of police torture had thus shifted from the Philippines to Vietnam. In fact, Burge had joined the police after having served in Vietnam. He had enlisted in the army in 1966 and worked in the 9th Infantry Division's military police. The military police had been responsible for prisoners of war who were interrogated and sometimes tortured by military intelligence officers. While the military police did not do the interrogation, they sometimes stood by and witnessed. Burge completed his service in 1970 and then joined the Chicago police force. He was first assigned to sections covering the mostly Black areas of Chicago's South Side.[215] Traveling from Vietnam to the South Side, he thus carried the horrific tactics of empire with him, ostensibly to protect and serve.

# 6

# Cycles of Policing and Insurgency
# in Britain, 1960s–1980s

In April 1981, Brixton erupted in violence.* Residents of the impoverished
London district rose up. Most were Black Britons: immigrants or descendants
of immigrants from Britain's ex-colonies and territories in the Caribbean. With
righteous indignation, they looted shops, set fire to buildings, and hurled bricks,
bottles, and gasoline bombs. It resulted in eighty-two arrests, more than five
hundred injuries, and scores of buildings or automobiles being destroyed by fire.
Splashed across the front page of the *Sun* newspaper the next day were images
of besieged policemen with the headline "To Think This Is England."[1] But the
uprising did not stop there. It spread to other urban neighborhoods populated
by racialized minorities. In July, the Toxteth area of Liverpool, Chapeltown in
Leeds, Handsworth in Birmingham, and Moss Side in Manchester all erupted.[2]
Other towns also saw uprisings. It was "a prolonged spasm of urban rioting of
a severity not seen in England for a century and a half."[3] James Anderton, chief
constable of the Greater Manchester Police, was taken aback, calling it "anarchy"
on the streets of Britain.[4]

The 1981 uprisings formed a watershed of sorts, resulting in a new wave of
police militarization. In response to the violence, the British police acquired
tear gas, riot shields, armored cars, rubber bullets, and new training in crowd
management. Some scholars call this Britain's "paramilitary turn," but it was,
more precisely, an effect of the imperial boomerang.[5] The new materials that
police received had long been part of Britain's imperial-military regime. They
included tools, tactics, and training from, among other forces, the Royal Ulster
Constabulary (RUC) and the Hong Kong Police. This was militarization through
imperial feedback all over again. More precisely, it was an explicit *colonial
counterinsurgenization* of policing—a variant of militarization by which police
domesticate the particular tools of colonial counterinsurgency to steel themselves against perceived subversion and insurgency at home.

This chapter will trace the circuits and process by which this imperial feedback
and transformation in policing occurred in Britain. As we will see, it happened in

---

* Parts of this chapter have appeared previously in Go 2020.

*Policing Empires.* Julian Go, Oxford University Press. © Oxford University Press 2024.
DOI: 10.1093/oso/9780197621653.003.0007

familiar ways, reiterating the logic of racialized threat and imperial importation that we have seen in previous chapters. We will also see that the militarization of the police in the wake of the Brixton Riots of 1981 was the perverse result of an earlier process. As with the uprisings in Watts in the United States, the uprisings in Brixton and the subsequent wave of militarization had been preceded by an earlier round of police militarization in the early 1970s. At that time, the London Metropolitan Police led the way in adopting counterinsurgency tools and tactics from the empire through a new unit, the Special Patrol Group. This domestication of colonial counterinsurgency was then extended to other police units across Britain's cities in the early 1970s, leading to bellicose, militarized policing of poor Black urban districts through the 1970s that in turn contributed to the uprisings of 1981.

The militarization of policing in the early 1970s thereby led to the very thing it was meant to suppress in the first place: insurgency from Britain's abject racialized minorities and internal colonies. The uprising in Brixton in 1981 was a self-fulfilled prophecy—one moment in a longer cycle of racialized threat and police militarization. In the last part of the chapter we will see how that cycle carried through the 1980s up to 2011, when residents of besieged communities across England—most of whom were nonwhite—again rose up against police brutality, this time in response to the police killing of Mark Duggan, a twenty-nine-year-old mixed-race male in Tottenham, north London.

To fully understand this larger cycle, we need to first expose the earlier round of police colonial counterinsurgenization that was unleashed in the early 1970s. In light of previous chapters, this round of police militarization poses a puzzle of sorts. As we have seen, British policing by the 1970s had already undergone different phases of militarization. The founding of the London Metropolitan Police was itself a form of militarization. Then, in the late nineteenth and early twentieth centuries, militarization was limited in the absence of racialized threats to order. Even when commissioners Charles Warren in the 1880s and Hugh Trenchard in the 1930s added some more militaristic components to policing, their efforts were stopped short. The colonial boomerang faced barriers coming home. The crucial question here arises: by what magic was the barrier broken in the early 1970s? In other words, why and how did this new wave of the 1970s happen? And what form did it take? Answering these questions will require a deep investigation into the conditions in Britain in the late 1960s that helped trigger the wave. It will also require charting the counterinsurgency repertoire of the British Empire amid its relative decline. We can then better understand the cycle of which the 1981 revolt was one part.

## Global Insurgency and Racial Threat

The late 1960s and early 1970s were a turbulent period in Britain. Workers' strikes, student protests, antiwar demonstrations, and radical groups of various stripes proliferated in London and other major cities in Britain. The 1968 antiwar protest at Grosvenor Square, which devolved into violent clashes with the police; the 1972 miners' strike in Birmingham, later called "the Battle of Saltley Gate"; bomb threats from the radical leftist group the Angry Brigade; various terrorist actions from the Irish Republican Army—all of these events and more made it appear as though Britain was under siege. The empire was burning.

Britain had seen its fair share of protests, demonstrations, and labor agitation before. But two features of this historical moment were crucial for triggering a new wave of militarization in the early 1970s. The first was the global context of anticolonial unrest and imperial decline. By the late 1960s, the sun had set on Britain's colonial empire. The end of the Second World War had galvanized anticolonial insurgency as never before while undermining colonial regimes. In its wake, Britain's imperial-military regime faced unprecedented pressures. Insurgencies erupted in quick succession; Palestine (1946–1948), Malaya (1948–1960), Kenya (1952–1955), Oman (1957–1959), and Cyprus (1954–1958) were just some of the largest conflicts. There were many more. According to one estimate, the British Army from the end of the Second World War through the 1970s was involved in more than fifty counterinsurgency campaigns and conflicts.[6] This taxed colonial police forces too, compelling the Colonial Office to hold the Conference of Commissioners of Police in the 1950s, with police officials from across the empire, spanning Aden to Uganda, Hong Kong to the Bahamas. The goal was to develop standardized procedures for controlling crowds and dispersing riots in order to form a unified front against the rising tide of anticolonial unrest.[7] Still, by the 1960s, the writing was on the wall: none of these efforts could salvage the empire. The decolonization of most of the African continent, the transition to Commonwealth associations with former colonies, the Aden "emergency" (1963–1968), persistent unrest in Hong Kong (1966–1967), political instability in Britain's neocolonial territories like Anguilla (1968–1969): these and more were signs of a new global field over which Britain no longer exercised control.

Beyond the British Empire, the whole world was on edge. Anticolonial nationalists, galvanized after the Bandung Conference in 1955, had continued their transnational organizing and enjoyed success. Nearly all of the European colonial powers were dismantling their colonial holdings (or those holdings were being dismantled). Meanwhile, the emergence of the Black Panthers in the United States and other Black militant groups in England revealed one of the many ways in which the anticolonial spirit could come back to the metropole's inner sanctums. From the United States and France to China and the countries of Southeast Asia, change was in the air. Workers, students, militants, communists, Black nationalists, anticolonialists, and anti-imperialists—all of these groups and many more were taking to the streets or seizing power.

The British political and economic elite thus felt new threats. Britain's imperial complacency and pride were shaken to the core. Insurgency appeared everywhere. On the one hand, this fear was warranted by the reality of terrorism. The eruption of the Troubles in Northern Ireland in the late 1960s brought new attacks in London. The IRA bombs at Aldershot (1972) and the Old Bailey (1973), along with James Roche's tossing of tear gas onto the floor of the House of Commons (1970), were arguably unprecedented, and not only did such incidents shake the British establishment, but they confirmed fears that anticolonialism was coming home. "What happened at Aldershot, what happened at the Old Bailey," declared Conservative MP John Biggs-Davidson before the Royal United Services Institute for Defence Studies in 1973, "reminds us that what happens in Londonderry is very relevant to what can happen in London, and if we lose in Belfast we may have to fight in Brixton or Birmingham."[8]

On the other hand, terrorism from the IRA was not the only concern. Many officials saw all the protests, demonstrations, and terrorist acts as part of a larger series marking total social breakdown. "There is a clearly perceptible trend in this country," noted the otherwise left-leaning *Observer* in 1972, "reflecting a more universal malaise, towards violence, anarchy and a contempt for established order. This is a genuine crisis in our own social system which needs radical and imaginative remedies."[9] Officials saw the 1970–1972 bomb attacks by the far-left Angry Brigade and the Saltley miners' strike in 1972 as manifestations of the larger global trend. Some observers linked the eight thousand antiwar protesters marching on Grosvenor Square in 1968 to other protests around the world and communist agitation from outside. The *Police Review* reported with horror that "foreigners" were part of the Grosvenor Square protest.[10] By the time of the miners' strike in 1972, senior army officials were openly discussing "'subversive forces' and 'growing pressures' on British society"—and, as the *Times* reported, they were not referring to the IRA: "Anarchy is a word used often [by British officials] and taken quite seriously."[11]

What was happening was, in the words of Erik Linstrum, the collapse of "the long-standing distinction between colonial and metropolitan dangers."[12] In the minds of British officials, anticolonial insurgency was coming home from everywhere. In an emblematic speech, Prime Minister Edward Heath declared to the United Nations General Assembly in 1970: "We must recognise a new threat to the peace of nations, indeed to the very fabric of society. We have seen in the last few years the growth of the cult of political violence, preached and practised not so much between states as within them. . . . [I]t may be that in the 1970s, the decade which faces us, civil war, rather than between nations, will be the main danger we face."[13] The Brigadier General Staff, Brian Watkins, stated: "We are worrying about society a hell of a lot more than we ever used to. This concern has escalated dramatically over the past three years and I am sure it will continue."[14]

There was a second new development that would contribute to the return of the boomerang in the 1970s: immigration. As Westminster had encouraged immigration from the Commonwealth countries in the immediate aftermath of the war to meet pressing labor needs, migrants came from the Caribbean, Africa, and Asia in unprecedented numbers. It had begun with the arrival of the passenger ship *Windrush* in 1948 from Jamaica. While it only carried 492 passengers, it was seminal. Unfortunately, data on immigration is inconsistent, but various statistics can be arrayed to provide the bigger picture. By 1950, the estimated number of nonwhite people in Britain was 30,000.[15] From around 1951 to 1959, the number of persons categorized as "Black" per 1,000 population increased from 1.70 to 7.30. The West Indian population grew from an estimated 15,300 in 1951 to 171,800 in that period. In 1961 there were 48,000 immigrants from India and Pakistan alone.[16] In 1968, the estimated number of Black Caribbeans in England and Wales was just over 1 million (the total population of the United Kingdom in 1968 was 55,132,596).[17] In 1972, a confidential Home Office report claimed that there were an estimated 1.5 million "coloured people living in this country," of whom only a third "have been born here."[18]

As with the earlier waves of immigration to Britain, the new immigration was met with official concern. In 1950, Prime Minister Clement Atlee called for a committee to consider "means which might be adopted to check the immigration into this country of coloured people from the British colonial territories." The committee ultimately concluded that restricting immigration at that time was not necessary, as they did not see it as a problem.[19] But many white Britons did. As most had barely ever met racialized minorities, and as their cities had been "almost entirely white," they greeted the new arrivals with consternation.[20] Surveys revealed most white Britons exhibited "extreme prejudice" and "disapproval" toward "black people."[21] "Colonial racism," as Benjamin Bowling explains, "was transformed into indigenous racism."[22] Discrimination in employment and housing followed.[23] Violent attacks on immigrants spread. White nationalists such as the members of the White Defence League and the Union Movement, led by the parliamentarian Oswald Mosley, fanned the flames of hatred. The riots of 1958 in Notting Hill, where many of the new immigrants resided near white working-class residents, signified the times. There, a mob of up to four hundred whites attacked West Indian residents for five nights straight. Many among the mob had been associated with a movement called Keep Britain White.

The initial police response to the new immigrants was cautious calm. In the early 1950s, Met officers' reports on London's African Caribbean communities referred to those communities as "the colonies of London" but expressed little concern. One report noted that the Jamaicans "give practically no trouble" (while adding that "the same cannot be said of [the West Africans]").[24] Another claimed that the "coloured colonials" were lacking in "moral conduct" and were "lazy and of poor education," but generally there was little to be concerned about.[25] Nonetheless, as the 1950s wore on, the number of Black Caribbean immigrants swelled, and the police and the government grew concerned in proportion. Black Caribbean leaders charged the police with abuse and maintained that the Met sided with white residents during the Notting Hill riots. In response, the Met blamed the fact of immigration itself. In 1959, Metropolitan Police commissioner Joseph Simpson claimed that while Notting Hill had always been "disorderly," the "concentration of Colonial immigrants" was the culprit behind law-and-order problems.[26]

Things worsened through the 1960s, as officials and the public came to associate the new immigrants with criminality. In 1968, home secretary James Callaghan insinuated this when he told the Police Federation: "We must all face the fact that we have over a million coloured citizens living among us. . . . I hope you will accept that you have got a problem with this large number of coloured citizens."[27] By the early 1970s, studies conducted by the police and Scotland Yard purported to find that 80 percent of street crime was committed by Black people.[28] Noting these and other statistics, Robert Mark of the Metropolitan Police later said such crime naturally increased because of the "larger and more mixed population" of England.[29] Police officials feared that criminality among Britain's Black populations would turn London into a crime-infested pit, presumably like New York. They complained of "small, violent highly mobile gangs" in London as leading the crime wave and called for stronger judicial penalties on violent crime.[30] A moral panic over "mugging" by Black youths erupted.[31]

The increase in London's immigrant population became especially worrisome to police officials and state authorities, who swiftly twinned it with their imperial anxieties over domestic insurgency. Perceived criminality in this context became a multivocal sign, not just of bad morals and practices but also of a refusal by Black Britons to submit to Britain's legal order—a defiance of white imperial authority. The menace that Black Caribbeans represented to white elites was thus articulated with the perceived threats to order, and the new immigration became articulated with the global threat. British officials did not see the rise in crime in the United States as disconnected from the African American riots in Detroit, Watts, Newark, and elsewhere, nor did they see any of these as isolated from anticolonial movements in Africa, communist grabs for power in Britain's former Caribbean colonies, or social decay in London. In 1970, the acting chief of defense intelligence pondered the "internal unrest in the United States" and linked together "Northern Ireland, Aden, Hong Kong, and Detroit" as one seamless string of revolutionary sites.[32] By 1968, likely half of all of England's Black population resided in London's Metropolitan District, which contributed to the notion that the city would explode as so many of America's cities had.[33] An editorial in the *Police Review* warned in the wake of the African American riots in the United States in 1969: "There is going to be much suffering in the United States; and some of the events in recent years are also almost certain to come home to roost here."[34] British authorities likewise felt besieged by Black Power protests and related demonstrations. They began to see Black Caribbean immigrants as potential subversives, just as they had assumed that they were always already criminals. Racializing the threat of insurgency. the *Police Review* warned that "race riots" in the United Kingdom as well as in the United States "are likely to be . . . more organized than before. Black power politicians . . . give thrust and violence to protest, producing dangerous situations out of very little." The *Police Review* similarly responded to the ghetto uprisings in the United States in the summer of 1967 by stating that soon there would be "blood on our streets too."[35] Officials were especially worried that Black Power movements in London were organizing with Black Power organizations in the United States and communist movements in Africa. The press even speculated that the rebellion in Britain's neocolonial territory of Anguilla in 1969 was "joined by American gangsters and Black Panthers, the trigger-happy wing of the Black Power movement."[36]

By the early 1970s, the stage was set for a new state strategy for countering the global racialized threats to British society that were keeping officials and the British upper classes awake at night. But what kind of strategy? White nationalist groups advocated for more immigration controls, and in 1971 more restrictive legislation was passed. To help enforce it, a new national police unit was set up within the Metropolitan Police, purportedly to track illegal immigration.[37] Furthermore, the London Metropolitan Police stepped up its surveillance and harassment of Black communities and movements, exemplified in their consistent raids of Frank Crichlow's Mangrove restaurant in Notting Hill. The police justified the raids by claiming that the restaurant was a center of drug dealing, but the real reason was that the Special Branch took it to be a center for Black Panther organizing.[38]

As early as 1965, the Conservative Party had promised an "all-out attack on lawlessness and violence."[39] One year later MP Quintin Hogg portended a violent state response: "In the complex urban society of our day the part of the sword cannot be ultimately dispensed with."[40] By 1972, Metropolitan commissioner Robert Mark had internalized the messaging. He declared nothing less than a "war on crime."[41] But as the racialized menace persisted and domestic unrest continued, high-level government officials were compelled to ponder more drastic alternatives to restore "law and order." Initially, they looked to Continental models of state coercion. They considered a national riot unit or a "third force": a coercive organization that was neither the military nor the civil police but rather a paramilitary internal defense force akin to the Continental gendarmerie or to riot control police like the French Compagnies Républicaines de Sécurité. The discussions heightened after the 1968 demonstrations at Grosvenor Square. They were opened up again after the Saltley miners' strike in 1972. In the wake of the miners' strike, the Brigadier General Staff, Brian Watkins, lamented that the police forces in England have been "based on the fundamental philosophy that we are a law-abiding country, but things have now got to the state where there are not enough resources to deal with the increasing numbers who are not prepared to respect the law."[42] Some kind of new force, he and others concluded, was needed.

In the end, the third force was never created. In the high circles of government, there were concerns over how the English public would take to such a new and potentially tyrannical force. They feared that it would reawaken all the fears of a gendarmerie that had circulated ever since the founding of the London Metropolitan Police in 1829 (see Chapter 1). Officials thus concluded that a third force would be impossible: the public would not accept such a European-style paramilitary force.[43] Instead, something else had to be done. Their solution, ultimately, was not unlike the solution that Sir Robert Peel had landed upon after he and his colleagues had rejected the idea of creating a British gendarmerie in 1829. The solution came from the colonies.

## Falling Empire, Rising Insurgencies

While Britain's colonial empire was falling apart in the 1950s and 1960s, its modalities and methods of power were not. They had been refined and modulated, serving to expand the imperial repertoire that would later influence the new 1970s wave of police militarization in the metropole. There were at least two fundamental developments in Britain's imperial-military repertoire that would resonate domestically.

First were new forms of colonial policing of crowds, riots, strikes, and mass disorder. In Britain, the standard methods of crowd control from the nineteenth century had included the "baton charge," which was extended to Ireland and other parts of the empire. But in the wake of the Jallianwala Bagh Massacre of 1919 (also known as the Amritsar Massacre), colonial officials began devising new approaches.[44] In the late 1920s, the colonial administration in India created reserve police units in Madras to be used in the event of riots, strikes, and unruly demonstrations. Trained by European sergeants, these new units were armed with the latest weaponry and given motorized transport to increase their mobility and striking power. Around the same time, in Malabar a new police unit called the Malabar Special Police was created to deal with outbreaks of social disorder. Armed with Lewis guns and .303 rifles, it too was commanded by European officers and run "on strict military lines." It played a leading role in quelling the uprisings in the Eastern Ghats in 1922–1924 and in Madras city in 1928–1929, among others. Sometimes referred to as "striking forces," these units deviated from conventional policing of India's rural villages.[45] As the historian David Arnold explains, they were urban, "well armed, highly disciplined units which could be quickly sent to deal with any variety of disturbance or resistance to colonial control." Their mobility made them much more like military units than standard police patrols, which tended to operate within their own beats, and unlike earlier mobile beat patrols they were organized as reserve forces, to be called upon when most needed. Perhaps more than any other features of colonial police, these units represented "the alien and repressive character of the colonial government."[46]

Across the British Empire similar tactical units emerged under a variety of names—notably "mobile strike forces," "police field forces," or "police mobile units."[47] All of these units were elite, specially trained, and mobile. Their arsenal included truncheons, firearms, riot shields, and by the 1950s, tear gas, along with special nonlethal bullets or new tools of public order like water cannons that were developed in the 1960s.[48] The Uganda Police Service Unit, established in 1942, had special training in drill and musketry and was created for "special duties" to complement the general police's "ordinary police duties." It wielded Brent guns and rode in armored cars.[49] The Mobile Strike Force in Palestine was created in 1940 to provide "mobile concentrations at strategic points."[50] In the colony of Aden, the unit known as the Armed Police was trained by British officers in the use of Brill and Lewis guns, riot control, and tear gas.[51] One particularly noteworthy unit was in the Shanghai International Settlement. As discussed in Chapter 5, the Shanghai Reserve Unit was a heavily armed mobile "riot squad." It became widely influential in the imperial world. Along with its Indian precedents, it provided a model for other police units in the British Empire, such as the Singapore Reserve Unit (formed in 1951) and the Hong Kong Police Tactical Unit, among many others. The SRU and these subsequent colonial units influenced policing forms and strategies in the US empire as well, while police from Malaya, Burma, Sri Lanka, and Vietnam trained with Singapore's Reserve Unit. Later variants in Ireland included the Ulster Special Constabulary (or "B-Specials").

Mobile units became increasingly important for the British in the late 1950s as the cracks of empire widened and postwar anticolonial dissidence exploded. The Singapore police commissioner reported in 1957 that the Singapore Reserve Unit and associated "specialised riot units" were vital for handling the colony's "large multi-racial, multi-lingual population" and served as "one of the major factors in preventing civil disturbances from erupting into large scale rioting."[52]

In turn, the conditions of late colonialism compelled innovations in crowd control methods, which tactical police units and the military deployed to great effect. A Gold Coast Police pamphlet in 1949 on "riot drill" codified some of these tactics for instruction and diffusion. The tactics included wedge formations (or "arrowhead formations" or "V" formations) for police to penetrate and disperse crowds, effective baton use, and "snatch squads," which were also employed by the British Army.[53]

By 1975, Major General Anthony Deane-Drummond referred to snatch squads as a standard army method of riot control.[54] These were small teams that would penetrate a crowd during demonstrations (typically after their colleagues had opened up space using wedge formations) to grab leaders and haul them to a secure place for interrogation and jailing. Snatch squads might also mount stealth assaults upon residences of anticolonial leaders to raid and seize. Both the Singapore police and the Hong Kong Police Tactical Unit used snatch squads successfully in response to the riots of 1956 and through the 1960s.[55] By the late 1960s the tactic had spread to other colonial forces and the army in Northern Ireland. In 1969 the army in Belfast touted it as a "new method" for crowd control that had been "used by British troops in various parts of the world" and that would, according to the *Belfast Telegraph*, help "nip Ulster riots in the bud."[56] US military strategists were particularly impressed with the use of snatch squads in Ulster.[57] The technique was then used regularly across Northern Ireland, spanning "Londonderry, Armagh and Lurgan," enabling soldiers to "make lightning arrests of ring-leaders" and disperse crowds.[58]

The other key development within the empire was part and parcel of the new policing units: counterinsurgency theory. Before the 1960s, colonial police and the British Army engaged in multiple campaigns against riots, disorder, and uprisings but they had not yet developed a formal counterinsurgency doctrine or universal method for so-called small wars. At most, the British Army had adopted a pragmatic "*ad hoc* approach to colonial conflicts . . . adapting its methods to the particular circumstances of each conflict." There were some shared principles, but officer training in counterinsurgency principles or tactics was absent; missing too were unified doctrines connecting conflicts in Malaya with those in Oman or Northern Ireland.[59] Accumulated experience in putting down the rebellions of the 1940s through the 1960s served to change things, offering the basis for new thinking. Campaigns conducted in Palestine, Kenya, and Malaya among other sites served as some of the bloody laboratories for new thinking. Lessons were learned.

Major General Richard Clutterbuck, a veteran of the Palestine and Malaya campaigns, emerged as one especially enterprising counterinsurgency thinker, vocalizing the view that the type of uprisings that occurred in the colonies would also happen in "London, Liverpool, Cardiff or Glasgow."[60] Underpinning this fear was a revised understanding of the character of insurgencies. In conventional thought, most insurgencies were rural. Clutterbuck stressed instead that insurgencies could just as well be urban, erupting in the heart of cities like Algiers or even London, Manchester, Los Angeles, and New York. Clutterbuck thus studied Britain's internal history of political violence, constructing a list of political groups in Britain purported to have insurgent tendencies, and theorized the best methods for countering the "urban guerilla."[61] When the public, the press, and officials expressed fears that the barbarians were at the gates, they were wittingly or unwittingly voicing Clutterbuck's concerns.

Other counterinsurgency thinkers included Major General Deane-Drummond and General Frank Kitson. Deane-Drummond had served in the Second World War and helped put down rebellions in Palestine, Cyprus, Malaya, and Oman. Starting in 1968 he was assistant chief of defense staff in the Ministry of Defence and later codified lessons from colonial insurgencies in his book *Riot Control* (1975), the first line of which foretold that "the control of riots presents an acutely difficult problem for the governments of modern, democratic states" and "presents a challenge to the authority of the state."[62] Kitson had served in Kenya, Malaya, and Cyprus and drew upon his experience to theorize distinct "phases" or stages of insurgency and counterinsurgency. He later put his theories to use in Northern Ireland where he served as an operational commander. Kitson's theories were not radically new; they merely codified "the methods that had been used against the Malayan *maquisards,* the Kenyan nationalists, the Algerian fighters, or the Vietcong."[63] But what *was* new, besides the formalization of these theories, was their direct or potential application to the home context. Based upon the shared premise that the fire was ablaze at home, the new doctrines of counterinsurgency were popularized and modified for domestic practice.

Most importantly, the new counterinsurgency theorizing shaped how British authorities viewed metropolitan policing. Three basic ideas were important. The first is that rebellion could happen "here" as easily as "there." This was one of the fundamental premises of Clutterbuck's book *Protest and the Urban Guerilla,* in which Clutterbuck went so far as to warn that "the great majority of urban revolutionaries are neither peasants nor ex-peasants nor industrial workers but intellectuals"—some of whom were immigrants who had studied or trained overseas.[64] The second was the notion that insurgencies could not be met with direct force alone but had to be managed through nonmilitary methods alongside military ones. A "politico-military strategy" was needed.[65] This was a lesson that was learned in the colonies by the 1950s, after disastrous years of treating rebellion and uprisings as only military problems. Cooperation between the civil government, its police, and the military was essential.

The third idea would prove particularly pernicious. This was the idea that rebellions can develop even from the most seemingly innocuous events or political groups. Revolution lurked behind the most benign-appearing shadows. On this point, Kitson borrowed from Sir Robert Thompson, another counterinsurgency expert who wrote about Malaya and Vietnam, to differentiate between "subversion" and "insurgency." While insurgency refers to the use of armed force to overthrow a government "or force them to do things they don't want to do," "subversion" refers to "all illegal measures short of the use of armed force." Involving "the use of political and economic pressure, strikes, protest marches, and propaganda," subversion can be a corollary to insurgency or a first phase of it—a "non-violent phase" of the ostensibly looming revolt.[66] Seemingly innocent protests or demonstrations, therefore, could be Trojan horses rather than legitimate expressions of opinion. "It must now be regarded as normal," Clutterbuck wrote, "for any major demonstration to be exploited for wider revolutionary aims."[67] The counterinsurgency principle followed: subversions must be monitored and entirely repressed if need be, thereby preventing them from becoming insurgencies. Rebellion must be nipped in the bud. This is where the civil government, and hence policing, was to play a role. In consistent consultation with the military, civil authorities needed to take action from the first sign of trouble, if not before. Kitson called this the "preparatory phase" of counterinsurgency, whereby the state created a "machinery" for civil-military coordination and counterinsurgency infrastructure. This was a "countersubversion" strategy, whereby the state ensured clear channels of communication between the civilian and military branches of the government, created the legal infrastructure for thwarting subversives and/or establishing "emergencies," and began "psychological operations" that used the media and other institutions "to promote its own cause and undermine that of the enemy."[68]

The implications for policing were profound. For if insurgency happened at home, if it could begin with seemingly innocuous demonstrations or protests, and if countersubversion therefore was not primarily a matter for the military but one for the civil government, the civil police had to play a direct role in counterinsurgency. More than fight crime, it also had to help prevent subversion. Clutterbuck put it simply: in "fascist and communist countries," insurrection and terrorists could be thwarted by direct military repression, but in democracies, what was needed was "efficient police work." The police needed to identify, monitor, and help contain subversives.[69] The army would wait in the background, but the police had to be the main mechanism. Sir Robert Thompson, who influenced Kitson and in turn internalized Kitson's views, declared in 1973: "The military may have to intervene and must be prepared to intervene, but God help us if they have to; this eventuality must be kept as far away as possible by having the right police forces."[70]

Notably, this theory about the role of the police marked a colonial boomerang effect in itself. It was the same philosophy of colonial policing that had been circulating through the empire ever since the Jallianwala Bagh Massacre, if not before. As a former officer of the Malaya police explained in 1969, the police's role in the colonies was not merely "the prevention and detection of crime." The notion that crime-fighting was the "primary duty of the police" in the colonies "is a myth which can be safely disregarded." While crime was still an issue, the real function of the police in the colonies was to "ensure that the government is not overthrown by violence or subversion."[71] Hence the proliferation of specialized anti-riot units in Britain's imperial periphery: these were exactly about nipping subversion, and hence revolution, in the bud. Policing was countersubversion, and countersubversion was counterinsurgency—which was also policing.

## Policing Subversion

Colonial policing methods and counterinsurgency theory did not reside only at the periphery of empire. They became well known to the British police on beloved home soil. Officials such as Robert Mark, commissioner of the Met (1972–1977), had already had military experience, and Mark actively recruited ex-military for the London Met.[72] Colonial policing and counterinsurgency theory also flowed into domestic policing circles through conferences, forums, and lectures held by organizations such as the Institute for the Study of Conflict (ISC).[73] The curriculum at the Metropolitan Police College included lessons on colonial policing. Senior police officers took courses at the Imperial Defence College. Clutterbuck and other experts lectured directly to police officials in various forums.[74] The British government facilitated such exchanges, instantiating Kitson's "preparatory" phase. The 1970 Ministry of Defence Working Party charged with reviewing military aid to civil governance included military officials such as Deane-Drummond and Mark (who was then assistant commissioner of the London Metropolitan Police). Mark also joined Home Office and Ministry of Defence representatives on a special committee to coordinate police-military actions dealing with civil disorder.[75]

Through these and other forums, British police officers and other high-level government officials internalized the new imperial-military mindset on counterinsurgency. John Alderson, commandant of the Bramshill Police College and later chief constable of Devon and Cornwall, gave an address to the Royal United Services Institute declaring: "The reality of malevolent activities of a society of extremist groups . . . marxists of every brand, anarchists, nihilists and at least some elements of the various nationalist movements, all these have a determined interest in subverting existing British society."[76] Military strategists and counterinsurgency theorists like Deane-Drummond in turn quoted Alderson to justify their view that revolution was happening from within rather than only from without.[77] Leading officials also internalized the view that the police, more than merely fighting street crime, should play a leading role in fighting insurgency by fighting subversion (just as counterinsurgency theory counseled). According to one ISC participant, it was through the ISC's meetings and lectures that many police officials came to the belief that insurgency grew from "the early stages of subversion and it was the responsibility of police" to deal with it.[78]

The views of Robert Mark, commissioner of the London Met, are exemplary. In various speeches and writings, he breathlessly stitched together revolution, disorder, and everyday crime while specifying the police's distinct role in managing it all. An "increasingly diverse and turbulent society" and the "shrinking world," he wrote, have "brought many problems" to the "doorstep" of the London police.[79] Insisting that the danger at home was real, he declared that one thing the police had learned from "events in Northern Ireland, Pakistan, the Middle East, Cyprus, Algeria, Czechoslovakia, Hungary and Vietnam" is "the greater sophistication and striking power of the violent inspired by political motives." And because "few, if any countries can these days exist in isolation . . . for those of us actively involved in the containment of violence, whether at home or abroad . . . our role is never likely to diminish in importance."[80] For the police, the "most serious problem today is the containment or absorption of social unrest arising from a number of factors, unemployment, political and industrial strife, racial problems, vandalism and hooliganism . . . The police are therefore very much on their own in attempting to preserve order in an increasingly turbulent society."[81]

Here lie the roots of the government's decision in the early 1970s to eschew a "third force" or national gendarmerie. Rather than create a third force, the government found an alternative in counterinsurgency theory and models of colonial policing. The alternative was this: use the existing police in Britain to take on countersubversion and hence counterinsurgency functions. The Home Office Working Party concluded in 1971 that rather than create a new force, the "existing forces [should] be retrained and re-equipped to cope better with serious civil unrest."[82] The 1972 National Security Committee likewise suggested that while a third force was not desirable, a newly empowered police force would be. It recommended that the police retrain in riot control and firearms usage, that regular exercises between police and military should be held to prepare for emergencies, and that clearer guidelines for when the army could be called in should be drawn up.[83] Notably, this was around the time Robert Mark called for an all-out "war on crime."

In short, to quell the radical disorder of the time and face down insurgency at home, the British imperial state adopted the approach it had taken in the periphery of empire. After all, in the eyes of British officialdom, the new threat at home was not only similar to but seemingly connected to that in the periphery. The tools, tactics, and theories of colonial counterinsurgency were deemed not only appropriate for Britain but vital, an imperative of survival. This had radical implications for policing in the late 1960s onward. One implication was a new police unit in London. It was called the Special Patrol Group.

## London's Tactical Unit, aka the Special Patrol Group

The Special Patrol Group (SPG) was founded in 1965 as a special unit within the London Metropolitan Police. It was the work of senior Met officers, including Douglas Webb and Commissioner Joseph Simpson (the latter was the same commissioner who had, in 1959, blamed the "concentration of Colonial immigrants" for aggravating law-and-order problems). Modeled after tactical police units like those in the colonies and New York's Tactical Patrol Force, the SPG was a special unit to manage perceived rises in "housebreaking and hooliganism" and "localized outbreaks of crime."[84] Initially it consisted of a hundred officers, chosen from five hundred volunteers from the Met, "divided into four units, each with two vans and a car . . . all equipped with radio."[85] "By this means," Simpson explained in his annual report, "I hope to be able to nip in the bud any marked shift in the territorial incidence of crime."[86]

The SPG began its career without controversy. In the first year of its operation, Londoners were almost bemused at the sight of SPG officers riding around in their special vans or walking the streets with the latest radio technology on offer. A local newspaper wrote of their sightings in the neighboring of Chelsea: "They are not spacemen in helmets and radios who come to invade Chelsea—they are, in fact, Scotland Yard's Special Patrol Group of uniformed policemen . . . seen since Friday patrolling Chelsea streets, with their walkie-talkie radios and aerials in their top pockets."[87] In its first nine months of operation, the SPG was credited with conducting "278 arrests for crime, 118 for non-criminal offences, and the recovery of a substantial quantity of stolen property."[88] In 1967 it was credited with quelling crime enough to cause a "dip" in the crime rate.[89]

The initial remit of the SPG was to handle crime. This is where it was not exactly like colonial police units. But as the global turbulence of the 1960s hit home, and as counterinsurgency theory became increasingly popular among police, SPG officials began wondering if crime control was what the SPG should be about. In his 1966 report, Superintendent Powis of the SPG wrote: "I feel certain the Metropolitan Police will soon pass through a testing period in respect of industrial and political disorder."[90] In his annual report for 1967, after British territories including Hong Kong had erupted in violence and as African Americans rioted in Detroit and Newark, Superintendent P. J. Flynn mused: "It may be that in the future this Force will have to deal with a type of disorder, prevalent abroad but not yet experienced in this country, which requires special measures and a particularly high degree of adroit handling. In the event, a body such as the Special Patrol Group . . . would be a valuable asset to the Force."[91] Two years later, Chief Inspector Atkins made a similar prediction and accordingly called for more personnel, more equipment, special planning groups, and additional training programs. He added the view that revolution abroad was connected with unrest at home:

> Bearing in mind the periodic upheaval, political and territorial throughout the world; the upthrust of student power and the emergence of racialistic factions, it naturally follows that repercussions will be felt in this country where the policy of free speech is advantageous to militant groups who, under the guise of pacifists are the main cause of disorder accompanying public demonstrations. Consequently the SPG will be increasingly called upon to perform duty in connection with these events.[92]

By 1972, as the government decided to rely upon police to manage countersubversion, the future was written: the SPG would be the key policing unit for domestic counterinsurgency, fulfilling the role that counterinsurgency theorists laid down for police. In essence, London would have its own colonial tactical police unit.

According to colonial counterinsurgency doctrine, there were at least two important functions of the police that the SPG would help fulfill. The first was the proper management of riots, demonstrations, and protests. Since the most innocuous-looking protests could harbor insurgents and revolutionaries, the police had to handle public demonstrations or other outbursts of civil disorder with the larger countersubversive strategy in view. This meant that police had to treat demonstrations and protests in a way that would not harm the image of the civil government and its larger mission of "propaganda" (as Kitson had called it simply).[93] This was the doctrine of minimum force with which the civil police would have been familiar and which Commissioner Mark repeated over and again. The goal was to prevent protests or demonstrations from spreading revolutionary propaganda and winning converts. Too much force or violence would undermine the effort.[94] This countersubversive approach to demonstrations also meant that the police had to target movement leaders. Rather than using violence to squash the protests and the movements they represented, police should cut off the heads of the movements entirely by arresting the subversives or would-be revolutionaries, thus separating them from the protests and followers. Leaders needed to be isolated from the population, arrested, and jailed; their influence would be weakened and their ideas discredited.[95] According to the theory, once movements lost their leaders, they would die out of their own accord.[96]

The second key function of the police was to gather intelligence. Identifying and thwarting subversion required information. Information, according to Kitson, was the "essential requisite . . . [for] countering non-violent subversion . . . [and] dealing with all forms of insurgency."[97] Civil governments therefore needed an organization for the task. The police were it. The police had to survey the terrain, identify possible insurgent movements, and collect information on subversives. This was especially crucial for containing leaders who would otherwise transform subversion into outright revolution. "Most police intelligence work," asserted Clutterbuck, "is . . . usually about identifying the people who are leaders and violence provokers."[98] This "intelligence work" was straightforward enough when "demonstrations and riots are rife," according to Kitson, "because the ringleaders during such events will be more visible and known.[99] But the police had to gather intelligence consistently and constantly. Sir Charles Jeffries, deputy undersecretary of state for the colonies in the 1950s, claimed that in periods of calm the most important thing police could do was to collect intelligence and pass it on to the army.[100] Army officials even asserted that the police was better than the army for such intelligence gathering because of the police's appearance of normality and its embeddedness within local communities.[101] This was one of the lessons from the Palestine Police Force's counterterrorism efforts: the police needed to collect intelligence for the army *before* the insurgency occurred and hence before the army got involved.[102]

The only problem was that the SPG, founded as an anticrime unit, was woefully ill-prepared for these new functions. In 1967, the chief superintendent of the Royal Hong Kong Police observed the London Metropolitan Police and registered surprise at its inadequate riot control training and inferior equipment.[103] Even as some police officers lauded the British Army's "great experience in controlling civil disorder" and insisted that "[the army's] methods could doubtless be adopted for police use," neither the London police nor the SPG specifically was receiving formal training in colonial or army methods.[104] The SPG needed retooling, and through a number of mechanisms this soon came about. One mechanism was overseas service. In 1969, to put down a coup d'état in the West Indies island of Anguilla, whose foreign relations Britain still controlled, forty members of the SPG armed with Walther automatics were sent along with the 16th Parachute Brigade and other army forces to invade the island. After British forces secured control and a friendly government was installed, more SPG officers were sent to serve as the island's police force until a new local force was created. During this time, SPG officers were rebranded as the Anguilla Police Unit (APU) under the direct supervision of a British officer with colonial experience.[105] The APU trained under a former member of the Malayan Police so that it could become, as one official in the Foreign Office put it, an "effective riot control squad trained on traditional Colonial Service lines."[106]

Back in England, high-level police officials received their own training of sorts. British chief constables across the country trained in Northern Ireland and met with the Royal Ulster Constabulary.[107] In 1969, Robert Mark, then assistant commissioner of the London Metropolitan Police, went with the chief constable of Hampshire and army officials to Northern Ireland to learn from the Royal Ulster Constabulary and its "paramilitary" B-Specials.[108] In 1970, Mark again joined other police and military officials, including Deane-Drummond, to travel to Ulster, Berlin, Paris, Hong Kong, and cities in the United States and Cyprus, among other places. As Mark later recalled, the trip offered "valuable . . . insight into police methods elsewhere."[109] In 1971, John Henry Gerrard, deputy assistant commissioner of the Met and a member of the SPG, traveled to the United States to discuss riot control methods. According to newspaper accounts, he also had "special training in riot control and wedge formation tactics based on the Army's experience in Ulster."[110] Subsequently, beginning in 1972, Gerrard and Mark instituted new training modules for the SPG. Some of these modules included annual joint exercises with the British Army.[111] The modules also included courses on counterinsurgency. Kitson's work was assigned, and Kitson and other army officials were invited to speak to police colleges. Meanwhile, the ISC created a "manual of counter insurgency" that was disseminated to police colleges.[112] Starting in 1973 if not earlier, members of the Special Branch and the SPG even took courses in "urban guerilla containment" (UGC). "I suppose the real tragedy," a policeman reportedly said about UGC training, "is that we have to learn such things. But we do, and that's that."[113]

## Colonial Counterinsurgenization in Black and Brown London

Through these experiences and channels, the SPG was trained in the new art of counterinsurgency. The stage was set for its transformation in practice, not just in theory, marking as much of a counterinsurgenization of policing as militarization.[114] For instance, the SPG soon became the leader in domestic counterterrorism. "Some form of security or anti-terrorist duty," reported the SPG inspector in 1974, "has become a permanent feature of the Group's activities."[115] The SPG also became the primary unit for any operations or disturbances in London involving firearms. Eventually, 80 percent of the SPG's members were trained in firearms. This was a "much higher proportion than in general in the Uniform Branch," as one report noted.[116] Furthermore, the SPG became the primary unit for the London Met's snipers and the first responder for bomb threats. By the early 1980s SPG members were found in armored personnel carriers equipped with plastic bullets and tear gas.[117] The SPG also became London's riot squad, hence resembling almost exactly the "mobile strike forces" in the colonies. In 1972, the SPG undertook about 109 "special operations," and the vast majority of them were public order events.[118] During the years 1972, 1973, and 1974, there were 1,321 demonstrations that involved police presence, and the SPG's participation in public order events rose accordingly.[119] In 1974, the SPG commanding officer fretted about the implications of this for crime control: "While there is no doubt that the Special Patrol Group has developed an impressive expertise in handling violent events . . . there is a danger of over specialization to the detriment of its real purpose."[120]

No longer appearing as a group of quaint "spacemen in helmets" or a praiseworthy crime unit, the SPG swiftly acquired a reputation for being an elite militarized force with a leading role in crowd control. It was notably aggressive in many demonstrations, such as the Red Lion Square protest, the picketing at the Grunwick factories in northwest London in 1976–1978, and the National Front meeting in Southall in 1979 when one anti-Nazi protester was killed by an SPG officer. Critics denounced the SPG's role in demonstrations and strikes, accusing it of being trained "to behave like the CRS of France"—the heavily aggressive and militarized Compagnies Républicaines de Sécurité.[121]

In fact, the SPG was less like the CRS of France and more like its colonial counterparts across the British Empire. This is clear in its adoption of colonial-military tactics such as snatch squads. As mentioned already, this tactic of arresting ringleaders of protests was an innovation of colonial tactical police units, and it followed counterinsurgency principles. It was a way to stop rioting and the entire movement at once. Snatch squads could be used at different moments of the protest cycle. One was during the riot itself. According to Clutterbuck, the best way to stop riots was to "arrest the leaders . . . after the crowds have taken to the streets" so that replacements could not jump in too early. Wedge formations were often used to aid the squad. But leaders could also be "snatched" after the first day of demonstrations in the middle of the night, a tactic that was used by the Singapore police in 1956, when 234 leaders were arrested at night, leaving demonstrations the next day without any heads.[122] Clutterbuck had found these snatch squads to be especially "effective in Ulster."[123] When Commissioner Mark visited Ulster, he witnessed the Royal Ulster Constabulary's use of snatch squads and subsequently ordered the London SPG to be trained in their use.[124]

The SPG deployed snatch squad tactics throughout the 1970s. According to newspaper reports, the police used snatch squads at a Black Power demonstration of about "200 coloured men and women" in London in 1970, seizing leaders and throwing them into vans to be taken to West End Central.[125] Later, Black residents of some of London's Black Caribbean communities condemned the snatch squads who "went round late at night" to arrest suspects.[126] At the 1974 Red Lion Square demonstration, where counterprotesters engaged marchers from the right-wing National Front organization, SPG officers were seen using the snatch tactic on members of the International Marxist Group.[127] In 1980, the London SPG even boasted about its skill at removing ringleaders from crowds using snatch methods—going after "the real nasties," as one SPG officer put it.[128] The SPG further added to its repertoire "dawn raids" of ringleaders' houses in order to seize and arrest them, mimicking the nighttime operations of the Singapore police that military strategists had so admired.[129]

Another part of this new countersubversion approach was the use of closed-circuit television (CCTV). The London Met had already been using CCTV since the 1950s. As Chris A. Williams notes, the centralized command structure and information room created earlier by Trenchard served as the center.[130] While CCTV had been originally introduced for traffic control, the London Met eventually enlisted the technology as part of its countersubversion strategy. In the 1960s the Met began experimenting with its use for crowd control. Meanwhile, police in Northern Ireland used CCTV to identify and indict protesters who hurled rocks during violent demonstrations. By 1972, the police had nine cameras in central London for crowd control purposes, linked to the existing system of traffic cameras. In 1974, assistant deputy commissioner and SPG member John Gerrard "openly acknowledged for the first time that the purpose of the [CCTV] system was crowd control," as it would serve "to identify unsafe 'pressure points' in crowds and to manage them more efficiently with fewer officers." It was not yet used to target individuals, he claimed, though other police forces appeared to use it for those purposes.[131] By the end of the decade, CCTV along with helicopters had become a vital part of riot control policing.[132]

While the SPG increasingly took on a public order role and deployed colonial methods to fulfill it, it nonetheless remained attentive to crime control. But the methods for crime control now differed. One method was saturation: flooding high-crime neighborhoods with a visible police presence to intimidate criminals into submission. As officials debated whether such saturation worked sufficiently, they twinned it with other operations like stop-and-search.[133] The strategy was to saturate an area and to stop and search as many residents as possible, using cordons, roadblocks, or checkpoints to divert foot or automobile traffic to areas for searching. In 1975, SPG's own annual report noted that such stops, searches, and roadblocks were among the SPG's "most favoured tactics."[134]

As critics like Anderson later noted, the effect of saturation operations like these was to turn the police into an "occupying army."[135] To be sure, in the colonies, the same operations and tactics had long served countersubversion and counterinsurgency functions. Stop-and-search had been a means by which to locate rebels, their accomplices, and their supplies or weapons at the height of the rebellion. Cordons and searches had been a preferred method of the armies in Malaya, Vietnam, and Algeria, when entire neighborhoods or villages might be cordoned. Used with checkpoints and barbed wire, cordoning served to divide entire cities or regions into "coloring areas" (black for insurgent territory, gray where some army control had been established, and white where the police and army had full control).[136] Kitson used such methods extensively in Northern Ireland—for example, deploying barbed wire and checkpoints in Derry during Operation Motorman in 1972, which involved the army as well as the Gardai (national police).[137] In the aftermath of the Kowloon disturbances of 1966, the Hong Kong Police, working with soldiers from the Queen's Regiment and Edinburgh's Own Gurkha Rifles, successfully deployed cordons and searches to arrest hundreds of presumed rioters and raid the homes of subversives.[138]

Cordons, roadblocks, and searches were also useful for collecting information, thereby helping to meet Kitson's imperative that the nonviolent phase of countersubversion should involve intelligence gathering by the civil rather than the military arms of the state.[139] Colonial police forces set up checkpoints or roadblocks to conduct snap searches and identification checks, or they created observation posts around known subversive territory to monitor possible contact between guerrillas and local civilians.[140] In Northern Ireland, the army's Special Investigation Branch created card files for nearly one-third of Northern Ireland's population by 1974 for a new army computer. Much of the information was collected, cross-checked, and supplemented through random checks and searches.[141] The Ulster Special Patrol Group regularly used roadblocks and searches, inspiring Robert Mark to train the London SPG in their use as well.[142]

Given the SPG's colonial training and new remit, it is fitting that the London SPG began using cordons, roadblocks, and related stop-and-search tactics on a regular basis. Random stops and searches had been permitted by the so-called sus (suspected person) laws under the Vagrancy Act of 1824, and as early as 1966 the SPG had utilized them for crime control.[143] The SPG began deploying the stop-and-search tactic more extensively amid a wave of new saturation operations in the 1970s. And following the racialization of crime and disorder, the SPG tended to use stop-and-search tactics in Black Caribbean communities. The SPG often conducted saturation campaigns using roadblocks, street checks, and dawn raids in areas like Brixton, Peckham, and Lewisham. The saturation operations sometimes took the form of outright occupation. In one instance, in 1973 the SPG was called in to saturate the predominantly Black community of Brixton for two months due to reports of high crime. In 1975, the SPG conducted another saturation operation, this time in Lewisham, where it used roadblocks to stop and question fourteen thousand individuals. The SPG also became adept at raiding nightclubs frequented by Black youths in search of one suspect or another, blocking off the surrounding streets and charging into the venues with full force.[144]

Complaints from Black residents about the SPG soon proliferated. In 1972, residents in north London accused the SPG of "indulging in 'blitz' tactics and making arrests in peculiar circumstances."[145] In 1973, Brixton residents reported that "they consider that their right to walk the streets freely and to be politically involved has been taken away."[146] The Parliamentary Select Committee on Race Relations reported widespread "dissatisfaction" with the police among London's West Indian population due to "regular harassment by the police of coloured people, unnecessary stopping in the streets," and the "employment of unnecessary and intimidating force by extra numbers of police."[147]

The racially disproportionate deployment of the London SPG for saturation operations cannot be underestimated. By the late 1970s, SPG incursions into Black areas of London had become so commonplace that, as one journalist reported, "it is scarcely newsworthy. You can guarantee that at any one time they will be in operation against the Black community. They seem to travel continuously back and forth between Notting Hill, Stoke Newington, Brixton, Peckham, Islington, Hackney and Tooting."[148] In his annual report for 1975, London Met commissioner Robert Mark himself noted that most of SPG's divisional assignments were in the L and P Divisions, which covered the main districts where Black Caribbean immigrants had settled, which is why Mark referred to them as the "racially sensitive Divisions."[149] Around the same time, the SPG focused heavily on the drug trade and drug possession—becoming "extremely knowledgeable, in the drugs field," as one internal report for 1974 noted, making "outstanding arrests and recovering substantial amounts of drugs." This, of course, was a racialized form of criminality, as most authorities at the time assumed that drugs dominated Black Caribbean communities.[150] Furthermore, by the end of the 1970s, the SPG had become active in arresting "illegal immigrants." In 1978, for example, the London SPG arrested fifty-two individuals suspected of being "illegal immigrants" (compared to nineteen arrests for begging and thirty-six for prostitution).[151] All the while, the SPG paid little mind to other dangers such as white nationalists. In the summer of 1978, the same year that the SPG arrested fifty-two so-called illegal immigrants, the SPG failed to protect Asian residents of Brick Lane from angry white nationalists who reportedly killed three Bengalis. In another series of attacks, 150 white youths assaulted Bengali shop owners, but the SPC did little to nothing.[152]

On its face, the SPG's racially disproportionate saturation operations and use of stop-and-search were meant to prevent crime.[153] Officials operated from the assumption that most crime happened in Black immigrant communities.[154] But something else was going on. SPG commanders, in fact, found in 1972 that saturating neighborhoods increased arrests by up to 19 percent but only reduced crime by 1 percent at best, and so they concluded that saturation operations "had little effect on reducing crime."[155] Even voices within the police admitted that their saturation efforts were not just about crime.

Rather than stopping crime, the SPG's saturation operations were most likely part of its new countersubversion strategy. The SPG used cordoning, roadblocks, and searches as colonial police and military forces had used them: not only to hunt for suspects but also to survey populations and collect information as countersubversion measures. This followed from police officials' call to gather intelligence on presumed Black Caribbean subversives. One British police officer, Frank Elmes, wrote in 1968 in the *Police Review* that "race riots" in America's cities were "bound to occur in some form or other" in Britain and claimed that "Black power politicians" were already beginning to cause trouble during protests in Britain. Echoing theories of the police's role in counterinsurgency and almost paraphrasing Kitson, Elmes then laid out what was needed to thwart the Black Power movement. "Inflammatory elements," he wrote, "must plainly be neutralised by surveillance."[156] Two years later, in 1970, the British Black Panthers claimed that there was a deliberate police campaign to "'pick off' Black militants."[157] It was revealed that same year that the Special Branch had indeed been monitoring Black communities for subversive activity and that it regarded Black Power as a movement "worthy of extremely tight surveillance."[158]

This surveillance of potential Black subversives emerged around the same time that the British government created its National Security Plan. That plan had sought to instantiate Kitson's "preparation" phase of counterinsurgency. It called for the police to collect intelligence on subversive leaders and criminals and make it available to the army.[159] The plan capitalized on the police's new surveillance capabilities. In 1970, the National Police Computer—the police equivalent to the army's new computer—was created. Put into full operation by 1974, it stored data on criminals, suspects, and all vehicles in Britain.[160] The *Police Review* boasted that the National Police Computer was "far more comprehensive than any other computerised intelligence service in the world."[161] In 1972, a new National Drugs Intelligence Unit and a new National Immigration Intelligence Unit were added to the surveillance machine, authorized to collect and share data on known or suspected offenders. Their data was to be coordinated with the other data in the National Police Computer.[162]

The character of the SPG's operations in the African Caribbean communities of London fits with the army's and colonial police's countersubversion surveillance operations. It is as if the cordon and searches were not only about finding criminals but also about collecting information to fulfill countersubversion functions. In 1973, for example, the SPG stopped and searched more than 34,000 individuals and vehicles, and only about 3,000 arrests were made. In 1974, the SPG conducted 41,304 stop-and-search actions, yielding only 3,262 arrests.

In 1976, the SPG made almost 61,000 stops in total across London, but only 4,000 arrests were made.[163] Many of these stops were made in London's non-white communities even though crime rates in these communities were the same or even lower than in other parts of the city—hence the relatively low number of arrests compared to stops.[164] Not surprisingly, in the early 1980s, critical criminologists found that

> the gathering of information on people in the community, and particularly in inner city "high crime" areas, is now becoming a matter of course regardless of whether the person is engaged in unlawful activity. It is, in effect, a major shift from just gathering and recording information on those suspected of being engaged in criminal activity to one of building up a street-by-street profile on all inhabitants regardless of its relevance to crime. By then, the police around the country had been collecting data on millions of individuals who had not even committed crimes.[165]

It appears that the SPG in London was the vanguard in this trend. When discussing the Lewisham operation and others at the end of 1975, Commissioner Mark reported that "the fullest use was made by the Group of the powers to stop and question people" and that there was an increase of 48 percent in total stops of persons and an increase of 64 percent in vehicle stops from the previous year. This massive increase, he wrote, "arises from the intensive use of selective road blocks to combat general crime and *terrorist activities*."[166] The fact that Mark here spoke of roadblocks and searches as a way to handle "terrorist activities" along with crime betrays the police's belief that Black Caribbean communities harbored subversives and "terrorists." Mark's statement was a near admission that the SPG was using cordons and stop-and-search as part of its countersubversion function rather than its crime control function. This was thus a *colonial counterinsurgenization* of policing. Not only had the London SPG militarized, drawing upon the forms and features of armies; it also adopted the postwar theories and tactics, as well as the forms and functions, of colonial policing and imperial counterinsurgency. And the trigger was a perceived racialized threat.

## Spreading the Boomerang

The Special Patrol Group of the London Metropolitan Police was not alone. It was part of a larger wave of police counterinsurgenization triggered by the perceived threats of the time. Other cities created their own versions of the SPG. By 1980, SPGs or similar units under different names had been created in at least thirty other police forces in the United Kingdom, or close to half of the country's police forces.[167] Their spread likely reflected the decision of the British government in the late 1960s and early 1970s, following counterinsurgency doctrine, that a "third force" should not be created and that the police should play a leading role in preventing insurgencies. It is not accidental that the majority of the SPGs around Britain were formed after the Home Office Working Party's rejection of the third force idea in 1971. The only ones formed before 1972 were the Tactical Patrol Group units in Hertfordshire (1965), Thames Valley (1969), and Derbyshire (1970). The rest were formed afterward.[168]

A version of the SPG was also created in Northern Ireland in 1969, upon advice from an advisory committee (which included Robert Mark) to the minister of home affairs of the government of Northern Ireland. This new Ulster SPG replaced the discredited Royal Ulster Constabulary. On the surface, the replacement was meant to be a demilitarization of sorts—an effort to quell criticisms of the RUC by putting civilian authorities in control. Unlike the RUC, the Ulster SPG was to be placed "under the command of a police officer who had practical experience of police operations in Great Britain."[169] But on a deeper level, it was the enactment of the new counterinsurgency doctrine. As the advisory committee responsible for recommending the creation of the Ulster SPG noted, it was a way for the police to better manage "the growing cult of violence in society, the increasing tendency of a minority to flout the law, [and] undermine authority and create anarchy"—a "trend not peculiar to Northern Ireland" and which also included "more recent agitations which are more widespread." In the face of "agitations," the committee continued, the "police force can and should play a leading part, not only in enforcing law and order, but in helping to create a new climate of respect for the law."[170] It followed that the Ulster SPG was given riot control training and upgraded weaponry by the army.[171] The Ulster SPG was also supposed to have "closer relationships with other police forces in Great Britain" than did its predecessor.[172]

The creation of the Ulster SPG was part of a larger string of SPGs spanning Britain and extending up to Ulster—in effect, a colonial counterinsurgency force, though under civilian control, traversing metropole and colony alike. Soon enough, other tactical police units besides Special Patrol Groups were created. Known as Police Support Units (PSUs), these units were akin to the SPG but, unlike the SPG, were formed on an emergency basis upon order of the Home Office, typically for public order events rather than for crime control. They were not meant to be long-standing elite forces within departments. They were a reserve force, consisting of police who were specially trained but otherwise carried out regular duties. This idea of mobilizing police for emergency situations was not itself new. It was rooted in the long tradition of militias and, in the 1950s at the height of the Cold War, mobile columns that were to be summoned in the event of nuclear war. But they were expanded and transformed subsequent to the government's decision to retool and repurpose the police for counterinsurgency in the early 1970s. *The Police Manual of Home Defence*, put out by the Home Office in 1974, called for their creation and specified their expanded role for riot control.[173] From 1974 to 1980, at least twenty-eight police forces created new PSUs.[174] Organized on a divisional basis and consisting of a unit commander and three sections that each comprised a sergeant and ten constables, they were specially trained in riot control and firearms and were conveyed in special vans. The boomerang again returned: these were metropolitan versions of colonial riot squads.[175]

## The 1981 Riots and the Cycle of Colonial Counterinsurgenization

Police tools and tactics are not only modular but resilient as well. They can be applied to contexts different from the contexts of their birth; they can persist even after they surpass their original function. Therefore, even after the perceived threat of the Black Panthers and earlier "terrorism" had waned in the early 1970s, the London SPG continued its racialized operations. This led to continued criticism. Protests by Black community activists, including the renowned activist Olive Morris, proliferated. In 1980 in Brixton, which had been the center of the Black Panther movement years earlier, activists charged the London Metropolitan Police with being an "army of occupation."[176] But the criticisms fell upon deaf ears. The SPG persisted in its ways.

The line from police counterinsurgenization in the 1970s to the 1981 riots can now be seen. Though the immediate cause of the Brixton uprising in 1981 was police brutality against a young resident, Michael Bailey, tensions in the community had been rising for years, not least due to the SPG's militaristic operations. One such operation had been mounted earlier in April 1981. Dubbed "Swamp '81," it was a response to a rise in "muggings" in the area. More than a hundred police officers saturated the area over the course of the four days, stopping close to a thousand people but only finding grounds to make 118 arrests.[177] The majority of those stopped were Black.[178] In his official report on the riots, Lord Scarman found that the SPG's treatment of Brixton's Black community had caused many in the neighborhood "to lose confidence in, and respect for, the police." Swamp '81 was "well known to the young Blacks: for it was upon them that it had a direct and unwelcome impact." It "was a factor which contributed to the great increase in tension" leading to the uprisings. The SPG's "allegedly abusive approach" over the years must be seen as a cause of the riots.[179] Even Scarman recognized that militaristic policing was one cause of the 1981 riots.

Aggressive policing also played a role in triggering the uprisings in other cities in 1981. While not all of the disorder had been precipitated by SPG operations, they had been preceded by years of militaristic policing using stop-and-search and related tactics. Police patrols or SPG-type mobile units typically carried out the operations.[180] In Liverpool, for example, the local version of the SPG had directed much of its attention at Liverpool's Toxteth area, also known as "Liverpool 8." This was where many Black Caribbean immigrants and long-standing working-class residents lived, some of whom had labored for generations at the port but who had been cast out of the economy, relegated to the status of the city's abject racialized subproletariat.[181] The successor to the Liverpool SPG was called the Operational Support Division—a new SPG in all but name—and the rebranding did little to resolve long-standing tensions between police and the Toxteth community.[182] The police continued to saturate the area, making liberal use of spl (suspected person loitering) laws, the Liverpool equivalent of the sus laws used by the London SPG. They allowed the police to stop and search almost anyone. Meanwhile, Merseyside chief constable Kenneth Oxford justified the aggressive policing of Toxteth by referring to the residents as "half-castes," children of Black seaman and white prostitutes, who were prone to crime.[183] In 1981, this aggressive policing led to the arrest of a "youth who had been riding on a motorcycle," summoning an angry response from a larger group of residents who in turn created a barricade against police.[184] Tensions mounted. The police continued to provoke. The uprising began.[185]

In short, the perverse outcome of the colonial counterinsurgenization of policing in cities such as London and Liverpool was that it led to the very thing that it was designed to prevent: urban rebellion. But the uprisings of 1981 were not only the manifestation of this. In fact, they were part of a larger cycle, as the uprisings of 1981 themselves triggered yet another round of counterinsurgenization.

It all began with the immediate police response to the 1981 uprisings. To contain rioting, police used colonial tactics. In Manchester, police launched a campaign of mass arrests and deployed fifty-four vans of snatch squads.[186] In Liverpool, police also deployed a colonial technology that had never before been used on metropolitan soil: tear gas. Tear gas had been a colonial counterinsurgency tool. As noted in Chapter 4, officials in England had always stopped short of deploying it against domestic demonstrators. As the historian Erik Linstrum shows, using it on home soil had been taboo. The *Observer* magazine in 1973 noted that while counterinsurgency tools "may not sound particularly controversial applied to, say, Mau Mau in Kenya or the communists in Malaya, it is heady stuff when the enemy is among your own people." But the perceived racial menace of rioters in July 1981 managed to break the taboo once and for all. The site where the taboo was broken was Liverpool's Toxteth area. As intimated earlier, this was not a space of white Englishmen. It had been racialized by the police as a disorderly district where putatively criminal "half-castes" and nonwhites lived, an impoverished part of the city that the press referred to as "the Jungle." When the uprisings began, it must have seemed that way to the mostly white police force. Chief Constable Kenneth Oxford called the rioters "a crowd of black hooligans" who had gone on an "uncivilized rampage."[187] The press added that the rioting was "on a Belfast scale."[188] Perhaps making the matter even more threatening, "half-castes" and some white youths participated in the rioting. "White working-class disorder," Linstrum explains, "never appeared so menacing as it did when conjoined with nonwhite violence."[189] After a series of failed attempts by the police to ram through the barricades and disperse the crowds, typically using the standard baton charge method, Chief Constable Oxford ordered that his forces launch tear gas canisters. As the press noted at the time, this was "the first time the gas has been used against rioters on mainland Britain."[190]

The use of tear gas marked the beginning of the next part of the cycle. In the wake of the police response to the 1981 uprisings, the police embarked on yet another round of counterinsurgenization. To many, the riots proved that the police were weak. Conventional approaches such as the baton charge were inadequate; it was the failure of those methods that led to the need for tear gas. On paper, the existing Special Patrol Groups and other units like Public Protection Units (PPUs) or PSUs were meant to help handle crowds, but not all cities had them. Therefore, after the Brixton uprising in April, the Police Federation, representing constables and other police officials across the country, demanded that all police forces, not just the SPGs, be provided with new riot gear, such as "helmets, visors, flak jackets and other riot gear to protect against mob violence," along with the freedom to use water cannons and rubber bullets against rioters.[191] But officials were cautious to avoid the appearance that the police were going to turn into a "French-style riot police" or gendarmerie.[192] In early May 1981, Home Secretary William Whitelaw and other officials said that some change was needed but that "any departure from traditional policing methods was undesirable."[193]

Then came July 1981 and the spread of the riots to other cities. This changed everything. First, it evoked yet more racialized fears of societal breakdown. Society had become "sick," said one police official from Durham.[194] Many blamed the sickness on nonwhite communities. The uprisings were nothing else than acts of wanton violence by "thugs and hooligans" with irresponsible parents.[195] Merseyside's chief constable, Kenneth Oxford, exclaimed, "Let's get back to some basic civilized discipline and get the parents to pick up their responsibilities."[196] Others firmly believed foreign subversive forces had been conspiring to foment "anarchy" and "guerrilla warfare," as the chief constable of Greater Manchester, James Anderton, put it.[197] Meanwhile, right-wing Tory MPs were so convinced that the uprisings were the fault of barbaric nonwhites that they suggested that the best policy to prevent future rioting was to get all immigrants to leave Britain at once.[198]

Second, justified by these racialized renderings of threat, officials decided that the police needed to be strengthened. Paul Middup, chairman of the Constables' Section of the Police Federation, said: "It is time for police to move into an offensive role."[199] Invoking "the burning names of Bristol and Brixton," Middup added: "We have always resisted the idea of water cannon, etc., but how much longer can we pretend the traditional methods of coping with disorder on modern scales can cope with disorder on major scales?" The police, he lamented, had had enough of "being asked to face mindless mobs armed with acid bombs, petrol bombs and bricks."[200] Chief Constable Oxford asserted defiantly: "In the light of our experiences, whilst the paramilitary concept is anathema to the precepts of British policing, we have a duty to the officers under our command to protect them against those with criminal propensities who wish to attack them and society."[201] Robert Mark, as former London Met commissioner, added his views in an editorial in the *Times*. To his mind, the riots got out of control only because "the police are very few in number and of limited mobility" and because "their present powers under the law are strictly limited and do not in any case afford an effective deterrent to communal disorder."[202]

Politicians and others of the governmental establishment also demanded change. MP Eldon Griffiths, parliamentary advisor to the Police Federation, claimed that "the time has come ... to set up specially trained squads of men with all the support of helmets, fireproof uniforms, armoured cars—yes, and even guns if necessary."[203] Major General Richard Clutterbuck weighed in with his suggestions, calling for more Police Support Units and a Special Patrol Group in every city. And just as they had done in the early 1970s, officials raised the prospect of creating a "third force" or Continental-style national riot police. Police Federation head James Jardine (who had been in the London Met after serving in the British Army) stated, "For the riot situation, we have got to have uniformity throughout the country with equipment and tactics, and it's got to be controlled centrally."[204] The press tracked these discussions with eager anticipation. "The image of the British Bobby—for long the envy of the world—is at the crossroads," declared the *Newcastle Journal* in July 1981.[205]

In the end, the government rejected the idea that a new paramilitary national force akin to a French gendarmerie should be created, just as they had done a decade earlier. *Police Officer Magazine* noted that many constables were against this idea because such a force would interfere with local chief constables' power. However, police did support a more "active rather than passive" approach to public order. The "active approach," *Police Officer Magazine* clarified, "would probably involve the use of plastic bullets (or baton rounds), snatch squads and armoured vehicles."[206] As Jardine of the Police Federation highlighted, a national riot police would not be necessary so long as existing police forces could get their "new riot equipment and new tactics."[207]

This was the approach was that police and high governmental officials landed upon after meetings between the Home Office, Prime Minister Margaret Thatcher's cabinet, and police chiefs in late July 1981.[208] The plan, in essence, was to retrain and retool the entire police force along the lines of colonial counterinsurgency—to, in effect, make all police forces like the Special Patrol Group by having the entire police undergo colonial counterinsurgenization. Police were to be equipped with protective helmets, new anti-riot batons, plastic or rubber bullets, and "Ulster-type armoured Land-Rover police vehicles" carrying tear gas and water cannons. As conventional police vehicles, noted Merseyside chief constable Kenneth Oxford, had been rendered "useless," the tanks of the Royal Ulster Constabulary were the preferred solution.[209] Police forces were also to be trained directly by advisors from the Royal Ulster Constabulary. The tactics from colonial forces that the SPG had been using, like snatch squads and wedge formations, were to be privileged. Leading officials were to be dispatched to Belfast for training in weaponry, equipment, and tactics to bring the lessons home.[210] Furthermore, the Home Office was to create a national reporting center to enable national coordination for police responses to riots, facilitating the movement of "police riot squads from different parts of the country to be moved at short notice to trouble spots—the first time such action had been taken in police history," according to the *Belfast Telegraph*. Finally, the Home Office, as if to unabashedly signal the militaristic turn, announced that it was considering using army camps as detention centers for rioters convicted of crimes.[211]

The novelty of these colonial counterinsurgency tactics and armature for the British police cannot be overestimated. The SPG had been the vanguard adopter of some of them, but prior calls for the regular police to have access to them had been rejected for years. After the Grosvenor Square protest in 1968, which involved mostly white demonstrators, some officials counseled the importation of colonial-military tools and tactics, including tear gas and water cannons. But the calls were not heeded.[212] Later, in the mid- to late 1970s, military strategists such as Deane-Drummond and police officials including Kenneth Sloan of the Manchester Police (and an editor at the *Police Review*) called for renewed training in army methods, new equipment such as "riot shields," "long staves and firearms," "armoured vehicles," and, generally, various tools enabling "military-style police action."[213] But their calls, like others, had fallen upon deaf ears. The SPG remained the closest to having the sort of military-grade equipment and training that Sloan was demanding for his entire force.

The calls for water cannons and rubber bullets after 1981 were particularly novel. Rubber bullets, and then plastic bullets, had been an imperial-military innovation. The Hong Kong Police first deployed the first versions of such nonlethal baton rounds, using wooden pegs—a tool that US authorities in the late 1960s admired. In the early 1970s, the British Army in Northern Ireland began using rubber and then plastic versions of the wooden baton rounds on the grounds that they were more controllable. These were often used along-side snatch squads: once targets were hit and demobilized, snatch squads could enter the fray and extract individuals.[214] Water cannons had been used by the British in Cyprus in the 1950s. They were then deployed extensively in Northern Ireland, first by the Royal Ulster Constabulary and then by the British Army, who borrowed their initial vehicle-mounted cannons from the RUC.[215] In the mid-1970s, British police officials suggested that their own police forces use water cannons and rubber bullets like their counterparts in Northern Ireland. In 1977, in the aftermath of the white nationalist demonstrations by the National Front, police authorities again considered equipping their forces with rubber bullets and water canons. They also suggested that their forces receive training in colonial methods like snatch squads. But nothing came of these suggestions, perhaps because police did not see white nationalists as much of a threat.[216] It was only after the revolt of Black communities in 1981 that officials finally warmed to colonial counterinsurgenization for the entire British police.

The aftermath of the 1981 uprisings also brought other imperial importations. The Association of Chief Police Officers (ACPO) spearheaded them. Funded by the Home Office, the ACPO was an association of chief constables and other police officials who met regularly to agree upon shared policies and practices. At their September meeting at Preston in the wake of the 1981 uprisings, they brought in members of the Royal Ulster Constabulary to speak about the RUC's anti-riot methods. They also brought in the commissioner of the Royal Hong Kong Police, Roy Henry, to discuss the methods of the Hong Kong Police, offering—as one journalist put it—a "distillation of British Colonial policing as practiced in the most important remaining outpost of the empire." He discussed the Hong Kong Police's computerized command-and-control system, the Police Tactical Unit, and riot control weaponry, and handed out copies of the Hong Kong Police's colonial police manual. He also suggested that each police department in Britain create its own version of the Police Tactical Unit that would focus exclusively on quelling disorder and suppressing riots.[217] While none of this was new for large urban police departments that already had SPG units, it was radically new for most other departments in small towns or rural areas. As the *Police Review* observed: "Now, even the rural policeman can be armed in riot gear one day and the next be required to return to his benevolent 'Evening, all' attitude."[218]

The larger goal was to steel police forces against insurrection and standardize tactics, techniques, and technologies across all departments in the country.[219] To further facilitate such standardization the ACPO created a new manual modeled after the Hong Kong colonial police manual. It codified many of the new anti-riot tactics and instructions from Britain's colonial-military regime and was circulated to police forces across Britain.[220]

This colonial boomerang was initially kept secret. Lord Scarman's November 1981 report on the Brixton Riots, which roundly criticized the police, had put many police officials on the defensive. That, along with the continued criticisms of the police from Black communities and labor groups, likely contributed to the secrecy. In any case, we now know the result. The next year, police across the country were trained in "offensive operations" regarding crowd control, adopting the counterinsurgency methods and "special shock tactics" of the army and police in Hong Kong and Northern Ireland. This included "specialized snatch-squad training" for about 10 percent of personnel in each police force. As the *Sunday Times* later discovered, these new squads consisted of small teams commanded by an inspector and two sergeants, all "equipped with short riot shields" and donning "Nato-style helmets which contain small earphones" and flame-proof uniforms with padding.[221]

The snatch squads were the tip of the iceberg. Other anti-riot tactics taken from colonial police and codified in the *Public Order Manual of Tactical Options and Related Matters* became part of basic training. Head officials began visiting Hong Kong regularly, and in turn officials from Hong Kong came to Britain to keep police forces up to date, with a formal agreement made in 1983 for operational officers to be exchanged regularly. The exchange continued in earnest thereafter. In 1987, the Hong Kong Police advertised in the *Police Review* for British police to join them, with the slogan "Royal Hong Kong Police—the proving ground for natural leaders." One British police official observed: "If something new should evolve in Hong Kong I am sure that it would flow to the United Kingdom—and vice versa. If there should be new equipment, new thoughts, new tactics, then both sides will gain on a mutual exchange of information."[222] Fittingly, British police were trained to mobilize into large-scale counterinsurgency units upon order from headquarters, just as in Hong Kong.[223] And following the decisions by the government in July, departments across the country could receive tear gas and plastic bullets, to be used according to strict guidelines, and armored vehicles and water cannons upon request. Police Federation head Jardine explained the rationale: "It is no good beating about the bush. This is a war that we are waging and it is one that the police and the rule of law and order have got to win."[224] If the line between colonial and domestic policing had always been porous (as the scholars Georgina Sinclair and Chris A. Williams also argue), the events of 1981 nearly dissolved it entirely.

In 2015, Douglas Tsui Yiu-kwong, former chief superintendent of the Royal Hong Kong Police, reflected upon his past experiences with policing in Britain. During prior travels to Britain, he had noticed how weak and ineffective the London Metropolitan Police was. "What amazed me was the total lack of suitable anti-riot equipment and tactics," he wrote. However, the "subsequent Brixton Riots in 1981" changed everything. "There are now," he wrote, "more specialist armed police units and more aggressive and better equipped anti-riot formations, signaling an albeit reluctant departure from the traditional 'civilian in uniform' model of British policing."[225]

Yiu-kwong was right to note the transformation. He was also right to underscore that it was caused by the Brixton Riots in 1981. But one thing he missed is that the transformation after 1981 was simply one part of a larger cycle that began earlier, in the first years of the 1970s.

* * *

We can now put that cycle in the longer durée of waves of police militarization in Britain. It begins in 1829, when Peel created the first "civil" police that was meant to be an alternative to the military. In earlier chapters we have seen that even this force was militarized through imperial feedback from the outset: Peel and his colleagues, facing the perceived racialized threat of the Irish in England, modeled the London Metropolitan Police and subsequent forces around the country after colonial police in Ireland and elsewhere in the empire. Subsequent rounds of additional militarization unfolded over the course of the nineteenth century as Irish immigration proceeded and the perceived Irish threat persisted. But militarization stalled through the early twentieth century. As seen in Chapter 4, other small racialized threats surfaced in the 1890s to summon the colonial boomerang again. But for the most part, militarization was kept in check. As the earlier Irish-oriented racialized threats subsided, and as immigration slowed and indeed receded, so too did police militarization; the attempts to further militarize the police by Warren in the 1880s or Trenchard in the 1930s were stopped short.

The 1970s cycle of militarization-as-counterinsurgenization enters here. The long stall of militarization in the early decades of the twentieth century gave way to a renewed round of imperial feedback. The trigger, as ever, was racialized threat—the sort of racialized threat that had previously summoned the boomerang in the nineteenth century and which resurfaced in the late 1960s through the early 1970s. But if this was a reiteration of the logic of racialized threat, it took on a somewhat new form in this period. By the 1960s, migrants from across the empire were entering Britain at rates unseen for over a century. And they did so amid global turbulence and imperial decline. The racialization of crime and disorder followed as in previous waves, but now—in the eyes of British authorities at least—it was tethered to global problems, and putatively induced by Brown and Black colonial subjects whose presence in Britain had barely been felt before. The perceived menace was sufficient to overcome earlier barriers to militarization and set off a new round, beginning with the London SPG but extending later throughout Britain. This launched a cycle of racialized threat, insurgency, and militarization through the 1980s.

This chapter has examined that shorter durée, illuminating the particular cycle that militarization-as-counterinsurgenization set off in the early 1970s. There are two further things to note about this cycle by way of conclusion. First, the effects of the post-1981 wave of the colonial counterinsurgenization of policing reverberated through later years. Yiu-kwong noticed the transformation in 2015, but to most of the British public it was first evidenced to the public during the miners' strike in 1984, when close to six thousand police personnel, including PPUs, violently confronted eight thousand miners at what became known as the Battle of Orgreave. Prior to the battle, Prime Minister Thatcher had compared the mostly white strikers to the Argentines on the Falkland Islands who, two years earlier, had disputed Britain's claims of sovereignty, thus sparking the Falklands War. Having defeated the Argentines, she told her fellow Conservatives, it was now time to defeat the "Enemy Within."[226] Thatcher's wish was apparently fulfilled, as the police indeed acted as an army, using their new tools and tactics taken from the colonies. In a detailed article in the *Guardian*, the miners' solicitor, Gareth Peirce, later characterized the "brutality" of the police as an exercise in "absolute power" wielded by the police.[227] What Peirce recognized, in short, was colonial countersubversion policing on the fields of England. John Alderson, then a retired chief constable who became critical of the police's conduct at the Battle of Orgreave, noted that the police's tactics and equipment amounted to a "carbon copy of the Hong Kong riot squad." As journalist Gerry Northam later wrote, "Orgreave represented the unveiling of colonial policing tactics in mainland Britain."[228] We might add that the Battle of Orgreave also reveals the modularity of the police's colonial tools and tactics. Imperial feedback had been triggered initially by racialized unrest, but the tools and tactics it bequeathed to the police were easily deployed on white workers. They were also mobilized against other white populations, such as those at Manchester University and Stonehenge in 1985.[229]

Second, even as counterinsurgenization impacted white populations, its racialized component did not entirely dissipate. Neither did the cycle of which it was a part. In London, despite the warnings registered in the Scarman Report about the dangers of aggressive policing of Black Britons, racialized policing continued. In 1982, Sir Kenneth Newman became the Met's new commissioner. Having served in the Palestine Special Branch in the 1940s and as chief constable of the Royal Ulster Constabulary, he did not hesitate to apply the colonial lens to London as his predecessors had long done, claiming that "policing inner-city ghettos had much in common with policing terrorism."[230] Under his watch, racialized policing proceeded almost unabated, contributing to yet another round of riots in Brixton in late September 1985 that lasted two days.

The SPG also continued its saturation operations as before. One area where the SPG focused its attention was the Broadwater Farm Estate. This had been declared by police officials as a trouble spot. As the deputy assistant commissioner put it, Broadwater Farm had "long been a haven for the wrongdoer." This emboldened SPG operations, which in turn garnered criticisms from the many Black residents of the estate. "Whenever there was a spate of burglaries on the estate," exclaimed one resident, "they'd send in the SPG and clamp down on everybody, especially Black people."[231] In October 1985, one week after the riots in Brixton, residents protested the death of Cynthia Jarrett, an African Caribbean woman who died from a heart attack during a police raid of her home after her son had been stopped and searched by the police. Tensions escalated to a full-blown riot. A PSU was sent in. One police officer was killed. The result? The London police carried out an operational review, leading the government to expand the police's arsenal, giving it twenty-four new bulletproof vehicles and eighty personnel carriers.[232] The cycle of insurgency and police counterinsurgenization continued.[233]

If London in the mid-1980s saw the recurrence of previous patterns, there was at least one major difference: the London SPG was eventually disbanded due to its controversial status. It was then replaced by new militarized units called Territorial Support Groups. These were SPGs in all but name, rebranded to try to deflect mounting public criticism. A similar process occurred across Britain's police forces, as new units with new names replaced the older, tarnished ones. Upon recommendation of the Home Office, provincial police forces created new specialist firearms teams. Specially trained in a range of firearms, they were to be available for calls twenty-four hours a day.[234] Even with the dismantling of the SPG, therefore, the militarization of Britain's civil police continued, though under different labels.[235]

This did not stop the cycle either. In 2011, from August 6 to August 11, thousands of Britons across England rose up against police brutality. It began in London and spread to Birmingham, Bristol, Coventry, Leicester, Liverpool, Manchester, and Wolverhampton, among other cities and towns. The result was nearly three thousand arrests and yet more police raids, brutality, and harassment summoning further resistance from Black and Brown communities.[236] The uprisings were sparked by various high-profile police killings of Black Britons. Reggae artist Smiley Culture died in March 2011 during a police raid on his home in Warlingham. The same month, Kingsley Burrell died while in police custody in Birmingham. And on August 4, Mark Duggan from Broadwater Farm in Tottenham, London, was shot by police. After the demands of protesters at the

Tottenham police station for information were ignored, the area erupted in violence. And though these killings were the spark, long-standing militarized police treatment of Black and Brown communities was the precondition. Protestors later clarified: they had been provoked by aggressive stop-and-search tactics and saturation campaigns of the Territorial Support Group that had replaced the SPG in the 1980s.[237]

# Conclusion

## Policing Beyond Empire?

> The ultimate mark of power may be invisibility; the ultimate challenge, the exposition of its roots.
>
> —Michel-Rolph Trouillot (2015)

When the British Parliament debated the bill that would create the London Metropolitan Police in 1829, Sir Robert Peel told his fellow legislators that, with the new police, they would "be able to dispense with the necessity of a military force in London."[1] We can now see that Peel was both right and wrong in his assertion. He was right in the sense that British authorities no longer turned to the "military force" for managing public order. While they have called on the army in exceptional circumstances, the army has been the last resort. Authorities instead turn to the civil police. But Peel was wrong to suggest that a *militarized* force would no longer be deployed in the metropolis. As the police in both Britain and the United States have repeatedly borrowed and deployed a range of imperial-military forms, functions, tools, templates, and tactics, the police have become an army on home territory. This is a "military force" indeed.

This book has explored this seemingly magical transformation from the civil police ideal to a militarized reality. It has shown that, from the beginning, the police in both Britain and the United States turned to the military for inspiration to conduct their work. This book has also shown how and why this has occurred. By the logics of racialization and imperialism, police in Britain and the United States have militarized during heightened historical moments of perceived racialized threat. And they have militarized by appropriating from Britain and America's imperial-military formations. What we call "police militarization" is the effect of the imperial boomerang.

We can now see the perverse outcome of it all. In the colonies, as Frantz Fanon observed, the line between the "police" and the "military" was always blurred. The police power was militarized power, and vice versa—a single formation of power designed to create and sustain a racialized social and economic order. Fanon also observed that the police in the colonies were always violent rather than pacific. Facing down colonized populations deemed intrinsically

*Policing Empires.* Julian Go, Oxford University Press. © Oxford University Press 2024.
DOI: 10.1093/oso/9780197621653.003.0008

inferior and unworthy, colonial police typically spoke the "language of pure force."[2] What we can now see is that, by the boomerang effect, metropolitan civil policing has become akin to, if not just like, military-imperial policing in colonial zones. The so-called civil police uses many of the same tactics, tools, and technologies as colonial forces, and the function is the same: to maintain a racialized socioeconomic order. The metropole is the colony. The colony is the metropole.

Given this, the term "civil police" should be used with caution. Its referent is both real and ideological. Yes, it refers to an actually existing institution called "the police" that is different from "the military." But that institution does not live up to its founding myths. It is "civil" in name only; its practices and forms betray its pretensions. Likewise, the concept of "militarization" must be questioned. Though useful as a shorthand, it obscures the subterranean workings of imperialism and the colonial boomerang that underpins it. The coercive assemblage of policing today needs to be understood for the racialized imperiality that has given it force, form, and function. The word "militarization" does not fully capture this.

This book has not tried to expose the racialized imperiality of police militarization by bearing witness. It has not related painful personal experiences of encounters with police. This it cannot do; its author cannot claim such experiences. What this book has tried to do, rather, is render police militarization in the United States and Britain intelligible by charting its development, identifying its logics of emergence, and tracking its recurrences. The result is a history that is irreducible to either individual experience on the one hand or the abstract grand narrative of capitalism on the other. It is instead a history of how logics of racialization and empire shaped militarized policing. This is a history of different logics converging to produce unique outcomes that nonetheless recur, hence a history of continuities and discontinuities. It is a history of waves of militarization and their relative abatement, of imperial appropriation triggered by moments of heightened racialized fear; a history of emergence and formation, of the deployment of colonial and militarized modalities alongside performances of "the civil," of violent exercises of police power punctuated by gestures of care and civility that ultimately prove meaningless to the victims of police brutality. This is a history that continues today, into our painful present. The militarization of the civil police in the United States and Britain may appear by now fully accomplished, but in fact it has not ceased. Nor has its entanglement with empire dissipated. The racialized imperiality of policing continues.

Something of this persistent history will be sketched shortly below, as will something of its possible futures. But it might help first to review and clarify the story already told. Let us begin with method and theory.

## Patterns of Policing: Method and Theory Reconsidered

We have seen that the militarization of policing through imperial feedback was not a singular event of recent years. It has occurred through multiple waves over time. Nor has it been restricted to one place: it has unfolded in different cities in Britain and the United States. In Britain, the first wave was the emergence of modern policing with the birth of the London Metropolitan Police. A series of smaller waves in the nineteenth and early twentieth centuries served to add more layers of militarized policing until the late 1960s through the early 1970s, when another major wave was unleashed. In the United States, the first wave of modern policing came with the birth of police departments in New York and Savannah. The next wave came in the early twentieth century with the so-called reform era, led by August Vollmer. In the late 1950s and early 1960s another wave began, leading to the infamous phase of vigorous militarization during the late 1960s.

Recognizing these waves has raised questions. How and why have these waves occurred? Why militarization? Addressing these questions has been the organizing motive of this book. Rather than seeking to uncover and examine everything about militarized policing, this book has sought to identify and explain waves of militarization in Britain and the United States. This book thereby offers a historical sociology of militarization, a mode of analysis that identifies and compares patterns over time and space and explains them by identifying causal processes.[3]

A key methodological principle of the examination has been comparison. Preceding chapters have compared waves of militarization to identify their conditions of emergence. They have also compared these waves with moments when militarization did *not* happen. The comparisons, therefore, have been both temporal (comparing the ebbs and flows of militarization in the same site over time) and spatial or cross-sectional (comparing waves and troughs of militarization across different sites). In the temporal register, this book has compared moments when police imported the tools of empire for home use in both Britain and the United States, and it asks what factors, events, or social conditions these moments shared, as opposed to the historical moments when militarization did not happen. Why, for example, did the British police begin to militarize in the late 1960s after years of relative indifference to militarization? Why did militarization happen in the United States in the early twentieth century (amid the so-called professionalization-reform movement) and not earlier or later? In the spatial register, this book has looked at cities or other places where militarization happened first, compared to those where it did not happen at that moment. Why, for instance, did New York City police commissioner Stephen P. Kennedy, who was not a veteran, create a tactical unit in the late 1950s, while the head of the Vermont Department of Public Safety, Merritt Edson, who was a veteran, did not? Why was London and not another city the site of the creation of the first Special Patrol Group in the early 1970s?

The comparative-historical examination in this book differs from existing studies of policing that tend to focus on one or another nation or empire, or on one or another historical era. If we restrict our lens in that way, it becomes harder to identify patterns over time and across space, which in turn makes it difficult to identify the logics that explain the patterns.[4] Admittedly, comparing processes at distinct historical moments and across different cases is a monumental task that sacrifices depth for breadth. But the benefit is that we look more broadly across time and space. We have thus been able to see how seemingly exceptional events (such as the militarization of policing in the United States in the 1960s) are in fact not exceptional but reflect deeper ongoing structures. We have also been to detect the multiple ways in which imperial feedback happens—not just through veterans but through a wider array of importers. And we have been able to track similarities across time and space that help us make causal inferences and illuminate the deeper causal forces at work.[5]

In all, therefore, the comparative-historical approach of this book has permitted us to see that police militarization is a *social* product, generated under definite social conditions. Police militarization does not just appear out of thin air. But neither is it the result of unique individuals only, whether they be racist police officers or overzealous military veterans striving to become entrepreneurs in "violence work."[6] Police militarization happens under certain historical conditions and particular social arrangements. In brief, the police-militarization-as-boomerang effect results from the conjuncture of imperialism on the one hand and metropolitan racialization on the other. Empire makes new tools and tactics available to police; police turn to them as they face racialized threats to law and order that construct equivalences between colonized subjects abroad and minority populations at home.[7]

While this book offers a comparative-historical sociology of police militarization, it also offers a sociology that centers something that most accounts of policing overlook entirely: empire. This, then, is a postcolonial historical sociology of the present.[8] One imperative of postcolonial theory is to draw on the insights of anticolonial thinkers who have highlighted the entanglements of metropole and colony wrought by empire, revealing among many other things that imperialism shapes the center as much as the periphery. The story related in this book abides. Rather than unfolding only in metropolitan centers, the story has encompassed the colonies and fringes of empire. This is a history that takes into account the "foreign" as well as the "domestic"; it is a story of "overlapping territories, intertwined histories" (as renowned cultural critic Edward Said once said in a different context).[9] "The work of the police," writes the French anthropologist Didier Fassin, "cannot be understood, as it usually is, purely in the moment of their interaction with the public. It is set within a history. It articulates relations of domination that extend beyond the individual actions of officers."[10] The analysis in this book concurs, but it urges us to also recognize that the "work of the police" must be set within a more global imperial history that illuminates colonial and hence racialized relations of domination. In short, while the historical sociological approach of this book was initially inspired by comparative analysis, it has ended up as a transnational and transimperial one—an analysis that puts the British and American police into the same observational field with colonial and military-imperial forms.[11]

This postcolonial historical sociology cautions of certain blinders in existing historical sociologies of states and power. Policing is a crucial dimension of states. To paraphrase the sociologist Max Weber's classic definition of a "state," policing is the coercive arm of the state that claims a monopoly over the legitimate use of violence in the territories it covers.[12] To extend Siegel's concept, policing claims the monopoly of "violence work" in the state's sovereign territory.[13] The problem is that too many studies of state formation fail to problematize the territorial aspect of this definition. They focus on the mechanisms and processes of state development internal to the "domestic" territory of states, thereby overlooking imperialism and the colonial or ex-colonial spaces it touches. This is especially true for classic sociological work on states that social scientists have inherited. Such scholarship examines how European, British, or American states formed over time but barely if ever reckons with the fact that those "states" are in fact empires whose activities reach beyond imperial metropoles to shape and reshape the "domestic" sphere.

Even exceptional scholarship that does take empires and colonialism seriously does not always help. Many such studies tend to focus only on the state's overseas arms—that is, the state's imperial policies or colonial governments. While this is a salutary analytic departure from conventional studies, it elides the entanglements of colonial and metropolitan states. To focus only on colonial states risks insinuating the dubious bifurcation of metropole and colony, separating the analysis of metropolitan state formation from the logics of peripheral or colonial state formation, as if these were two separate entities rather than mutually reciprocal and mutually entangled processes.[14]

The analysis of police militarization in this book explodes such analytic bifurcations, revealing how important empire and colonialism have been in the making of metropolitan modernities—how empire and colonialism have been *constitutive* of modernity—and how the logics and operations of racialized power in the frontiers and peripheries of empire and those in the center are intimately braided together. This helps fulfill what I take to be one of the main affordances of a postcolonial sociological imagination: to chart the connectedness of being.[15]

The postcolonial historical sociology offered in this book also speaks to critical structuralist thinking on policing. As critical structuralist thought would have it, the postcolonial history told here shows how policing is entangled with logics of capital accumulation and class repression. But this does not mean that we should see militarized policing as a tool for disciplining the metropolitan white working class only. On the one hand, there can be no doubt that militarized policing was often directed at the largely white industrial working class. Police in the United States and Britain monitored working-class neighborhoods, crushed strikes, repressed labor unions, and cajoled or disciplined vagrants who refused to sell their labor. Police have long tried to manage the unpredictable unruliness of laborers or would-be proletarians who dare defy the imperatives of capital accumulation. On the other hand, we have seen that police militarization in Britain and the United States was not originally triggered by concerns over these workers. The new civil police in Britain and the United States—with their hierarchical formation, uniforms, beat patrols, and weapons taken from Ireland and American plantation colonialism—were meant to regulate the presumably unwashed mass of Irish workers and Black laborers underpinning the transatlantic cotton economy. The use of firearms and new surveillance systems drawn from the colonies in nineteenth-century Britain was triggered by panics about the anticolonial Irish and, later in the century, destitute and ostensibly devilish Jewish immigrants in London's East End. The so-called reform era of policing in the early twentieth-century United States was sparked by concerns over the Asian, African American, and European immigrant workers foregathered in America's urbanizing spaces. The creation of New York's tactical unit, Los Angeles's SWAT, and the Special Patrol Group in London, along with a range of other militarized forms and tools from India, Ulster, Hong Kong, or Vietnam, were aimed at the unemployed or casually employed Puerto Ricans, Black Americans, and Black Caribbeans who dared enter metropolitan spaces and critique the status quo.

In short, militarized policing was triggered by concerns over particular segments of the working class: the racialized subproletariat in the metropole and the peripheries of empire; those subject to expropriation as well as exploitation; the teeming Black, Brown, and Yellow colonial subjects put under imperial control; the "dirty" immigrants and menacing "underclass" that society debases, renders inferior, loathes, and criminalizes.[16] This is the "wretched of the earth," to draw on Frantz Fanon's famous phrasing: the abject alters spanning the metropole and colony whose labor is essential for capital accumulation but whose status is irreducible to that of the metropolitan working class racialized as "white."[17]

The history of policing, and hence of militarized policing (for we have seen they are the same), cannot be adequately told without recognizing these subjects of empire. And these subjects of empire, these racialized alters that militarized policing has sought to subdue, have not only been located within metropolitan centers like London or New York or Los Angeles. They extend across metropole and colony and traverse different empires. Militarized policing, born in the colonies and brought to the centers of metropolitan "civilization," has been part of the larger imperial project to create, enforce, and reproduce what W. E. B. Du Bois famously called the "global color line." As historian Robin Kelley might have it, while militarized policing serves the needs of capitalism, it more precisely serves the needs of *racial* capitalism.[18]

This book, finally, has endeavored to offer a postcolonial historical sociology of militarized policing, casting our eyes on cyclical and linear temporalities. The first, the *cyclical*, refers to the recurrence over expansive swaths of time of the same logic of racialized triggers, imperial feedback, and militarization—that is, repeated waves of militarization. Tied to these waves are subcycles of militarization, rebellion, and militarized response. For instance, in Chapters 5 and 6 we saw how the police-militarization-as-boomerang effect can trigger a cacophony of other generative historical processes, transforming the very conditions under which society's members lived. In 1950s America and 1970s Britain, the police adopted the tools and tactics of imperial-military regimes and wielded them aggressively, in turn arousing rightful anger among the police's victims. That rightful anger often triggered rebellion and then more militarized responses. This cycle of militarization, insurgency, and renewed militarization has occurred repeatedly, with no end in sight. Police militarization, therefore, must be seen not just as an effect of social processes but also as their driver, serving not only to "fabricate order," as Mark Neocleous puts it, but also to fabricate the very disorder that it is ostensibly meant to suppress.[19] This is a cyclical history that bears telling and retelling.

The other temporality, the *linear*, refers to the unidirectional development of militarized policing—that is to say, its continued accumulation and growth. While there have been waves, the periods in between waves (troughs) do not mark regression from militarization but rather a temporary stall. Over longer swaths of time, militarized means and methods have been continually added to policing, layer by layer, thereby increasing and expanding the militarized capacities of policing to create a vast imperial-militarized formation. One example of this linear development is the fact that many of the first civil police forces did not wield firearms or hide their truncheons, but today the police are more likely to openly carry military-grade weapons. It used to be controversial for police to openly wield a truncheon; today it is common and accepted for police to carry assault rifles and ride in MRAPs. Police militarization has thus been naturalized by its linear growth. It is telling that critical observers of policing often focus on the weapons of the police rather than teasing out the deeper militarized forms and cultures that constitute policing. Some might stand appalled at the images of MRAPs on the streets of Ferguson or Armed Police Units in London but then fail to consider how so much more about the police—its hierarchical command-and-control structure, titles such as "sergeant," beat patrols, crime mapping, mobile units—has emerged from imperial-military regimes too. The historical accumulation of militarization has gotten to the point where militarized policing is almost taken for granted. We forget, in other words, the racialized imperial provenance of policing, which marks an imperial unconscious. We barely register the fact that today, police have layers on layers of imperial-military forms, operations, tools, and tactics accumulated since the very birth of modern policing.

Understanding this linear trend, peeling back the layers, and digging into the depths of militarized policing can help us see new things. For example, it can help us better fathom what Stoughton calls the "warrior mentality." Police officers, he explains, believe themselves to be "locked in intermittent and unpredictable combat with unknown but highly lethal enemies." As a result, "officers learn to be afraid. . . . Fear is ubiquitous in law enforcement."[20] This is akin to what sociologist Michael Sierra-Arévalo calls the "danger imperative," something to which Arthur Rizer, former police officer and military veteran, also attests: "We have for years told American police officers to regard every civilian encounter as potentially deadly, and that they must always be prepared to win that death match."[21]

The story told in this book offers a friendly amendment to this idea of a "warrior mentality" and "danger imperative." It suggests that the deeply seeded warrior mentality should also be considered a colonial counterinsurgency mentality, one that does not see "danger" as racially neutral. Birthed from the outset of policing, and continually reproduced through multiple waves of imperial feedback since then, this is a mentality that racializes crime while criminalizing racial difference. It likens dark criminals in Los Angeles or Manchester to dark rebels in the colonies. It imagines the streets of Brixton or the South Side of Chicago to be zones of insurgency like Kabul or Fallujah, assuming that mortal danger lurks around every corner and behind every passing Brown or Black face. It remains to be seen if this mentality is reducible to "racism" that can be expunged through "anti-bias" training. This book offers instead the hypothesis that the counterinsurgency mentality reflects a deep habitus of colonial-military policing baked into the very nature of what "policing" means in Britain and the United States.[22]

## Flows and Logics of Militarized Policing

The analysis in this book has focused on waves of militarization, but it has also led us to see a range of related logics. We have seen, for example, how coercive means and methods undergo modulation as they are imported from imperial peripheries in the interests of performing civility. This is what some critical studies of policing overlook amid their overzealous equations between war abroad and policing at home: the tools of imperial-military regimes are indeed brought home, but they are never brought home wholesale, nor do they go without some modification. Peel and Rowan were inspired by colonial forces in Ireland and light infantry in the Caribbean when they created the London Met, but they did not arm London constables exactly as colonial-military forces. And they insisted truncheons be hidden from view. We have seen that this has been a crucial part of police militarization generally. Police borrow imperial-military means and methods but domesticate them, adjusting them for use at home. Sometimes they try to hide militarization entirely, seeking to keep it all secret— as ACPO officials in Britain did in the early 1980s (Chapter 6)—so as to portray the police as a civil force. This is one sense in which we can say that the "civil police" has always been a ruse. It is also why it is worth speaking of the *imperiality* of policing: the term, though a mouthful, helps break through the ruse.

We have seen variations in the strength and duration of the waves of militarization that imperial feedback ushers in. These loosely correspond to the extent or depth of the racialized threat to order. In extreme cases, often in the wake of especially violent crime waves or heavily racialized protests that converge with transnational threats to order, the threat is widespread and extreme. In such cases, the colonial boomerang is hastily summoned back and militarization ensues with vigor. But sometimes racialization is more subtle, and officials only dimly perceive a serious threat. In these cases, officials might still seek out new means and methods of policing from the imperial-military apparatus, but militarization will be muted, the wave fleeting and of relatively lower intensity. We have further seen how the specific racial images matter; the type of perceived racialized threat dictates the particular tactics, technologies, and templates that are sought out. In nineteenth-century Britain, the image of unruly and indignant urban insurgents seeking to violently overthrow the white order conjured methods and modalities of military power from the scenes of colonial counterinsurgency (Chapter 6). Alternatively, in the late nineteenth century, the image of the criminal alter as cunning, sneaky, and elusive invited the search for new technologies of surveillance, such as fingerprinting (Chapter 4).

It should also be clear that the flows of militarized policing have been global, hence multiscalar and multidirectional. Not only have police forces in the major metropolises in Britain and the United States influenced each other, and not only have those police forces been influenced by colonial-military forces in imperial peripheries, but the relationship has gone in the other direction as well. British police forces drew from colonial models, but they also shipped policing models back to the colonies and across the empire. The Royal Irish Constabulary influenced not only the London Metropolitan Police and England's rural constabularies but also police forces in colonies across the British imperial sphere. August Vollmer imported tactics from the Philippines, but he also advised police officials in Havana, Ceylon, and Japan (to name just a few overseas lands). Later in the twentieth century, after World War II, US police forces were sent all around the world to aid and advise newly independent countries through programs sponsored by the State Department's Office of Public Safety.[23] And as seen in Chapter 6, officers of the London Metropolitan Police in the 1960s were sent to British territories in the Caribbean, such as Anguilla, to train new police departments. The colonial boomerang has not just come "home"; it has flowed across and through transnational, transimperial, and intraimperial spaces in all directions.

Understanding this sheds light on the formation of the civil police itself, as well as on its subsequent militarization, but it also illuminates a range of other related connections. We might see more clearly the connections between the police responses to BLM protestors in Minneapolis and Ferguson from 2016 to 2020 and the so-called rioters in London in 2011. We might see how the tactics of the Hong Kong and Singapore tactical units in the 1950s and 1960s not only influenced British policing but also flew from there to other countries, including back to Hong Kong itself (manifest in the police repression of protestors there in 2019 and 2020). We might also perceive how the militarization of policing as a result of the "war on drugs" and the "war on gangs" in the United States and Britain is entangled with the militaristic modalities of violence used during the Vietnam War, the "war on terror" in the Middle East, and the "war on drugs" in the Philippines, Mexico, Colombia, and South Africa.[24] The forms and functions of colonial policing seemingly appear everywhere at once.

In exposing the boomerang effect, this book does not deny that these other flows occur. Nor does it deny that different factors, forces, and functionalities have been entwined with militarized policing. For example, political, bureaucratic, or professional factors have probably been important in shaping militarization. When Sir Robert Peel created the London Metropolitan Police, he likely had political and professional goals in mind. The structure of governance plays a role too. America's policing assemblage consists of multiple layers of law enforcement agencies, from municipal and county to state and federal levels, and is arguably more complexified than that of Britain's. This might shape the extent and speed to which militarized tactics can spread.[25] Or consider business interests and weapons manufacturers. They too have interests in police militarization, thus contributing to the construction of an entire police-military-industrial complex costing the public billions of dollars.

Gender is another social force worth considering. When Progressive-era reformers in the United States embarked on aggressive "anti-vice" campaigns, or when police in late nineteenth-century London fretted over prostitution among incoming immigrants from eastern Europe, among their goals was to control women's bodies—a control covered under the rhetoric of "protecting" them from prostitution, drugs, or Black, Brown, and Asian men. "Women's bodies," writes the historian Anne Gray Fisher, "are an important and overlooked site on which police power . . . has been built."[26] Elliott-Cooper reveals another way in which aggressive policing and gender are entwined: police authorities in Britain in the 2000s have often justified militarized policing as a form of noble masculinity while constructing crimes like knife attacks and drug dealing as criminal expressions of Black masculinity. Assertions of masculine domination by the state and its white allies, such as in the form of police aggression, are assumed to be valid, while any assertions of masculinity by nonwhites are denigrated, criminalized, and policed.[27]

These and other factors, forces, and functionalities have probably played a part in police militarization alongside imperialism and racialization. Rather than claiming these other logics are irrelevant, this book has endeavored to expose, excavate, and explore the logics of racialization and empire that have been crucial for militarized police yet typically overlooked. Rather than a replacement of other knowledges about the history of policing, this book is meant as a remediation, uncovering the forces of imperialism and racialization that have been previously unnoticed or underexplored.

## The Presence of Recurrence in the United States

What, then, of the present? It would not be a stretch to say that by now, police militarization in the United States and Britain is almost axiomatic.[28] The repeated historical turn to the military by the police has made it such that imperial feedback and police militarization are ingrained, almost habitual practices that no longer require racialized triggers. An analogy is Max Weber's analysis of how the Protestant ethic has shaped capitalism. According to his thesis, modern capitalism was first triggered by a Protestant work ethic: laboring for profit and reinvestment was infused with deep religious motivation. But as capitalism further developed over time, it no longer required religious motivation to keep it going. In capitalist society today, people work hard because of habit rather than spiritual orientation.[29] Similarly, it may be that police militarization today no longer requires racial triggers. The weight of history silently presses down on the present; centuries of police officials turning to imperial-military regimes and attendant centuries of racialized justifications have ingrained in them a deep habitus of militarization.[30]

Consider the policing of protests. By now, police departments across the United States have fully embraced the crowd control measures invented and deployed by colonial police and counterinsurgency units. During the 2020 protests that raged across America's cities in the wake of the killing of George

Floyd, police from Portland to New York City used plainclothes versions of "snatch squads" to make "pop-up" arrests of unsuspecting leaders on the streets, thus reenacting the tactics London's SPG used in the 1970s, which had come from Ulster, Hong Kong, and Singapore (Chapter 6).[31] New York City's Strategic Response Group (SRG), created in 2015, is the clearest example: it used snatch squad tactics on BLM protestors in 2020 while also, as the unit's training manual reveals, deploying wedge formations of the sort that had been first perfected by British colonial police and military counterinsurgency forces.

Besides protest policing, the "war on drugs" has served as another node for continued militarization in the United States. While the ghetto uprisings of the 1960s sparked the creation of the first SWAT unit in Los Angeles, officials across the country used the war on drugs as a rationale for creating more SWAT teams in the 1970s and 1980s. By the late 1990s, about 90 percent of all large cities in the United States had SWAT units. The same trend is evident in small towns. In the 1980s, about 20 percent of small towns had SWAT units, but by the early 2000s, about 80 percent had them. Officials have also used the war on drugs as a reason to repurpose these units over time. Initially, some SWAT units were created to serve as emergency "reactive" teams (responding to emergencies, riots, and large-scale upheaval), but they have increasingly taken on "proactive" roles on the front lines of the drug war.[32] In 2011 and 2012, the majority of SWAT deployments across the country (62 percent) were initiated in order to execute warrants to search for drugs.[33]

The war on drugs has also helped police continue to obtain military-grade tools. During his administration, President George H. Bush renewed Richard Nixon's earlier war on drugs, declaring drug use to be "the most pressing problem facing the nation" in 1989. Around the same time, the Department of Defense (DoD) was tasked with serving as "the single lead agency of the Federal Government for the detection and monitoring of aerial and maritime transit of illegal drugs into the United States."[34] The National Defense Authorization Act then allowed the DoD to make military equipment available to law enforcement agencies. This set the conditions for the National Defense Authorization Act of 1990–1991, which facilitated the transfer of yet more excess military equipment to law enforcement agencies. In 1997, Section 1033 of the National Defense Authorization Act renewed and expanded the program.[35]

The transfer of military equipment to law enforcement agencies continued through the early 2000s.[36] From 1990 to 2021, at least $7.5 billion worth of surplus military equipment was transferred to subnational policing agencies.[37] This included blankets, office equipment, health supplies, riot gear, night-vision goggles, rifles, aircraft, armored vehicles, and MRAPs. In terms of value, the majority of these, about 82 percent of the total value of all such surplus materials, are "controlled equipment," the most dangerous military gear associated with war and counterinsurgency. The category includes riot gear, explosives, specialized firearms and ammunition under .50 caliber, breaching equipment, aircraft, armored vehicles, tactical vehicles, and command and control vehicles. Evidently, most were drawn from America's imperial-military apparatus in the Middle East.[38]

The so-called war on terror, which took on unprecedented urgency in the wake of 9/11, has also served as a pretense for recent bouts of imperial feedback. A federal program created in 2003 allowed the Department of Homeland Security to spend $740 billion from 2003 to 2016 to promote collaboration among federal, state, and local law enforcement agencies in counterterrorism intelligence gathering. It also provided military-style vehicles, weapons, and gear to local police. This included powerful surveillance cameras kitted out with facial recognition software, acoustic devices for crowd control, armored vehicles called BearCats, spy drones, and other surveillance technologies, many developed initially for the military. The Intelligence Division unit of the NYPD has used such technologies to target and surveil Muslim religious leaders, student associations, organizations, and businesses, while the LAPD has used military-grade computer software for its "big data" surveillance initiatives.[39]

Still, while militarization can happen today habitually, without the racialization of crime and disorder, these more recent bouts of militarization do appear to have been triggered by racialization. The war on drugs, for example, was a notoriously racialized policy. Nixon's domestic policy chief, John Ehrlichman, later admitted that the drug war was an attempt to "disrupt" Black communities.[40] The spread of military equipment in the 2000s under the auspices of the Section 1033 program likewise followed racialized logics. Studies show that police agencies in towns that received military equipment from the program had higher rates of violent crime, and the towns with the highest rates received the most military equipment. But the same studies show that crime rates were not the only factor. Even accounting for levels of violent crime, the cities and towns receiving the most military equipment had higher proportions of racialized minorities in their populations.[41] This suggests that police agencies requesting and receiving militarized equipment have only partly responded to actual crime rates: they have also been motivated by *perceived* racialized threats—militarization as a tactic of anticipation fueled by racist assumptions of who criminals are.

Triggered by racialization or not, the boomerang continues to return. For example, since the early 2000s at least, police officers and police chiefs from various US towns—including San Bernardino, California; Orlando, Florida; and Haverhill, Massachusetts—have traveled to Israel to observe and learn about counterterrorism from the Israeli military and Israeli National Police.[42] In one trip in 2017, a delegation of officers from towns in Massachusetts toured the West Bank, East Jerusalem, the border with Syria, and Israel's municipal police academy to learn about intelligence-gathering and tactics such as roadblocks, making "for an exchange of ideas between Israeli and Massachusetts law enforcement."[43] At the same time, veterans of the Iraq and Afghanistan wars of the early 2000s have also served as new conduits for continued imperial importation. In Savannah, the beat cop Patrick Skinner has imported military methods for policing, thus picking up the mantle left by William G. Austin, the Army veteran who, in the early twentieth century, joined Savannah's police department and initiated a new round of militarization (Chapter 3). Before becoming a Savannah cop, Skinner had worked as a case officer in the US Central Intelligence Agency to help coordinate and conduct counterterrorist operations. He told a journalist that policing at home and overseas counterterrorism are "the same side of the coin, only looked at from different angles." Crime, he claimed, is "exactly like terrorism."[44] Accordingly, Skinner applies counterterrorist principles to what is sometimes called "community policing" but is actually a form of counterinsurgency.[45] It is about "getting the local community on your side" and developing "area familiarization" in order to identify and capture criminals. Skinner also praised the counterinsurgency tactic of "targeted raids," which, he asserts, prove useful in both overseas counter-terrorist campaigns and "policing at home."[46]

Skinner joins many other military veterans and counterinsurgency experts who have brought the "war on terror" and counterinsurgency campaigns from the Middle East back home in the 2010s.[47] Kevin Kit Parker, another veteran of the Middle East campaigns, sees similarities between insurgent networks and street gangs. "Gangs rely upon the passive support of the population," he said. "They move into at-risk neighborhoods the same way Al-Queda would go into Sudan rather than Switzerland."[48] He and other ex-military created a "counterinsurgency laboratory" in Salinas, California, to advise local police on employing counterinsurgency tools to quell gang activity in the largely Mexican communities of the city. Parker has worked with another veteran, Mike Cutone, who conducted counterinsurgency operations in Haiti, Jordan, Kosovo, Kuwait, Iraq, and Afghanistan, to expand the program to other cities. Cutone has named his program C3 and trademarked the name.[49] The project's website explains that "C3" stands for "counter criminal continuum." C3 is based on the premise that "gang members and criminals act similarly to insurgents," and therefore "draws on strategies used in US military campaigns against insurgents in Iraq and Afghanistan" to eliminate gang violence and crime.[50]

Computer analysis and new software platforms are part of many of these policing efforts; they are deployed for intelligence-gathering and metric-based interventions. These too have roots in the military.[51] As the sociologist Sarah Brayne reveals, both the LAPD and NYPD have adopted "big data" policing using "analytic platforms originally designed for counterinsurgency efforts in Iraq and Afghanistan."[52] In fact, the US Army itself has created new software platforms to help police conduct their anti-gang operations. In the early 2000s, the army increasingly used "social network analysis" in its counterinsurgency efforts in the Middle East (a form of analysis now enshrined in counterinsurgency manuals). The strategy necessitated new software designed to analyze networks of insurgents (so that the army could best attack them). Based on the dubious claim made by army experts and police that criminal gangs operate through social networks just like terrorists, police have adopted these same software platforms.[53] One result has been the creation of gang databases. Police feed information on gang members, suspected gang members, their relatives, friends, neighbors, and even passing acquaintances into the database, even if they do not have a criminal record. Police then use that database in their counter-gang strategy, which, as one member of the Chicago Police Department explains, "blends traditional law enforcement competencies with military intelligence and targeting practices."[54] The effects have not been salutary. Innocent people have been targeted by the police just because they happened to have spoken with a suspected gang member or live in the same neighborhood.[55]

## The Persistent Boomerang Effect in Britain

Across the Atlantic, Britain has also seen recent rounds of the police-militarization-as-boomerang effect. One recent round has to do with armed police units. The London Special Patrol Group in the 1970s was the earliest version, giving way to Territorial Support Groups in the 1980s and specialized firearms units known as Armed Response Units (ARUs), trained by officers from the School of Infantry at Hythe. This opened the floodgates for further developments. In the 1990s, Armed Response Units were given Armed Response Vehicles (ARVs) and put on permanent patrol, available twenty-four hours a day. The units were also given military-grade firearms to be held in secure cases in the boot of the ARV. ARUs have access to a variety of weapons, from handguns and shotguns to sniper rifles and submachine guns such as Heckler & Koch MP5 carbines.[56] The first ARV in London hit the streets in 1991, manned by London's firearms unit, now known as SO19. The ARV, or "Trojan," attended twenty-five calls per day across London in that decade. In 1993, thirty-three of the forty-three police forces in England and Wales had ARVs. In 2020, there were 19,372 police firearms operations in England and Wales, 91 percent of which involved an ARV.[57]

Another significant development unfolded in London in the 1990s along with the rise of these ARUs and ARVs. In 1994, in response to the killing of police officers in Brixton, the London Metropolitan Commissioner gave permission for SO19 officers to openly carry firearms on their belts and deploy them at their own discretion.[58] Previously officers had had to store their weapons in the boot of the Trojan and could only fire their weapons after being given permission by the senior officer. Meanwhile, the Police Federation called for all officers "in certain inner-city troublespots" to be routinely armed.[59]

The arming did not cease. By the early 2000s, London's SO19 wielded Glock pistols, Heckler & Kock machine guns, and G3 short-barreled rifles in their shoulder holsters.[60] By 2021, the unit also carried Sig MCX carbines and magazines, baton guns, and "stunnies" or stun grenades, as well as rams for forced entry, helmets, and bulletproof shields.[61] That same year, London had forty ARVs, with twenty on patrol at any given time. Meanwhile, ARVs were involved in 16,713 police firearms operations across England and Wales. This marked a "gradual increase in the proportion of operations involving ARVs since records began in the year ending March 2009."[62]

The increasing use of ARUs and ARVs has been tied to a newer racialized policing project in Britain: the war on so-called gangs. While ARVs are meant to attend major incidents like terrorist attacks and active shooters, it is often difficult to determine beforehand whether an incident is of this character. In effect, ARVs have served on the "front line of the war on gang violence."[63] In the wake of the 2011 riots, Prime Minister David Cameron announced this war, proclaiming an "all out war on gangs and gang culture."[64] He articulated the view of most authorities that the riots were primarily led by gangs in inner-city districts (Mark Duggan, whose shooting by the police sparked the 2011 riots, had been accused by the police of being a gang member). In the end, it was proven that gangs did not in fact play a significant role in the 2011 uprisings. But this fact did not stop the official discourse from generating a near moral panic about gangs. As Adam Elliot-Cooper explains, the official and popular discourse on gangs was heavily racialized and drew on British counterinsurgency categories.[65]

While ARUs and their new ARVs have been deployed for this war on gangs, another part of the campaign has involved the use of surveillance and identification techniques originally drawn from counterinsurgency operations in Northern Ireland. Earlier versions of the techniques had been imported to England beginning in the 1970s by the Special Patrol Group and other police units. The SPG used stop-and-search tactics to register automobiles and individuals into the national databases (see Chapter 6). In the 2000s, the use of counterinsurgency-style surveillance techniques was reanimated by the police amid their new war on gangs. This time the police generated a new surveillance system called the Gang Matrix. Formed in 2012, and akin to the gang databases used by US police departments, the Matrix contained information on individuals presumably associated with gangs. From its inception until at least 2018, about 80 percent of the individuals listed in the Matrix were Black, even as London's Black population was only around 13 percent.[66] Individuals in the Matrix need not be proven to be actual "gang members"; as with similar gang databases in the United States, they need only be associated with suspected gang members or live in the same housing estates as those marked as having heavy gang activity.[67]

The threat of Islamic terrorism in Britain has generated further militarization. Police have intensified surveillance efforts of Muslim populations using Automated Number Plate Recognition (ANPR) and CCTV cameras, whose maintenance was subcontracted out to a company called Olive Group—the same group that had conducted surveillance operations in Iraq and Afghanistan.[68] Furthermore, after the September 11, 2001, attacks, British officials searched for new ways to manage terrorist threats and ended up implementing novel tactics, doctrines, and operations for firearms use. One of those tactics, Operation Kratos, was modeled on shoot-to-kill tactics by British Army forces in Northern Ireland, Israeli forces operating in the Occupied Territories, and Israeli forces inside Israel itself. It was drawn up by the British government upon consultation with Israeli security officials.[69] Kratos transgresses the presumption of innocence, inviting police officers to shoot terrorist suspects in the head (as opposed to prior Met policy, which counseled aiming for the chest) even without confirmation that the suspect is carrying explosives.[70] Islamic activist groups in London were rightly critical. "We have raised concerns about the Met sending officers to learn from the Israelis about suicide bombers," said Massoud Shadjareh of the Islamic Human Rights Commission. "They have a policy of assassinating people—why should our police learn these tactics and these values?"[71]

Shadjareh's criticism was on the mark. The first known use of the new Kratos tactics came in July 22, 2005, when SO19 was dispatched to a tube station in South London to hunt for a suspected terrorist. At the station they shot and killed a man named Jean Charles de Menezes. He was a twenty-seven-year-old Brazilian electrician later found to have nothing to do with terrorism. The police mistook Jean Charles for a terrorist based less on factual information or even behavior than on coincidence and appearance. Jean Charles looked Middle Eastern.[72] Later the Met admitted Jean Charles was innocent, but no individual police officers faced prosecution over his death. Police officials defending the killing pointed out that "these police were acting according to their training and orders from above"—that is, they were simply acting "in accordance with the Kratos guidelines."[73]

## Convergence and Comparison

These most recent waves of militarization in the United States and Britain reveal significant similarities between them. Both countries have embarked on racialized "wars" on gangs that draw on similar tactics of highly technical computerized surveillance systems ("big data") and that in turn come from imperial counter-insurgency operations. Both countries have also converged on similar firearms tactics: as noted above, the racialized threat of Islamic terrorism and the "war on terror" have generated a near "shoot to kill" policy for the British police (i.e., Operation Kratos) that approximates firearms use policy for US police.

This convergence is both surprising and not. It is surprising given the very real and long-standing differences in the two empires' militarized regimes of metropolitan policing. Throughout the preceding chapters we have seen some of these differences. The US police adopted firearms relatively early, while the British police overcame their initial hesitation to wield firearms only later—and even then, in a more limited manner than in the United States. Accordingly, while police in the two countries now use similar militarized tactics, technologies, and tools drawn originally from colonial peripheries and the battlefields of empire, they differ significantly in firearms usage. Police killings are more prominent in the United States than in Britain. The best estimates suggest that between 2015 and 2021, there were 5,367 fatal police shootings in the United States and only 20 in England and Wales (or roughly 33.5 people killed in the United States per 10 million people, compared to 0.5 people per 10 million in England and Wales).[74] Relatedly, militarized policing in the United States has been seemingly more racially disproportionate than in Britain. Born from efforts to control, contain, and coerce Indigenous peoples, slaves, and ex-slaves, policing in the United States has variously taken aim at Mexican immigrants, Asian minorities, Puerto Ricans, Muslims, and African Americans. It is true that militarized policing in Britain has also been racialized, beginning with the Irish in the nineteenth century and carrying through to the surveillance of Jewish immigrants later in the century. But the relatively smaller numbers of racialized minorities in the British metropole, at least until World War II, had arguably rendered racialized policing in Britain much less pronounced. To be sure, as seen in Chapter 4, perceived racialized threats to law and order after the Fenian disturbances subsided in the late nineteenth century, making for a muted militarization of police at best. Exactly when Vollmer led the radical militarization of policing in the United States, the militarism of his counterparts like Commissioner Warren and Lord Trenchard in Britain was stopped short.

These sorts of differences between American and British policing contribute to long-standing claims of exceptionality. It can seem that only the United States has been plagued by militarized policing, police brutality, and race problems, with Britain appearing exempt from such horrors. As Elliott-Cooper notes, this British exceptionalist claim was on full display during a 2020 discussion between BBC *Newsnight* anchor Emily Maitlis and Black British artist George the Poet. The discussion was about the Black Lives Matter protests in the United States. George the Poet suggested that there were "disturbing parallels between the

Black British experience and the African American experience" in terms of policing especially. Maitlis responded: "You're not putting America and the UK on the same footing. . . . Our police aren't armed, they don't have guns, the legacy of slavery is not the same."[75]

On the other hand, the analysis of policing offered in this book counsels caution when it comes to claims of exceptionality or fundamental difference between British and US policing. The police in both countries, embedded in similar transnational and imperial circuits, have been militarized along very similar lines. And they have long borrowed from and even emulated each other. The founders of the civil police in the United States emulated the London model in the nineteenth century; US police borrowed criminal identification systems from England in the early twentieth century; innovators like Trenchard in London were partly inspired by Vollmer's "scientific policing"; in the 1960s, the London Metropolitan Police looked not only at British imperial forms to create the Special Patrol Group but also at New York's Tactical Unit, which was in turn inspired by British colonial forces and Vollmer's mobile units. In the late 1960s, British police officials facing domestic urban upheaval looked to cities like New York and Los Angeles as they fretted about Black revolt. Furthermore, convergences in militarized tactics between the US and British police have come from shared imperial experiences rather than just cross-imperial emulation. Together, the US and British imperial states conducted campaigns in Iraq and Afghanistan amid the so-called war on terror in which new surveillance systems, counterterrorism theories, and counterinsurgency tactics were developed and thus made available.

Any claims about fundamental differences in the racial dimensions of militarized policing between the United States and Britain should also be qualified. As seen in this book, militarization in both countries has been caused by racialized triggers. And due to post-*Windrush* migration to Britain, British cities and America's cities are demographically less different from each other today than they were in the nineteenth century. Racialized minorities make up significant proportions of the population in both countries. And in both countries they have been demonized and denounced. Blamed for urban decay, crime, and disorder, racialized immigrants in Britain today have come to serve as the repository of many residents' anxieties about social change, just as in the United States. It is not shocking that British officials have responded with forms of racialized warfare that duplicate America's bellicose policing campaigns, such as the "war on drugs," the "war on gangs," and the "war on terror." In both the United States and Britain, crime and disorder have been continually and literally colored by colonial racism. Similarities in militarized policing between the two metropolitan nations have followed in tow.

Return, then, to the claims of exceptionality by BBC *Newsnight* anchor Emily Maitlis. While Maitlis intimated that racist police brutality in Britain did not match that of the US police, she overlooked important similarities. For instance, despite the small number of fatal police shootings in Britain compared to the United States, racial disparities in policing remain high in Britain. In the United States, Black people are 2.5 times more likely to be fatally shot by police than those coded as white, while Native Americans are 3 times more likely and Latinx people are 1.5 times more likely to be fatally shot. But in England and Wales, Black people are more than 6 times more likely to die from policing shootings than whites.[76] Of course, the raw numbers are small (only twenty in Britain killed between 2015 and 2021), but the disproportionalities remain large. And even if we let the small raw numbers dispel claims of equivalence with the United States, other figures are compelling. From April 2019 to March 2020, for example, there were 492,000 recorded incidents in England and Wales where a police officer used force; of these, about 31 percent of the subjects involved were nonwhite (with 11 percent of the total population being Black or Asian). At the same time, Black people were more than nine times as likely to be stopped and searched by the police than white people. Asians were twice as likely than whites.[77] Racialized policing in Britain is real.

Racialized disparities in incarceration in Britain are also evident. In 2019 (before a decrease in incarceration for all groups given the COVID-19 pandemic), Black men were 228 percent more likely than white men "to be arrested, plead not guilty and be sent to prison by the Crown Court than their white counterparts." When you include not just Black men but also Asians, "mixed" individuals, and other ethnic groups, the percentage still remains higher than for whites, at 75 percent. In all, in 2019, over 25 percent of the entire prison population in England and Wales was from a minority ethnic group (the largest being "Black or Black British" and "Asian or Asian British," who constitute only 11 percent of the total population in England and Wales).[78] According to some measures, this "disproportionate imprisonment of Black people in Britain is greater than that of the US."[79] In 2010, the proportion of Black prisoners in the United States was four times greater than their population share, while in the United Kingdom, the proportion of Black people in jail was seven times their share of the population.[80] Just as tragically, Black residents in Britain are more likely to be left to die while being held by police than white residents are, and racial disproportionalities in rates of deaths while in police custody are worse in Britain than in the United States.[81]

In all, therefore, the so-called civil police in Britain and the United States share a history of policing and hence exhibit key similarities that are too often overlooked in the popular imagination. The civil police in both countries have been militarized from the beginning, eagerly adopting the racialized tools of empire. And they have done so consistently, often with vigor. Yes, comparative statistics on racialized policing in the United States and Britain may be mobilized to make claims of exceptionality, to highlight the supposedly benign British "bobby" as opposed to the racist, bellicose American cop. But such statistics simply cover up a shared racialized imperiality and a martial approach to racialized minorities that cannot be overlooked. As one member of BLM in Britain put it: "There may be fewer guns issued in the U.K. but there is still a war against black people."[82]

\* \* \*

But if there has been such a "war," will it end? Can the continued expansion and intensification of militarized policing be halted? Can it be resisted, fought, and undone? This book does not explore the full scope of historical resistance to police brutality. Nor does it serve as a handbook on how to change policing or suggest detailed policy prescriptions. But the postcolonial historical sociology of policing offered in preceding chapters does yield some thoughts about resistance and possible futures.[83]

Consider resistance. The history of racialized minorities fighting against police brutality is a long one, reaching all the way back to their opposition to slave patrols in the Caribbean and southern United States. In the preceding chapters we have seen more recent resistance from racialized minorities in the form of mass uprisings in urban communities, from Watts and Queens to Brixton and Bristol. Sometimes connected to movements like the Black Panther Party (and, most recently, Black Lives Matter), these uprisings stand as direct responses to police violence and aggression. They remind us that aggressive militarized policing has not gone unchallenged.

Of course we know the tragic outcomes of these uprisings: they have typically been met with yet more militarized policing. At best, officials have responded by further militarizing the police while covering up their tracks, such as when officials in London dismantled the Special Patrol Group only to replace it with new militarized units under different names, or when they retrained police in Hong Kong–style tactics behind closed doors. As seen, "civil" policing from its birth has been a performance covering up occult militarizing moves—and performativity depends on incessant repetition.

Look at what happened in the wake of the 2011 riots in Britain. Soon after the riots, the Home Office purchased new water cannons for the police, and public criticism mounted. In response, Home Secretary Theresa May halted the purchases and denounced the cannons, stating, "Our police have never and will never routinely carry guns or hide behind military-style equipment." But what May did not state is that police had long had access to water cannons, along with a range of other military-grade equipment, and she did not denounce any of it.[84] In this case, therefore, public outrage and critique compelled authorities to momentarily back off, but it did not lead to a fundamental change in militarized policing. It was just more of the same, another scene in an extended play of "civil" policing.

On the other hand, the potential and productivity of resistance, critique, and outrage must not be ignored. The civil police have to be performed, but sometimes performances fail. And as repeated performances of the civil police are met with relentless resistance and critique, new possibilities are pried open. Public protests and urban uprisings have challenged authority, exposed lies, and cast a light on problems hitherto unseen by average citizens. Speaking truth to power, these campaigns have helped alter the terms of debate. One response to the urban uprisings of the 1960s in the United States was the Kerner Commission in 1968, which pinpointed structural problems that had led to the uprisings, including racial inequality and violent policing. The commission's report did not lead to fundamental change; its social components were ignored, and authorities instead seized on its recommendations for colonial policing. But at the very least it offered an aperture for an awakening and allowed for the discourse about policing to slowly shift.[85] Similarly, in Britain, the Scarman Report of 1981, written in response to the Brixton riots, did not launch an era of change, but it did help cast a new light on police aggression and helped shift perceptions.[86] Furthermore, while it is true that police officials have responded to mass uprisings with yet more militarization in new guises or in secret, the fact that those officials feel the need to rebrand the police or remilitarize behind closed doors is itself notable. It highlights that relentless resistance and public critique can put the police on the defensive. It underscores the fragility of their power.

Another lesson from preceding chapters is this: resistance must be not only relentless but also systematic and global. Some challenges to police militarization have only targeted the weaponry of police. They critique the acquisition of water cannons, military-grade firearms, MRAPS, and other tools of violence work. In the United States, with support from both the right and the left, this movement has mostly focused on the Department of Defense's 1033 Program.[87] But we now know that police militarization is much deeper than the arms police wield. As seen throughout this book, the militarization of policing extends to the very core of policing itself—from its form and structure to its operations and culture. It includes mindsets like the counterinsurgency mentality, which sees danger everywhere and compels police to stand ready to react with violence at the slightest provocation. Such mindsets reach back to the beginnings of policing. More than manifested in police weaponry, the racialized imperiality of policing is deeply entrenched, baked into its very existence. To only criticize the weaponry of policing is to miss the bigger picture. The entire militarized culture of policing must also be scrutinized. This means that "policing" itself needs to be questioned.

There have been small victories on this front. In 2018, the city council of Durham, North Carolina, unanimously voted to pass a measure that banned all training and exchange between the Israeli military and Durham's police department; Durham was the "first US city to ever explicitly take such a measure."[88]

Still, undoing the police's training and access to military-grade weaponry does nothing to change the structural conditions that give rise to militarized policing in the first place. These conditions are not just about the police's mindsets but also about the racialized perceptions held by state officials and the public more broadly. They have to do with the tightly interwoven links between perceived racialized menace and criminality—links that have historical and imperial roots. Whiteness is taken to signify lawfulness and citizenship; nonwhiteness is taken to signify lawlessness, violence, and menace.[89]

With the findings of this book, we can see that this is not a new set of equations; it is a colonial discourse that has given shape to policing historically and has served to trigger militarized policing in the first place. The assumption that all nonwhites are criminals and all criminals are nonwhite; that they are all evil deviants hell-bent on violence and insurgency; that they only respond to physical coercion and violent force—these are long-standing ideas that the public perpetuates along with the police, and they have helped give birth to and justify militarized policing. From this we can see that any attempt to change or abolish policing must also interrogate society's deep-rooted racial assumptions, along with the socioeconomic inequalities wrought by colonial capitalism and its contemporary neoliberal variant that help perpetuate those assumptions. And it follows that movements to undo governmental programs or policies that provide military equipment and weaponry are promising but limited, for they target an effect of empire—that is, surplus military weapons and tools—rather than empire itself. If there has been a military-industrial complex, by now it has become an imperial-military-policing complex, and "demilitarizing" policing without demilitarizing the military and struggling for a postimperial world will be futile.

This brings us to the final point. It is to be hoped that if this book has done anything, it has convincingly demonstrated that resistance to policing must be as global as policing itself. We have seen that the discourses of racial difference, disorder, and crime that both trigger and justify militarized policing in the United States and Britain did not emerge within the confines of the United States and Britain. They emerged from and in relation to colonial discourses of difference, indexing a global color line. And the tools and techniques that militarized policing employs are also part of a larger global imperial formation of coercion, both past and present. Struggles against racialized and militarized policing in the metropole, therefore, must also target militarized policing around the world, and they must target imperial formations everywhere. If modern policing in Britain and the United States has been inspired by empire, then struggles against policing must join with and become anti-imperial struggles—and vice versa. Policing must be not only dearmed but decolonized as well. Post-policing futures must be informed by postcolonial and postimperial imaginaries where neither police nor empire exists at all.

# Notes

Abbreviations: Primary Documents and Archives

| | |
|---|---|
| AVP | August Vollmer Papers, Bancroft Library, University of California at Berkeley, Collection BANC MSS C-B 403 |
| BPD | Berkeley Police Department Papers, Bancroft Library, University of California at Berkeley, Collection BANC MSS 72/227c |
| CPD | Chicago Police Department, Annual Reports, City of Chicago, Illinois |
| CSPD | Police Department Records, City of Savannah, Research Library and Municipal Archives, Savannah, Georgia |
| GP | Sheldon Glueck Papers, Series XII, General Correspondence, Harvard Law Library, Cambridge, MA |
| HCP | Howell Cobb Papers, University of Georgia Library, Athens |
| HO | Home Office (UK) |
| HPD | *Hansard's Parliamentary Debates*, PP (UK) |
| IACP | International Association of Chiefs of Police, *Proceedings* of the Annual Conventions of the International Association of Chiefs of Police (Grand Rapids, MI: Seymour and Muir) |
| JHP | James Harper Papers, New York City Historical Society |
| LAPD | Los Angeles Police Department, Annual Reports, City of Los Angeles, California. |
| MCSAV | Mayor of Savannah, *Report of the [Mayor of Savannah, GA], Together with the Reports of the City Officers* (Savannah, GA: Morning News Print) |
| MEPO | Records of the Metropolitan Police Office (London), PRO |
| MYB | Municipal Yearbook, Chicago: International City Managers Association |
| PCM | Police Commissioner, Manchester, Annual Reports, 1829–1942, Manchester Central Library |
| PEC | Papers of Sir Edwin Chadwick, Special Collections, University College London |
| PP | Parliamentary Papers (UK) |
| PRO | Public Records Office, National Archives, Kew, United Kingdom |
| PRP | Papers of Sir Robert Peel, Manuscript Collections, British Library |
| RCDC | Commissioners of District of Columbia, Annual Reports (Washington, DC: US Government Printing Office) |

| | |
|---|---|
| RCPMET | *Report of the Commissioner of Police of the Metropolis* (London), various publishers |
| RMP | *Report of the Mayor of Philadelphia with the Annual Reports of the Directors of Departments* (Philadelphia: Dunlap Printing) |
| SPD | Records of the Savannah Police Department, Savannah Municipal Archives, City of Savannah, Georgia |

## Abbreviations: Newspapers and Periodicals

| | |
|---|---|
| *BDE* | *Brooklyn Daily Eagle* |
| *BT* | *Belfast Telegraph* |
| *CDC* | *Charleston Daily Courier* |
| *DM* | *Daily Mirror (UK)* |
| *DMA* | *Daily Mail (UK)* |
| *LAEE* | *Los Angeles Evening Express* |
| *LAT* | *Los Angeles Times* |
| *LQR* | *Quarterly Review (London)* |
| *NYDH* | *New York Daily Herald* |
| *NYDN* | *Daily News (New York)* |
| *NYTRI* | *New York Tribune* |
| *NYT* | *New York Times* |
| *OT* | *Oakland Tribune* |
| *PI* | *Philadelphia Inquirer* |
| *PMG* | *Pall Mall Gazette (London)* |
| *POM* | *Police Officer Magazine (Essex, UK)* |
| *PR* | *Police Review (London)* |
| *SDG* | *Savannah Daily Georgian* |
| *SDN* | *Savannah Daily News* |
| *SDR* | *Savannah Daily Republican* |
| *SMN* | *Savannah Daily Morning News* |
| *SR* | *Saturday Review of Politics, Literature, Science and Art* (London) |
| *SRB* | *State Research Bulletin* |
| *ST* | *Sunday Times (London)* |
| *TL* | *The Times (London)* |
| *WP* | *Washington Post* |

## Introduction

1. Lynch 2014.
2. Tolan 2017.
3. Kraska and Kappeler 1997, 4. See also Balko 2013 on militarization.

4. Wiechselbaum and Schwartzapfel 2017, para. 13.

5. The distinction was even enshrined in law: the 1878 Posse Comitatus Act limited the federal government's ability to use the military as a domestic police force.

6. Reingle Gonzalez et al. 2018.

7. Stoughton 2015, 228.

8. Delehanty et al. 2017; Lawson 2018; Mummolo 2018.

9. American Civil Liberties Union 2014.

10. Khan-Cullors and Bandele 2018, 200.

11. Khan-Cullors and Bandele 2018, 187.

12. Fassin 2013), 229.

13. Foucault 1979, 31.

14. I discuss the postcolonial theoretical underpinnings in the conclusion.

15. Quoted in Reith 1943, 140, emphasis added. Peel is attributed with writing the principles but the real authorship is unclear, as is the date when they were written.

16. Emsley 1999b, 36; also Emsley 1999a.

17. Reith 1952, 20.

18. Miller 1977, 17. European states have this type too, alongside their national gendarmerie. Besides the Gendarmerie Nationale, France's towns and cities also have municipal police forces and the Paris police, which follow this state-civilian type modeled after the London Metropolitan Police.

19. To this day, rank-and-file police as well as high-level officials in the United States still recite "Peel's Principles" of law enforcement. "Sir Robert Peel's Nine Principles of Policing" 2014.

20. Bayley 1975, 327–328.

21. Else 2014.

22. Alderson 1979, 5.

23. BLM Transparency Center 2021.

24. Singh 2017, 45.

25. Randhawa 2016.

26. Such as with the death of Smiley Culture in 2011, discussed in Elliott-Cooper 2021, 111.

27. Hall 2021, 92.

28. Home Office 2015.

29. See Home Office 2020b, 2021. These are discussed in the conclusion to this book. Here and throughout, "Britain" refers to England and Wales, as opposed to "Great Britain," which includes Scotland.

30. Elliott-Cooper 2021, 184–163; Network for Police Monitoring 2020.

31. Ascoli 1979, 1.

32. From the Slaughterhouse Cases of 1873, quoted in Dubber 2005, xi.

33. For a blog entry that expresses this view, see Lamartina Palacios 2015.

34. Harring 1983, 1, 13. See also Gourevitch 2015. Histories of policing in this vein thus unveil the police's role in repressing labor strikes and regulating working-class life. The literature is large, but regarding the United Kingdom, see Storch 1976 and Swift 2007b. For the United States, see Harring 1983 and Mitrani 2013.

35. Dubber 2005; Neocleous and the Anti-Security Collective 2021; Neocleous 2021.

36. Neocleous 2021, 7, 14. Bittner (1970, 36–47) long ago noted that the capacity to use force is a key function of the police. As Seigel (2018) puts it, police work is "violence work."

37. Unfortunately, this claim about the persistent militarized character of policing is typically assumed in some existing critical structuralist works. Rather than induced from empirical analysis, it is deduced from theoretical categories.

38. Claims that the police have always been militarized fail to account for why some tools and tactics are appropriated while others are not (the tactics of trench warfare used by the British Army during the First World War were different from those used by the British forces during the Malayan Emergency of 1948). Can we explain such variation by deducing principles of policing from a theory of capital accumulation?

39. A notable exception in the critical structuralist tradition is Brucato 2021.

40. Dulaney 1996, 2.

41. Du Bois 1935; also Brown 2019 and Kelley 2020. On slave patrols as early forms of militarized policing, see Brucato 2021, Hadden 2001, and Rousey 1996.

42. Kelley 2020, 33.

43. Maher 2021; Vitale 2017.

44. Purnell 2021, 66.

45. Kelley 2020, 14.

46. By speaking of "racialized minorities" or "racialized communities," I am referring to how some people get classified as a distinct inferior "race." This typically means marginalized groups seen as "nonwhite." Of course, the idea of a "nonwhite" race also implies that there is a superior "white" race, so people seen as "white" are also "racialized" (Roediger 1992). In this book, when speaking of racialized communities as primarily nonwhite, I by no means wish to imply that whites are not racialized. I use the descriptor "racialized" as a shorthand to refer to racialized groups who are also seen as inferior (who in the United States and British contexts tend to be nonwhite).

47. I discuss these different forms in Go 2011.

48. Fanon 1968 (1961), 40, 52.

49. Barder 2015, 6. This literature is extensive, but see the early discussion in Rabinow 1989. I theorize this further as "imperial feedback" or the "boomerang effect" below.

50. Blanchard 2014, 1838. See also Blanchard et al. 2017.

51. Elliott-Cooper 2021, 139.

52. Kuzmarov 2012; Schrader 2019.

53. Barkawi 2017.

54. Katznelson 2002.

55. The boomerang effect, or imperial feedback, is not the same as "blowback" (Johnson 2000), which refers to the negative side effects of imperial war and expansion at home rather than how forms or practices are imported from the colonies to the metropole.

56. Arendt 1970, 54.

57. Foucault 1997, 103.

58. In addition, understanding police militarization as the product of imperial feedback illuminates the *types* of militaristic tools and tactics that police adopt, not just the timing. What police import depends upon what is happening in the peripheries of empire and hence upon the content of the imperial-military regime at the time; the tools, tactics, and technologies in empire's *repertoire of force*.

59. It thereby helps fulfill one of the tasks of a critical social science: to dispel myths. If the term "civil police" does ideological work, masking deeper or more nefarious militaristic and violent policing practices, the term "militarization" also does its own kind of ideological work, functioning to cover up the global and racial underpinnings of militarized policing. Recognizing the imperial origins of police militarization sheds light on those underpinnings.

60. The term "coloniality" is used by decolonial philosophers rooted in Latin American thought to refer to the effect of colonial legacies upon modernity (Quijano 2000; Mignolo 2011). I use the term to refer to the condition of an institution, organization, policy, social practice, or social form having colonial origins, influences, meanings, and/or functionalities. I use the term "imperiality" similarly, to refer to the way in which something has imperial origins, influences, meanings and/or functionalities.

61. Sinclair and Williams 2007. See also Brogden 1987.

62. See Schrader 2019; Kuzmarov 2012; Harcourt 2018; Hinton 2017; McCoy 2009. Much of this work focuses on federal governance rather than local-level policing. Also, much of it focuses on recent history (e.g., McCoy 2009) to discuss federal programs and policies in the mid- to late twentieth century. Earlier waves of militarization are left undetected.

63. Other studies show that policies such as the 1033 Program or President Johnson's "war on crime" provide the impetus for police departments to militarize. This too, as we will see, has also been an important path toward militarization, generating new waves of transformation in policing. But it is very different from the agency of military veterans who return home to militarize on their own accord. Taken together, these examples from the extant historiography on militarization suggest that there are possibly different paths to militarization.

64. Also, much of the existing scholarship analyzes individuals who imported things from colonial sites but give less attention to what the things are—the actual tools, tactics, materials, and mentalities they brought back with them and how these transformed policing at home.

65. For an analysis of the boomerang effect upon various aspects of state-formation, see also Coyne and Hall 2018.

66. Newton 1967, 4.

67. Omi and Winant 1986, 111.

68. Go 2004.

69. Asst. Commissioner to HO, April 10, 1952, MEPO 2/9047, PRO.

70. Bhabha 1994.

71. Mbembe 2017, 10.

72. Nijjar 2018.

73. Fanon 1968 (1961), 40.
74. The classic work is Becker 1963.
75. Muhammad 2010.
76. Magubane 2004; Stoler 1995.
77. Asst. Commissioner to HO, April 10, 1952, MEPO 2/9047, PRO.
78. The racialization of crime and disorder and subsequent police responses relate to "racial threat" theory and research that shows that police expenditures increased in US cities with a greater proportion of racial minorities, or at historical moments when more racial minorities are present (Jackson and Carroll 1981). Research also shows how police use of force increases for the same reason (Parker et al. 2005). For the literature, see Smith 2021.
79. The critical interrogation by Hall et al. (1978) of the moral panic in London in the early 1970s is informative. Hall and coauthors meticulously chart how incidents of pickpocketing turned into a full-scale crisis of so-called mugging assumed to be practiced by Black Caribbean youths. This process relates to but is not reducible to "moral panics" (Cohen 1972).
80. I am informed in particular by critical realism in historical sociology (Gorski 2013; Steinmetz 1998) about which there is much to say. But simply put, I take from critical realism the following principles: (1) against radical constructivism, there is a social reality that can be accessed by observers; (2) the levels of that social reality are multiple; (3) there are patterns in that reality that manifest as events and that can be explained by examining the often invisible causal mechanisms shaping those patterns and the multiple causes shaping events.
81. I here follow principles of comparative social science that aim to uncover causal processes by looking across cases. See Go (2014b) and Mahoney (2003).
82. Go and Lawson (2020); Go (2014c).

# Chapter 1

1. Clarkson and Richardson 1889, 71.
2. Clarkson and Richardson 1889, 70.
3. Reith 1956, 154–155.
4. *The Standard*, April 26, 1831, 4.
5. Ascoli 1979, 7.
6. Critchley 1978, 31; see also Harris 2004, 16, and Emsley 1986, 70.
7. Critchley 1978, 34.
8. Palmer 1977, 637.
9. Lyman 1964, 154.
10. Reiner 2000, 51; Gash 1961, 52; Fuld 1910, 20–22; Hay and Snyder 1989, 5.
11. The financial district, known as the City, retained a different police organization and jurisdiction (Harris 2004).
12. *TL*, September 25, 1829, 2; italics in original. See also "Return of All General Orders Issued by the Secretary of State," House of Commons, June 7, 1830, 4–5, PP.

13. House of Commons, April 15, 1829, vol. 21, col. 883, HPD.

14. *NYTRI*, April 27, 1902, 5.

15. Bayley 1975, 328–329.

16. Miller 1977, 49.

17. Critchley 1978, 51; Miller 1977, 33.

18. Waddington 1991, 125.

19. Philips 2003.

20. Palmer 1988, 381–382, 287–288.

21. Gatrell 2008, 250–251.

22. Select Committee on the Police of the Metropolis 1828, 46.

23. McDonald 1982.

24. *Morning Chronicle*, April 16, 1829, 2.

25. Peel and Parker 1899, I:432.

26. Lyman 1964, 151.

27. Colquhoun 1806, 316–317, 352, 354.

28. Colquhoun 1806, 358.

29. Mainwaring 1821, 6–8; Silver 1965, 6.

30. Quoted in Gatrell 2008, 251.

31. Lees 1979, 29; Ó Gráda 1988, 68.

32. Lewis 1836, 7; Virdee 2014, 12.

33. George 1965, 140, 358–359.

34. Lees 1979, 45–47.

35. Bermant 1975, 43. For the concept of the "subproletariat," I am drawing partly from Oppenheimer (1974), who distinguishes the subproletariat from the "lumpenproletariat" as well as the higher-paid unionized working class and who stresses that the subproletariat is typically racialized or ethnically different from the higher-paid and regularly employed working class.

36. George 1965, 113–114.

37. George 1965, 125. A report in 1796–1797 on London beggars found that there were about 5,097 such beggars and that the Irish were disproportionately represented (2,862 Irish out of 5,097).

38. Quoted in Belchem 1985, 87.

39. *LQR* 37 (January–March 1828): 563.

40. Quoted in King 2013, 393.

41. Quoted in George 1965, 121.

42. Lewis 1836, 7–8.

43. Ó Tauthaigh 1985; MacRaild 1999, 58; Renshaw 2018, 20; King 2013, 393–394.

44. *Manchester Times*, July 9, 1836, 4.

45. MacRaild 1999, 58; Renshaw 2018, 20; Curtis 1971, 21.

46. Hickman 1995, 49.

47. Curtis 1971, 100.

48. Kay-Shuttleworth 1832, 25, 12.

49. *LQR* 37 (January–March 1828): 575.

50. The influx of Irish immigrants in the wake of 1815, and the concomitant anxieties it fueled, led to the formation of various parliamentary committees, investigations, and hearings.
51. Jackson 1963, 57–58.
52. Quotes from George 1965, 119, 124; see also Select Committee on Mendicity in the Metropolis 1815, 240.
53. *LQR* 37 (January–March 1828): 565.
54. Quoted in Swift 1989, 163 (originally in *The Scotsman*, December 27, 1828).
55. Committee on the State of the Police of the Metropolis 1817, 340.
56. George 1965, 120.
57. Colquhoun 1806, 354.
58. Colquhoun 1806, 13–15 (quote on 353).
59. Crymble 2018; Renshaw 2018, 19.
60. King 2013, 402.
61. King 2018, 25, 44; Swift 1989, 165.
62. Swift 1989, 166.
63. George 1965, 119.
64. Quoted in Crossman 1991, 309.
65. Peel and Parker 1899, I:239.
66. Peel and Parker 1899, I:236.
67. Quoted in Ellison and Smyth 2000, 9.
68. Lebow 1976, 43, 46.
69. Renshaw 2018, 18.
70. Quoted in King 2013, 394.
71. Committee on the State of the Police of the Metropolis 1817, 151.
72. Jackson 1963, 57, 135–136.
73. Nelson 2012.
74. *LQR* 37 (January–March 1828): 567.
75. Lees 1979, 237–241.
76. Belchem 1985, 88.
77. E. P. Thompson as quoted in Berresford Ellis 1996, 136.
78. Quoted in MacRaild 1999, 129.
79. Quoted in Virdee 2014, 30.
80. Quoted in Palmer 1988, 288–289.
81. Ó Catháin 2019; Philips 1980, 182; Reith 1943, 26–28.
82. King 2018, 6.
83. Quoted in Palmer 1988, 288–289.
84. Peel and Parker 1899, I:405; also Hay and Snyder 1989, 10.
85. Quoted in Palmer 1988, 288–289.
86. Emsley 1996, 23.
87. Colquhoun 1806, 358.
88. Kay-Shuttleworth 1832, 21.
89. The other perceived problem was worse: many of the watch were actually Irish. This would later feed into Rowan and Mayne's notion that officers should not be

appointed from within their own residential districts. See Select Committee on the Police of the Metropolis 1828, 25, and Miller 1977, 32.

90. Quoted in Lewis 1836, 86–87.
91. Lewis 1836, 86.
92. Swift 1989, 166.
93. Select Committee on the Police of the Metropolis 1828, 25–26, 28, 61, 67, 95, 193, 197.
94. Peel and Parker 1899, II:111–112.
95. MacRaild 1999, 48.
96. Peel and Parker 1899, II:111–112, quotes on 113.
97. Of course, there were other factors to the formation of the new police, including political competition (Watts Miller 1987). The point here has been to highlight factors that have received less attention (specifically, racialized threats).
98. Lees 1979, 215–219.
99. Summerfield and Law 2016, 191.
100. Cusick 2013, 207.
101. Soulsby 2018, 32; Summerfield and Law 2016, 62. Moore's innovations were partly codified in the official *1789 Irish Regulations* (Summerfield and Law 2016, 170).
102. Quoted in Palmer 1988, 151. On the Dublin police, see Dukova 2016.
103. Peel and Parker 1899, I:121–122, 236.
104. Broeker 1961, 366, 372.
105. "Plan of Police for Ireland, 1816," PRP, Add. MS 40202, vol. XXII, ff. 71–74. Also Gash 1961, 184.
106. Whitworth to Dismouth, April 21, 1814, PRO HO 100/177, 60. See also Ellison 2000, #4345, 5–15; King 2013, 393.
107. Palmer 1988, 152.
108. Peel to Wellesley, April 12, 1822, PRP, Add. MS 40324, ff. 33–45.
109. "Plan of Police for Ireland, 1816," PRP, Add. MS 40202, vol. XXII, f. 76.
110. Broeker 2017, 193.
111. Quoted in Hoppen 2016, 57.
112. Clarkson and Richardson 1889, 4.
113. Maitland 1885, 108.
114. Peel and Parker 1899, II:136.
115. Peel and Parker 1899, II:124.
116. Existing scholarship has pointed to some of the connections between the London Metropolitan Police and colonial Ireland (Brodgen 1987; Williams 2003). Here I flesh out the connections in greater detail and point to other colonial influences that existing scholarship has not yet detected.
117. "A bill for the more effectual administration of the office of a justice of the peace [for the] Dublin metropolis," PP, 1808, Bills and Acts series, no. 151; cf. "A bill . . . for improving the police in and near the metropolis," PP, 1829, Bills and Acts series, no. 245. Notably Peel also justified the force's financing by making the same argument had had made to used to justify his Peace Preservation Force: it would protect landowners' property and trade (Peel and Parker 1899, II:113).

118. *Courier*, September 29, 1829, 1; "General Instructions," in Ascoli 1979, 43, 85.
119. Reith 1956, 131.
120. Palmer 1988, 409–411.
121. Peel to Gregory, May 29, 1829, in Peel and Parker 1899, II:114.
122. See "Minutes of Evidence" in House of Commons 1834, 9.
123. Palmer 1988, 299–300; Broeker 2017, 147; House of Commons 1834, 5.
124. Peel and Parker 1899, I:151.
125. Fosdick 1915, 200–204.
126. Miller 1977, 32.
127. Lyman 1964, 153.
128. Dukova 2016.
129. Palmer 1988, 418.
130. *London Courier and Evening Gazette*, September 29, 1829, 3.
131. House of Commons 1834, 3. Rowan would have been familiar with the beat system of the militia patrols in the West Indies and the South from his army experience.
132. Quoted in Hadden 2001, 43.
133. Williams 2004, 40.
134. Hadden 2001, 15–17, 105–121; Reichel 1988, 61–62.
135. Stauffer 1987, 110.
136. McCord 1841, 358.
137. Quoted in Weir 1997, 195.
138. McCord 1841, 658.
139. Ascoli 1979, 85.
140. House of Commons 1834, 3.
141. Steedman 1984, 4.
142. Ascoli 1979, 82. Also, at Shorncliffe, light infantry officers were instructed to drill alongside the men, when previously most officers did very little or even no training (Summerfield and Law 2016, 155–159; Reith 1956, 29–59).
143. Moylan 1929, 102; Miller 1977, 41.
144. House of Commons 1830, 6. The instructions were officially signed by Peel but, as historians note, the details and the language were mostly written by Rowan, with legal language supplied by Mayne (Reith 1956, 135–150).
145. Prominent police reformer Edwin Chadwick reckoned the likeness. The only difference was that the "Irish Constabulary is a superior military force adapted to the suppression of riots & insurrections" but it "is not essentially a civil preventive police." Therefore, the London Met marked "a great advance upon the Irish Constabulary for the ordinary purposes of a Police" (Palmer 1988, 754).
146. Claeys 1989, 184.
147. See Campion 2005.
148. On the surveillance of the Irish nationalists by Dublin Castle, see Bartlett 1998.
149. Miller 1977, 124.
150. House of Commons 1834, 241.
151. House of Commons 1834, 11.
152. Watts 1864, 161–162, 165.

153. *TL*, March 13, 1886, 4.

154. House of Commons 1834, 266.

155. Quoted in Hodder 1877, 197–198.

156. House of Commons 1834, 32.

157. Inwood 1990, 135, 130, 134.

158. Wade 1837, 174–175, 177.

159. These figures are from random samples from 1830 to 1838 of the "Daily Reports" of the Metropolitan Police Office (MEPO 4, Office of the Commissioner). The reports do not give ethnicity or place of birth, which I then estimated using the surnames method developed by Crymble (2014).

160. Judicial statistics suggest that the Irish were arrested at higher rates *and* sent to prison at higher rates (Fitzpatrick 1989, 25; Swift 1989, 164–165).

161. *TL*, March 13, 1886, 11.

162. Reproduced in Reith 1956, 140. Whether these are actually the exact same "principles" Peel spelled out for his force remains disputed by historians. On their "invented" character, see Lentz and Chaires 2007. If they were in fact retrospectively "invented," this speaks to the larger point about the ideology, and performativity, of the "civil police."

163. As quoted in Miller 1977, 16.

164. Miller 1977, 13.

165. Miller 1977, 49; Reiner 2000, 50.

166. Moore 1992, 155–156.

167. Wallas 1925, 9. See also Smith 1985, 117, and *The Guardian*, June 26, 1930, 9.

168. Moore 1992, 156.

169. *TL*, April 15, 1829.

170. Quoted in Jefferson 1990, ix.

171. Quotes from Emsley 1996, 26. See also Clarkson and Richardson 1889, 63.

172. None of this is to say that the new police *only* targeted Irish immigrants or Irish-Anglo laborers. Once created in response to perceived racialized threats, the tools and tactics of the new police could be used on anyone, and they were directed at other parts of the working class too. See Inwood 1990 and Miller 1977, 120–139.

173. Peel and Parker 1899, II:113.

# Chapter 2

1. *NYDH*, March 4, 1845, 2; see also January 9, 1843, 2, and July 17, 1843, 1.

2. See Monkkonen 1981, 55.

3. Beckert 2014, 121, ix; Clapham 1932, 24–37; Bailey 1994, 37.

4. Bailey 1994, 37.

5. Floud and Johnson 2004, 186; Hall 2017; PP 1826–1827 (290), XVIII, 265.

6. Hood 2016, 86–88.

7. Hall 2017.

8. Kay-Shuttleworth 1832, 7.

9. Reimers et al. 2019, 29.

10. Ignatiev 1995, 109–110.

11. Bancroft 1848, 5.

12. Shoemaker 1990, 4.

13. Fraser 2003, 273.

14. Ayers 1985, 80.

15. Lewis 1836, 7–8.

16. Hadden 2001; Elliott and Strobel 1835, iv, ix, x. For an earlier reference to "beat companies" in South Carolina, see the *Columbian Herald*, March 17, 1788, 3.

17. Hadden 2001, 19–20, 42–47.

18. Cooper 1838, vol. 3, part 1, 396.

19. Quoted in Hadden 2001, 67.

20. Quote in Rousey 1996, 17.

21. Rousey 1996, 16–17, 22; Wagner 2009, 63.

22. Rousey 1996, 13–19.

23. Some militia, patrol, and watch members even developed their own incipient if not prescient forms of military counter insurgency operations. For instance, they patrolled on horseback as well as on foot, and in the towns they surveiled suspects as spies later would. See Hadden 2001, 121–124.

24. Levinson 2005.

25. Swanson 2021.

26. The law creating the new police in Manchester, Birmingham, and Bolton was meant to be temporary; after it expired, the new police forces were maintained.

27. Hewitt 1979, 67; Busteed 2016, 14; Pooley 1989, 66.

28. Busteed 2016, 15–16.

29. Quoted in Werly 1973, 353.

30. Lewis 1836, 518–519.

31. Kay-Shuttleworth 1832, 24–28.

32. Kay-Shuttleworth 1832, 26.

33. Kay in Lewis 1836, 7.

34. Kay-Shuttleworth 1832, 7.

35. Kay-Shuttleworth 1832, 21, 27–28.

36. Lewis 1836, 46.

37. Lewis 1836, 88.

38. "First Report of the Commissioners appointed to inquire as to the best means of establishing an efficient Constabulary Force in the counties of England and Wales," PP 1839, XIX, 88.

39. "First Report," PP 1839, XIX, 87; also see Kay-Shuttleworth 1832, 26.

40. Quoted in Hewitt 1979, 67.

41. O'Higgins 1961, 83.

42. Palmer 1988, 412.

43. Palmer 1988, 413. This practice of sending London police to help advise local forces and in some cases serve as auxiliary powers followed Rowan's initial vision for the

London Metropolitan Police—a vision informed by Peel's counterinsurgency operations in Ireland, whereby members of his Peace Preservation Force were dispatched to so-called troubled areas.

44. Palmer 1988, 415.

45. Bouverie to HO, May 6, 1829, HO 40/23/239, PRO; see also Palmer 1988, 415.

46. Quotes from Lewis 1836, 87, 89.

47. Petitions in HO 40/30/2/113–116, PRO; Col. Shaw (via Bouverie) to HO, February 5, 1832, and Shaw to Crawford, February 5, 1832, HO 40/30/2/114, PRO. See also Palmer 1988, 415.

48. *Manchester Times*, January 7, 1837, 4.

49. Quoted in Palmer 1988, 416; see also Hewitt 1979, 48–49.

50. "First Report . . . ," PP 1839, vol. 19, XIX, 87.

51. Kay-Shuttleworth 1832, 26, emphasis added.

52. Quotes from Lewis 1836, 43, 47.

53. Pooley 1989, 66.

54. Weaver 1994.

55. Palmer 1988, 416–417.

56. Quoted in Mather 1959, 121.

57. Palmer 1988, 418.

58. Palmer 1988, 418.

59. Channing 2018, 175–176.

60. Weaver 1994, 295.

61. Weaver 1994, 295, quotes on 296.

62. Weinberger 1991, 70; 1851 Irish population from Pooley 1989, 66–67.

63. Philips 1977, 65.

64. *Manchester Guardian*, September 7, 1839, 2; Davies 1985, 31, 34.

65. Mather 1959, 123.

66. Quoted in Hewitt 1979, 56.

67. Palmer 1988, 400.

68. *Manchester Guardian*, June 15, 1850, 8.

69. Hewitt 1979, 58.

70. Watch Committee Bourough of Manchester 1844, 31; "Number of Persons Taken into Custody . . ." for 1840 to 1843, ref. 352.2.M1, PCM; Hewitt 1979, 60–67. It is not clear whether "Irish" in these figures refers to Irish-born only or if it includes those born of Irish-born parents, but given the typical classifications of the time, it is likely "Irish-born." Over the next decades, 80 percent of all arrests in Manchester were in the "A" police division, one of the main working-class parts of town (Davies 1985, 39).

71. In 1839, Parliament also passed the County Police Act, which enabled county magistrates to appoint constables to replace the existing system of parish constable, led by an appointed chief constable. The subsequent county forces were heavily militarized, and their creation was likely also sparked by fears of Irish disorder and crime. See Midwinter 1968, 8, 12, 16; Philips and Storch 1999; and the testimonies in Royal Commission 1839.

72. In 1838, the city of Boston established a new police corps to replace the constables and to work alongside the existing watchmen, copying London's model, but because the new corps did not replace the constable-watch system, it was not the same as modern police forces today. Similarly, while it has been claimed that slave patrols in New Orleans were the first real police forces in the United States, these did not replace the constable-watch system or militia and they mainly enforced the slave codes. Slave patrols did not represent a centralization and monopolization of the functions of crime management and the repression of social disorder. Slave patrols were an early *form* of policing, but they were not the same as current police departments.

73. Calculated from data in New York City Board of Aldermen 1844. For comparison, parliamentary reports on crime in London suggested that crime increased in the London and Middlesex areas from 1811 to 1827 by about 55 percent, while the population increased at a rate of only 19 percent (Select Committee on the Police of the Metropolis 1828, 5–7).

74. Hood 2016, 86–87.

75. Quoted in Costello 1885, 76.

76. Richardson 1970, 26.

77. Richardson 1974, 19.

78. New York City Board of Assistants. 1836. Doc. no. 81, September 12, 1836, 213–225.

79. Richardson 1974, 20.

80. Lardner and Reppetto 2000, 17.

81. Quoted in Richardson 1970, 27.

82. Dolan 1940, 859–860.

83. Costello 1885, 77.

84. Ignatiev 1995, 38; on the almshouse, see Hirota 2017, 60.

85. New York City Board of Aldermen 1827, 564.

86. New York City Board of Aldermen 1827, 562–563.

87. *NYDH*, July 1, 1844, 2.

88. *NYTRI*, March 13, 1844, 2.

89. Richardson 1974, 23; Costello 1885, 76.

90. New York City Board of Alderman 1837, 562–563.

91. *NYDH*, January 12, 1843, 2, emphasis added.

92. New York City Board of Aldermen 1844, 692.

93. Richardson 1970, 25–26.

94. *NYDH*, January 31, 1843, 1.

95. This was the party that was most likely responsible for circulating racialized derogatory images of European immigrants before those immigrants had become "whitened" later in the century.

96. Quotes in Reimers et al. 2019, 37.

97. Ibid.

98. Quotes in Dolan 1940, 859, and Richardson 1970, 27.

99. *NYTRI*, May 15, 1844, 1. For more on the nativists' views of Catholics, see Hirota 2017, 49, and Canny 1973.

100. Reimers et al. 2019, 38.

101. On these policies and views, see *NYDH*, April 4, 1844, 1; Hirota 2017, 54–55; Scisco 1901, 243; and Binder and Reimers 1996, 71.

102. Richardson 1970, 47.

103. *Evening Post*, October 1, 1844, 2; *NYDH*, October 1, 1844, 1.

104. "An Act Relative to the Police," in New York City Board of Aldermen 1837, 580–581. On other Democrats' plans, see *Evening Post*, March 26, 1844, 2; "Report of the Special Committee," December 27, 1843, doc. 19, 183–196, in New York City Board of Aldermen 1843; and Richardson 1970, 42–44.

105. *Brooklyn Evening Star*, April 17, 1844, 2; *NYDH*, April 12, 1844, 3.

106. *NYDH*, February 6, 1845, 2; also Richardson 1970, 47–48, and Gerard 1853, 18.

107. *NYDH*, February 6, 1845, 2; quotes from *NYT*, June 4, 1871, 8, discussing the police retrospectively.

108. *NYDH*, March 4, 1845, 2.

109. Richardson 1970, 297n36.

110. Cotton to Harper, June 8, 1844, JHP.

111. Roach to Harper, November 23, 1844, JHP.

112. *Evening Post*, April 27, 1844, 2, and May 1, 1844, 1; Costello 1885, 100; New York City Police Department 1851, 26–33.

113. *NYDH*, January 22, 1845, 2. See the important discussion of this issue in Miller 1977, 35–36.

114. On the uniforms, see Costello 1885, 129. Quotes from *New York Daily Times*, June 24, 1853, 4, and Costello 1885, 127. See also *NYDH*, April 25, 1853, 4; *Brooklyn Evening Star*, December 13, 1855, 2; and Richardson 1970, 64.

115. *NYDH*, April 25, 1853, 4.

116. *Brooklyn Daily Eagle*, November 15, 1853, 2; "An Act in Relation to the Police Department April 13, 1853," doc. no. 24, Board of Aldermen, vol. 20, 1, no. 1–34 (January–June 1853), 501–511. Also see Costello 1885, 127–131, and Palmer 1978, 384.

117. Rules and regulations of the New York police quoted in Forte 2000, 20; see also Palmer 1978, 384.

118. *NYTRI*, May 28, 1855, 5.

119. *NYT*, March 22, 1855, 2.

120. Miller 1977, 29–30, 51; Richardson 1970, 68.

121. *NYDH,* February 5, 1856, 2.

122. Quote from Miller 1977, 22.

123. *NYDH*, June 5, 1852, 4.

124. Richardson 1970, 51; Glazer and Moynihan 1974, 219.

125. Quoted in Ignatiev 1995, 111.

126. Miller 1968, 163.

127. Quoted in Wei Tchen 1996, 130; see also Ernst 1948, 176–182, and Hirota 2017, 59, 66–67. Some historians suggest that city politics in the 1850s remained divided between two main sides: nativists who had been previously represented in the American Nativists (who in the 1850s became the Know Nothings) and Democrats.

The Democrats, according to this view, were the party of the Irish Catholics (Richardson 1970, 71). But this is misleading, for it overlooks how a more virulent anti-immigrant discourse spread from nativists to the mainstream Whig Party and the Democratic Party too. This is also partly because the demise of the American Republicans as a party organization sent some former members to the ranks of the Whigs.

128. *NYDH*, January 8, 1852, 7.

129. Quoted in Chadwick 2017, 242.

130. Gerard in *NYDH*, April 9, 1853, 2, and Gerard 1853, 8.

131. *NYDH*, February 5, 1856, 2.

132. E.g., *NYDH*, June 5, 1852, 4, and November 22, 1852, 3; *NYT*, April 6, 1853, 4, and June 24, 1853, 4; Chadwick 2017, 258.

133. Gerard 1853, 8, 9, 23–24.

134. Gerard 1853, 14.

135. Gerard 1853, 17, 23–24.

136. Hirota 2014, 16.

137. *NYTRI*, May 28, 1855, 5.

138. *NYDH*, February 5, 1856, 2.

139. Walling 1887, 48; *Brooklyn Daily Eagle*, August 1, 1853, 2.

140. Chadwick 2017, 224; *NYTRI*, March 17, 1853, 3; on Irish arrests, see Miller 1977, 153.

141. *NYT*, January 23, 1852, 4, and March 18, 1853, 3; Costello 1885, 131.

142. New York City Board of Metropolitan Police 1866, 33. The wealthy were rarely arrested (Chadwick 2017, 230).

143. The correlation coefficient of Irish residents and police per capita: Pearson's $r = .465$, sig. at $< .05$ level, two-tailed. This excludes the Second Ward, which is an outlier (and probably due to the fact that it was a major manufacturing district). The Fifteenth and Second Wards did not have many Irish, but they were wealthy residential and commercial areas that would have required more police to "protect" the wealthy. Patronage politics might have also played a role, but even then, as Miller (1977, 53) shows, Irish police officers tended to arrest Irish residents disproportionately and treat them harshly.

144. *SDR*, April 19, 1855, 2, and June 9, 1854, 4.

145. As quoted in Wade 1964, 101.

146. Haunton 1968, 244; *SDR*, January 30, 1852, 2.

147. Haunton 1968, 67–75.

148. Fraser 2003, 282–284.

149. Quoted in Haunton 1968, 3.

150. Haunton 1968, 78.

151. Johnson 1999, 93.

152. For these figures, see Ayers 1985, 77; Fraser 2003, 254; Shoemaker 1990, 4; and Anbinder 2015, 7.

153. Ayers 1985, 80.

154. Fraser 2003, 305; see also Shoemaker 1990 and Anbinder 2015.

155. Ignatiev 1995, 41.

156. Gleeson 2001, 105.
157. Ayers 1985, 80; Haunton 1968, 76–78.
158. Parsons 1855, 23.
159. Quote in Shryock 1929, 45. *Savannah Daily Journal and Courier*, February 6, 1855, 2; Haunton 1968, 252.
160. Quoted in Wade 1964, 86.
161. *SDR*, January 30, 1852, 2.
162. *SDR*, March 24, 1855, 2.
163. *SDG*, May 17, 1854, 2. The majority of defendants in the courts for violent crimes against the person and property in the 1850s were unskilled laborers, mainly Irish (Ayers 1985, 100, 298). A report on crime in 1854 noted that crime statistics relating to the Black population are always going to be misleading because so "many offences committed by slaves . . . never appear on public records" because they are "punished by the master or his agent." This report also asserted that more serious crimes would never be reported by the master for fear of their slave being jailed, thus depriving them of their labor (*SDN*, February 3, 1854, 1.
164. Haunton 1972, 9–10.
165. Bancroft 1848, 20; Gamble 1900, 25, 58–68, 198–199; Shoemaker 1990, 192–193.
166. Bancroft 1848, 20; Gamble 1900, 198.
167. Harden 1934, 17.
168. Quoted in Haunton 1968, 14.
169. Quoted in Ayers 1985, 83. See also *SDG*, May 17, 1854, 2; *SDR*, January 24, 1851, 2.
170. Gamble 1900, 198, 239.
171. Dr. W. C. Daniel to Hon. Howell Cobb, January 4, 1850, in HCP. See also Haunton 1972, 4.
172. *SDR*, October 2, 1852, 2; see also *SDN*, September 14, 1852, 1.
173. *SDG*, May 21, 1854, 2.
174. *SDG*, July 1, 1854, 4; *SDN*, January 25, 1856, 2; report, Anderson, year ending October 31, 1856, 4, MCSAV; *SDR*, February 21, 1856, 2.
175. *SDR*, April 19, 1855, 2.
176. Report, Anderson, year ending October 31, 1856, 5, MCSAV.
177. *SDN*, January 25, 1856, 2.
178. *SDR*, April 19, 1855, 2, and April 21, 1855, 2.
179. *SDG*, July 1, 1854 4; *SMN*, November 21, 1854, 2.
180. Gamble 1900, 239.
181. Report, Anderson, year ending October 31, 1856, 5, MCSAV.
182. *SDR*, April 19, 1855, 2; *Charleston Daily Courier*, January 15, 1856, 1.
183. *SDN*, November 21, 1854, 2.
184. *CDC*, January 15, 1856, 1.
185. Roth 1998, 708; Gould and Waldren 1986, 15.
186. *CDC*, January 15, 1856, 1.
187. Hadden 2001, 121–122. A notable exception is in the early 1800s, when the city of New Orleans had also formed an urban mounted unit as part of its force. City officials in Savannah, like Anderson, had become familiar with this tradition of

mounted patrols not only from their connections to frontier wars in Mexico and Florida but also since they were leaders of local militia units.

188. *CDC*, January 15, 1856, 1.

189. *CDC*, January 15, 1856, 1.

190. *SDG*, July 1, 1854, 4.

191. Farley 1969, 71.

192. Quoted in Shoemaker 1990, 357. See Anderson's letter to Charleston officials about the new police in *SDR*, February 21, 1856, 2.

193. Ayers 1985, 88.

194. *SDR*, March 24, 1855, 2.

195. Random sample of arrest entries, "Jail Records," 1855–1858, SPD.

196. Ayers 1985, 75; Gleeson 2001, 48. The sample is 234 defendants in the 1850s, the majority of whom (230) were white (only 4 were Black).

197. *NYDH*, July 17, 1843, 1.

198. *NYDH*, March 4, 1845, 2; see also *NYDH*, January 9, 1843, 2; *NYDH*, July 17, 1843, 1.

199. *NYDH*, March 4, 1845, 2.

200. Miller 1977, 53.

201. Palmer 1978, 383–385.

202. Miller 1977, 51.

203. Miller 1977, 49–50; see also Ingleton 1996, 36.

204. Palmer 1988, 441.

205. Ingleton 1996, 38.

206. Quoted in Satia 2019, 3.

207. See Satia 2019, 4, and Dunbar-Ortiz 2018.

208. Quoted in Miller 1977, 53.

209. The same logic would explain why, within the United States, the SPD was armed from the get-go: given the long history of slave insurrection, armed forces were much more common, and the public had become accustomed to them (e.g., Rousey 1996 and Wintersmith 1974, 37). Fittingly, Savannah's was the first police force in the United States that looked more like the Caribbean and Irish colonial forces of the British empire—fitted with firearms, other weapons, and mounted patrols—than the police of London, Manchester, or New York. If this was a colonial boomerang effect, it was also a historical *continuation* of previous colonial-military forms.

210. Mitrani 2013, 25–27; Swift 1984.

211. Burgess-Parker n.d.

212. Monkkonen 1981.

# Chapter 3

1. Address, July 8, 1927, Box 48, BPD.

2. Vollmer to Smith, January 3, 1930, Box 40, AVP.

3. Quoted in Leichtman 2014, 64.

4. Fogelson 1977; Harring 1983, 30; Walker 1977.

5. *The Crisis,* October 1911, 311, and November 1911, 20.

6. National Commision on Law Observance and Enforcement 1931, 4.

7. *Albuquerque Journal,* December 30, 1912, 4.

8. National Commission on Law Observance and Enforcement 1931, 67.

9. *Chicago Tribune,* February 27, 1907, 6;

10. National Commission on Law Observance and Enforcement 1931, 56.

11. Monkkonen 1992, 554–555; Walker 1977, 8–10.

12. Harring 1983, 26–30, Walker 1977, 3–31, Williams 2004, 125.

13. Walker 1977, 8–28; Monkkonen 1992, 554–555.

14. Fogelson 1977, 58–59, 97–98.

15. Vollmer 1933, 163–175, Graper 1921, 128–122.

16. Fosdick 1920, 298–302.

17. Harring 1983, 34.

18. Graper 1921, 276–305.

19. Paynich and Hill 2010, 10–12.

20. Vollmer 1939, 3–4; Vollmer 1933, 166.

21. US Bureau of the Census 1916, 17–18.

22. Vollmer quoted in Shaw, ch. 37, n.p. Microfilm 3089, AVP.

23. US Bureau of the Census 1910, 101; US Bureau of the Census 1916, 18.

24. Graper 1921, 165.

25. Vollmer 1933, 166.

26. Fuld 1910, 461–462.

27. National Commission on Law Observance and Enforcement 1931, 86; see also Vollmer 1933, 165.

28. Walker 1977; Monkkonen 1981, ch. 4; Monkkonen 1992, 556; Wertsch 1992.

29. Go 2011, 38–39, 54–66; Immerwahr 2016.

30. Katznelson 2002.

31. Williams 1981, 310.

32. Linn 2000.

33. Go 2011, 61–62, 83–93.

34. Cosmas 1998, 14.

35. Williams 1981, 309.

36. On these reforms, see Ball 1984; Clark 2017, 167–196; Kaplan 2001; Nenninger 1978; White 1995.

37. Jamieson 1994, 101.

38. Quoted from Williams 1981, 311; Birtle 2009, 114–115.

39. Hernandez 2010.

40. Birtle 2009, 114. On how continental frontier experiences shaped the US military's approach to the new colonies, see Bjork 2019.

41. Linn 1991, 98.

42. Birtle 2009, 115.

43. Linn 2000, 325.

44. McCoy 2015, 7.

45. Linn 1991, 101.
46. McCoy 2015, 7.
47. Bickel 2001, 42.
48. Bickel 2001, 81–87; Kuzmarov 2012, 41. See also Chapter 5.
49. Cosmas 1998.
50. Birtle 2009, 100. It was partly through the organizational transformations attendant on empire that the US military became the globally oriented force smoothing America's entry into the First World War (Kaplan 2001, 2).
51. Thompson 2010.
52. United States Philippine Commission 1901, I:59.
53. Kuzmarov 2012, 25; Forbes 1928, I:204–205.
54. Quoted in McCoy 2009, 134. The US colonial state also created the Philippine Scouts, a unit of the US Army that incorporated locals under white officers (Laurie 1989).
55. United States Philippine Commission 1901, I:59.
56. United States Philippine Commission 1904, I:85.
57. Governor of Porto Rico 1901, 33.
58. *LAEE*, September 20, 1899, 8. On crime and policing in early US colonial Puerto Rico, see Santiago-Valles 1994.
59. Governor of Porto Rico 1901, 5.
60. Governor of Porto Rico 1901, 64.
61. *LAEE*, September 20, 1899, 8.
62. Oliver 2017.
63. Wilson 1953, 97.
64. Wilson 1953, 97.
65. Carte and Carte 1975, 23.
66. Schutt 1922.
67. "Police Progress," June 28, 1930, and "Minutes," February 25, 1927, Box 48, BPD.
68. Vollmer and Schneider 1917, 881.
69. Carte 1973, 278; *Chicago Tribune*, October 1, 1929, 3.
70. Walker 1977, 162–165.
71. Mason 1935.
72. Shaw, ch. 2, n.p., Microfilm 3089, AVP.
73. Vollmer to O'Reilly, January 6, 1930, Box 40, AVP.
74. "Important Events," Carton 1, AVP.
75. Oliver 2017, 162.
76. Fuld 1910, 339.
77. Vollmer to Greening, June 9, 1933, Box 42, AVP.
78. Wilson 1995, 97; "Police Organization," Box 3, AVP.
79. *Honolulu Star Bulletin*, June 5, 1923, 1.
80. Vollmer to Mills, August 24, 1923, Box 40, AVP.
81. *LAT*, August 2, 1923, 2.
82. Shaw, ch. 37, n.p., Microfilm 3089, AVP.
83. "Police Organization," Box 3, AVP.
84. Vollmer to Jenkins, November 30, 1929, Box 40, AVP.

85. Oliver 2017, 381.
86. "Police Progress," June 28, 1930, Box 48, BPD.
87. Bidwell 1986, 63–64; Moseley 1904. The connections between crime mapping and military mapping are not yet explored in conventional histories (cf. Kindynis 2014). Police expert Fuld later noted the military origins of crime mapping (1910, 339).
88. Vollmer to J.S. Mills, August 24, 1923, Box 40, AVP; *Tulsa Tribune*, November 23, 1923, 22.
89. Quoted in Shaw, ch. 37, n.p. Microfilm 3089, AVP; *LAT*, October 13, 1923, 21.
90. "Minutes," February 25, 1927, Box 48, BPD.
91. "Police Progress," June 28, 1930, Box 48, BPD.
92. Vollmer, "The Police Beat," ms., 12, Carton 3, AVP.
93. Vollmer to Mills, August 24, 1923, Box 40, AVP; *Tulsa Tribune*, November 23, 1923, 22.
94. *LAEE*, August 21, 1923, 1; *Long Beach Press-Telegram*, January 14, 1924, 1.
95. Shaw, ch. 38, n.p. Microfilm 3089, AVP.
96. *LAEE*, September 13, 1923, 19; *OT*, January 22, 1924, 19.
97. *LAEE*, August 22, 1923, 55.
98. Parker 1961, 144.
99. Vollmer to Greening, June 9, 1933, Box 42, AVP; Carte et al. 1983, xi n. 9. One of his students, Carte, later wrote, "He came to admire the organizational skills of the professional army corps, and frequently referred to his army experience in later years when discussing the strategy of police operations" (Carte et al. 1983, v).
100. Vollmer to Glueck, December 2, 1932, Series XII, "General Correspondence," GP.
101. "Minutes," February 25 and March 1, 1929, Box 48, BPD.
102. "Minutes," September 24, 1926, Box 48, BPD.
103. Carte et al. 1983, 3; IACP 1920, 65–66.
104. Vollmer, "Police Organization and Administration," ms., C-B403, Box 3, 22, AVP
105. IACP 1909, 8; 1914, 98, 1900, 5.
106. IACP 1909, 44–47. On Los Angeles policing and the "hobo" problem, see Lytle Hernández 2014.
107. IACP 1904, 6. In 1895, terms like "army," "soldier," "war," "battle," or "military" began to appear at the rate of 1.6 per 100 total words; in 1897 at a rate of 5.1 per 100 total words; in 1903 and 1904 at a rate of 5.6 per 100 words; in 1907, 1910, and 1914 at a rate of 8.3 per 100 words (calculated from the *Proceedings* of the IACP). A search of the biggest newspapers of the time reaching back to the 1850s (*New York Times, Boston Globe, Los Angeles Times, Chicago Daily Tribune,* and *Washington Post*) shows that the phrase "war on crime" does not appear until 1897, where it is used once to refer to a new police initiative in St. Louis. It appears again in 1900; thereafter it becomes used more often.
108. Sylvester 1910, 16–17.
109. Leonard Felix Fuld, a member of the New York Civil Service board and a prominent police reformer, promoted centralized police structures by referring to the military as his model (Fuld 1910, 340). The words "army," "soldier," or "military" appear on at least eighty-five pages of Fuld's book on policing.

110. New York Committee on the Police Problem 1905, 220, 120.

111. New York Committee on the Police Problem 1905, 105.

112. New York Committee on the Police Problem 1905, 12.

113. Vollmer 1933, 163–175; Graper 1921, 128–122; Fosdick 1920, 298–302.

114. IACP 1903, 53–54.

115. RMP 1912, 282.

116. Berman 1987, 61–62.

117. IACP 1899, 17.

118. Berger 2014, para. 10.

119. *SMN*, January 23, 1907, 12; MCSAV 1892, 12, and 1893, 13.

120. Berger 2014, para. 9.

121. E.g., IACP 1910, 18–19.

122. In the 1870s, the army gave the NRA surplus weapons, and in the early 1900s the NRA set up training programs at military schools and shaped the US Army's own instruction programs.

123. LAPD 1925, 1, 9.

124. Fosdick 1920, 303.

125. Vollmer to White, February 11, 1930, Box 40, AVP.

126. Vollmer 1933, 165.

127. *BDE*, February 5, 1906, 24, and April 22, 1906, 24. For the influences on the Pennsylvania State Police, which current scholars tend to assume rather than demonstrate, see Forbes 1928, I:58–59; Reinsch 1911, 217–221; Johnstone 2014, 51; Mayo 1917; Mayo 1922, 70, 91, 110, 132; Toland 2007, 12; United States Commission on Industrial Relations 1916, 10935.

128. Quotes from *PI*, November 11, 1906, 2; see also Mayo 1917, 59, 70–71; Conti 1977, 52.

129. *BDE*, February 5, 1906, 24.

130. *BDE*, April 22, 1906, 24.

131. *NYT*, July 8, 1905, 1.

132. *BDE*, February 5, 1906, 24. Previous labor troubles had been dealt with by hiring a private police force, the Pinkertons.

133. Williams 1921, 78.

134. Vollmer wrote positively about the Pennsylvania State Police's military orientation in his book on state police, comparing it to the colonial police of the Philippines, Puerto Rico, and the Panama Canal Zone (Vollmer and Parker 1935, 96–97, 140–141).

135. Vollmer also popularized and promoted his innovations through lectures, consulting work, and his leading role in the IACP.

136. It is difficult to determine how many of the rank and file of the police were military veterans, as records remain only at the city level. But one study of the St. Louis police suggests that the ranks were not overwhelmed by veterans (Watts 1981). My own investigation into the records of the Savannah police department shows that veterans serving in the rank and file of the police in the early twentieth century were the exception rather than the rule (Personnel Record books Sub-series 5600PL-060, SPD).

137. Go 2020.
138. *NYT*, December 4, 1898, 1.
139. Whalen and Whalen 2014, 17–26.
140. IACP 1912, 84.
141. *Indianapolis News*, July 16, 1920, 36.
142. Columbus Police Benevolent Association 1908, 95, 97.
143. Fogelson 1977, 58.
144. MCSAV 1893, 13; *SMN*, January 23, 1907, 12.
145. *SMN*, January 23, 1907, 12.
146. MCSAV 1907, 53; *SMN*, January 1, 1907, 16.
147. MCSAV 1907, 53; *SMN*, January 31, 1907, 16.
148. MCSAV 1908, 42; *SMN*, January 23, 1907, 12.
149. MCSAV 1908, 55.
150. *PI*, October 16, 1902, 2; September 12, 1909, 7.
151. *PI*, July 17, 1903, 5.
152. *PI*, September 5, 1912, 1.
153. Philadelphia Bureau of Police 1913, 6–7; Hershler 1900, 9.
154. RMP 1913, 107.
155. Toland 2007, 48–49.
156. United States Commission on Industrial Relations 1916, 10967.
157. IACP 1912, 89.
158. Yonkers Police Department n.d.
159. Katz 2021, 209–219.
160. Leichtman 2014, 65.
161. Kuzmarov 2012, 40.
162. *NYT*, January 21, 1924, 2.
163. RCDC 1899, 182–188; IACP 1915, 15; *WP*, June 24, 1901, 2, and March 19, 1902, 10.
164. *WP*, October 18, 1899, 12; *Washington Evening Star*, December 3, 1905, pt. 2, 8.
165. IACP 1920, 12.
166. *NYT*, April 9, 1910, 2.
167. Another explanation is that the reforms were a "natural if not inevitable, adjustment to changed social circumstances" brought about by industrialization and urbanization (Liebman and Polen 1978, 346).
168. Conti 1977, 31.
169. Feigenbaum 2017. The first use of tear gas in the United States was by the army in 1932.
170. Harring 1983; Donner 1990.
171. Go 2004.
172. Go 2004; Kramer 2006; Gossett 1997, 310–338.
173. Quoted in Go 2007, 79.
174. Kennan 2001, 82.
175. Davis 1899, 19–21, quote on 20.
176. Moehling and Piehl 2009, 740.
177. Beach 1932, 15.

178. Baldoz 2011.
179. Escobar 1999, 20–21.
180. Sacks 2005, 800.
181. Lane 1986, 7.
182. Miller 1975, 189–190.
183. Allen 2012; Johnson 2003, 59–60; Ignatiev 1995, 163; Roediger 1992; Jacobson 2000.
184. Muller 2012, 294; Richardson 1974, 53.
185. Muhammad 2010, 7. On empire and "Anglo-Saxons," see Kramer 2003.
186. Muhammad 2010, 3; Sacks 2005, 801.
187. Miller 1975, 184.
188. Beach 1932.
189. Quoted in Oliver 2017, 163. On race, crime, and opium, see Courtwright 2001, 111–140.
190. Foster 2010.
191. Turner 1968, 77; Turner 1971, 222.
192. IACP 1913, 98, 103.
193. IACP 1908, 124.
194. IACP 1899, 16.
195. Fosdick 1920, 9, 26.
196. On this colonial discourse, see Go 2004.
197. Carte and Carte 1975, 3.
198. IACP 1907, 9.
199. IACP 1920, 97.
200. IACP 1897, 29.
201. IACP 1899, 17.
202. IACP 1903, 54.
203. IACP 1902, 68.
204. OT, May 15, 1905, 11; San Francisco Call, January 31, 1905, 6.
205. Shaw, ch. 2, n.p. Microfilm 3089, AVP.
206. Shaw, ch. 2, n.p. Microfilm 3089, AVP. On the term "gugu," see Miller 1982, esp. 269–275.
207. Oakland Post-Enquirer article as quoted in Shaw, ch. 3, n.p. Microfilm 3089, AVP.
208. Berkeley Daily Gazette, April 27, 1905, 1.
209. Quoted in Shaw, ch. 3, n.p. Microfilm 3089, AVP. See also Wilson 1953, 94.
210. San Francisco Call, April 24, 1905, 4. See also San Francisco Examiner, June 18, 1906, 9, and Berkeley Daily Gazette, April 24, 1905, 1.
211. OT, May 15, 1905, 11.
212. OT, December 11, 1905, 12. Beach (1932) showed that in the 1920s Chinese and Japanese in California tended to be arrested for offenses relating to drugs, prostitution, and gaming and that "police prejudice" was likely the source (5). The police in San Francisco had already been monitoring Chinatown for decades and had even created its own "Chinatown Squad."
213. Vollmer and Schneider 1917, 886–887.
214. Vollmer to Dalton, September 4, 1936, Box 45, BANC C-B 403, AVP.

215. Castellanos to Vollmer, December 7, 1934, Microfilm 2266, AVP.

216. Vollmer to Castellanos, December 7, 1934, "Letters," Box 43, BANC MSS C-B 403, AVP. Later, though, in the 1930s, Vollmer praised the Chinese "character." See Vollmer to Hsieh, February 8, 1934, "Letters," Box 43, AVP.

217. On Vollmer and eugenics, see Oliver 2017, 499–502.

218. Gessel 2003, 11; Miller 1975, 190.

219. MCSAV 1908, 54–55.

220. MCSAV 1908, 55.

221. Calculated from MCSAV 1895, 1906.

222. *SMN*, August 12, 1916, 6.

223. MCSAV 1915, 480. It is not unlikely that the new militarized capacities of the police in the South were also used to try to control the labor of former slaves. As Muller (2018) shows, securing African American labor was a problem for white employers in the South, and so police arrested African Americans at high rates in ways that enabled white employers to pull them out of prison in exchange for labor. Something akin to this sort of labor control happened in 1916 in Savannah, when the police tried to prevent scores of Black workers from leaving the city for the North during the onset of the Great Migration (Gessel 2003, 37, 54–57, 96–97, 114–117, 134–135).

224. US census data from 1890 and 1910. On race and crime, see Muhammad 2010.

225. Adams 2015, 82–85; IADP 1914, 28; RMP 1913, 182–173.

226. RMP 1911, 1913, 1914.

227. Adams 2015, 166.

228. Adams 2015, 113; see also Fisher 2022, 193.

229. Muhammad 2010, 193.

230. Thompson 1926, 254.

231. *WP*, September 25, 1898, 11; also October 18, 1899, 12, and October 22, 1899, 12.

232. *WP*, October 22, 1899, 12. Sylvester actively supported the anti–"white slavery" movement, which assumed that immigrants, racial minorities, and intermingling in urban settings corrupted white women (IACP 1913, 94)

233. *WP*, September 11, 1903, 11.

234. *Washington Evening Star*, December 17, 1905, pt. 5, 4; also December 10, 1905, pt. 5, 3.

235. *The Coloured American*, June 12, 1902, 8, See also RCDC 1900, I:190, and *WP*, November 28, 1899, 2. My study of over one hundred cities in the United States from the 1890s to 1915 reveals that Sylvester's case is not unique. The racialization of crime and disorder was crucial for triggering militarization as imperial feedback, regardless of whether police chiefs were veterans (Go 2022).

236. Quotes from Mayo (1917), 32, 25.

237. Quoted in Conti (1977), 33–34, 36; emphasis added.

238. United States Commission on Industrial Relations 1916, 10966.

239. *Mount Union Times*, May 4, 1906, 2; *West Schuylkill Herald*, May 4, 1906, 2, which claimed that the town consists of "9,500 foreigners," many of whom were "drinking heavily."

240. Quotes from *BDE*, April 22, 1906, 24; Mayo 1917, 37–39.

241. Williams 1921, 78.

242. "Address," July 8, 1927, Folder "Speeches, Statements," BANC MSS 72/227c, BPD.

243. Sylvester 1910, 18–19.

244. IACP 1910, 14. For more on the "third degree," see IACP 1910, 50, 59, 60–73, 100–105.

245. *Boston Globe*, May 21, 1920, 14; *Gettysburg Times*, May 9, 1921, 2.

246. *Honolulu Star-Bulletin*, October 14, 1920, 6.

247. United States Senate Committee on the Philippines 1902, 1539–1540 (testimony of William Lewis Smith).

248. *Albuquerque Journal*, December 30, 1912, 4.

# Chapter 4

1. *Illustrated London News*, May 1, 1886, 449.

2. Go 2011, 170–174; Go 2014a; Knepper 2010, 43–44.

3. Jones 1982, 117; Churchill 2017, 42; London Metropolitan Police 1871, 4–6.

4. Most of the rank and file before the First World War had been agricultural laborers rather than soldiers or colonial police officers. In London prior to 1900, most recruits had been manual laborers coming from rural areas; only about 14 percent or less were military veterans. By 1927, candidates for the London Metropolitan Police were mostly nonmilitary, with only 2.7 percent having been soldiers (Smith 1985, 33, 46–47; Moylan 1929, 101; Shpayer-Makov 2002). For the non-London police, see Emsley 1996, 178–181, and Palmer 1988, 564–565.

5. Taylor 2015, 37.

6. Roycroft 2016, 90.

7. Quoted in Taylor 2015, 37–38. On other major cities and county police forces, see Stallion et al. 1999; Taylor 2015, 36–40; Wall 1998, 238–251.

8. Ascoli 1979, 178–179.

9. Porter 1987, 17.

10. By 1862, Britain's regular troops consisted of about 534,527 men, plus a reserve force of about 228,240 men that included the Irish Constabulary, militia, yeomanry, and volunteers, up from around 162,000 in the 1790s (*NYT*, January 3, 1862, 2). Native soldiers were also increasingly incorporated (McElwee 1974, 72).

11. Another set of changes were the Cardwell reforms, beginning in 1868. Not entirely unlike the Root Reforms in the United States later, they involved new criteria for staff promotion and recruitment, among other things (Spiers 1992, 2–24).

12. Hutton 1886, 695–696. While light cavalry had been a long-standing part of the British Army's tactics—and had influenced the formation of the beat patrol system of policing—the idea of auxiliary mounted infantry units was connected to renewed interest in combining mobility with firepower. Dragoons had previously used firearms but were dismounted for engagement. The new aim was to have armed

mounted capacities (which was realized partly through the creation of lighter firearms). See Robinson 2008, 140–141.

13. Winrow 2017.

14. Robinson 2008; Winrow 2017.

15. Quotes from Goodenough and Dalton 1893, 171, and Hutton 1886, 703. Reserve or auxiliary mounted forces were crucial for offering relief to "English horses of our Cavalry" exhausted from the "tropical and uncongenial climate" of the imperial frontiers (Hutton 1886, 703).

16. *Naval and Military Gazette and Weekly Chronicle of the United Service*, May 16, 1877, 395; *Bradford Weekly Telegraph*, November 6, 1869, 3. The breech-loading revolver was widely advertised in outlets such as *Home News for India, China and the Colonies* (e.g., August 28, 1868, 28).

17. Palmer 1988, 762. The .442 was copied in other countries, and Custer carried it at his famous battle at the Little Big Horn. See also *Times of India*, April 18, 1888, 1.

18. Satia 2018, 345–390; Wagner 2018, 7–8.

19. Callwell 1906, 21; Whittingham 2020, 45.

20. Knepper 2010, 43.

21. On these forces, see Anderson and Killingray 1991, 4; Clayton and Killingray 1989; Jeffries 1952, 32; Ellison and O'Reilly 2008, 402; Sinclair 2006, 16–25. Hawkins 1991 assesses the influence of the "Irish model."

22. Dowbiggin 1928, 205.

23. Sinclair and Williams 2007, 223.

24. Finnane 2005, 55; Mukhopadhyay 1998, 254; Arnold 1986, 3.

25. The Met did conduct political surveillance and gathered intelligence through plainclothes officers, as the Popay affair revealed, but public fears of a French-style political police kept its surveillance and intelligence-gathering activities in check, compelling Commissioners Rowan and Mayne to restrict it. See Clutterbuck 2006, 97–98.

26. Andrew 1985, 16. See also Porter 1987, 16, and Dublin Metropolitan Police documents, CAB 37/24/21, PRO.

27. Metcalf 1996, 338–340.

28. Brückenhaus 2017.

29. Swift 1987, 1989, 1997, 2007a.

30. Shannon 1935, 81, 83. The Irish tended to migrate instead to the United States (MacRaild 1999, 15). The migration data does not account for the number of ethnically Irish living in England, which was sizable (Lees 1979, 47–48). But of relevance here is whether there was an increase in Irish migration that might have sparked a racialized panic.

31. Jones 1982, 180–183.

32. Quoted in Ó Tuathaigh 1981, 156. For the changing class fortunes of the Irish in London, see Lees 1979, 89–122.

33. On the Irish in police, see Swift 1989, 178; on the Irish electorate, see O'Day 1989a.

34. For instance, *LQR* 129 (1870): 108–109.

35. Mayhew and Binny 1862, 386. While they suggested that the Irish committed the majority of crime in London, they were just reporting on what was popularly said. Notably, their own statistics on the prisoners of the Cold Bath Fields prison in 1856 revealed that out of 1,393 prisoners, only 100 were Irish (282). Mayhew further tempered any simple equation between criminality and the Irish by constant reference to multiple other groups who made up the "criminal class," from Scots to Jews and Englishmen. The Irish were no longer singled out as responsible for crime (165).

36. On Booth's observations regarding crime and immigrants, see Englander 1989, 551–552.

37. Emsley 2005, 173. The classic is Tobias 1979; more recent discussions are in Bailey 1993; Philips 2003; Stanford 2007, 27–43; and Bach 2020.

38. London Metropolitan Police annual report, 1869, 3, PP.

39. Mayhew and Binny 1862, 45; Knepper 2010, 53. This racial discourse was connected to "biological positivism" in Europe associated with Cesare Lombroso (considered by some to be the father of modern criminology; Leps 1992, 41–63).

40. Anderson 1907, 104, 114–115; Knepper 2010, 49.

41. Wiener 1990, 216–217.

42. The classic and still relevant literature on crime figures during this period is discussed in, among others, Emsley 2005, 21–55; Gatrell 2008; Taylor 1998; and Jones 1982, 4–10, 119–122.

43. Quoted in Jones 1982, 120.

44. Quoted in Wiener 1990, 216.

45. Quoted in Sengoopta 2003, 12.

46. For more on these perceptions, including outside London, see Jones 1982, 148; Miller 1977, 110–111.

47. See Wiener 1990, 217; Jones 1982, 120; Anderson 1907, 104.

48. Emsley 2005, 73; Wiener 1990, 217–218.

49. *LQR* 129 (1870): 91.

50. On "ticket-of-leave," see Bartrip 1981. On the "garroting" scares, see Davis 1980 and Sindall 1987. For the 1919 moral panic that did not happen, see Emsley 2008. On legal and punitive systems in this period see Bailey 1981b and Petrow 1994.

51. On humanitarianism toward criminals rather than dehumanization, see Anderson 1907 and Wiener 1990.

52. We might also consider cities where the Irish presence remained strong, such as Liverpool, which maintained one of the largest Irish-born populations per capita in the country. Police officials like Commissioner Nott-Bower thought of Liverpool as similar to Irish cities like Belfast, and drew upon his experience in the Royal Irish Constabulary to meet the persistently perceived Irish threat. Among his reforms of 1885, Nott-Bower created a new mounted unit, reflecting the RIC's mounted forces and the growing importance of mounted army units across the empire. See Nott-Bower 1926, 56–57, 91–93, 149. For Liverpool policing in the Victorian period, see Archer 2011.

53. Emsley 1996, 70.

54. On the Chartists, see the classic by Mather (1959). On other major public order issues, see Smith 1985 and Vogler 1991. For workers' strikes in this period, see Weinberger 1991.

55. Ascoli 1979, 191.

56. *Sun* (London), December 13, 1867, 3.

57. Steward and McGovern 2013.

58. *TL*, December 14, 1867, 6.

59. This is noted by Porter 1987, 16.

60. Curtis 1997, 37.

61. London *Weekly Dispatch*, December 15, 1867, 16; Ascoli 1979, 134.

62. Quoted in Nott-Bower 1926, 70–71.

63. Quoted in Nott-Bower 1926, 8.

64. *Weekly Standard*, December 15, 1867, 16.

65. *SR*, January 16, 1869, 76, and January 2, 1869, 4–5.

66. *SR*, December 12, 1868, 766.

67. Emsley 1985, 127.

68. As quoted in Gould and Waldren 1986, 23.

69. *TL*, December 18, 1867, 8.

70. *SR*, January 16, 1869, 76.

71. Quoted in Emsley 1985, 136.

72. Miller 1977, 49–50.

73. Gould and Waldren 1986, 25.

74. Home Office 1868, 119–123.

75. Chamberlain 1976.

76. *Surrey Comet*, September 1, 1883, 5; *PMG*, August 31, 1883, 3; Palmer 1988, 762; Gould and Waldren 1986, 30–44.

77. RCPMET, 1870, 12.

78. Ascoli 1979, 140; *SR*, December 12, 1868, 766.

79. Quoted in Clutterbuck 2006, 97.

80. Anderson 1910, 22.

81. Clutterbuck 2006, 98.

82. *TL*, January 20, 1883, 9, and January 26, 1885, 9.

83. Clutterbuck 2006, 102.

84. Gould and Waldren 1986, 30.

85. Porter 1987, 41.

86. Clutterbuck 2006, 103–112, Porter 1987, 41–49.

87. Porter 1987 tells the complete story of the Special Branch and how its creation marked the overcoming of Victorian political fears.

88. Ascoli 1979, 156; Bailey 1981a, 95–96; *PMG*, February 9, 1886, 8; *TL*, February 10, 1886, 5.

89. *Globe*, February 9, 1886, 3.

90. *TL*, February 10, 1886, 5; Clarkson and Richardson 1889, 204; also see *SR*, February 13, 1886, 219; Bailey 1981a, 96.

91. *SR*, February 20, 1886, 246, and February 13, 1886, 220; Porter 1987, 20–49; Knepper 2010, 128–158.

92. *TL*, March 13, 1886, 4.

93. *SR*, February 13, 1886, 220, and February 20, 1886, 246; *PMG*, February 9, 1886, 1.

94. House of Commons 1886.

95. Williams 1941, 195.

96. *TL*, March 13, 1886, 11.

97. Clarkson and Richardson 1889, 82.

98. House of Commons 1886, 4; Williams 1941, 197.

99. *Sunderland Daily Echo and Shipping Gazette*, November 1, 1886, 2.

100. Warren 1888, 591.

101. "Drill Instruction," 1888, MEPO 2/170; Bailey 1981a, 106–107; *SR*, November 6, 1886, 605.

102. *London Evening Standard*, January 10, 1887, 5.

103. House of Commons 1886, 5. For more on mounted units, see Roth 1998.

104. Clarkson and Richardson 1889, 83–84.

105. *SR*, May 26, 1888, 622–623.

106. Ascoli 1979, 159; *Justice*, June 4, 1887, 1.

107. Bailey 1981a, 117.

108. Clarkson and Richardson 1889, 207–208.

109. *SR*, May 5, 1888, 534; *SR*, May 26, 1888, 623.

110. Williams 1941, 209.

111. *Evening News* (London), November 14, 1887, 2; *Illustrated London News*, November 19, 1887, 605. See also Vogler 1991, 64; "military formation" in *Daily Telegraph and Courier* (London), November 14, 1887, 5. Warren may have had the recent Belfast riots (of 1886) on his mind, when the police and the army faced down angry protestors for almost a week.

112. *TL*, November 14, 1887, 6.

113. Ascoli 1979, 160; Vogler 1991, 65.

114. Williams 1941, 205.

115. Williams 1941, 209.

116. Clarkson and Richardson 1889, 198.

117. Quoted in Williams 1941, 209.

118. Quoted in Bailey 1981a, 108.

119. Ascoli 1979, 160.

120. Quoted in Clarkson and Richardson 1889, 212.

121. *Justice*, July 24, 1886, 1, and June 4, 1887, 1; *Daily Telegraph and Courier*, November 14, 1887, 5.

122. Bailey 1981a, 110–113.

123. Porter 1987, 81.

124. *PMG*, November 9, 1887, 1.

125. House of Commons, March 2, 1888, vol. 322, col. 89, col. 1, HPD.

126. House of Commons, March 2, 1888, vol. 322, col. 69–70, HPD.

127. House of Commons, March 2, 1888, vol. 322, col. 1146–1147, HPD.

128. Quoted in Bailey 1981a, 102.
129. *Murray's* IV, no. XXIII (November 1888): 578.
130. *SR*, November 3, 1888, 515, and November 6, 1886, 605.
131. Bailey 1981a, 96–97.
132. O'Day 1989b, 187–188. Even in Liverpool, which had the largest Irish-born population per capita throughout the late nineteenth and early twentieth centuries, the earlier threats passed away (Nott-Bower 1926, 85).
133. PMG, November 9, 1887, 1.
134. Quoted in Williams 1941, 196.
135. Moylan 1929, 46.
136. House of Commons, November 13, 1888, col. 1147–1148, HPD.
137. Anderson in *NYTRI*, April 27, 1902, 5.
138. "Memorandum on the Working of the Finger Print System," July 1, 1904, 2, 11, MEPO 4/270.
139. Macnaghten 1914, 147.
140. Committee to Inquire into the Best Means Available for Identifying Habitual Criminals 1894, 5; Petrow 1994, 90–96; *Police Review and Parade Gossip*, May 12, 1905, 223.
141. Arnold 1976, 5.
142. Cole 2001, 65; Sengoopta 2003, 57–62.
143. Quoted in Sengoopta 2003, 110.
144. *Home News for India, China and the Colonies*, July 14, 1893, 18.
145. Simhadri 1991, 121.
146. The problem was that some were mobile and "people with no fixed residence of any kind came automatically under suspicion of being criminals," according to Sengoopta (2003, 127).
147. Quoted in Cole 2001, 70.
148. Sengoopta 2003, 109–111.
149. After the Indian mutiny, Herschel had begun using handprints in ink and later began using tips of the fingers only. This did not, however, amount to a system that the police could use at the time. See Cole 2001, 65–66.
150. Quoted in Sengoopta 2003, 135.
151. "Memorandum . . . Finger Print System," July 1, 1904, 1, MEPO 4/270.
152. Sengoopta 2003, 195.
153. Anderson 1907, 88, 102–103.
154. Anderson 1907, 93–96.
155. Knepper 2010.
156. Wiener 1990, 224.
157. Committee to Inquire into the Best Means Available for Identifying Habitual Criminals 1894, 6.
158. Anderson 1907, 94–95; Spearman 1890, 364–371.
159. Englander 1989, 551 (citing Lipman 1954, 97–100, 157–160).
160. Gartner 2001, 216.
161. Englander 1989; Knepper 2007, 63.

162. Sweeney and Richards 1904, 306.

163. Quoted in Ewence 2019, 137.

164. Quoted in Ewence 2019, 166.

165. Royal Commission on Alien Immigration 1903, I:5.

166. Knepper 2007, 65.

167. Anderson 1907, 106.

168. Lee 1980, 115–116 (quotes from 115)

169. Sweeney and Richards 1904, 312.

170. Emsley 1996, 159.

171. Sweeney and Richards 1904, 314; Royal Commission on Alien Immigration 1903, II:256; also Knepper 2007, 64.

172. On the connection with anarchism, see Knepper 2008 and Anderson 1911. On Jewish women as prostitutes, see Royal Commission on Alien Immigration 1903, II:526.

173. Anderson 1910, 137.

174. Spearman 1890, 364; Committee to Inquire into the Best Means Available for Identifying Habitual Criminals 1894, 2–36, 61. Bertillon's method had also helped identify Jean Pauwels in Paris, the anarchist Belgian and hence a foreigner to France.

175. *LQR* 129 (1870): 99.

176. Petrow 1994, 89.

177. Spearman 1890, 371.

178. Spearman 1890, 376.

179. *TL*, September 28, 1887, 3.

180. Sweeney and Richards 1904, 314.

181. Cole 2001, 99–103; Sengoopta 2003, 93–95.

182. *St. James's Gazette*, December 1, 1892, 18.

183. A chief clerk to the lord mayor said that photography would suffice for tracking the "foreigners from abroad—German and Polish Jews" (Committee to Inquire into the Best Means Available for Identifying Habitual Criminals 1894, 46).

184. Quoted in Sengoopta 2003, 17.

185. Committee to Inquire into the Best Means Available for Identifying Habitual Criminals 1984, 6, 9, 26–27.

186. Henry 1901, 6.

187. Royal Commission on Alien Immigration 1903, II:526, 617.

188. Royal Commission on Alien Immigration 1903, II:862–863.

189. Henry quoted in Sengoopta 2003, 194.

190. Metropolitan Police annual report for 1932, 3, 8, MEPO 4/180.

191. *Daily Herald*, May 29, 1933, 9; *Daily News* (London), August 28, 1933, 7; *DM*, September 15, 1932, 2, and September 6, 1932, 2. Athelson Popkess, the commissioner in Nottingham, was among the first to implement Q cars modeled after the navy system (Williams 2014; also *DM*, September 6, 1932, 2, and Taylor 2015, 44).

192. Metropolitan Police annual reports for 1932, 19, MEPO 4/180, and for 1934, 16–17, MEPO 4/182.

193. Williams 2014, 154.

194. *Police Journal* 6, no. 3 (1933), 269.
195. Taylor 2015, 35–36.
196. *DM*, May 4, 1933, 1; Wall 1998, 208–210.
197. Taylor 2015, 46; Wall 1998, 212.
198. Taylor 2015, 35–36, 49–50; Metropolitan Police annual report for 1933, 15, MEPO 4/181; see also *Police Journal* 6, no. 3 (1933), 276; *Times of India*, July 3, 1934, 10.
199. *Daily Herald*, May 29, 1933, 9.
200. Ascoli 1979, 225–231.
201. House of Commons, May 2, 1932, vol. 265, c. 875, HPD.
202. House of Commons, May 2, 1932, vol. 265, c. 865, HPD.
203. As reported in *DM*, January 13, 1933, 20.
204. *Nottingham Journal*, June 27, 1933, 7.
205. *The People*, August 6, 1933, 10. When Trenchard met with delegates from the Police Federation in 1933 to explain his proposals for the new elite school, they mocked his proposals by giving Nazi salutes (Taylor 2015, 48).
206. *Birmingham Daily Gazette*, June 23, 1933, 6.
207. Another example is the proposal in 1919 to centralize all police into a single command and control structure, akin to Ireland. This proposal failed.
208. Linstrum 2019, 575.

## Chapter 5

1. Hinton 2017, 89.
2. Quoted in Horne 1995, 164.
3. *LAT*, January 16, 1970, 116.
4. American Civil Liberties Union 2014; Kraska and Kappeler 1997.
5. Gates 1992, 109–110.
6. Clinton 2010.
7. Kohler-Hausmann 2011, 48; Horne 2003, 165.
8. *NYDN*, July 20, 1964, 3; Johnson 2003, 234–238.
9. *NYDN*, July 19, 1964, 2.
10. *NYDN*, July 20, 1964, 18.
11. *NYDN*, July 24, 1964, 3.
12. President's Commission on Law Enforcement and Administration of Justice 1967b, 97; Wilson 1963, 250.
13. *Newsweek*, June 27, 1966, 24.
14. Knights 1969, 202.
15. Johnson 1967; Hinton 2021, 96.
16. Leonard 1951, 332–333.
17. Leonard 1951, 334.
18. President's Commission on Law Enforcement and Administration of Justice 1967b, 97.

19. Wilson 1963, 437.
20. Leonard 1962, 34.
21. Anne Arundel County, Maryland n.d.
22. United States Senate Committee on the Judiciary 1973, 352, based upon the claim that tactical units reduced crime (President's Commission on Law Enforcement and Administration of Justice 1967a, 95).
23. IACP, proceedings for 1956, 128.
24. Reiss 1992, 51.
25. Leonard 1951, 335.
26. Balto 2019, 147. Tactical units also differed from specialized task-specific "squads" aimed at specific problems, like drugs, gambling, or presumed communists as opposed to crime and disorder broadly. Fogelson 1977, 78; Donner 1990.
27. Leonard 1951, 355.
28. IACP, proceedings for 1962, 63.
29. Reynolds 2020, 274.
30. *NYT*, July 21, 1968, SM7.
31. *St. Louis Globe-Democrat*, December 22, 1958, 7.
32. Coyne and Hall 2018, 107.
33. Quoted in Schrader 2019, 223.
34. *Kansas City Star*, December 6, 1959, 29.
35. *Newsweek*, June 27, 1966 24.
36. Turner 1968, 64.
37. Poka 2020, 265.
38. Eastman 1960, 15.
39. IACP, proceedings for 1956, 128.
40. *Lansing State Journal*, April 25, 1956, 25.
41. IACP, proceedings for 1958, 40–41.
42. In the 1950s the Army's Special Forces were created, including the Green Berets, to which some police tactical units were compared (Doughty 1979).
43. Go 2011, 9, 121–126; Kuzmarov 2012, 37–52.
44. *Kansas City Star*, October 29, 1952, 22.
45. *Kansas City Star*, March 23, 1953, 26. This approach of course required a global network of bases, which the United States did construct, though first by creating bases in Europe's colonies (Go 2011, 143–145).
46. Wilson 1998, 414.
47. Edwards 1912, 408. The limits of the existing territorial distribution of the military were most starkly revealed in 1911 during the ad hoc mobilization of the brigades ordered by President Taft to Texas and California in response to the outbreak of civil war in Mexico. Just before the outbreak of the First World War, Congress approved a reorganization that would help solve these problems by creating permanent tactical divisions. The divisions would provide much-needed flexibility and power, enabling the army to be deployed to wherever it was most needed, with rapidity and power (Huebner 1997, 70).

48. *The Spectator*, May 1, 1936, 794; Rowley 1932.
49. See Vollmer to Wolfsperger, November 20, 1939, Box 45, and Vollmer to Leonard, June 22, 1940, Box 46, BANC MSS C-B 403, AVP.
50. Bickel 2001, 49.
51. Bickel 2001, 155–162, 162; Brooks 1989; Bryan and Wood 2015, 34–53.
52. Doughty 1979, 35.
53. Jackson 2017, 114.
54. Cassidy 1978, 46–47; Thompson 2012, 121.
55. Jackson 2017, 122.
56. Wakeman 1996, 59–61.
57. Martin 1936, 41.
58. Thompson 2012, 77.
59. Cassidy 1978, 49.
60. Thompson 2012, 110; Wakeman 1996, 337; Cassidy 1978, 48.
61. Thompson 2012. Cassidy (1978, 46) makes a similar claim.
62. *Salt Lake Tribune*, November 29, 1942, 24.
63. Since the US Marines also had responsibility for internal security within the settlement, it worked with the SRU and developed their own riot company, copying the SRU, that consisted of ninety Marines and had its own "riot truck" filled with arms. It learned riot formations and the use of tear gas from the SRU (Thompson 2012, 186–188).
64. Thompson 2012, 184.
65. Wukovits 2009.
66. Whitaker 2017; Vollmer to Fairburn, June 9, 1933, "Letters," Box 42, June 1933, AVP.
67. *Chicago Tribune*, March 31, 1930, 13.
68. Strecker 2011, 98–99.
69. LAPD annual report for 1951, 10.
70. Schrader 2021, 174.
71. Thompson 2012, 6; *NYT*, July 27, 1998, A15.
72. *NYT*, July 27, 1998, A15; Schrader 2019, 147.
73. Applegate 1964, 206–245.
74. This was later named the Reserve Detail, part of the Metropolitan Division, which Davis also created. The Reserve Unit also appears to have existed before 1933, under Davis' predecessor, Chief Steckel, but it is likely Davis created it when he was chief prior to Steckel (he and Steckel alternated chief positions in these years). See LAPD annual report for 1933, 14–15; *Los Angeles Evening Citizen News*, August 18, 1933, 1.
75. *LAT*, March 27, 1930, 23.
76. *LAT*, September 24, 1933, 7, 19.
77. LAPD annual report for 1933, 14–15.
78. Vollmer's mobile unit operated in plain clothes to maintain the military element of surprise. Davies' Reserve Unit wore plain clothes when dispatched to high crime areas but wore uniforms when handling riots, as did the SRU (LAPD annual report for 1933, 14–15).

79. LAPD annual report for 1957, 13, annual report for 1952, 12–13, and annual report for 1949, 15; also LAT, June 21, 1955, 12. On connections between the Crime Crushers, the Reserve Unit and the Metro Division, see LAT, February 6, 1961, 14.

80. Webb 1958, 136.

81. Jacobs 1968, 155.

82. Cannon 1999, 66.

83. LAT, February 6, 1961, 14.

84. International City Managers' Association 1954, 90.

85. Carte, Carte, and Robinson 1983, 23.

86. Wilson 1963, 167–168, 436–437.

87. President's Commission on Law Enforcement and Administration of Justice 1967b, 97.

88. As Schrader (2019, 227–232) notes, in 1962 members of the LAPD were enlisted by the United States Office of Public Safety to help train police in the Dominican Republic; later, in 1965, the OPS urged the creation of a "strike force" to help the National Police there. This shows that tactical units were shipped abroad, but as argued in this chapter, they were initially an effect of the imperial boomerang, imported and *then* reexported.

89. Leonard 1951, 337.

90. NYPD annual report for 1961, 2, and annual report for 1959, 2.

91. Quoted in Elkins 2017, 89.

92. Eastman 1960, 15; Knights 1969, 202.

93. Giarruso 1961, 4–5.

94. IACP proceedings for 1959, 85.

95. St. Louis Post Dispatch, February 24, 1959, 1, and March 8, 1959, 7.

96. CPD annual report for 1956, 7.

97. Chicago Sunday Tribune Magazine, August 12, 1956, 20.

98. Latrobe Bulletin, April 3, 1968, 13.

99. NYT, July 21, 1968, 51.

100. IACP proceedings for 1956, 127.

101. Chicago Sunday Tribune Magazine, August 12, 1956, 20.

102. Leonard 1951, 343.

103. NYDN, December 1, 1959, C2, December 2, 1959, 5, and December 4, 1959, B1. For Chicago, see CPD annual report for 1958, 34.

104. Balto 2019, 129; Chicago Tribune, June 24, 1946, 1.

105. Burlington Free Press, August 12, 1947, 9.

106. Barre Daily Times, April 19, 1947, 1.

107. On Edson's experiences, see Alexander 2000.

108. Vermont Department of Public Safety 1950, 37–39, Burlington Free Press, August 12, 1947, 9.

109. St. Albans Daily Messenger, September 29, 1947, 1, 9.

110. Vermont Department of Public Safety 1950, 36–37, 40.

111. It is not that state police forces or rural county sheriffs would never create their own tactical forces. Johnson County, Missouri, created one in 1964 (see *Kansas City Star*, September 9, 1964, 4A).
112. Smith 1960, 144–154, 306–307.
113. Agee 2014, 5.
114. Chicago Commission on Human Relations 1961, 1.
115. Agee 2014, 6.
116. Felker-Kantor 2018, 13; Tullis 1999, 205. On the policing of Mexicans in Los Angeles in the early twentieth century, see Escobar 1999.
117. Schnore and Sharp 1963, 248.
118. Coe 1959, 195. In fact, though, the new migration was not entirely new; it was a continuation of prior trends, which suggests that white residents fell into a moral panic of sorts. See Schnore and Sharp 1963.
119. Bogue 1955, 474–475.
120. Watts 1982, 296.
121. MYB for 1958, 402.
122. IACP proceedings for 1957, 11.
123. While conventional scholarship on "big-city policing" in the 1940s through the early 1960s ignores race issues (e.g., Fogelson 1977), a range of excellent new scholarship shows how urban police were concerned about the changing racial composition of cities demographics and correlated it with rising crime rates. See Balto 2019, Felker-Kantor 2018, and Escobar 1999.
124. IACP proceedings for 1958, 155.
125. Quoted in Rudwick 1960, 66.
126. The attempts by some police officials to deal with charges of racism reveal the racist assumptions they were trying desperately to not betray. One increasingly common strategy was to try to employ more "Negro" officers. This reflected a characteristic of colonial police forces more generally, in that the Insular Police in Puerto Rico, the Philippine Constabulary, the Gendarmerie of Haiti under General Smedley Butler, the Shanghai Municipal Police, and the various police forces in British India had all relied upon "native" personnel. The assumption was that criminality was predominantly a "Negro" matter (Balto 2019, 129).
127. Wilson 1950, 3.
128. Parker and Wilson 1957, 187; see Felker-Kantor 2018, 20–26, for a succinct overview of Parker's approach.
129. Parker and Wilson 1957, 39.
130. Quoted in Felker-Kantor 2018, 46.
131. Liska, Lawrence, and Benson 1981, 413.
132. Chronopoulos 2018, 652.
133. Parker and Wilson 1957, 161; Felker-Kantor 2018, 22.
134. See Felker-Kantor 2018, 20–23.
135. Lassiter and the Policing and Social Justice History Lab 2021.
136. IACP proceedings for 1957, 11.

137. *NYDN*, September 2, 1959, 3.

138. Johnson 2003, 194–228.

139. *NYT*, May 29, 1964, 1.

140. *New York Age*, August 1, 1959, 4.

141. *NYT*, July 15, 1959, 13.

142. *NYT*, July 6, 1959, 1; Chronopoulos 2018, 654.

143. Chronopoulos 2018, 652.

144. On the "gangs," see Schneider 1999.

145. *NYT*, September 6, 1959, E2.

146. Schneider 1999, 9.

147. Quoted in Barnosky 2006, 316.

148. *New York Age*, February 28, 1959, 1.

149. *NYDN*, September 4, 1959, 29.

150. *NYDN*, September 13, 1959, 8C. For claims that Black and Puerto Rican youth committed "a huge percentage of the crime and violence," see Barnosky 2006, 316. The NYC Youth Board, an agency for preventing juvenile delinquency, estimated that there were 150 "fighting gangs in the city, of which one-third are Puerto Rican, one-third Negro, and one-third white or mixed" (*NYT*, September 6, 1959, E2).

151. *NYT*, March 2, 1954, 19.

152. *NYDN*, September 3, 1959, C3.

153. *NYDN*, December 4, 1959, B1.

154. *NYDN*, September 4, 1959, 29. This was a snide remark in response to Governor Rockefeller's claim that the island of Puerto Rico did not have a disproportionate amount of crime. On the racialization of youth criminality in New York in this period, see Suddler 2019.

155. *NYDN*, September 3, 1959, C3.

156. *New York Age*, September 12, 1959, 6.

157. *NYDN*, September 2, 1959, C3.

158. *NYDN*, September 3, 1959, C3.

159. The *NYDN* wrote that a congressman in the District of Columbia suggested that the US Marines be called in to handle that city's "gang" problem (September 13, 1959, C8).

160. *NYT*, September 6, 1959, E2; *NYDN*, September 2, 1959, C3, and September 4, 1959, 3–4.

161. *NYDN*, December 1, 1959, C2, December 2, 1959, 5, and December 4, 1959, B1.

162. *NYDN*, December 2, 1959, 5.

163. *NYDN*, December 2, 1959, C13.

164. CPD annual report for 1956, 7; *Chicago Defender*, March 31, 1956, 2.

165. Balto 2019, 125–137.

166. *Newsweek*, June 26, 1966, 24.

167. CPD annual report for 1956, 7; Balto 2019, 146–147.

168. *NYDN*, December 2, 1959, 5; *NYDN*, December 4, 1959, B1.

169. NYPD annual report for 1961, 2.

170. *NYT*, May 29, 1964, 13.

171. Stramberg 2020, 353.

172. *Pottsville Republican,* July 24, 1967, 1.

173. Reynolds 2020, 276.

174. *NYDN,* July 24, 1964, 3.

175. *NYT,* May 29, 1964 p. 13.

176. *Chicago Defender,* April 26, 1958, 9.

177. Balto 2019, 130.

178. Jacobs 1968, 28.

179. LAPD annual report for 1957, 14.

180. LAPD annual report for 1960.

181. Cannon 1999, 67.

182. Quoted in Jacobs 1968, 25.

183. Tullis 1999, 205–206.

184. Quoted in Tullis 1999, 207.

185. *Los Angeles Sentinel,* September 2, 1965, B11; also *LAT,* February 19, 1962.

186. Felker-Kantor 2018, 25.

187. Tullis 1999, 216.

188. Governor's Commission on the Los Angeles Riots 1965, 27–29.

189. Felker-Kantor 2018, 20.

190. Tullis 1999, 208.

191. Lawyers' Committee for Civil Rights Under Law 1973, 363.

192. Editorial in *The Movement* 3, no. 2 (February 1967): 2.

193. Felker-Kantor 2018, 21.

194. For more on this, see Tullis 1999.

195. Quoted in Rosenau 2014, 118.

196. Kohler 2011, 48.

197. Quoted in Rosenau 2014, 118.

198. Gates 1992, 91, 109–110.

199. Kohler-Hausmann 2011, 48–49. One critical report on the LEAA program fretted that many of the funding grants "have gone to states such as Vermont, Montana, Idaho and Maine which—without the funding—never would have considered the possibility of a riot" (Lawyers' Committee for Civil Rights Under Law 1973, 353).

200. President's Commission on Law Enforcement and Administration of Justice 1967a, 118–120.

201. Sorenson 1965, 6–7.

202. Cherry 1975, 55.

203. National Action Research on the Military Industrial Complex 1971, 98.

204. Sinclair 2006, 177, 179.

205. Malkin 2019; Thompson 2012, 186–187.

206. Jeffries 1952, 210.

207. Tullis 1999, 26.

208. United States National Advisory Commission on Civil Disorders, 26–26, 278.

209. United States National Advisory Commission on Civil Disorders, 277, 281.

210. McPhail et al. 1998, 63.

211. Hinton 2017, 91.
212. *Latrobe Bulletin*, April 3, 1968, 13.
213. Kohler-Hausmann 2011, 49.
214. Conroy 2005.
215. For more on the Burge horrors, see Baer 2020. The full archive of documents related to Burge's activities is available online at https://chicagopolicetorturearchive.com/documents.

# Chapter 6

1. Quoted in Shivsdani 2021.
2. Scarman 1981, 111.
3. Quoted in Palmer 1988, 4.
4. *TL*, July 10, 1981, 2.
5. Northam 1988; Waddington 1991, 1987. On the term "paramilitary," see Hills 1995; Jefferson 1990, 1993; Waddington 1991.
6. Faligot 1983, 11.
7. Jeffries 1952, 210–217.
8. Quoted in Gilroy 1982, 153.
9. *Observer*, May 25, 1972, 14.
10. *PR*, March 22, 1968, 245.
11. *TL*, May 23, 1972, 6.
12. Linstrum 2019, 577.
13. Quoted in Bunyan 1977, 268n32.
14. *TL*, May 23, 1972, 6.
15. *TL*, January 2, 1982, 11; Kettle and Hodges 1982, 40.
16. Rich 1986, 188; Foner 1979, 289; Kettle and Hodges 1982, 41.
17. Whitfield 2004, 3–4.
18. "Measures Against Illegal Immigration," 1972, HO 344/427, PRO.
19. *TL*, January 2, 1982, 1.
20. Spencer quoted in Watson 2018, 330.
21. Bowling 1996, 186.
22. Bowling 1996, 187.
23. Kettle and Hodges 1982, 42.
24. Asst. Commissioner to HO, April 10, 1952, MEPO 2/9047.
25. Commander Paddington, March 31, 1952, MEPO 2/9047; Whitfield 2003, 145–146.
26. Quoted in Collings-Wells 2019. See also Cashmore and McLaughlin 1991, 23–24; Gordon 1983, 17. On the Met and London's Black community, see Whitfield 2004; on "community relations" attempts that copied colonial models of "indirect rule," see Rich 1986, 161.
27. *PR* 76 (November 22, 1968): 990.
28. Keith 1991, 192–194.

29. Mark 1973, 14.
30. *TL*, August 24, 1971, 2; RCPMET for 1970. On the racialized and colonial discourse of Black "gangs," see Elliott-Cooper 2021, 135–163.
31. Hall et al. 1978, 50–52.
32. Quoted in Linstrum 2019, 578.
33. Whitfield 2004, 105.
34. *PR* 77 (June 6, 1969): 476.
35. *PR* 76 (April 5, 1968): 290; *PR* 76 (June 7, 1968): 482.
36. *DMA*, March 18, 1969, 2.
37. "Establishment of National Police Intelligence Unit on Illegal Immigration," HO 287/2215, PRO; Gordon 1985, 22–23.
38. Humphry 1972, 13–17, 52.
39. *TL*, February 20, 1965, 8.
40. *DMA*, October 14, 1966, 6.
41. *DMA*, April 24, 1972, 6.
42. *TL*, May 23, 1972, 6.
43. Jefferson 1990, 2–3.
44. Arnold 1977, 103–105.
45. Arnold 1977, 109; see also 8–10.
46. Arnold 1976, 9.
47. Sinclair 2006, 153.
48. Sinclair 2006, 152–153.
49. Quotes from Jeffries 1952, 121–122.
50. Kroizer 2004; Jeffries 1952, 157.
51. Willis 2011, 213.
52. Commissioner of Police, Singapore, "Handling Students Taking Part in Unlawful Assemblies," 1957, ADM 156/180, PRO.
53. Clayton and Killingray 1989, 22.
54. Deane-Drummond 1975, 114.
55. Commissioner of Police, Singapore, "Handling Students Taking Part in Unlawful Assemblies," 1957, PRO, ADM 156/180; Sinclair 2006, 178.
56. *BT*, October 2, 1969, 69.
57. Shea 1973.
58. *Guardian*, April 2, 1970, 1; *ST*, January 24, 1971, 1.
59. Kennedy-Pipe and McInnes 1997, 2–3.
60. Clutterbuck 1973, x.
61. Clutterbuck 1973, x; *Guardian*, December 11, 1973, 5.
62. Deane-Drummond 1975, 7.
63. Faligot 1983, 1. See more in Ackroyd et al. 1977, 90–124.
64. Clutterbuck 1973, 145.
65. Kennedy-Pipe and McInnes 1997, 3; Kitson 1991 (1971), 49–52.
66. Kitson 1991 (1971), 3, 82–94; also Bunyan 1977, 268, and Hall et al. 1978, 289–290. On "subversion" first in colonial administrations, see Thomas 2008, 16–17.
67. Clutterbuck 1973, 35.

68. Kitson 1991 (1971), 68–71.

69. *Guardian*, May 20, 1975, 8.

70. Ackroyd et al. 1977, 109. For disagreements, see Dixon 2009, 361.

71. Hutchinson 1969, 56.

72. British policing saw a decline in the number of ex-military leading police departments in this period. Mark was an exception. While over 51 percent of all county chief constables had held senior military rank in 1951, by 1964 that figure had dropped to 8 percent, and by 1990, military ranks ceased to be important at all. It was not until 1959 that a Metropolitan chief commissioner had come up from the ranks rather than the military; it was Joseph Simpson (Vogler 1991, 105).

73. Jeffries 1952, 217; J. Deegan, Deputy Inspector General of Colonial Police, November 13, 1957, ADM 156/180, PRO; *SRB* 9, no. 1 (1978): 129–134.

74. Taylor 2015, 21–22; Sinclair and Williams 2007, 231.

75. *ST*, February 2, 1971, 4; see especially Mark's own reflections in Mark 1973, 1977.

76. Quoted in Gilroy 1982, 165.

77. Deane-Drummond 1975, 50–51.

78. *Guardian*, July 16, 1976, 15.

79. Robert Mark to Mountbatten, February 25, 1970, MEPO 10/30.

80. Mark 1973, 22–23.

81. Mark 1978, 244.

82. Jefferson 1990, 2.

83. *SRB* 2, no. 13 (1979): 132.

84. Quotes from Keene 1967, 155, and *TL*, July 22, 1966, 12; see also "Recommendations," J. Flynn, June 5, 1967, 5, MEPO 2/10364, and *PR*, December 17, 1965, 640.

85. *PR*, January 29, 1965, 94, and May 21, 1965, 444.

86. *Guardian*, July 23, 1965, 4.

87. *Chelsea News and General Advertiser*, November 17, 1965, 1. The use of these small radios or "walkie-talkies" also had a military-imperial lineage, having been previously part of a new policing plan proposed earlier by Trenchard and Popkess (Williams 2014, 154–161).

88. *TL*, July 22, 1966, 12.

89. *TL*, July 6, 1967, 11.

90. Report of Superintendent, Special Patrol Group, December 23, 1965, MEPO 2/10364.

91. Special Patrol Group annual report, December 11, 1967, MEPO 2/10364.

92. Atkins, "Recommendation," April 16, 1969, MEPO 2/10364.

93. Kitson 1991 (1971), 83.

94. Kennedy-Pipe and McInnes 1997, 4; Jeffries 1952, 210.

95. Mark 1977, 87–96; Ackroyd et al. 1977, 104–107; Deane-Drummond 1975, 117.

96. Clutterbuck 1973, 35–42.

97. Kitson 1991 (1971), 91.

98. Clutterbuck 1973, 36; see also Kitson 1991 (1971), 91.

99. Kitson 1991 (1971), 92.

100. Jefrries 1952, 198.

101. Dixon 2009, 361; Kitson 1991 (1971), 92.

102. Hoffman 2013.

103. Yiu-kwong 2015, xvii.

104. Sloan 1978, 24; *PR*, March 29, 1968, 267.

105. On the "invasion," see *TL*, March 20, 1969, 1, 10; *DMA*, April 18, 1969, 2; Special Patrol Group, annual report, December 13, 1969, MEPO 2/103064; *PR* 77 (March 28, 1969): 254.

106. Quoted in Sinclair 2006, 100. Later, police officials praised the operation in Anguilla, along with others, as an early example of cooperation between police and the army. "Malaya, Anguilla and Northern Ireland," said Kenneth Steele of the Somerset and Bath Constabulary, "have already shown the value of the Army and Police working side by side"; *PR* 78 (April 10, 1970).

107. Ackryod et al. 1977, 139; *SRB* 4, no. 25 (August-September 1981): 165.

108. Mark 1978, 105; *DMA*, August 16, 1969, 2.

109. Mark 1978, 112.

110. *ST*, March 2, 1974, 49.

111. *Morning Star*, August 16, 1974, clipping in HO 325/371; *TL*, on March 17, 1973, 1, also reported that the SPG was training with the City's equivalent, the City Special Operations Group, set up under Commissioner Robert Mark. Ackroyd et al. 1977, 134.

112. SRB 1978; *Guardian*, July 16, 1976, 15.

113. *Guardian*, February 21, 1973, 13.

114. Northam (1988) claims that the British police underwent a "paramilitary drift" in terms of riot control in the early 1980s. I find that the SPG led the way and underwent a change earlier (in the 1970s).

115. Special Patrol Group annual report, December 31, 1974, MEPO 2/10364; *TL*, July 9, 1974, 1.

116. Special Patrol Group annual report for 1976, doc. 29B, MEPO 2/10364.

117. Special Patrol Group annual report, December 31, 1972, 8, MEPO 2/10364; *Mail on Sunday*, October 13, 1985, 4.

118. "Special Tasks Undertaken—1970," April 27, 1972, MEPO 2/10364.

119. Mark 1977, 97–98.

120. Special Patrol Group annual report, December 31, 1974, MEPO 2/10364. A later internal investigation in 1980 admitted that during the 1970s the SPG had shifted much of its attention toward policing public order "at the expense of their original primary functions" ("Report" by B. Kavanagh, Deputy Commissioner, HO 325/371).

121. *TL*, November 6, 1974, 4.

122. Clutterbuck 1973, 37.

123. Clutterbuck 1973, 39.

124. *Morning Star*, August 16, 1974, 2.

125. *Guardian*, April 27, 1970, 1. The Ulster Special Patrol Group was also seen using wedges and snatch squads (*Reading Evening Post*, August 20, 1979, 8).

126. *Guardian*, August 9, 1972, 12.

127. *TL*, September 28, 1974, 2; *Guardian*, September 18, 1974, 6.

128. *ST*, June 1, 1980, 17.

129. *DM*, February 20, 1978, 5; *ST*, February 19, 1978, 3.

130. Williams 2014, 163–164.

131. Quote in Taylor 2015, 127.

132. Kettle and Bunyan 1980, 354.

133. Special Patrol Group annual report 1966, 5–6, MEPO 2/103064; *PR*, July 11, 1969, 586–587.

134. Special Patrol Group annual report 1974, 5, MEPO 2/103064.

135. *PR*, April 6, 1979, 534.

136. Kitson 1991 (1971), 100–101, 5.

137. Faligot 1983, 117–118.

138. Sinclair 2006, 182.

139. Kitson 1991 (1971), 71.

140. Hutchinson 1969, 60–61.

141. Bunyan 1977, 280; *TL*, December 5, 1974, 1; Hillyard 1985, 180.

142. *Reading Evening Post*, August 20, 1979, 8.

143. Special Patrol Group annual reports 1966 and 1967, MEPO 2/103064.

144. Special Patrol Group annual reports 1974, 1975, 1976, MEPO 2/103064; see also Rollo 1980, 189–190; Humphry 1972, 9; and Institute of Race Relations 1979.

145. *Guardian*, June 30, 1972, 9.

146. *Guardian*, June 12, 1973, 15; *TL*, March 12, 1973, 12.

147. *Guardian*, August 9, 1972, 12.

148. Quoted in Rollo 1980, 191–192.

149. RCPMET for 1975, ms. version, MEPO 2/103064.

150. Special Patrol Group annual report, 1974, 3, MEPO 2/103064.

151. Appendix C of "Report of the Deputy Commissioner of the Special Patrol Group," 1980, HO 325/371.

152. Rollo 1980, 193–194.

153. *DMA*, January 22, 1973, 23.

154. RCPMET for 1975, MEPO 2/103064.

155. "Special Patrol Group—Crime Analysis," June 27, 1972, MEPO 2/10364; also "Divisional Commanders' Conference," minutes, April 6, 1972, MEPO 10/41.

156. *PR*, April 5, 1968, 290.

157. Quoted in Hall et al. 1978, 281.

158. *Guardian*, August 12, 1970, 5; also Fryer 2010, 394.

159. Bunyan 1977, 278–280.

160. Bunyan 1977, 83–86; RCPMET for 1973, 58, 79–80.

161. *PR*, May 5, 1972, 256.

162. Bunyan 1977, 88.

163. Special Patrol Group Superintendent annual reports 1973, 1974, 1976, MEPO 2/103064.

164. *Guardian*, September 8, 1972, 12; Rollo 1980, 192.

165. Bridges and Bunyan 1983, 97–98.

166. RCPMET for 1975, MEPO 2/103064.

167. Kettle and Bunyan 1980, 353; Bridges and Bunyan 1983, 100.

168. *Morning Star*, August 16, 1974, clipping in HO 325/371.

169. *Birmingham Daily Post*, November 10, 1969, 13.

170. Government of Northern Ireland 1969, 3.

171. Ellison and Smyth 2000, 105.

172. *Birmingham Daily Post*, November 10, 1969, 1.

173. Joyce 2016, 27–28.

174. Kettle and Bunyan 1980, 352–353; Bridges and Bunyan 1983, 100.

175. Police departments also created specialist firearms units separate from the SPGs and PPUs. See Kettle and Bunyan 1980, 352–354; Bridges and Bunyan 1983, 101.

176. *TL*, June 3, 1981, 3; "Final Report . . . Community Police Relations in Lambeth," 1981, HO 266/68, PRO.

177. Scarman 1981, 29–41; Vogler 1991, 116–117.

178. Peplow 2019, 109–110.

179. Scarman 1981, 23, 51,59, 150.

180. Hall et al. 1978, 46–48.

181. Rex 1982; Vogler 1991, 131.

182. Bunyan 1981, 166.

183. McMahon 2022, para. 22 d.

184. Scarman 1981, 13.

185. Peplow 2019, 152–153.

186. Peplow 2019, 168.

187. Quotes in Linstrum 2019, 582.

188. *Newcastle Journal*, July 7, 1981, 6.

189. Linstrum 2019, 582.

190. *Aberdeen Evening Express*, July 6, 1981, 1.

191. *DM*, April 30, 1981, 2.

192. *Newcastle Journal*, July 7, 1981, 6.

193. *Aberdeen Press and Journal*, May 2, 1981, 5.

194. *BT*, May 20, 1981, 9.

195. *BT*, July 6, 1981, 11.

196. *DM*, July 8, 1981, 2; *Newcastle Journal*, July 7, 1981, 6. In response to the Liverpool rioting, home secretary William Whitelaw pointed out that white nationalists were involved, and decried them as "cowardly racists," but he did not join the many African Caribbean community groups who later criticized police violence for stirring up resentment (*DM*, July 8, 1981, 2).

197. *TL*, July 10, 1981, 2.

198. *DM*, July 6, 1981, 5. Robert Mark, as former London Met commissioner, wrote an editorial in the *Times* to say that the riots should not be seen as coming from "blacks" only, but also whites. He nonetheless decried them all as "criminals" (*Observer*, July 12, 1981, 14).

199. *DM*, April 30, 1981, 2.
200. *BT*, May 20, 1981, 9.
201. *BT*, July 6, 1981, 11.
202. *Observer*, July 12, 1981, 14.
203. *SRB* 4, no. 25 (August–September 1981): 165.
204. *Reading Evening Post*, July 12, 1981, 8.
205. *Newcastle Journal*, July 7, 1981, 6.
206. *POM* 1 (December 1981): 4. See also *DM*, April 30, 1981, 2.
207. *TL*, July 10, 1981, 2.
208. Kettle and Hodges 1982, 233; *POM* 8 (July 1982): 16; *TL*, November 27, 1985, 36.
209. *Newcastle Journal*, July 7, 1981, 6.
210. *DM*, July 7, 1981, 6; *Daily Express*, July 9, 1981, 24.
211. *BT*, July 14, 1981, 4; "Civil Disturbances," July 16, 1981, vol. 8, col. 1397–1503, HC, PP; also *DM*, July 14, 1981, 1.
212. Taylor 2015, 124–125. On bringing in tools from "the former colonies," see *PR* 76 (March 22, 1968): 245.
213. Quotes in Sloan 1978, 22–24.
214. Shea 1973, 49–50. On baton rounds in Northern Ireland, see Drohan 2018. For a list of their usage and other riot control tools, see Deane-Drummond 1975, 147–155.
215. Ackroyd et al. 1977, 205–207.
216. *ST*, August 21, 1977, 1.
217. Northam 1988, 40, quote on 39.
218. Quoted in Northam 1988, 63.
219. Northam 1988, 40–41.
220. Northam 1988, 40–41.
221. *ST*, March 28, 1982, 4.
222. Northam 1988, 46, 135, quote on 132.
223. Kettle and Bunyan 1980, 353.
224. *Aberdeen Press and Journal*, July 10, 1981, 1.
225. Yiu-kwong 2015, xvii.
226. Quoted in Northam 1988, 53.
227. *Guardian*, August 12, 1985, 7.
228. Northam 1988, 59.
229. Cashmore and McLaughlin 1991, 34–35.
230. Cashmore and McLaughlin 1991, 34.
231. Gifford 1986, quotes on 44 and 45.
232. *Guardian*, July 3, 1986, 1; Cashmore and McLaughlin 1986, 33.
233. For more on the riots' impact, see Peplow 2019.
234. Ingleton 1996, 58.
235. *Hammersmith and Shepherds Bush Gazette*, July 18, 1986, 5; *Pinner Observer*, February 19, 1987, 10.
236. Eliott-Cooper 2021, 111–134.
237. Newburn et al. 2016, 214–217; Lewis et al. 2011; Wain and Joyce 2012, 131.

# Chapter 7

1. House of Commons, April 15, 1829, vol. 21, col. 883, HPD.
2. Fanon 1968 [1961], 40.
3. Speaking more technically, I have used a method that might be thought of as "comparative process tracing." Process tracing is a within-case procedure for testing hypotheses and thus making causal inferences (Mahoney 2003, 2012). Comparative process tracing begins as a within-case study identifying the hypothesized causal variables and then sees how they might be connected to outcome variables. It proceeds to between-case analyses, comparing how the relationships among variables apply or not in other cases (Bengtssoon and Ruonavaara 2016, 47–48).
4. Meanwhile, it has become too easy to make grand theoretical gestures and claims without empirically validating them or by basing them on observations of one set of events or sites—to employ deductive logic rather than explanations induced from careful empirical analyses of a wider set of cases.
5. Does not comparison militate against postcolonial, transnational, transimperial, or global studies? In some sectors of the critical academy, comparative analysis has become untrendy exactly on these grounds. However, to say that comparison is necessarily opposed to the analyses of more global processes is an unfortunate if not naive assumption that should be dispatched at once. The examination in this book, exploring police militarization in the United States and Britain, began as a seemingly conventional cross-national comparison that would appear to militate against excavations of transnational processes. But, as we have seen, it has ended up *comparing* transnational processes—in this case, it has compared processes of imperial importation from metropole to colony in the United States and British empires that have underpinned police militarization. It has thus compared processes within each empire while nonetheless remaining attentive to flows across them. See Go and Lawson 2017, 2020.
6. Seigel 2018.
7. The analysis has focused on *initial* moments of militarization in particular cities or agencies. Once a vanguard police department adopted a new militarized tactic, tool, or technique, it became further available for other departments to copy. The analysis in this book has focused only on the moment of initial adoption.
8. My views on postcolonial theory and its relevance for social science can be found in Go 2016, among other places. For existing scholarship that explicitly adopts a postcolonial perspective on policing, though in somewhat different ways, see Hönke and Müller 2020 and Brogden and Ellison 2013.
9. Said 1979.
10. Fassin 2013, 44.
11. The takeaway is not that imperialism is a new causal "variable" that can explain cross-national differences. We cannot, for instance, assume that because a country was not imperialistic, its police are not militarized. Nor is the analysis here meant to explain why, say, the French police are militarized. The focus here is on the "civil police" of the

United States and Britain. Other paths to militarization, particularly in Europe, have included Napoleonic conquest. I discuss this in Go 2020, 53–54.

12. Weber 1946, 77–128.

13. Siegel 2018.

14. See Go 2016, esp. 88–91 and 103–142.

15. Go 2016.

16. On the uses and abuses in social science of the concept "underclass," see Wacquant 2022. For the concept of the "subproletariat," I am drawing partly from Oppenheimer (1974), who distinguishes the subproletariat from the "lumpen proletariat" as well as the higher-paid unionized working class. On the "expropriation" vs. "exploitation" concept, see Fraser 2016.

17. Fanon 1968 [1961].

18. DuBois 2005 [1906]; Kelley 2020. The literature on "racial capitalism" is no doubt extensive; my own views are offered in Go 2021a.

19. Neocleous 2000. See Hinton 2021 for more on this cycle in the United States in the later twentieth century.

20. Stoughton 2015, 227.

21. Sierra-Arévalo 2021; Rizer 2022.

22. One might conclude that police training, the use of military equipment, and the military culture of policing today serve to reproduce and reinforce this warrior mentality, which is likely true. But we must not overlook the fact that such militaristic training and culture are deeply entrenched, reaching all the way back to when Sir Charles Rowan drew from military models to develop his training programs.

23. See Kuzmarov 2012, Schrader 2019, and Seigel 2018. For an excellent collection of essays on various multidirectional flows at more global scales, see Hönke and Müller 2020. The "exportation" of policing models is well studied. This book has focused upon one important phase in that process: the prior stage of importation. This book argues that many if not most of the models imported have come from the imperial periphery.

24. On the "war on drugs" and policing in a global context, see Koram 2019.

25. The difference in centralization and autonomy in police agencies between the United States and Britain, according to Bayley (1992), is in fact not large. In both countries, local police agencies have wide autonomy and the central government plays similarly weak roles (with the exception of Parliament's control over the Met). Another difference is that only in the United States are citizens subjected to overlapping police jurisdictions, whereas in Britain it makes much more sense to speak of a single coordinated policing system across the country.

26. Fisher 2022, 4; Adams 2015.

27. Elliott-Cooper 2021, 101–104. See also, on the policing of sexuality, Lvovsky 2020. On the inherently patriarchal character of counterinsurgency, see Owens 2015.

28. The same goes for militarized policing in America's long-standing colonies like Puerto Rico (LéBron 2019).

29. Weber 1992.

30. For "habitus," I refer to Bourdieu 1990.

31. *Pittsburgh Post-Gazette,* August 19, 2020, A1.
32. Kraska 2007, 7.
33. Kraska 2007, 6; American Civil Liberties Union 2014, 31.
34. Bush quote from Beckett 2000, 59–61; DoD quote from Else 2014, 2.
35. Else 2014, 2–3.
36. Radil et al. 2017.
37. Friedman et al. 2021, 5.
38. Davenport et al. 2018, 27–28. American intervention in the Middle East generated untold amounts of weaponry and equipment; the demobilization of US forces from Iraq in 2007 coupled with Section 1033 provided the DoD with this surplus military equipment for police (Radil et al. 2017, 208).
39. Murray 2016; American Civil Liberties Union n.d.; Brayne 2020.
40. Quoted in Baum 2016, 22–23. On the "war on drugs" as a racial project, see esp. Alexander 2010.
41. Ramey and Steidley 2018.
42. Eisenbud 2016.
43. Francis 2017; see also Graham and Baker 2020.
44. Cruikshank 2018.
45. The practices that come under the term "community policing" are varied, but recent efforts at community policing have drawn upon counterinsurgency principles since the Vietnam war era at least. See Hodge 2009, Senik 2010, Rosenau 2014, and Schrader 2016.
46. Cruikshank 2018.
47. Hodge 2009, para. 5.
48. From the podcast at: https://www.whoop.com/thelocker/podcast-2-kevin-kit-parker-mad-scientist-harvard/.
49. Berry 2013.
50. The Measured Group n.d.; Bertetto 2013.
51. Senik 2010.
52. Brayne 2020, 7.
53. Crocker 2017.
54. Bertetto 2013.
55. CST Editorial Board 2012.
56. Ingleton 1996, 59; *DM,* July 23, 2005, 7.
57. Rufford 2021; Ingleton 1996, 58; Home Office 2020a.
58. Ingleton 1996, 58.
59. *DMA* 17 May 1994, 2.
60. *DM,* July 23, 2005, 7.
61. Rufford 2021.
62. Home Office 2021, para. 4.
63. Rufford 2021.
64. Amnesty International 2018, 5; Perera 2019, 20.
65. Elliot-Cooper 2021. See also Nijjar 2018 and Williams and Clarke 2018.
66. Densley and Pyrooz 2019, 11–12; Amnesty International 2018.

67. Amnesty International 2018, 15–18. For more on the Matrix, "gangs," race, and crim-inalization, see Williams and Clarke 2016.
68. Elliott-Cooper 2021, 160.
69. McCulloch and Sentas 2006, 97–98; *DM,* July 23, 2005, 7; *Evening Standard,* July 23 2005, 6; *Guardian,* July 23, 2005, 2.
70. *TL,* July 23, 2005, 4; *DM,* July 23, 2005, 7.
71. *Guardian,* July 23, 2005, 2.
72. McCulloch and Sentas 2006, 100.
73. *Express,* January 3, 2006, 1; *Express,* January 13, 2006, 1.
74. Inquest n.d.; cf. Jones and Sawyer 2020.
75. Elliott-Cooper 2021; Lewis 2020.
76. Open University 2021. This refers to data from England and Wales between 2004 and 2019.
77. HO 2020b, 2021, 2022. For the 1990s, see Peplow 2019, 220.
78. Prison Reform Trust 2019, 7.
79. Elliot-Cooper 2021, 150.
80. Ramesh 2010.
81. Macfarlane 2020.
82. Macfarlane 2020.
83. At least two other books are especially insightful on how to move beyond police "re-form" and address systemic change: Vitale 2017 and Maher 2021.
84. Dodd 2015.
85. Gillon 2018.
86. Benyon 1984.
87. In 2021, the Black Lives Matter Global Network Foundation began embarked a cam-paign to end the program. Sen. Rand Paul (R-Kentucky) has sponsored legislation seeking to end the Section 1033 program.
88. Younes 2018. See also Schrader's (2017) discussion of an early attempt to reform po-licing that targeted militarized cultures—though in this case the attempts failed.
89. Besides the historians' work on this matter, see also Wacquant 2001, 117–119.

# References

Ackroyd, Carol, Karen Margolis, Jonathan Rosenhead, and Tim Shallice. 1977. *The Technology of Political Control*. London: Pluto Press.

Adams, James H. 2015. *Urban Reform and Sexual Vice in Progressive-Era Philadelphia*. Lanham, MD: Lexington Books.

Agee, Christopher Lowen. 2014. *The Streets of San Francisco: Policing and the Creation of a Cosmopolitan Liberal Politics, 1950–1972*. Chicago: University of Chicago Press.

Alderson, John C. 1979. *Policing Freedom*. Plymouth, UK: Macdonald and Evans.

Alexander, Joseph H. 2000. *Edson's Raiders: The 1st Marine Raider Battalion in World War II*. Asheville, NC: Edson's Raiders Association.

Alexander, Michelle. 2010. *The New Jim Crow: Mass Incarceration in the Age of Colorblindness*. New York: The New Press.

Allen, Theodore. 2012. *The Invention of the White Race, Volume I*. New York: Verso.

American Civil Liberties Union. 2014. *War Comes Home: The Excessive Militarization of American Policing*. New York: American Civil Liberties Union.

American Civil Liberties Union. n.d. "The NYPD Muslim Surveillance Program." https://www.aclu.org/other/factsheet-nypd-muslim-surveillance-program. Accessed April 5, 2022.

Amnesty International. 2018. *Trapped in the Matrix: Secrecy, Stigma, and Bias in the Met's Gangs Database*. London: Amnesty International, United Kingdom Section.

Anbinder, Tyler. 2015. "Irish Origins and the Shaping of Immigrant Life in Savannah on the Eve of the Civil War." *Journal of American Ethnic History* 35, no. 1: 5–37.

Anderson, David M., and David Killingray. 1991. "Consent, Coercion and Colonial Control: Policing the Empire, 1830–1940." In *Policing the Empire*, edited by David M. Anderson and David Killingray, 1–15. Manchester: Manchester University Press.

Anderson, Robert. 1907. *Criminals and Crime*. London: James Nisbet.

Anderson, Robert. 1910. *The Lighter Side of My Official Life*. London: Hodder and Stoughton.

Anderson, Robert. 1911. "The Problem of the Criminal Alien." *Nineteenth Century* 69: 217–224.

Andrew, Christopher. 1985. *Secret Service: The Making of the British Intelligence Community*. London: Heinemann.

Anne Arundel County, Maryland. n.d. "History of Anne Arundel County Police Dept." https://www.aacounty.org/departments/police-department/about-us/history/index.html. Accessed July 2, 2020.

Applegate, Rex. 1964. *Crowd and Riot Control*. Harrisburg, PA: Stackpole.

Archer, John E. 2011. *The Monster Evil: Policing and Violence in Victorian Liverpool*. Liverpool: Liverpool University Press.

Arendt, Hannah. 1970. *On Violence*. New York: Harcourt.

Arnold, David. 1976. "The Police and Colonial Control in South India." *Social Scientist* 4, no. 12: 3–16.

Arnold, David. 1977. "The Armed Police and Colonial Rule in South India, 1914–1917." *Modern Asian Studies* 11, no. 1: 101–125.

Arnold, David. 1986. *Police Power and Colonial Rule: Madras, 1859–1947*. Delhi: Oxford University Press.

Ascoli, David. 1979. *The Queen's Peace: The Origins and Development of the Metropolitan Police, 1829–1979*. London: Hamish Hamilton.

Ayers, Edward. 1985. *Vengeance and Justice: Crime and Punishment in the Nineteenth-Century American South*. New York: Oxford University Press.

Bach, Matthew. 2020. *Combating London's Criminal Class: A State Divided, 1869–95*. London: Bloomsbury.

Baer, Andrew S. 2020. *Beyond the Usual Beating: The Jon Burge Police Torture Scandal and Social Movements for Police Accountability in Chicago*. Chicago: University of Chicago Press.

Bailey, Ronald. 1994. "The Other Side of Slavery: Black Labor, Cotton, and Textile Industrialization in Great Britain and the United States." *Agricultural History* 68, no. 2: 35–50.

Bailey, Victor. 1981a. "The Metropolitan Police, the Home Office and the Threat of Outcast London." In *Policing and Punishment in Nineteenth Century Britain*, edited by Victory Bailey, 94–125. New Brunswick, NJ: Rutgers University Press.

Bailey, Victor, ed. 1981b. *Policing and Punishment in Nineteenth Century Britain*. New Brunswick, NJ: Rutgers University Press.

Bailey, Victor. 1993. "The Fabrication of Deviance: 'Dangerous Classes' and 'Criminal Classes' in Victorian England." In *Protest and Survival: The Historical Experience*, edited by John Rule and Robert Malcomson, 221–256. London: Merlin Press.

Baldoz, Rick. 2011. *The Third Asiatic Invasion*. New York: New York University Press.

Balko, Radley. 2013. *Rise of the Warrior Cop: The Militarization of America's Police Forces*. New York: PublicAffairs.

Ball, Harry. 1984. *Of Responsible Command: A History of the U.S. Army War College*. Carlisle, PA: Alumni Association of US Army War College.

Balto, Simon. 2019. *Occupied Territory: Policing Black Chicago from Red Summer to Black Power*. Chapel Hill: University of North Carolina Press.

Bancroft, Joseph. 1848. *Census of the City of Savannah*. Savannah, GA: Edward J. Purse.

Barder, Alexander D. 2015. *Empire Within: International Hierarchy and Its Imperial Laboratories of Governance*. New York: Routledge.

Barkawi, Tarak. 2017. *Soldiers of Empire: Indian and British Armies in World War II*. Cambridge, UK: Cambridge University Press.

Barnosky, Jason. 2006. "The Violent Years: Responses to Juvenile Crime in the 1950s." *Polity* 38, no. 3: 314–344.

Bartlett, Thomas. 1998. "Informers, Informants and Information: The Secret History of the 1790s." *History Ireland* 6, no. 2: 23–26.

Bartrip, Peter W. J. 1981. "Public Opinion and Law Enforcement: The Ticket-of-Leave Scares in Mid-Victorian Britain." In *Policing and Punishment in Nineteenth Century Britain*, edited by Victor Bailey, 150–181. New Brunswick, NJ: Rutgers University Press.

Baum, Dan. 2016. "Legalize it All." *Harper's Magazine*, April 2016, 22–32.

Bayley, David H. 1975. "The Police and Political Development in Europe." In *The Formation of National States in Western Europe*, edited by Charles Tilly, 328–379. Princeton, NJ: Princeton University Press.

Bayley, David H. 1992. "Comparative Organization of the Police in English-Speaking Countries." *Crime and Justice* 15: 506–545.

Beach, Walter G. 1932. *Oriental Crime in California: A Study of Offenses Committed by Orientals in That State 1900–1927*. New York: AMS Press.

Becker, Howard. 1963. *Outsiders: Studies in the Sociology of Deviance*. London: Free Press of Glencoe.

Beckert, Sven. 2014. *Empire of Cotton*. New York: Vintage Books.

Beckett, Katherine. 2000. *Making Crime Pay: Law and Order in Contemporary Politics*. Oxford: Oxford University Press.

Belchem, John. 1985. "English Working-Class Radicalism and the Irish, 1815–50." In *The Irish in the Victorian City*, edited by Roger Swift and Sheridan Gilley, 85–97. London: Croom Helm.

Bengtsoon, Bo, and Hannu Ruonavaara. 2016. "Comparative Process Tracing: Making Historical Comparison Structured and Focused." *Philosophy of the Social Sciences* 47, no. 1: 44–66.

Benyon, John, ed. 1984. *Scarman and After: Essays Reflecting on Lord Scarman's Report, the Riots and Their Aftermath*. Oxford: Pergamon Press.

Berger, Knute. 2014. "The Militarization of Seattle's Police." *Crosscut*, October 27, 2014. https://crosscut.com/2014/10/militarization-seattle-police-knute-berger.

Berman, Jay Stuart. 1987. *Police Administration and Progressive Reform*. New York: Greenwood Press.

Bermant, Chaim. 1975. *London's East End*. London: Macmillan.

Berresford Ellis, Peter. 1996. *A History of the Irish Working Class*. London: Pluto Press.

Berry, Conor. 2013. "Springfield Receives More than $700,000 to Help Fight Crime in City's North End." MassLive, January 19, 2013. https://www.masslive.com/news/2013/01/springfield_receives_more_than.html.

Bertetto, John A. 2013. "Counter-Gang Strategy." *Small Wars Journal*, November 11, 2013. https://smallwarsjournal.com/jrnl/art/counter-gang-strategy-adapted-coin-in-policing-criminal-street-gangs.

Bhabha, Homi K. 1994. *The Location of Culture*. London: Routledge.

Bickel, Keith. 2001. *Mars Learning: The Marine Corps' Development of Small Wars Doctrine, 1915–1940*. Boulder, CO: Westview Press.

Bidwell, Bruce. 1986. *History of the Military Intelligence Division, Department of the Army General Staff: 1775–1941*. Frederick, MD: University Publications of America.

Binder, Frederick, and David Reimers. 1996. *All the Nations Under Heaven: An Ethnic and Racial History of New York City*. New York: Columbia University Press.

Birtle, Andrew. 2009. *U.S. Army Counterinsurgency and Contingency Operations Doctrine, 1860–1941*. Washington, DC: US Army Center of Military History.

Bittner, Egon. 1970. *The Functions of the Police in Modern Society*. Chevy Chase, MD: National Institute of Mental Health.

Bjork, Katharine. 2019. *Prairie Imperialists: The Indian Country Origins of American Empire*. Philadelphia: University of Pennsylvania Press.

Blanchard, Emmanuel. 2014. "French Colonial Police." In *Encyclopedia of Criminology and Criminal Justice*, edited by Gerben Bruinsma and David Weisburd, 1836–1846. New York: Springer.

Blanchard, Emmanuel, Marieke Bloembergen, and Amandine Lauro, eds. 2017. *Policing in Colonial Empires*. Brussels: Peter Lang.

BLM Transparency Center. 2021. "BLM Global Network Foundation Launches Campaign to Stop Militarization of Police." Black Lives Matter, April 21, 2021. https://blacklive smatter.com/blm-global-network-foundation-launches-campaign-to-stop-militarizat ion-of-police/.

Bogue, Donald J. 1955. "Urbanism in the United States, 1950." *American Journal of Sociology* 60: 471–486.

Bourdieu, Pierre. 1990. *The Logic of Practice*. Palo Alto, CA: Stanford University Press.

Bowling, Benjamin. 1996. "The Emergence of Violent Racism as a Public Issue in Britain, 1945–81." In *Racial Violence in Britain in the Nineteenth and Twentieth Centuries*, edited by Panikos Panayi, 184–220. London: Leicester University Press.

Brayne, Sarah. 2020. *Predict and Surveil*. Oxford: Oxford University Press.

Bridges, Lee, and Tony Bunyan. 1983. "Britain's New Urban Policing Strategy—The Police and Criminal Evidence Bill in Context." *Journal of Law and Society* 10, no. 1: 85–107.

Broeker, Galen. 1961. "Robert Peel and the Peace Preservation Force." *Journal of Modern History* 33, no. 4: 363–373.

Broeker, Galen. 2017. *Rural Disorder and Police Reform in Ireland, 1812-36*. London: Routledge.

Brogden, Mike. 1987. "The Emergence of the Police—The Colonial Dimension." *British Journal of Criminology* 27, no. 1: 4–14.

Brogden, Mike, and Graham Ellison, eds. 2013. *Policing in an Age of Austerity: A Postcolonial Perspective*. London: Routledge.

Brooks, David C. 1989. "US Marines, Miskitos and the Hunt for Sandino: The Rio Coco Patrol in 1928." *Journal of Latin American Studies* 21, no. 2: 311–342.

Brown, Robert A. 2019. "Policing in American History." *Du Bois Review* 16, no. 1: 189–195.

Brucato, Ben. 2021. "Policing Race and Racing Police: The Origin of US Police in Slave Patrols." *Social Justice* 47, nos. 3–4: 115–136.

Brückenhaus, Daniel. 2017. *Policing Transnational Protest: Liberal Imperialism and the Surveillance of Anticolonialists in Europe, 1905-1945*. New York: Oxford University Press.

Bryan, Joe, and Denis Wood. 2015. "Weaponizing Maps: Indigenous Peoples and Counterinsurgency in the Americas." New York: Guilford Press,.

Bunyan, Tony. 1977. *The History and Practice of the Political Police in Britain*. London: Quartet.

Bunyan, Tony. 1981. "Police Against the People." *Race and Class* 23, nos. 2–3: 153–170.

Burgess-Parker, A. G. M. n.d. "The Formation of the Bristol Police Force and Its First Three Years of Existence." Pol/HM/1/1, Bristol Collections, Bristol Archives, Bristol, UK.

Busteed, Mervyn. 2016. *The Irish in Manchester, c. 1750-1921*. Manchester: Manchester University Press.

Callwell, C. E. 1906. *Small Wars: Their Principles and Practice*. London: His Majesty's Stationery Office.

Campion, David. 2005. "'Policing the Peelers': Parliament, the Public, and the Metropolitan Police, 1829-33." In *London Politics, 1769-1940*, edited by Matthew Cragoe and Antony Taylor, 38–56. London: Palgrave Macmillan.

Cannon, Lou. 1999. *Official Negligence: How Rodney King and the Riots Changed Los Angeles and the LAPD*. New York: Basic Books.

Canny, Nicholas. 1973. "The Ideology of English Colonization: From Ireland to America." *William and Mary Quarterly* 30, no. 4: 575–598.

Carte, Gene E. 1973. "August Vollmer and the Origins of Police Professionalism." *Journal of Police Science and Administration* 1, no. 3: 274–281.

Carte, Gene E., and Elaine H. Carte. 1975. *Police Reform in the United States: The Era of August Vollmer, 1905–1932*. Berkeley: University of California Press.

Carte, Gene E., Elaine Carte, and Jane Howard Robinson. 1983. *August Vollmer: Pioneer in Police Professionalism, Volume II*. Berkeley: Regional Oral History Office, Bancroft Library, University of California.

Cashmore, Ellis, and Eugene McLaughlin. 1991. "Out of Order?" In *Out of Order? Policing Black People*, edited by Ellis Cashmore and Eugene McLaughlin, 10–41. London: Routledge.

Cassidy, William. 1978. "Historical Origins of the Special Weapons and Tactics Concept." *Police Journal* 45: 45–51.

Césaire, Aimé. 1955. *Discours sur le colonialisme*. Paris: Présence Africaine.

Chadwick, Bruce. 2017. *Law and Disorder: The Chaotic Birth of the NYPD*. New York: St. Martin's Press.

Chamberlain, W. H. J. 1976. *Adam's Revolvers*. London: Barrie & Jenkins.

Channing, Iain. 2018. "Chief Constables and Public Order." In *Leading the Police: A History of Chief Constables 1835–2017*, edited by Kim Stevenson, David J. Cox, and Iain Channing, 174–190. London: Routledge.

Cherry, William. 1975. "The Military: A Source of Equipment and Training." *The Police Chief* 42: 53–55.

Chicago Commission on Human Relations. 1961. "Non-White Population Changes 1950–1960." *Human Relations News of Chicago* 3, no. 3: 1–16.

Chronopoulos, Themis. 2018. "Police Misconduct, Community Opposition, and Urban Governance in New York City, 1945–1965." *Journal of Urban History* 44, no. 4: 643–688.

Churchill, David. 2017. *Crime Control and Everyday Life in the Victorian City*. Oxford: Oxford University Press.

Claeys, Gregory. 1989. *Citizens and Saints: Politics and Anti-politics in Early British socialism*. Cambridge, UK: Cambridge University Press.

Clapham, John H. 1932. *An Economic History of Modern Britain*. Cambridge: Cambridge University Press.

Clark, Jason P. 2017. *Preparing for War: The Emergence of the Modern U.S. Army, 1815–1917*. Cambridge, MA: Harvard University Press.

Clarkson, Charles Tempest, and J. Hall Richardson. 1889. *Police!* London: Field and Tuer.

Clayton, Anthony, and David Killingray. 1989. *Khaki and Blue: Military and Police in British Colonial Africa*. Athens: Ohio Center for International Studies.

Clinton, Paul. 2010. "Daryl Gates and the Origins of LAPD SWAT." *Police Magazine*, April 16, 2010. http://www.policemag.com/blog/swat/story/2010/04/daryl-gates-and-the-origins-of-lapd-swat.aspx.

Clutterbuck, Linsday. 2006. "Countering Irish Republic Terrorism in Britain: Its Origin as a Police Function." *Terrorism and Political Violence* 18: 95–118.

Clutterbuck, Richard. 1973. *Protest and the Urban Guerilla*. London: Cassell.

Coe, Paul F. 1959. "The Nonwhite Population Surge to Our Cities." *Land Economics* 35, no. 3: 195–210.

Cohen, Stanley. 1972. *Folk Devils and Moral Panics*. London: MacGibbon and Kee.

Colquhoun, Patrick. 1806. *A Treatise on the Police of the Metropolis*. London: J. Mawman, Cadell and Davies.

Cole, Simon A. 2001. *Suspect Identities: A History of Criminal Identification and Fingerprinting*. Cambridge, MA: Harvard University Press.

Collings-Wells, Sam. 2019. "Policing the Windrush Generation." *History Today* 69, no. 11 (November). http: https://www.historytoday.com/archive/history-matters/policing-windrush-generation.

Columbus Police Benevolent Association. 1908. *History of the Police Department of Columbus, Ohio*. Columbus, OH: Columbus Police Benevolent Association.

Committee on the State of the Police of the Metropolis. 1817. *Second Report from the Committee on the State of the Police of the Metropolis*. London: House of Commons Parliamentary Papers.

Committee to Inquire into the Best Means Available for Identifying Habitual Criminals. 1894. *Report of a Committee Appointed by the Secretary of State to Inquire into the Best Means Available for Identifying Habitual Criminals; with Minutes of Evidence and Appendices*. London: Her Majesty's Stationery Office.

Conroy, John. 2005. "The Tools of Torture." *Chicago Reader*, February 3, 2005. https://chicagoreader.com/news-politics/tools-of-torture/.

Conti, Philip. 1977. *The Pennsylvania State Police: A History of the Service to the Commonwealth, 1905 to the Present*. Mechanicsburg, PA: Stackpole Books.

Cooper, Thomas. 1838. *The Statutes at Large of South Carolina*. Columbia, SC: A. S. Johnston.

Cosmas, Graham. 1998. *An Army for Empire: The United States Army in the Spanish-American War*. Shippensburg, PA: White Mane.

Costello, Augustine. 1885. *Our Police Protectors: History of the New York Police from the Earliest Period to the Present Time*. New York: Augustine Costello.

Courtwright, David T. 2001. *Dark Paradise: A History of Opiate Addiction in America*. Cambridge, MA: Harvard University Press.

Coyne, Christopher J., and Abigail Hall. 2018. *Tyranny Comes Home: The Domestic Fate of U.S. Militarism*. Palo Alto, CA: Stanford University Press.

Critchley, Thomas Alan. 1978. *A History of Police in England and Wales*. London: Constable.

Crossman, Virginia. 1991. "Emergency Legislation and Agrarian Disorder in Ireland, 1821–1841." *Irish Historical Studies* 27, no. 108: 309–323.

Crocker, Timothy. 2017. "The Power of Social Network Analysis." *Police Chief* (online). https://www.policechiefmagazine.org/power-social-network-analysis/.

Cruickshank, Paul. 2018. "A View from the CT Foxhole." *CTC Sentinel* 11, no. 10: 13–16. https://ctc.usma.edu/view-ct-foxhole-patrick-skinner-police-officer-savannah-georgia-former-cia-case-officer-afghanistan-iraq/.

Crymble, Adam. 2014. "Surname Analysis, Distant Reading, and Migrant Experience: The Irish in London, 1801–1820." PhD dissertation, Department of History and Digital Humanities, King's College, University of London.

Crymble, Adam. 2018. "How Criminal Were the Irish? Bias in the Detection of London Currency Crime, 1797–1821." *The London Journal: A Review of Metropolitan Society Past and Present* 43, no. 1: 36–52.

CST Editorial Board. 2012. "Chicago Takes a Much-Needed Step to Overhaul Police Gang Database." *Chicago Sun-Times*, November 21, 2021. https://chicago.suntimes.com/2021/11/21/22791798/chicago-police-gang-database-appeal-process-city-council-mayor-lightfoot-editorial.

Curtis, L. Perry. 1997. *Apes and Angels: The Irishman in Victorian Caricature*. Washington, DC: Smithsonian Institution Press.

Curtis, L. P. 1971. *Apes and Angels: The Irishman in Victorian Caricature*. Newton Abbott, UK: David and Charles.

Cusick, Ray. 2013. *Wellington's Rifles: The Origins, Development and Battles of the Rifle Regiments in the Peninsular War and at Waterloo from 1758 to 1815*. Barnsley, UK: Pen & Sword Books.

Davenport, Aaron, Jonathan Welburn, Andrew Lauland, Annelise Pientenpol, Marc Robbins, Erin Rebhan, Patricia Boren, and K. Jack Riley. 2018. *An Evaluation of the Department of Defense's Excess Property Program*. Santa Monica, CA: Rand Corporation.

Davies, Stephen. 1985. "Classes and Police in Manchester, 1829–1880." In *City, Class and Culture*, edited by Alan Kidd and Kenneth Roberts, 26–47. Manchester: Manchester University Press.

Davis, George. 1899. *Report of Brig. Gen. Geo. W. Davis on the Civil Affairs of Puerto Rico*. Washington, DC: US Government Printing Office.

Davis, Jennifer. 1980. "The London Garrotting Panic of 1862." In *Crime and the Law: The Social History of Crime in Western Europe Since 1500*, edited by V. A. C. Gatrell, Bruce Lenman, and Geoffrey Parker, 190–213. London: Europa Publications.

Deane-Drummond, Anthony. 1975. *Riot Control*. London: Thornton Cox.

Delehanty, Casey, Jack Mewhirter, Ryan Welch, and Jason Wilks. 2017. "Militarization and Police Violence: The Case of the 1033 Program." *Research and Politics* 4, no. 2: 1–7.

Densley, James, and David C. Pyrooz. 2019. "The Matrix in Context: Taking Stock of Police Gang Databases in London and Beyond." *Youth Justice* 20, nos. 1–2: 11–30.

Dixon, Paul. 2009. "'Hearts and Minds'? British Counter-Insurgency from Malaya to Iraq." *Journal of Strategic Studies* 32, no. 3: 353–381.

Dodd, Vikram. 2015. "Theresa May Rejects Use of Water Cannon." *The Guardian*, July 23, 2015. https://www.theguardian.com/uk-news/2015/jul/23/theresa-may-police-water-cannon-use-england-wales.

Dolan, Paul. 1940. "Rise of Crime in the Period 1830–1860." *Journal of Criminal Law and Criminology* 30, no. 6: 857–864.

Donner, Frank J. 1990. *Protectors of Privilege: Red Squads and Police Repression in Urban America*. Berkeley: University of California Press.

Doughty, Robert A. 1979. *The Evolution of US Army Tactical Doctrine, 1946–1976*. Fort Leavenworth, KS: Combat Studies Institute.

Dowbiggin, H. L. 1928. "The Ceylon Police and Its Development." *Police Journal* 1, no. 2: 203–217.

Drohan, Brian. 2018. "Unintended Consequences: Baton Rounds, Riots, and Counterinsurgency in Northern Ireland, 1970–1981." *Journal of Military History* 82 (April): 491–514.

Dubber, Markus Dirk. 2005. *The Police Power: Patriarchy and the Foundations of American Government*. New York: Columbia University Press.

DuBois, W. E. B. 1935. *Black Reconstruction in America*. New York: Russell & Russell.

DuBois, W. E. B. 2005 [1906]. "The Color Line Belts the World." In *W. E. B. Du Bois on Asia*, edited by Bill Mullen and Cathryn Mullen, 33–34. Jackson: University Press of Mississippi.

Dukova, Anastasia. 2016. *A History of the Dublin Metropolitan Police and its Colonial Legacy*. London: Palgrave Macmillan.

Dulaney, W. Marvin. 1996. *Black Police in America*. Bloomington: Indiana University Press.

Dunbar-Ortiz, Roxanne. 2018. *Loaded: A Disarming History of the Second Amendment.* San Francisco: City Lights Books.

Eastman, George D. 1960. "The Flexible Unit—A Unique Striking Force." *Police*, July–August 1960, 14–17.

Edwards, Clarence R. 1912. "What Is the Matter with Our Army: It Lacks Organization." *The Independent*, February 22, 1912, 406–411.

Eisenbud, Daniel. 2016. "US Police Chiefs Visit Israel to Learn Counter-Terrorism Techniques." *Jerusalem Post*, August 3, 2016. https://www.jpost.com/Israel-News/US-police-chiefs-visit-Israel-to-learn-counter-terrorism-techniques-463090.

Elkins, Alexander B. 2017. "Battle of the Corner: Urban Policing and Rioting in the United States, 1943–1971." PhD dissertation, Department of History, Temple University.

Elliott, Benjamin, and Martin Strobel. 1835. *The Militia System of South-Carolina, Being a Digest of the Acts of Congress Concerning the Militia, Likewise of the Militia Laws of This State* . . . Charleston, SC: A. E. Miller.

Elliott-Cooper, Adam. 2021. *Black Resistance to British Policing.* Manchester: Manchester University Press.

Ellison, Graham, and Conor O'Reilly. 2008. "From Empire to Iraq and the 'War on Terror': The Transplantation and Commodification of the (Northern) Irish Policing Experience." *Police Quarterly* 11, no. 4: 395–426.

Ellison, Graham, and Jim Smyth. 2000. *The Crowned Harp: Policing in Northern Ireland.* London: Pluto Press.

Else, Daniel. 2014. "The '1033 Program,' Department of Defense Support to Law Enforcement." Congressional Research Service Report No. R43701, Washington, DC.

Emsley, Clive. 1985. "The Thump of Wood on a Swede Turnip." *Criminal Justice History* 6: 125–149.

Emsley, Clive. 1986. "Detection and Prevention: The Old English Police and the New 1750–1900." *Historical Social Research* 37: 69–88.

Emsley, Clive. 1996. *The English Police.* London: Longman.

Emsley, Clive. 1999a. *Gendarmes and the State in Nineteenth-Century Europe.* Oxford: Oxford University Press.

Emsley, Clive. 1999b. "A Typology of Nineteenth-Century Police." *Crime, Histoire and Sociétés / Crime, History and Societies* 3, no. 1: 29–44.

Emsley, Clive. 2005. *Crime and Society in England 1759–1900.* 3rd ed. London: Longman.

Emsley, Clive. 2008. "Violent Crime in England in 1919: Post-war Anxieties and Press Narratives." *Continuity and Change* 23, no. 1: 173–195.

Englander, David. 1989. "Booth's Jews: The Presentation of Jews and Judaism in *Life and Labor of the People in London.*" *Victorian Studies* 32, no. 4: 551–571.

Ernst, Robert. 1948. "Economic Nativism in New York City During the 1840s." *New York History* 29, no. 2: 170–186.

Escobar, Edward. 1999. *Race, Police, and the Making of a Political Identitiy: Mexican Americans and the Los Angeles Police Department, 1900–1945.* Berkeley: University of California Press.

Ewence, Hannah. 2019. *The Alien Jew in the British Imagination, 1881–1905: Space, Mobility and Territoriality.* Cham, Switzerland: Palgrave Macmillan.

Faligot, Roger. 1983. *Britain's Military Strategy in Ireland: The Kitson Experiment.* London: Zed Press.

Fanon, Frantz. 1968 (1961). *The Wretched of the Earth.* New York: Grove Press.

Farley, M. Foster. 1969. "John Elliott Ward, Mayor of Savannah 1853–1854." *Georgia Historical Quarterly* 53, no. 1: 68–71.

Fassin, Didier. 2013. *Enforcing Order: An Ethnography of Urban Policing.* Cambridge, UK: Polity Press.

Feigenbaum, Anna. 2017. *Tear Gas: From the Battlefields of World War I to the Streets of Today.* London: Verso.

Felker-Kantor, Max. 2018. *Policing Los Angeles.* Chapel Hill: University of North Carolina Press.

Finnane, Mark. 2005. "Crimes of Violence, Crimes of Empire?" In *Crime and Empire, 1840–1940,* edited by Barry S. Godfrey and Garaeme Dunstall, 43–56. Cullumpton, Devon, UK: Willan.

Fisher, Anne Gray. 2022. *The Streets Belong to Us: Sex, Race and Police Power from Segregation to Gentrification.* Chapel Hill: University of North Carolina Press.

Fitzpatrick, David. 1989. "A Curious Middle Place: The Irish in Britain, 1871–1921." In *The Irish in Britain, 1815–1939,* edited by Roger Swift and Sheridan Gilley, 10–59. Savage, MD: Barnes and Noble Books.

Fletcher, Joseph. 1850. "Statistical Account of the Police of the Metropolis." *Journal of the Statistical Society of London* 13, no. 3: 221–267.

Floud, Roderick, and Paul Johnson. 2004. "Trade: Discovery, Mercantilism and Technology." In *The Cambridge Economic History of Modern Britain,* edited by Roderick Floud and Paul Johnson, 175–203. Cambridge, UK: Cambridge University Press.

Fogelson, Robert M. 1977. *Big-City Police.* Cambridge, MA: Harvard University Press.

Foner, Nancy. 1979. "West Indians in New York City and London: A Comparative Analysis." *International Migration Review* 13, no. 2: 284–297.

Forbes, W. Cameron. 1928. *The Philippine Islands.* Boston: Houghton Mifflin.

Forte, Matthew G. 2000. *American Police Equipment: A Guide to Early Restraints, Clubs and Lanterns.* Upper Montclair, NJ: Turn of the Century.

Fosdick, Raymond. 1915. *European Police Systems.* New York: Century.

Fosdick, Raymond. 1920. *American Police Systems.* New York: Century.

Foster, Anne. 2010. "Opium, the United States, and the Civilizing Mission in Colonial Southeast Asia." *Social History of Alcohol and Drugs* 24, no. 1: 6–19.

Foucault, Michel. 1979. *Discipline and Punish: The Birth of the Prison.* New York: Vintage Books.

Foucault, Michel. 1997. *"Society Must Be Defended." Lectures at the Collège de France, 1975–79.* New York: Picador.

Francis, Peter. 2017. "Haverhill Police Chief Travels to Israel on Training Trip." *Eagle-Tribune* (North Andover, MA), December 26, 2017. https://www.eagletribune.com/news/haverhill/haverhill-police-chief-travels-to-israel-on-training-trip/article_4c035 75f-e04b-5ad4-adcb-4a0cba7a2fb6.html.

Fraser, Nancy. 2016. "Expropriation and Exploitation in Racialized Capitalism: A Reply to Michael Dawson." *Critical Historical Studies* 3, no. 1: 163–178.

Fraser, Walter Jr. 2003. *Savannah in the Old South.* Athens: University of Georgia Press.

Friedman, Barry, Jessica W. Gillooly, Maria Ponomarenko, Karen L. Amendola, Tom Clark, Adam Glynn, and Michael Leo Owens. 2021. "Police Militarization: A 1033 Program Analysis." The Policing Project (New York University School of Law), Emory University, and the National Police Foundation.

Fryer, Peter. 2010. *Staying Power: The History of Black People in Britain.* London: Pluto Books.

Fuld, Leonard Felix. 1910. *Police Administration: A Critical Study of Police Organisations in the United States and Abroad*. New York: G. P. Putnam's Sons.

Gamble, Thomas. 1900. *A History of the Government of the City of Savannah, Ga., from 1790 to 1901*. Savannah: City Council.

Gartner, Lloyd P. 2001. *History of the Jews in Modern Times*. Oxford: Oxford University Press.

Gash, Norman. 1961. *Mr. Secretary Peel*. Cambridge, MA: Harvard University Press.

Gates, Daryl. 1992. *Chief: My Life in the LAPD*. New York: Bantam Books.

Gatrell, V. A. C. 2008. "Crime, Authority and the Policeman-State." In *The Cambridge Social History of Britain, 1750–1950*, edited by F. M. L. Thompson, 3:243–310. Cambridge, UK: Cambridge University Press.

George, M. Dorothy. 1965. *London Life in the Eighteenth Century*. New York: Harper and Row.

Gerard, James. 1853. *London and New York: Their Crime and Police*. New York: Wm. C. Bryant.

Gessel, Elizabeth A. 2003. "Nowhere but Heaven: Savannah, Georgia, During the Era of the First Great Migration." PhD dissertation, Department of History, University of California, Berkeley.

Giarruso, Joseph. 1961. "New Orleans Police Use Tactical Unit to Prevent Crime." *FBI Law Enforcement Bulletin* 30, no. 2: 3–7.

Gifford, Tony. 1986. *The Broadwater Farm Inquiry: Report of the Independent Inquiry into Disturbances of October 1985 at the Broadwater Farm Estate, Tottenham, Chaired by Lord Gifford*. London: Karia Press.

Gillon, Steven. 2018. *Separate and Unequal: The Kerner Commission and the Unraveling of American Liberalism*. New York: Basic Books.

Gilroy, Paul. 1982. "Police and Thieves." In *The Empire Strikes Back: Race and Racism in 70s Britain*, edited by Centre for Contemporary Culture Studies, 143–182. London: Hutchinson.

Glazer, Nathan, and Daniel P. Moynihan. 1974. *Beyond the Melting Pot: The Negroes, Puerto Ricans, Jews, Italians, and Irish of New York City*. Cambridge, MA: MIT Press.

Gleeson, David. 2001. *The Irish in the South, 1815–1877*. Chapel Hill: University of North Carolina Press.

Go, Julian. 2004. "'Racism' and Colonialism: Meanings of Difference and Ruling Practices in America's Pacific Empire." *Qualitative Sociology* 27, no. 1: 35–58.

Go, Julian. 2007. "The Provinciality of American Empire: 'Liberal Exceptionalism' and US Colonial Rule." *Comparative Studies in Society and History* 49, no. 1: 74–108.

Go, Julian. 2008. *American Empire and the Politics of Meaning*. Durham, NC: Duke University Press.

Go, Julian. 2011. *Patterns of Empire: The British and American Empires, 1688–Present*. Cambridge, UK: Cambridge University Press.

Go, Julian. 2014a. "Capital, Containment, and Competition: The Dynamics of British Imperialism, 1730–1939." *Social Science History* 38, nos. 1–2: 43–69.

Go, Julian. 2014b. "Comparing Societies." In *Concise Encyclopedia of Comparative Sociology*, edited by Masamichi Sasaki, Jack Goldstone, Ekkart Zimmerman, and Stephen Sanderson, 21–29. Boston: Brill.

Go, Julian. 2014c. "The Historical Sociology of Empire: Response to Critics of *Patterns of Empire*." *Comparative Studies of South Asia, Africa, and the Middle East* 34, no. 3: 644–651.

Go, Julian. 2016. *Postcolonial Thought and Social Theory*. New York: Oxford University Press.

Go, Julian. 2020. "The Imperial Origins of American Policing: Militarization and Imperial Feedback in the Early 20th Century." *American Journal of Sociology* 125, no. 5: 1193–1254.

Go, Julian. 2021a. "Three Tensions in the Theory of Racial Capitalism." *Sociological Theory* 39, no. 1: 38–47.

Go, Julian. 2021b. "From Crime Fighting to Counterinsurgency: The Transformation of London's Special Patrol Group in the 1970s." *Small Wars and Insurgencies* 33, nos. 4–5: 654–672.

Go, Julian, and George Lawson. 2017. *Global Historical Sociology*. Cambridge, UK: Cambridge University Press.

Go, Julian, and George Lawson. 2020. "Response to Reviewers—*Global Historical Sociology*." *Cambridge Review of International Affairs* 33, no. 6: 914–920.

Goodenough, William Howley, and James Cecil Dalton. 1893. *The Army Book for the British Empire*. London: Her Majesty's Stationery Office.

Gordon, Paul. 1983. *White Law: Racism in the Police, Courts and Prisons*. London: Pluto Press.

Gordon, Paul. 1985. *Policing Immigration*. London: Pluto Press.

Gorski, Philip S. 2013. "What Is Critical Realism? And Why Should You Care?" *Contemporary Sociology: A Journal of Reviews* 42, no. 5: 658–670.

Gossett, Thomas F. 1997. *Race: The History of an Idea in America*. New York: Oxford University Press.

Gould, Robert W., and Michael J. Waldren. 1986. *London's Armed Police*. London: Arms and Armour Press.

Gourevitch, Alex. 2015. "The Centrality of Labor Repression in American Political History." *Perspectives on Politics* 13, no. 3: 762–773.

Government of Northern Ireland. 1969. *Report of the Advisory Committee on Police in Northern Ireland*. Belfast: Her Majesty's Stationery Office.

Governor of Porto Rico. 1901. *First Annual Report of the Governor of Porto Rico*. Washington, DC: US Government Printing Office.

Governor's Commission on the Los Angeles Riots. 1965. *Violence in the City—An End or a Beginning?* Los Angeles: Governor's Commission on the Los Angeles Riots.

Graham, Stephen, and Alexander Baker. 2020. "Laboratories of Pacification and Permanent War." In *The Global Making of Policing: Postcolonial Perspectives*, edited by Jana Hönke and Markus-Michael Müller, 40–58. London: Routledge.

Graper, Elmer. 1921. *American Police Administration: A Handbook of Police Organization and Methods of Administration in American Cities*. New York: Macmillan.

Hadden, Sally. 2001. *Slave Patrols*. Cambridge, MA: Harvard University Press.

Hall, Nigel. 2017. "Liverpool's Cotton Importers, c. 1700 to 1914." *Northern History* 54, no. 1: 79–93.

Hall, Stuart. 2021. *Selected Writings on Race and Difference*. Durham, NC: Duke University Press.

Hall, Stuart, Charles Critcher, Tony Jefferson, John Clarke, and Brian Roberts. 1978. *Policing the Crisis*. London: Macmillan.

Harcourt, Bernard. 2018. *The Counterrevolution: How Our Government Went to War Against Its Own Citizens*. New York: Basic Books.

Harden, William. 1934. *Recollections of a Long and Satisfactory Life*. New York: Negro Universities Press.

Harring, Sidney. 1983. *Policing a Class Society: The Experience of American cities, 1865–1915*. New Brunswick, NJ: Rutgers University Press.

Harris, Andrew T. 2004. *Policing the City: Crime and Legal Authority in London, 1780–1840*. Columbus: Ohio State University Press.

Haunton, Richard. 1968. "Savannah in the 1850s." PhD dissertation, Department of History, Emory University.

Haunton, Richard. 1972. "Law and Order in Savannah, 1850–1860." *Georgia Historical Quarterly* 56, no. 1: 1–24.

Hawkins, Richard. 1991. "The 'Irish Model' and the Empire: A Case for Reassessment." In *Policing the Empire*, edited by David M. Anderson and David Killingray, 18–32. Manchester: Manchester University Press.

Hay, Douglas, and Francis Snyder. 1989. "Using the Criminal Law, 1750–1850: Policing, Private Prosecution, and the State." In *Policing and Prosecution in Britain 1750–1850*, edited by Douglas Hay and Francis Snyder, 3–54. Oxford: Clarendon Press.

Henry, Edward. 1901. *Classification and Uses of Finger Prints*. London: Her Majesty's Stationery Office.

Hernandez, Kelly Lytle. 2010. *Migra! A History of the US Border Patrol*. Berkeley: University of California Press.

Hershler, Nathanial. 1900. *The Soldier's Handbook for Use in the Army of the United States, Prepared by Direction of the Adjutant General of the Army*. Washington, DC: US Government Printing Office.

Hewitt, E. 1979. *A History of Policing in Manchester*. Manchester: Morten.

Hickman, Mary. 1995. *Religion, Class and Identity*. Aldershot: Avebury.

Hills, Alice. 1995. "Militant Tendencies: 'Paramilitarism' in the British Police." *British Journal of Criminology* 35, no. 3: 450–458.

Hillyard, Paddy. 1985. "Lessons from Ireland." In *Policing the Miners' Strike*, edited by Bob Fine and Douglas Millar, 177–187. London: Lawrence and Wishart.

Hinton, Elizabeth. 2017. *From the War on Poverty to the War on Crime*. Cambridge, MA: Harvard University Press.

Hinton, Elizabeth Kai. 2021. *America on Fire: The Untold History of Police Violence and Black Rebellion Since the 1960s*. New York: Liveright.

Hirota, Hidetaka. 2014. "'The Great Entrepot for Mendicants': Foreign Poverty and Immigration Control in New York State to 1882." *Journal of American Ethnic History* 33, no. 2: 5–32.

Hirota, Hidetaka. 2017. *Expelling the Poor: Atlantic Seaboard States and the Nineteenth-Century Origins of American Immigration Policy*. New York: Cambridge University Press.

Hodder, Edwin. 1877. *All the World Over: Sketches and Tales*. New York: Atheneum.

Hodge, Nathan. 2009. "'Counterinsurgency' to Fight U.S. Crime? No, Thanks." *Wired*, November 24, 2009. https://www.wired.com/2009/11/counterinsurgency-to-fight-us-crime-no-thanks/.

Hoffman, Bruce. 2013. "The Palestine Police Force and the Challenges of Gathering Counterterrorism Intelligence, 1939–1947." *Small Wars and Insurgencies* 24, no. 4: 609–647.

Home Office, UK. 1868. *Manual of Drill, Prepared for the Use of the County and District Constables*. London: W. Clowes & Sons.

Home Office, UK. 2015. "Police Use of Taser Statistics, England and Wales 2014." https://www.gov.uk/government/statistics/police-use-of-taser-statistics-england-and-wales-1-january-to-31-december-2014/police-use-of-taser-statistics-england-and-wales-2014#trends-in-taser-use-2010-to-2014.

Home Office, UK. 2020a. "Police Use of Firearms Statistics, England and Wales: April 2019 to March 2020." https://www.gov.uk/government/statistics/police-use-of-firearms-statistics-england-and-wales-april-2019-to-march-2020.

Home Office, UK. 2020b. "Police Use of Force Statistics, England and Wales: April 2019 to March 2020." https://www.gov.uk/government/statistics/police-use-of-force-statistics-england-and-wales-april-2019-to-march-2020.

Home Office, UK. 2021. "Police Use of Force Statistics, England and Wales: April 2020 to March 2021." https://www.gov.uk/government/statistics/police-use-of-force-statistics-england-and-wales-april-2020-to-march-2021/police-use-of-force-statistics-england-and-wales-april-2020-to-march-2021.

Home Office, UK. 2022. "Stop and Search." May 27, 2022. https://www.ethnicity-facts-figures.service.gov.uk/crime-justice-and-the-law/policing/stop-and-search/latest#main-facts-and-figures.

Hönke, Jana, and Markus-Michael Müller, eds. 2020. *The Global Making of Policing: Postcolonial Perspectives*. London: Routledge.

Hood, Clifton. 2016. *In Pursuit of Privilege: A History of New York City's Upper Class and the Making of a Metropolis*. New York: Columbia University Press.

Hoppen, K. Theodore. 2016. *Governing Hibernia: British Politicians and Ireland, 1800–1921*. Oxford: Oxford University Press.

Horne, Gerald. 1995. *Fire This Time: The Watts Uprising and the 1960s*. Charlottesville: University of Virginia Press.

Horne, Gerald. 2003. "Race from Power: U.S. Foreign Policy and the General Crisis of White Supremacy." In *Window on Freedom*, edited by Brenda Gayle Plummer, 45–66. Chapel Hill: University of North Carolina Press.

House of Commons, Parliament, UK. 1830. *Return of the Metropolitan Police Force, with the Number of Divisions, and an Estimate of Population in Each Division, 1st June 1830*. Parliamentary Papers.

House of Commons, Parliament, UK. 1834. *Report from the Select Committee on the Police on the Police of the Metropolis*. London: House of Commons.

House of Commons, Parliament, UK. 1886. *Disturbances (Metropolis): Report of the Committee Appointed by the Secretary of State for the Home Department to Inquire into the Administration and Organisation of the Metropolitan Police Force*. London: Eyre and Spottiswoode.

Huebner, Michael. 1997. "Base Alignment and Closure: A Historical Perspective." *Military Review* 77, no. 6: 68–73.

Humphry, Derek. 1972. *Police Power and Black People*. London: Panther Books.

Hutchinson, S. 1969. "The Police Role in Counter-Insurgency Operations." *Royal United Services Institution Journal* 114, no. 565: 56–61.

Hutton, E. T. H. 1886. "Mounted Infantry." *Royal United Services Institution Journal* 30, no. 135: 695–738.

Ignatiev, Noel. 1995. *How the Irish Became White*. London: Routledge.

Immerwahr, Daniel. 2016. "The Greater United States: Territory and Empire in U.S. History." *Diplomatic History* 40, no. 3: 373–391.

Ingleton, Roy. 1996. *Arming the British Police: The Great Debate*. London: Frank Cass.

Inquest. n.d. "Fatal Police Shootings." https://www.inquest.org.uk/fatal-police-shootings, accessed 12/2/2022.

Institute of Race Relations. 1979. *Police Against Black People: Evidence Submitted to the Royal Commission on Criminal Procedure*. London: Institute of Race Relations.

International City Managers' Association. 1954. *Municipal Police Administration*. 4th ed. Chicago: Intnernational City Managers' Association.

Inwood, Stephen. 1990. "Policing London's Morals: The Metropolitan Police and Popular Culture, 1829–1850." *The London Journal: A Review of Metropolitan Society Past and Present* 15, no. 2: 129–146.

Jackson, Isabella. 2017. *Shaping Modern Shanghai: Colonialism in China's Global City*. Cambridge, UK: Cambridge University Press.

Jackson, John Archer. 1963. *The Irish in Britain*. London: Routledge.

Jackson, P. I., and L. Carroll. 1981. "Race and the War on Crime: The Sociopolitical Determinants of Municipal Police Expenditures in 90 Non-Southern US Cities." *American Sociological Review* 46: 290–305.

Jacobs, Paul. 1968. *Prelude to Riot*. New York: Random House.

Jacobson, Matthew Frye. 2000. *Barbarian Virtues: The United States Encounters Foreign Peoples at Home and Abroad*. New York: Hill and Wang.

Jamieson, Perry D. 1994. *Crossing the Deadly Ground: United States Army Tactics, 1865–1899*. Tucsaloosa: University of Alabama Press.

Jefferson, Tony. 1990. *The Case Against Military Policing*. Milton Keynes, UK: Open University Press.

Jefferson, Tony. 1993. "Pondering Paramilitarism: A Question of Standpoints?" *British Journal of Criminology* 33, no. 3: 374–381.

Jefrries, Charles. 1952. *The Colonial Police*. London: Max Parrish.

Johnson, Chalmers. 2000. *Blowback: The Costs and Consequences of American Empire*. New York: Metropolitan Books.

Johnson, Lyndon B. 1967. "Annual Message to the Congress on the State of the Union." January 10, 1967. https://www.presidency.ucsb.edu/documents/annual-message-the-congress-the-state-the-union-28.

Johnson, Marilynn. 2003. *Street Justice: A History of Police Violence in New York City*. Boston: Beacon Press.

Johnson, Whittington. 1999. *Black Savannah, 1788–1864*. Fayetteville: University of Arkansas Press.

Johnstone, Peter. 2014. "Real Influence of Sir Robert Peel on Twenty-First Century Policing in America." In *Economic Development, Crime and Policing*, edited by Frederic Lemieux, Garth den Heyer, and Dilip K. Das, 39–66. Boca Raton, FL: CRC Press.

Jones, Alexi, and Wendy Sawyer. 2020. "Not Just 'a Few Bad Apples': U.S. Police Kill Civilians at Much Higher Rates than Other Countries." Prison Policy Initiative, June 5, 2020. https://www.prisonpolicy.org/blog/2020/06/05/policekillings/.

Jones, David. 1982. *Crime, Protest, Community and Police in Nineteenth Century Britain*. New York: Routledge.

Joyce, Peter. 2016. *The Policing of Protest, Disorder and International Terrorism in the UK Since 1945*. London: Palgrave Macmillan.

Kaplan, L. Martin. 2001. "Modernization in the Root Reform Era." US Army Center of Military History. https://www.history.army.mil/documents/1901/Root-Mod.htm.

Katz, Jonathan M. 2021. *Gangsters of Capitalism: Smedley Butler, the Marines and the Making and Breaking of America's Empire*. New York: St. Martin's Press.

Katznelson, Ira. 2002. "Flexible Capacity: The Military and Early American Statebuilding." In *Shaped by War and Trade: International Influences on American Political Development*, edited by Ira Katznelson and Martin Shefter, 82–110. Princeton, NJ: Princeton University Press.

Kay-Shuttleworth, James. 1832. *The Moral and Physical Condition of the Working Classes Employed in the Cotton Manufacture in Manchester*. London: J. Ridgway.

Keene, M. J. 1967. "The Metropolitan Police Special Patrol Group." *Police Journal* 40, no. 4: 155–167.

Keith, Michael. 1991. "'Policing a Perplexed Society?' No-Go Areas and the Mystification of Police-Black Conflict." In *Out of Order? The Policing of Black People*, edited by Ellis Cashmore and Eugene McLaughlin, 189–213. London: Routledge.

Kelley, Robin D. G. 2020. "Insecure: Policing Under Racial Capitalism." *Spectre* 1, no. 2: 12–37.

Kennan, Jerry. 2001. *Encyclopedia of the Spanish-American and Philippine-American Wars*. Santa Barbara, CA: ABC-CLIO.

Kennedy-Pipe, Caroline, and Colin McInnes. 1997. "The British Army in Northern Ireland, 1969–1972." *Journal of Strategic Studies* 20, no. 2: 1–24.

Kettle, Martin, and Tony Bunyan. 1980. "The Police Force of the Future Is Now Here." *New Society* 21 (August): 353–354.

Kettle, Martin, and Lucy Hodges. 1982. *Uprising! The Police, the People and the Riots in Britain's Cities*. London: Pan Books.

Khan-Cullors, Patrisse, and Asha Bandele. 2018. *When They Call You a Terrorist*. New York: St. Martin's Press.

Kindynis, Theo. 2014. "Ripping Up the Map: Criminology and Cartography Reconsidered." *British Journal of Criminology* 54, no. 2: 222–243.

King, Peter. 2013. "Ethnicity, Prejudice, and Justice: The Treatment of the Irish at the Old Bailey, 1750–1825." *Journal of British Studies* 52, no. 2: 390–414.

King, Peter. 2018. "Immigrant Communities, the Police and the Courts in Late Eighteenth and Early Nineteenth-Century London." *Crime, Histoire et Sociétés / Crime, History and Societies* 20, no. 1 (online). http://journals.openedition.org/chs/1639.

Kitson, Frank. 1991 [1971]. *Low Intensity Operations*. London: Faber and Faber.

Knepper, Paul. 2007. "British Jews and the Racialisation of Crime in the Age of Empire." *British Journal of Criminology* 47: 61–79.

Knepper, Paul. 2008. "The Other Invisible Hand: Jews and Anarchists in London before the First World War." *Jewish History* 22, no. 3: 295–315.

Knepper, Paul. 2010. *The Invention of International Crime: A Global Issue in the Making, 1881–1914*. Basingstoke, UK: Palgrave Macmillan.

Knights, P. D. 1969. "A Look at the United States Police." *The Police Journal* 42, no. 5: 199–209.

Kohler-Hausmann, Judith. 2011. "Militarizing the Police: Officer Jon Burge, Torture, and War in the 'Urban Jungle.'" In *Challenging the Prison-Industrial Complex: Activism, Arts, and Educational Alternatives*, edited by Stephen Josh Hartnett, 43–71. Urbana: University of Illinois Press.

Koram, Kojo, ed. 2019. *The War on Drugs and the Global Colour Line*. London: Pluto Press.

Kramer, Paul. 2006. *The Blood of Government: Race, Empire, the United States, and the Philippines*. Chapel Hill: University of North Carolina Press.

Kramer, Paul. 2003. "Empires, Exceptions, and Anglo-Saxons: Race and Rule Between the British and U.S. Empires, 1880–1910." In *The American Colonial State in the*

*Philippines: Global Perspectives*, edited by Julian Go and Anne Foster, 43–91. Durham, NC: Duke University Press.

Kraska, Peter. 2007. "Militarization and Policing—Its Relevance to 21st Century Police." *Policing* 1, no. 4: 501–513.

Kraska, Peter, and Victor Kappeler. 1997. "Militarizing American Police: The Rise and Normalization of Paramilitary Units." *Social Problems* 44, no. 1: 1–18.

Kroizer, Gad. 2004. "From Dowbiggin to Tegart: Revolutionary Change in the Colonial Police in Palestine During the 1930s." *Journal of Imperial and Commonwealth History* 32, no. 2: 115–133.

Kuzmarov, Jeremy. 2012. *Modernizing Repression: Police Training and Nation-Building in the American Century*. Amherst: University of Massachusetts Press.

Lamartina Palacios, Nicholle. 2015. "#WeCantBreathe": Peel's Principles of Policing Gone Wrong?" *Huffpost* blog, last updated February 9, 2015. https://www.huffpost.com/entry/wecantbreathe-peels-princ_b_6291374.

Lane, Roger. 1986. *Roots of Violence in Black Philadelphia, 1860–1900*. Cambridge, MA: Harvard University Press.

Lardner, James, and Thomas Reppetto. 2000. *NYPD*. New York: Henry Holt.

Lassiter, Matthew D., and the Policing and Social Justice History Lab. 2021. "Detroit Under Fire: Police Violence, Crime Politics, and the Struggle for Racial Justice in the Civil Rights Era." University of Michigan Carceral State Project. https://policing.umhistorylabs.lsa.umich.edu/s/detroitunderfire/page/sweep-the-streets.

Laurie, Clayton. 1989. "The Philippine Scouts: America's Colonial Army, 1899–1913." *Philippine Studies* 37, no. 2: 174–191.

Lawson, Edward. 2018. "Police Militarization and the Use of Lethal Force." *Political Research Quarterly* 72, no. 1: 177–189.

Lawyers' Committee for Civil Rights Under Law. 1973. *Law and Disorder III: State and Federal Performance Under Title I of the Omnibus Crime Control and Safe Streets Act of 1968. Submitted to the Committee on the Judiciary, United States Senate, for Hearing Before the Subcommittee on Criminal Laws and Procedures, Ninety-Third Congr., First Session on S. 977, S.1023, S. 1114, S. 1234, S. 1495, S. 1645 and S. 1796*. Washington, DC: US Government Printing Office.

Lebow, Richard Ned. 1976. *White Britain and Black Ireland: The Influence of Stereotypes on Colonial Policy*. Philadelphia: Institute for the Study of Human Issues.

LeBrón, Marisol. 2019. *Policing Life and Death: Race, Violence, and Resistance in Puerto Rico*. Oakland: University of California Press.

Lee, Alan. 1980. "Aspects of the Working-Class Response to the Jews in Britain, 1880–1914." In *Hosts, Immigrants and Minorities*, edited by Kenneth Lunn, 107–132. New York: St. Martin's Press.

Lees, Lynn Hollen. 1979. *Exiles of Erin: Irish Migrants in Victorian London*. Ithaca, NY: Cornell University Press.

Leichtman, Ellen. 2014. "Smedley D. Butler and the Militarisation of the Philadelphia Police, 1924–1925." *Law, Crime and History* 2: 48–69.

Lentz, Susan A., and Robert H. Chaires. 2007. "The Invention of Peel's Principles: A Study of Policing 'Textbook' History." *Journal of Criminal Justice* 35: 69–79.

Leonard, Glenford. 1962. "Our Tactical Police Unit." *The Police Chief* 29, no. 4: 34–37.

Leonard, V. A. 1951. *Police Organization and Management*. Brooklyn: Foundation Press.

Leps, Marie-Christine. 1992. *Apprehending the Criminal*. Durham, NC: Duke University Press.

Levinson, Irving. 2005. *Wars Within Wars: Mexican Guerillas, Domestic Elites, and the United States of America, 1846–1848*. Fort Worth: Texas Christian University Press.

Lewis, George Cornewall. 1836. *Report on the State of the Irish Poor in Great Britain*. London: C. Knight.

Lewis, Isobel. 2020. "George the Poet Refutes Emily Maitlis's Claims." *The Independent*, June 2, 2020. https://www.independent.co.uk/arts-entertainment/tv/news/george-the-poet-newsnight-emily-maitlis-black-lives-matter-george-floyd-a9544776.html.

Lewis, Paul, Tim Newburn, Matthew Taylor, Catriona Mcgillivray, Aster Greenhill, Harold Frayman, and Rob Proctor. 2011. *Reading the Riots*. London: London School of Economics and Political Science and The Guardian.

Liebman, Robert, and Micahel Polen. 1978. "Perspectives on Policing in Nineteenth-Century America." *Social Science History* 2, no. 3: 346–360.

Linn, Brian. 1991. "Intelligence and Low-Intensity Conflict in the Philippine War, 1899–1902." *Intelligence and National Security* 6, no. 1: 90–114.

Linn, Brian. 2000. *The Philippine War, 1899–1902*. Lawrence: University Press of Kansas.

Linstrum, Erik. 2019. "Domesticating Chemical Weapons: Tear Gas and the Militarization of Policing in the British Imperial World, 1919–1981." *Journal of Modern History* 91, no. 3: 557–585.

Lipman, V. D. 1954. *A Social History of the Jews in England, 1850–1950*. London: Watts.

Liska, A. E., J. Lawrence, and M. Benson. 1981. "Perspectives on Legal Order: The Capacity for Social Control." *American Journal of Sociology* 87, no. 2: 413–426.

London Metropolitan Police. 1871. *Instruction Book for the Use of Candidates and Constables of the Metropolitan Police Force*. London: G. E. Eyre and William Spottiswoode. PRO MEPO 4/36.

Lvovsky, Anna. 2020. "Cruising in Plain View: Clandestine Surveillance and the Unique Insights of Antihomosexual Policing." *Journal of Urban History* 46, no. 5: 980–1001.

Lyman, J. L. 1964. "The Metropolitan Police Act of 1829." *Journal of Criminal Law and Criminology* 55, no. 1: 141–154.

Lynch, Tim. 2014. "Ferguson, a War Zone or U.S. City?" Cato Institute, August 14, 2014. https://www.cato.org/commentary/ferguson-war-zone-or-us-city#.

Lytle Hernández, Kelly. 2014. "Hobos in Heaven: Race, Incarceration, and the Rise of Los Angeles, 1880–1910." *Pacific Historical Review* 83, no. 3: 410–447.

Macfarlane, Julia. 2020. "How Do British Black Deaths in Police Custody Compare with the US?" ABC News, June 6, 2020. https://abcnews.go.com/International/british-black-deaths-police-custody-compare-us/story?id=71054650.

Macnaghten, Melville L. 1914. *Days of My Years*. London: E. Arnold.

MacRaild, Donald. 1999. *Irish Migrants in Modern Britain, 1750–1922*. London: Palgrave.

Magubane, Zine. 2004. *Bringing the Empire Home: Race, Class, and Gender in Britain and Colonial South Africa*. Chicago: University of Chicago Press.

Maher, George. 2021. *A World Without Police: How Strong Communities Make Cops Obsolete*. New York: Verso.

Mahoney, James. 2003. "Strategies of Causal Assessment in Comparative Historical Analysis." In *Comparative Historical Analysis in the Social Sciences*, edited by James Mahoney and Dietrich Rueschemeyer, 337–372. Cambridge, UK: Cambridge University Press.

Mahoney, James. 2012. "The Logic of Process Tracing Tests in the Social Sciences." *Sociological Methods & Research* 4, no. 4: 570–597.

Mainwaring, George. 1821. *Observations on the Present State of the Police of the Metropolis*. London: John Murray.

Maitland, Frederic W. 1885. *Justice and Police*. London: Macmillan.

Malkin, Stanislav. 2019. "From Small Wars to Counterinsurgency: C. W. Gwynn, 'Imperial Policing' and Transformation of Doctrine." *Small Wars and Insurgencies* 30: 660–678.

Mark, Robert. 1973. "Social Violence." In *The Police We Deserve*, edited by J. C. Alderson and Philip John Stead, 11–24. London: Wolfe.

Mark, Robert. 1977. *Polcing a Perplexed Society*. London: Allen & Unwin.

Mark, Robert. 1978. *In the Office of Constable*. London: Collins.

Martin, R. M. J. 1936. "Police Work in Shanghai." *Metropolitan Police College Journal* 1: 41–50.

Mason, Max. 1935. "Presentation of the Public Welfare Medal to August Vollmer." *Science* 81, no. 2105: 416.

Mather, F. C. 1959. *Public Order in the Age of the Chartists*. Manchester: Manchester University Press.

Mayhew, Henry, and John Binny. 1862. *The Criminal Prisons of London, and Scenes of Prison Life*. London: Griffin, Bohn.

Mayo, Katherine. 1917. *Justice to All: The Story of the Pennsylvania State Police*. New York: G. P. Putnam's Sons.

Mayo, Katherine. 1922. *Mounted Justice: True Stories of the Pennsylvania Police*. Boston: Houghton Mifflin.

Mbembe, Achille. 2017. *Critique of Black Reason*. Durham, NC: Duke University Press.

McCord, D. J., ed. 1841. *Statutes at Large of South Carolina, Vol. 9, Part 2*. Columbia, SC: A. S. Johnston.

McCoy, Alfred W. 2009. *Policing America's Empire*. Madison: University of Wisconsin Press.

McCoy, Alfred W. 2015. "Policing the Imperial Periphery: The Philippine-American War and the Origins of U.S. Global Surveillance." *Surveillance and Society* 13, no. 1: 4–26.

McCulloch, Jude, and Vicki Sentas. 2006. "The Killing of Jean Charles de Menezes: Hyper-Militarism in the Neoliberal Economic Free-Fire Zone." *Social Justice* 33, no. 4: 92–106.

McDonald, Lynn. 1982. "Theory and Evidence of Rising Crime in the Nineteenth Century." *British Journal of Sociology* 33, no. 3: 404–420.

McElwee, William. 1974. *The Art of War: Waterloo to Mons*. Bloomington: Indiana University Press.

McMahon, Tony. 2022. "Memories of Liverpool in 1981—Part Five." *The 70s 80s 90s Blog*. January 24, 2022. https://thatchercrisisyears.com/2022/01/24/liverpool-police-riots/#_ftnref8.

McPhail, Clark, David Schweingruber, and John McCarthy. 1998. "Policing Protest in the United States: 1960–1995." In *Policing Protest*, edited by Donatella della Porta and Herbert Reiter, 49–69. Minneapolis: University of Minnesota Press.

The Measured Group. n.d. "Counter Criminal Continuum: The Story." https://measured.design/c3-counter-criminal-continuum/. Accessed June 2, 2019.

Metcalf, Thomas R. 1996. *Empire and Information*. Cambridge, UK: Cambridge University Press.

Midwinter, E. C. 1968. *Law and Order in Early Victorian Lancashire*. York, UK: St. Anthony's Press.

Mignolo, Walter. 2011. *The Darker Side of Western Modernity*. Durham, NC: Duke University Press.

Miller, Douglas. 1968. "Immigration and Social Stratification in Pre-Civil War New York." *New York History* 49, no. 2: 156–168.

Miller, Stuart Creighton. 1982. *"Benevolent Assimilation": The American Conquest of the Philippines, 1899–1903*. New Haven: Yale University Press.

Miller, Wilbur. 1977. *Cops and Bobbies: Police Authority in New York and London*. Chicago: University of Chicago Press.

Miller, Zane. 1975. "Urban Blacks in the South, 1865–1920: The Richmond, Savannah, New Orleans, Louisville and Birmingham Experience." In *The New Urban History: Quantitative Explorations by American Historians*, edited by Leo Francis Schnore, 184–204. Princeton, NJ: Princeton University Press.

Mitrani, Sam. 2013. *The Rise of the Chicago Police Department*. Urbana: University of Illinois Press.

Moehling, Carolyn, and Anne Morrison Piehl. 2009. "Immigration, Crime and Incarceration in Early Twentieth-Century America." *Demography* 46, no. 4: 739–763.

Monkkonen, Eric H. 1981. *Police in Urban America, 1860–1920*. Cambridge, UK: Cambridge University Press.

Monkkonen, Eric H. 1992. "History of Urban Police." *Crime and Justice* 15: 547–580.

Moore, Tony Michael. 1992. "Policing Serious Public Disorder: The Search for Principles, Policies and Operational Lessons." M. Phil. thesis, Department of Politics, University of Southampton.

Moseley, George Van Horn. 1904. "A Map-Card System." *Journal of the Military Service Institution of the United States* 34: 476–479.

Moylan, Sir John. 1929. *Scotland Yard and the Metropolitan Police*. London: G. P. Putnam's Sons.

Muhammad, Khalil Gibran. 2010. *The Condemnation of Blackness: Race, Crime, and the Making of Modern Urban America*. Cambridge, MA: Harvard University Press.

Mukhopadhyay, Surajit. 1998. "Importing Back Colonial Policing Systems? The Relationship Between the Royal Irish Constabulary, Indian Policing and Militarization of Policing in England and Wales." *Innovation* 11, no. 3: 253–265.

Muller, Christopher. 2012. "Northward Migration and the Rise of Racial Disparity in American Incarceration, 1880–1950." *American Journal of Sociology* 118, no. 2: 281–326.

Muller, Christopher. 2018. "Freedom and Convict Leasing in the Postbellum South." *American Journal of Sociology* 124, no. 2: 367–405.

Mummolo, Jonathan. 2018. "Militarization Fails to Enhance Police Safety or Reduce Crime but May Harm Police Reputation." *Proceedings of the National Academy of Sciences of the United States of America* 115, no. 37: 9181–9186.

Murray, Nancy. 2016. "Cops in the Commonwealth: The Pitfalls of Militarized, Federalized Policing." Privacy SOS. https://privacysos.org/cops/.

National Action Research on the Military Industrial Complex. 1971. *Police on the Homefront*. Philadelphia: National Action Research on the Military Industrial Complex.

National Commission on Law Observance and Enforcement. 1931. *Report on Lawlessness in Law Enforcement*. Washington, DC: US Government Printing Office.

Nelson, Bruce. 2012. *Irish Nationalists and the Making of the Irish Race*. Princeton, NJ: Princeton University Press.

Nenninger, Timothy. 1978. *The Leavenworth Schools and the Old Army: Education, Professionalism, and the Officer Corps of the United States Army, 1881–1918*. Westport, CT: Greenwood Press.

Neocleous, Mark. 2000. *The Fabrication of Social Order: A Critical Theory of Police Power*. Sterling, VA: Pluto Press.

Neocleous, Mark. 2021. *A Critical Theory of Police Power*. London: Verso.

Neocleous, Mark, and the Anti-Security Collective, eds. 2021. "A Critical Theory of Police Power in the Twenty-First Century." Special issue. *Social Justice* 47, nos. 3–4.

Network for Police Monitoring. 2020. "'Britain Is Not Innocent': A Netpol Report on the Policing of Black Lives Matter Protests." London: Network for Police Monitoring.

New York City Board of Aldermen. 1837. *Documents of the Board of Aldermen of the City of New York. Volume III*. New York: New York Common Council.

New York City Board of Aldermen. 1843. *Proceedings of the Board of Aldermen*. New York: Board of Aldermen.

New York City Board of Aldermen. 1844. *Report of the Special Committee of the New York City Board of Aldermen, January 3, 1844 . . . in Relation to a Re-organization of the Police Department. Document No. 53*. New York: City of New York.

New York City Board of Assistants. 1836. *Journal and Documents*. New York: James Van Norden.

New York City Board of Metropolitan Police. 1866. *Annual Report*. New York: Bergen & Tripp.

New York City Police Department. 1851. *Rules and Regulations for the Government of the Police Department of the City of New-York, with Instructions as to the Legal Powers and Duties of Policemen*. New York: Bowne.

New York Committee on the Police Problem. 1905. *Papers and Proceedings of Committee on the Police Problem*. New York: C. P. Young.

New York Secretary of State. 1855. *Census of the State of New York for 1855*. Albany: C. Van Benthuysen.

Newburn, Tim, Rebekah Diski, Kerris Cooper, Rachel Deacon, Alex Burch, and Maggie Grant. 2016. "'The Biggest Gang'? Police and People in the 2011 England Riots." *Policing and Society* 28, no. 2: 205–222.

Newton, Huey P. 1967. "In Defense of Self-Defense." *The Black Panther* 1, no. 3: 3–4.

Nijjar, Jasbinder. 2018. "Echoes of Empire: Excavating the Colonial Roots of Britain's 'War on Gangs.'" *Social Justice* 45, nos. 2–3: 147–162.

Northam, Gerry. 1988. *Shooting in the Dark: Riot Police in Britain*. London: Faber and Faber.

Nott-Bower, John William. 1926. *Fifty-Two Years a Policeman*. London: E. Arnold.

Ó Catháin, Martin. 2019. "Peterloo—An Irish Tragedy?" *History Ireland* 27, no. 4: 26–29.

Ó Gráda, Cormac. 1988. *Ireland Before and After the Famine: Explorations in Economic History, 1800–1925*. Manchester: Manchester University Press.

Ó Tuathaigh, M. A. G. 1981. "The Irish in Nineteenth-Century Britain: Problems of Integration." *Transactions of the Royal Historical Society* 5, no. 31: 149–173.

O'Day, Alan. 1989a. "The Political Organization of the Irish in Britain, 1867–90." In *The Irish in Britain, 1815–1939*, edited by Roger Swift and Sheridan Gilley, 183–211. Savage, MD: Barnes and Noble Books.

O'Day, Alan. 1989b. "The Political Organization of the Irish in Britain, 1867–90." In *The Irish in Britain, 1815–1939*, edited by Roger Swift and Sheridan Gilley, 183–211. Savage, MD: Barnes and Noble Books.

O'Higgins, Rachel. 1961. "The Irish Influence in the Chartist Movement." *Past and Present* 20 (November): 83–96.

Oliver, Willard. 2017. *August Vollmer: The Father of American Policing*. Durham, NC: Carolina Academic Press.

Omi, Michael, and Howard Winant. 1986. *Racial Formation in the United States*. New York: Routledge.

Open University. 2021. "Differences and Similarities: Policing in the US and the UK." February 23, 2021. https://www.open.edu/openlearn/education-development/race-and-ethnicity-hub/differences-and-similarities-policing-the-us-and-the-uk.

Oppenheimer, Martin. 1974. "The Sub-Proletariat: Dark Skins and Dirty Work." *The Insurgent Sociologist* 4, no. 2: 6–20.

Owens, Patricia. 2015. *Economy of Force: Counterinsurgency and the Historical Rise of the Social*. Cambridge, UK: Cambridge University Press.

Palmer, Stanley. 1977. "Before the Bobbies: The Caroline Riots, 1821." *History Today* 27, no. 10: 637–644.

Palmer, Stanley. 1978. "Cops and Guns: Arming the American Police." *History Today* 28, no. 6: 382–389.

Palmer, Stanley. 1988. *Police and Protest in England and Ireland, 1780–1850*. Cambridge, UK: Cambridge University Press.

Parker, Alfred. 1961. *Crime Fighter, August Vollmer*. New York: Macmillan.

Parker, Karen, John M. MacDonald, and Wesley Jennings. 2005. "Racial Threat Urban Conditions and Police Use of Force: Assessing the Direct and Indirect Linkages Across Multiple Urban Areas." *Justice Research and Policy* 7, no. 1: 53–79.

Parker, William H., and O. W. Wilson. 1957. *Parker on Police*. Springfield, IL: Thomas.

Parsons, C. G. 1855. *Inside View of Slavery*. Boston: J. P. Jewett.

Paynich, Rebecca, and Bryan Hill. 2010. *Fundamentals of Crime Mapping*. Sudbury, MA: Jones and Bartlett.

Peel, Robert, and Charles Stuart Parker. 1899. *Sir Robert Peel. From His Private Papers. Edited for His Trustees by Charles Stuart Parker. With a Chapter on His Life and Character by His Grandson, the Hon. George Peel*. London: J. Murray.

Peplow, Simon. 2019. *Race and Riots in Thatcher's Britain*. Manchester: Manchester University Press.

Perera, Jessica. 2019. *The London Clearances: Race, Housing and Policing*. London: Institute of Race Relations.

Petrow, Stefan. 1994. *Policing Morals*. Oxford: Clarendon Press.

Philadelphia Bureau of Police. 1913. *Patrolman's Manual*. Philadelphia: Department of Public Safety.

Philips, David. 1977. *Crime and Authority in Victorian England: The Black Country 1835–1860*. London: Croom Helm.

Philips, David. 2003. "Three 'Moral Entrepreneurs' and the Creation of a 'Criminal Class' in England, 1790–1840." *Crime, Histoire et Sociétés / Crime, History and Societies* 7, no. 1: 79–107.

Philips, David, and Robert Storch. 1999. *Policing Provincial England, 1829–1856*. London: Leicester University Press.

Poka, John. 2020. "Impressions of a Rookie Cop." In *A Time to Stir*, edited by Paul Cronin, 263–268. New York: Columbia University Press.

Pooley, Colin. 1989. "Segregation or Integration? The Residential Experience of the Irish in Mid-Victorian Britain." In *The Irish in Britain, 1815–1939*, edited by Roger Swift and Sheridan Gilley, 60–83. Savage: Barnes and Noble Books.

Porter, Bernard. 1987. *The Origins of the Vigilant State*. London: Weidenfeld and Nicolson.

President's Commission on Law Enforcement and Administration of Justice. 1967a. *The Challenge of Crime in a Free Society*. Washington, DC: US Government Printing Office.

President's Commission on Law Enforcement and Administration of Justice. 1967b. *Task Force Report: The Police*. Washington, DC: US Government Printing Office.

Prison Reform Trust. 2019. "Prison: The Facts." Bromley Briefings, Summer 2019. Prison Rerform Trust, London.

Purnell, Derecka. 2021. *Becoming Abolitionists*. New York: Penguin Random House.

Quijano, Anibal. 2000. "Coloniality of Power, Eurocentrism and Latin America." *Nepantla: Views from South* 1: 533–580.

Rabinow, Paul. 1989. *French Modern: Norms and Forms of the Social Environment*. Cambridge, MA: MIT Press.

Radil, Steven, Raymond J. Dezzani, and Lanny McAden. 2017. "Geographies of U.S. Police Militarization and the Role of the 1033 Program." *The Professional Geographer* 69, no. 2: 203–213.

Ramesh, Randeep. 2010. "More Black People Jailed in England and Wales Proportionately than the US." *The Guardian*, October 10, 2010. https://www.theguardian.com/society/2010/oct/11/black-prison-population-increase-england.

Ramey, David, and Trent Steidley. 2018. "Policing Through Subsidized Firepower: An Assessment of Rational Choice and Minority Threat Explanations of Police Participation in the 1033 Program." *Criminology* 56, no. 4: 812–856.

Randhawa, Kiran. 2016. "Revealed: The New Face of Anti-Terror Policing in London." *Evening Standard*, August 3, 2016. https://www.standard.co.uk/news/london/revealed-the-new-face-of-antiterror-policing-in-london-a3310691.html.

Reichel, Philip. 1988. "Southern Slave Patrols as a Transitional Police Type." *American Journal of Police* 7, no. 2: 51–77.

Reimers, David, Frederick Binder, and Robert Snyder. 2019. *All the Nations Under Heaven: Immigrants, Migrants, and the Making of New York*. Revised ed. New York: Columbia University Press.

Reiner, Robert. 2000. *The Politics of the Police*. Oxford: Oxford University Press.

Reingle Gonzalez, Jennifer M., Stephen A. Bishopp, Katelyn K. Jetelina, Ellen Paddock, Kelley Pettee Gabriel, and M. Brad Cannell. 2018. "Does Military Veteran Status and Deployment History Impact Officer Involved Shootings? A Case-Control Study." *Journal of Public Health* 41, no. 3: e245–e252.

Reinsch, Paul S. 1911. *Readings on American State Government*. Boston: Ginn.

Reiss, Albert J., Jr. 1992. "Police Organization in the Twentieth Century." *Crime and Justice* 15: 51–97.

Reith, Charles. 1943. *British Police and the Democratic Ideal*. London: Oxford Universty Press.

Reith, Charles. 1952. *The Blind Eye of History*. London: Faber.

Reith, Charles. 1956. *A New Study of Police History*. London: Oliver and Boyd.

Renshaw, Daniel. 2018. *Socialism and the Diasporic "Other": A Comparative Study of Irish Catholic and Jewish Radical and Communal Politics in East London, 1889–1912*. Liverpool: Liverpool University Press.

Rex, John. 1982. "The 1981 Riots in Britain." *International Journal of Urban and Regional Research* 6, no. 1: 99–113.

Reynolds, Mike. 2020. "Hats and Bats." In *A Time to Stir*, edited by Paul Cronin, 274–276. New York: Columbia University Press.

Rich, Paul B. 1986. *Race and Empire in British Politics.* Cambridge, UK: Cambridge University Press.

Richardson, James F. 1970. *The New York Police: Colonial Times to 1901.* Oxford: Oxford University Press.

Richardson, James F. 1974. *Urban Police in the United States.* Port Washington, NY: Kennikat Press.

Rizer, Arthur. 2022. "Police Militarization Gave Us Uvalde." *The Atlantic*, June 17, 2022. https://www.theatlantic.com/ideas/archive/2022/06/police-training-militarization-mass-shootings-uvalde/661295/.

Robinson, Peter. 2008. "The Search for Mobility During the Second Boer War." *Journal of the Society for Army Historical Research* 86, no. 346: 140–157.

Roediger, David. 1992. *The Wages of Whiteness.* New York: Verso.

Rollo, Joanna. 1980. "The Special Patrol Group." In *Policing the Police*, edited by Peter Hain, 2:153–208. London: John Calder.

Rosenau, William. 2014. "'Our Ghettos, Too, Need a Lansdale': American Counter-insurgency Abroad and at Home in the Vietnam Era." In *The New Counterinsurgency Era in Critical Perspective*, edited by Celeste Ward, David Martin Jones, and M. L. R. Smith, 111–126. Houndmills, UK: Palgrave Macmillan.

Roth, Mitchel. 1998. "Mounted Police Forces: A Comparative History." *Policing: An International Journal of Police Strategies and Management* 21, no. 4: 707–719.

Rousey, Dennis C. 1996. *Policing the Southern City.* Baton Rouge: Louisiana State University Press.

Rowley, H. V. 1932. "The Fighter Tactical Unit for Home Defence." *Journal of the Royal United Service Institution* 77: 598.

Royal Commission. 1839. *First Report of the Commissioners Appointed to Inquire as to the Best Means of Establishing an Efficient Constabulary Force in the Counties of England and Wales.* London: W. Clowes and Sons.

Royal Commission on Alien Immigration. 1903. *Report of the Royal Commission on Alien Immigration.* London: Her Majesty's Stationery Office.

Roycroft, Mark. 2016. *Police Chiefs in the UK: Politicians, HR Managers, or Cops?* London: Palgrave Macmillan.

Rudwick, Elliot. 1960. "Negro Crime and the Negro Press." *Police* 5, no. 3: 66–67.

Rufford, Nick. 2021. "On Patrol with 'the Trojans,' Britain's Armed Response Police." *Sunday Times*, March 15, 2021. https://www.thetimes.co.uk/article/on-patrol-with-the-trojans-britains-armed-response-police-ltg20w9zb.

Sacks, Marcy S. 2005. "'To Show Who Was in Charge': Police Repression of New York City's Black Population at the Turn of the Twentieth Century." *Journal of Urban History* 31, no. 6: 799–819.

Said, Edward. 1979. *Orientalism.* New York: Vintage Books.

Santiago-Valles, Kelvin. 1994. *"Subject People" and Colonial Discourses: Economic Transformation and Disorder in Puerto Rico, 1898–1947.* Albany: State University of New York Press.

Satia, Priya. 2018. *Empire of Guns.* Palo Alto, CA: Stanford University Press.

Satia, Priya. 2019. "What Guns Meant in Eighteenth-Century Britain." *Palgrave Communications* 5, no. 1: 104.

Scarman, Leslie. 1981. *The Brixton Disorders: Report of an Inquiry*. London: HMSO.

Schneider, Eric C. 1999. *Vampires, Dragons, and Egyptian Kings: Youth Gangs in Postwar New York*. Princeton, NJ: Princeton University Press.

Schnore, Leo Francis, and Harry Sharp. 1963. "Racial Changes in Metropolitan Areas, 1950–1960." *Social Forces* 41, no. 3: 247–253.

Schrader, Stuart. 2016. "Against the Romance of Community Policing." *Stuart Schrader* (blog), August 10, 2016. https://www.stuartschrader.com/blog/against-romance-community-policing.

Schrader, Stuart. 2017. "More than Cosmetic Changes: The Challenges of Experiments with Police Demilitarization in the 1960s and 1970s." *Journal of Urban History* 46, no. 5: 1002–1025.

Schrader, Stuart. 2019. *Badges Without Borders*. Berkeley: University of California Press.

Schrader, Stuart. 2021. "Cops at War: How World War II Transformed U.S. Policing." *Modern American History* 4: 159–179.

Schutt, Harold. 1922. "Advanced Police Methods at Berkeley." *National Municipal Review* 11, no. 3: 80–84.

Scisco, Louis Dow. 1901. "Political Nativism in New York State." PhD dissertation, Department of Political Science, Columbia University.

Seigel, Micol. 2018. *Violence Work: State Power and the Limits of Police*. Durham, NC: Duke University Press.

Select Committee on Mendicity in the Metropolis. 1815. *Report*. Great Britain, Parliamentary Papers, House of Commons Papers 1814–1815, Paper Number 473, Volume III.231.

Select Committee on the Police of the Metropolis. 1828. *Report from the Select Committee on the Police of the Metropolis, Ordered, by the House of Commons, to be Printed 11 July 1828*. London: Parliamentary Papers, House of Commons, 533, VI.1.

Sengoopta, Chandak. 2003. *Imprint of the Raj: How Fingerprinting Was Born in Colonial India*. London: Pan.

Senik, Troy. 2010. "The Surge Comes to Salinas." *City Magazine*, Winter 2010. https://www.city-journal.org/html/surge-comes-salinas-13263.html.

Shannon, H. A. 1935. "Migration and the Growth of London, 1841–1891." *Economic History Review* 5, no. 2: 79–86.

Shea, J. J. 1973. "Lessons Learned in Ireland." *Marine Corps Gazette* 57 (April): 49–50.

Shivdasani, Siddy. 2021. "We Must Acknowledge the Legacy of the Brixton Riots." *Metro* (UK), April 10, 2021. https://metro.co.uk/2021/04/10/40-years-later-we-must-acknowledge-the-legacy-of-the-brixton-riots-14353854/.

Shoemaker, Edward. 1990. "Strangers and Citizens: The Irish Immigrant Community of Savannah, 1837–1861." PhD dissertation, Department of History, Emory University.

Shpayer-Makov, Haia. 2002. *The Making of a Policeman: A Social History of a Labour Force in Metropolitan London, 1829–1914*. Burlington, VT: Ashgate.

Shryock, Richard. 1929. *The Letters of Richard D. Arnold, M.D., 1808–1876*. Durham, NC: Duke University Press.

Sierra-Arévalo, Michael. 2021. "American Policing and the Danger Imperative." *Law and Society Review* 55, no. 1: 70–103.

Silver, Allan. 1965. *On the Demand for Order in Civil Society*. Ann Arbor, MI: Working Papers of the Center for Research on Social Organization.

Simhadri, Y. C. 1991. *Denotified Tribes: A Sociological Analysis*. New Delhi: Classical Publishing.

Sinclair, Georgina. 2006. *At the End of the Line: Colonial Policing and the Imperial Endgame 1945–80*. Manchester: Manchester University Press.

Sinclair, Georgina, and Chris A. Williams. 2007. "'Home and Away': The Cross-Fertilisation Between 'Colonial' and 'British' Policing, 1921–85." *The Journal of Imperial and Commonwealth History* 35, no. 2: 221–238.

Sindall, R. 1987. "The London Garotting Panics of 1856 and 1862." *Social History* 12, no. 3: 351–359.

Singh, Nikhil Pal. 2017. *Race and America's Long War*. Berkeley: University of California Press.

"Sir Robert Peel's Nine Principles of Policing." *New York Times*, April 16, 2014. https://www.nytimes.com/2014/04/16/nyregion/sir-robert-peels-nine-principles-of-policing.html.

Sloan, Kenneth. 1978. *Public Order and the Police*. London: Police Review.

Smith, Bruce. 1960. *Police Systems in the United States*. New York: Harper & Brothers.

Smith, Justin. 2021. "Racial Threat and Crime Control: Integrating Theory on Race and Extending Its Application." *Critical Criminology* 29: 253–271.

Smith, Philip Thurmond. 1985. *Policing Victorian London*. Westport, CT: Greenwood Press.

Sorenson, John L. 1965. *Urban Insurgency Cases*. Santa Barbara, CA: Defense Research Corp.

Soulsby, Ian. 2018. "The Irish Military Establishment 1796–1798: A Study in the Evolution of Military Effectiveness." MA thesis, Department of History, University College Cork.

Spearman, E. J. 1890. "Mistaken Identity and Police Anthropometry." *Fortnightly Review* 53: 361–376.

Spiers, Edward M. 1992. *The Late Victorian Army, 1868–1902*. Manchester: Manchester University Press.

Stallion, Martin, David Wall, and Police History Society. 1999. *The British Police: Police Forces and Chief Officers, 1829–2000*. Bramshill, UK: Police History Society.

Stanford, Terence George. 2007. "The Metropolitan Police 1850–1914: Targeting, Harassment and the Creation of a Criminal Class." PhD dissertation, Department of History, University of Huddersfield.

Stauffer, Michael. 1987. "Volunteer or Uniformed Companies in the Antebellum Militia: A Checklist of Identified Companies, 1790–1859." *South Carolina Magazine* 88, no. 2: 108–116.

Steedman, Carolyn. 1984. *Policing the Victorian Community: The Formation of English Provincial Police Forces, 1856–80*. London: Routledge & Kegan Paul.

Steinmetz, George. 1998. "Critical Realism and Historical Sociology: A Review Article." *Comparative Studies in Society and History* 39, no. 4: 170–186.

Steward, Patrick, and Bryan McGovern. 2013. *The Fenians: Irish Rebellion in the North Atlantic World, 1858–1876*. Knoxville: University of Tennesee Press.

Stoler, Ann Laura. 1995. *Race and the Education of Desire: Foucault's History of Sexuality and the Colonial Order of Things*. Durham, NC: Duke University Press.

Storch, Robert. 1976. "The Policeman as Domestic Missionary: Urban Discipline and Popular Culture in Northern England, 1850–1880." *Journal of Social History* 9, no. 4: 481–509.

Stoughton, Seth. 2015. "Law Enforcement's 'Warrior' Problem." *Harvard Law Review Forum* 128: 225–234.

Stramberg, Peter. 2020. "From College Walk to Stonewall Inn." In *A Time to Stir*, edited by Paul Cronin, 349–354. New York: Columbia University Press.

Strecker, Mark. 2011. *Smedley D. Butler, USMC: A Biography*. Jefferson, NC: MacFarland.

Suddler, Carl. 2019. *Presumed Criminal: Black Youth and the Justice System in Postwar New York*. New York: New York University Press.

Summerfield, Stephen, and Susan Law. 2016. *Sir John Moore and the Universal Soldier*, volume 1, *The Man, the Commander, and the Shorncliffe System of Training*. Huntingdon, UK: Ken Trotman Publishing.

Swanson, Doug. 2021. *Cult of Glory: The Bold and Brutal History of the Texas Rangers*. New York: Penguin Random House.

Sweeney, John, and Francis Richards. 1904. *At Scotland Yard: Being the Experiences During Twenty-Seven Years' Service of John Sweeney*. London: Grant Richards.

Swift, Roger. 1984. "'Another Stafford Street Row': Law, Order and the Irish Presence in Mid-Victorian Wolverhampton." *Immigrants and Minorities* 3, no. 1: 5–29.

Swift, Roger. 1987. "The Outcast Irish in the British Victorian City: Problems and Perspectives." *Irish Historical Studies* 25, no. 99: 264–276.

Swift, Roger. 1989. "Crime and the Irish in Nineteenth-Century Britain." In *The Irish in Britain, 1815–1939*, edited by Roger Swift and Sheridan Gilley, 163–182. Savage, MD: Barnes & Noble Books.

Swift, Roger. 1997. "Heroes or Villains? The Irish, Crime, and Disorder in Victorian England." *Albion: A Quarterly Journal Concerned with British Studies* 29, no. 3: 399–421.

Swift, Roger. 2007a. *Irish Migrants and Crime in the Victorian City*. Chester, UK: University of Chester Press.

Swift, Roger. 2007b. "Policing Chartism, 1839–1848: The Role of the 'Specials' Reconsidered." *English Historical Review* 122, no. 497: 669–699.

Sylvester, Richard. 1910. "The Treatment of the Accused." *Annals of the Academy of Political and Social Science* 36, no. 1: 16–19.

Taylor, Ben. 2015. "Science and the British Police: Surveillance, Intelligence and the Rise of the Professional Police Officer, 1930–2000." PhD dissertation, Department of History, King's College London.

Taylor, Howard. 1998. "Rationing Crime: The Political Economy of Criminal Statistics Since the 1850s." *Economic History Review* 51, no. 3: 569–590.

Thomas, Martin. 2008. *Empires of Intelligence*. Berkeley: University of California Press.

Thompson, Anna. 1926. "A Survey of Crime Among Negroes in Philadelphia." *Opportunity* 4, no. 44: 251–254.

Thompson, Lanny. 2010. *Imperial Archipelago: Representation and Rule in the Insular Territories Under US Domination After 1898*. Honolulu: University of Hawai'i Press.

Thompson, Leroy. 2012. *The World's First SWAT Team*. London: Frontline Books.

Tobias, J. J. 1979. *Crime and Police in England, 1700–1900*. New York: St. Martin's Press.

Tolan, Sandy. 2017. "Taxpayer-Funded Horror at Standing Rock." *The Daily Beast*, last updated April 11, 2017. https://www.thedailybeast.com/taxpayer-funded-horror-at-standing-rock.

Toland, Harry. 2007. *Gentleman Trooper*. Westminster, MD: Eagle Editions.

Trouillot, Michel-Rolph. 2015. *Silencing the Past*. Boston: Beacon Press.

Tullis, Tracy. 1999. "A Vietnam at Home: Policing the Ghettos in the Counterinsurgency Era." PhD dissertation, Department of History, HH`HNew York University.

Turner, William W. 1968. *The Police Establishment*. New York: Putnam.

Turner, William W. 1971. *Power on the Right*. Berkeley, CA: Ramparts Press.

US Bureau of the Census. 1864. *Population of the United States in 1860; Compiled from the Original Returns of the Eighth Census.* Washington, DC: US Government Printing Office.

US Bureau of the Census. 1910. *Statistics of Cities Having a Population of Over 30,000: 1915.* Washington, DC: US Government Printing Office.

US Bureau of the Census. 1916. *General Statistics of Cities, 1915.* Washington, DC: US Government Printing Office.

United States Commission on Industrial Relations. 1916. *Industrial Relations: Final Report and Testimony, Volume 11.* Washington, DC: US Government Printing Office.

United States National Advisory Commission on Civil Disorders. 1967. *Report.* Washington, DC: Government Printing Office.

United States Philippine Commission. 1900–1915. *Annual Reports of the Philippine Commission.* Washington, DC: US Government Printing Office.

United States Senate Committee on the Judiciary. 1973. *Amendments to Title I (LEAA) of the Omnibus Crime Control and Safe Streets Act of 1968. Hearing Before the Subcommittee on Criminal Laws and Procedures of the Committee on the Judiciary.* Washington, DC: US Government Printing Office.

United States Senate Committee on the Philippines. 1902. *Affairs in the Philippine Islands, Hearings Before the Comm. on the Phil. of the U.S.S., 57th Cong.* Washington, DC: US Government Printing Office.

Valentine, D. T. 1855. *Manual of the Corporation of the Corporation of the City of New York,.* New York: D. T. Valentine.

Vermont Department of Public Safety. 1950. *Biennial Report of the Department of Public Safety.* Montpelier, VT: Department of Public Safety.

Virdee, Satnam. 2014. *Racism, Class and the Racialized Outsider.* Houndmills, UK: Palgrave Macmillan.

Vitale, Alex. 2017. *The End of Policing.* New York: Verso.

Vogler, Richard. 1991. *Reading the Riot Act: The Magistry, the Police and the Army in Civil Disorder.* Milton Keynes, UK: Open University Press.

Vollmer, August. 1933. "Police Progress in the Past Twenty-Five Years." *Journal of Criminal Law and Criminology* 24, no. 1: 161–175.

Vollmer, August. 1939. "The Police Beat." Unpublished ms. August Vollmer Papers, Bancroft Library, University of California at Berkeley.

Vollmer, August, and Alfred Parker. 1935. *Crime and the State Police.* Berkeley: University of California Press.

Vollmer, August, and Albert Schneider. 1917. "School for Police as Planned at Berkeley." *Journal of Criminal Law and Criminology* 7, no. 6: 877–898.

Wacquant, Loïc. 2001. "Deadly Symbiosis: When Ghetto and Prison Meet and Mesh." *Punishment and Society* 3, no. 1: 95–134.

Wacquant, Loïc. 2022. *The Invention of the "Underclass": A Study in the Politics of Knowledge.* Cambridge, UK: Polity Press.

Waddington, P. A. J. 1987. "Towards Paramilitarism? Dilemmas in Policing Civil Disorder." *British Journal of Criminology* 27, no. 1: 37–46.

Waddington, P. A. J. 1991. *The Strong Arm of the Law.* Oxford: Clarendon Press.

Wade, John. 1837. "Principles of Police, and Their Application to the Metropolis." *Fraser's Magazine* 16, no. 2: 169–178.

Wade, Richard. 1964. *Slavery in the Cities: The South, 1820–1860.* New York: Oxford University Press.

Wagner, Bryan. 2009. *Disturbing the Peace: Black Culture and the Police Power After Slavery*. Cambridge, MA: Harvard University Press.

Wagner, Kim. 2018. "Savage Warfare: Violence and the Rule of Colonial Difference in Early British Counterinsurgency." *History Workshop Journal* 85: 217–237.

Wain, Neil, and Peter Joyce. 2012. "Disaffected Communities, Riots and Policing: Manchester 1981 and 2011." *Safer Communities* 11, no. 3: 125–134.

Wakeman, Frederic E. 1996. *Policing Shanghai*. Berkeley: University of California Press.

Walker, Samuel. 1977. *A Critial History of Police Reform: The Emergence of Professionalism*. Lexington, MA: Lexington Books.

Wall, David. 1998. *The Chief Constables of England and Wales: The Socio-legal History of a Criminal Justice Elite*. Aldershot, UK: Ashgate.

Wallas, Graham. 1925. *The Life of Francis Place, 1771–1854*. London: Allen and Unwin.

Walling, George W. 1887. *Recollections of a New York Chief of Police*. New York: Caxton Book Concern.

Warren, Charles. 1888. "The Police of the Metropolis." *Murray's Magazine* 4, no. 23: 577–594.

Watch Committee Bourough of Manchester. 1845. *Statistical Returns of the Manchester Police for the Year 1844*. Manchester: Bradshaw and Blacklock.

Watson, Jake. 2018. "Family Ideation, Immigration, and the Racial State: Explaining Divergent Family Reunification Policies in Britain and the US." *Ethnic and Racial Studies* 41, no. 2: 324–342.

Watts, Eugene. 1981. "St. Louis Police Recruits in the Twentieth Century." *Criminology* 19, no. 1: 77–114.

Watts, Eugene. 1982. "Cops and Crooks: The War at Home." In *Reshaping America: Society and Institutions 1945–1960*, edited by Robert Bremner and Gary W. Reichard, 284–318. Columbus: Ohio State University Press.

Watts, W. H. 1864. *London Life at the Police Courts*. London: Levey.

Watts Miller, William. 1987. "Party Politics, Class Interest and Reform of the Police, 1829–1956." *Police Studies* 10: 42–60.

Weaver, Michael. 1994. "The New Science of Policing: Crime and the Birmingham Police Force, 1839–1942." *Albion: A Quarterly Journal Concerned with British Studies* 26, no. 2: 289–308.

Webb, Jack. 1958. *The Badge*. Englewood Cliffs, NJ: Prentice Hall.

Weber, Max. 1946. *From Max Weber: Essays in Sociology*. New York: Oxford University Press.

Weber, Max. 1992. *The Protestant Ethic and the Spirit of Capitalism*. Translated by Talcott Parsons, with an introduction by Anthony Giddens. New York: Routledge.

Wei Tchen, John Kuo. 1996. "Quimbo Appo's Fear of Fenians: Chinese-Irish-Anglo Relations in New York City." In *The New York Irish*, edited by Ronald Bayor and Timothy Meagher, 125–152. Baltimore: Johns Hopkins University Press.

Weinberger, Barbara. 1991. *Keeping the Peace? Policing Strikes in Britain, 1906–1926*. New York: St. Martin's Press.

Weir, Robert. 1997. *Colonial South Carolina: A History*. Millwood, NY: KTO Press.

Werly, John M. 1973. "The Irish in Manchester, 1832–49." *Irish Historical Studies* 18, no. 71: 345–358.

Wertsch, Douglas. 1992. "Resisting the Wave: Rural Iowa's War Against Crime, 1920–1941." PhD dissertation, Departmen of History, Iowa State University.

Whalen, Bernard, and Jon Whalen. 2014. *The NYPD's First Fifty Years*. Lincoln, NE: Potomac Books.

Whitaker, Robert. 2017. "From Cooperation to Neocolonialism: Colonial Police and International Policing, 1920–1960." In *Policing in Colonial Empires: Cases, Connections, Boundaries*, edited by Emmanuel Blanchard, Marieke Bloembergen, and Amandine Lauro, 161–175. Oxford: Peter Lang.

White, Richard D. 1995. "Civilian Management of the Military: Elihu Root and the 1903 Reorganization of the Army General Staff." *Journal of Management History* 4, no. 1: 43–59.

Whitfield, James. 2003. "The Metropolitan Police: Alienation, Culture, and Relations with London's Caribbean Community 1950–1970." *Crime, Histoire et Sociétés / Crime, History and Societies* 7, no. 2: 23–39.

Whitfield, James. 2004. *Unhappy Dialogue: The Metropolitan Police and Black Londoners in Post-war Britain*. Cullompton, UK: Willan.

Whittingham, Daniel. 2020. *Charles E. Callwell and the British Way in Warfare*. Cambridge, UK: Cambridge University Press.

Wiechselbaum, Simone, and Beth Schwartzapfel. 2017. "When Warriors Put on the Badge." https://www.themarshallproject.org/2017/03/30/when-warriors-put-on-the-badge.

Wiener, Martin J. 1990. *Reconstructing the Criminal: Culture, Law, and Policy in England, 1830–1914*. Cambridge, UK: Cambridge University Press.

Williams, Chris A. 2014. *Police Control Systems in Britain, 1775–1975: From Parish Constable to National Computer*. Manchester: Manchester University Press.

Williams, Dave. 1921. "State Police and the Irish 'Black and Tans.'" *The Bridgemen's Magazine* 21, no. 1: 76–78.

Williams, Kristian. 2004. *Our Enemies in Blue*. Brooklyn, NY: Soft Skull Press.

Williams, Patrick, and Becky Clarke. 2016. *Dangerous Associations: Joint Enterprise, Gangs and Racism*. London: Centre for Crime and Justice Studies.

Williams, Patrick, and Becky Clarke. 2018. "The Black Criminal Other as an Object of Social Control." *Social Sciences* 7, no. 11: 1–14.

Williams, Randall. 2003. "A State of Permanent Exception: The Birth of Modern Policing in Colonial Capitalism." *Interventions: International Journal of Postcolonial Studies* 5, no. 3: 322–344.

Williams, T. Harry. 1981. *The History of American Wars from 1745 to 1918*. New York: Alfred A. Knopf.

Williams, Watkin. 1941. *The Life of General Sir Charles Warren*. Oxford: Basil Blackwell.

Willis, John. 2011. "Colonial Policing in Aden, 1937–1967." In *Globalising British Policing*, edited by Georgina Sinclair, 209–246. Farnham, UK: Ashgate Publishing.

Wilson, John B. 1998. *Manuever and Firepower: The Evolution of Divisions and Separate Brigades*. Washington, DC: Center of Military History, United States Army.

Wilson, Kathleen. 1995. *The Sense of the People: Politics, Culture, and Imperialism in England, 1715–1785*. Cambridge, UK: Cambridge University Press.

Wilson, O. W. 1950. *Police Administration*. New York: McGraw-Hill.

Wilson, O. W. 1953. "August Vollmer." *Journal of Criminal Law and Criminology* 44, no. 1: 91–103.

Wilson, O. W. 1963. *Police Administration*. 2nd ed. New York: McGraw-Hill.

Winrow, Andrew Philip. 2017. *The British Regular Mounted Infantry 1880–1913*. London: Routledge.

Wintersmith, Robert F. 1974. *Police and the Black Community*. Lexington, MA: Lexington Books.

Wukovits, John. 2009. *American Commando*. New York: NAL Caliber.

Yiu-kwong, Doulas Tsui. 2015. "Foreword." In *Policing in Hong Kong: History and Reform*, edited by Kam C. Wong, xvii–xviii. London: CRC Press.

Yonkers Police Department. n.d. "Past Commander: Daniel Wolff." www.yonkersny.gov/live/public-safety/police-department/police-history/past-commanders/daniel-wolff. Accessed February 10, 2022.

Younes, Ali. 2018. "Durham First US City to Ban Police Training with Israeli Military." Al-Jazeera, April 19, 2018. https://www.aljazeera.com/news/2018/4/19/durham-first-us-city-to-ban-police-training-with-israeli-military.

# Index